Beverly McLeod

D1603073

The Mediating Person

Edited by
Stephen Bochner

The Mediating Person:
Bridges Between Cultures

G.K. Hall and Co. Boston, Massachusetts

Schenkman Publishing Company Cambridge, Massachusetts

Copyright © 1981 by Schenkman Publishing Company, Inc.

Library of Congress Cataloging in Publication Data

Main entry under title:

   The Mediating person.

   Includes indexes.
   1. Intercultural communication—Addresses, essays,
lectures.   2. Cross-cultural studies—Addresses, essays,
lectures.   3. Cultural relations—Addresses, essays,
lectures.   I. Bochner, Stephen.
HM258.M375   306'.4   81–6358
ISBN 0-8161-9016-X   AACR2

This publication is printed on permanent/durable acid-free paper.
MANUFACTURED IN THE UNITED STATES OF AMERICA

To Otto Klineberg

Mediating gentleman, friend, and teacher

Contents

Stephen Bochner

Preface and Overview

This book brings together the concepts, theory, empirical findings, and practical application of cultural mediation. At the center of the inquiry is the mediating person, defined as an individual who serves as a link between diverse cultural systems. His purpose is to insure that cross-cultural exchanges of people, ideas, and technology are mutually beneficial to the participating societies, as judged by the internal value systems of each culture.

The book has been organized into three parts. The first section defines terms and develops a working model of cultural mediation. The broad aim of the first section is to integrate the personal, situational, and institutional supports of cultural mediation into a social-psychological model of the mediating individual.

The second section deals with the experience of being a mediator, identifying the main stresses affecting individuals who link different cultures and the measures that can be taken to reduce them. Some of the roles that are treated in detail include overseas students, visiting professors, Peace Corps volunteers, foreign service personnel and their families, and technical experts.

The third section examines the mediator's role in cultural change, culture preservation, and culture building. The organization of the material reflects two interrelated aims: to consider the function of mediators in countries that are in the process of becoming multicultural societies, and to describe the participation of mediators in the transfer of cultural practices from one society to another. The conclusion suggests areas of further research and applies the principles of cultural mediation to the solution of real problems in the world of affairs.

This volume is the result of a collaborative effort which itself illustrates the mediating process in international social-science research. Each chapter is an original contribution by an authority in his or her field, written specially for this book at the request of the editor. The authors were invited to participate because of their expertise and because of the disciplines and cultures that they represented. Most of the writers attended an intensive two-week workshop coordinated by the editor that was held in June 1976 at the East-West Center in Honolulu under the auspices of the Culture Learning Institute.

At the workshop, participants critically reviewed each other's contributions, and wrote their final drafts in the light of that mediating experience.

The editor would like to reaffirm his gratitude to the distinguished men and women who gave so unstintingly of their wisdom, time, and enthusiasm to join in the creation of this book. I am also indebted to the Culture Learning Institute of the East-West Center for underwriting the authors' workshop, and to the director of the institute, Dr. Verner Bickley, for his continuing support and encouragement.

The preparation of the manuscript was carried out jointly at the East-West Center and at the University of New South Wales. Both institutions provided a congenial academic atmosphere in which to complete the task. Finally, I would like to acknowledge the cheerful and expert secretarial assistance of Patricia Kim and Jo Ann Oda in Honolulu, and of Louise Kahabka in Sydney. Their patience, good humor, and willing cooperation greatly eased the burden of producing this book.

Part I

Cultural Mediation:
Theory and Definition of the Field

Introduction

The contributions in this section define the theoretical terms for the present inquiry. In the first chapter, Bochner draws on the language and concepts of social psychology to develop an empirically based model of cultural mediation. The mediating person is an individual who serves as a link between two or more cultures and social systems. The essence of the mediating function is to shape the exchanges between the participating societies so that the contact will benefit both cultures, on terms that are consistent with their respective value systems.

The model regards these individuals as participants in culture-learning. The dual effect of culture-learning on the person is increasing heteroculturality and marginality induced by exposure to several cultures.

Bochner distinguishes among three types of culture-learning situations: (1) the accident-of-birth condition, in which individuals are brought up simultaneously in more than one culture; (2) culture-learning by adults as a result of an extended sojourn abroad; and (3) culture-learning by adults exposed to a specific culture-training experience. Bochner then distinguishes between two types of mediating functions: the translator and synthesizer roles. The purpose of the mediator-as-translator is to represent one culture to another faithfully and thereby contribute to mutual understanding and accurate cross-cultural knowledge. The purpose of the mediator-as-synthesizer is to reconcile disparate cultural practices, this type of mediation having special relevance to exchanges from which some action is to follow.

The major research question relates to the conditions under which persons in interface situations become mediating men and women rather than remaining monocultural or becoming marginal. Bochner's investigations reveal that the mediating person is an individual who enjoys a social network spanning many cultures, obtains personal and professional support from transcultural sources and has a positive attitude toward the various cultures that he operates in and/or belongs to; he is a cultural relativist.

Finally, Bochner discusses legitimization of the mediating role and the associated problem of training mediators. However, as McLeod shows in the following chapter, even if the mediating role is institutionalized, there is a problem of acceptance which goes well beyond the narrow institutional context of any particular mediating episode. That is because cultures vary greatly in the value that they place on the mediating function itself. It is therefore not sufficient for a mediator to have the correct training, motivation, and institutional support because the mediator's effectiveness ultimately depends on the acceptance or rejection of his role by the participating cultures.

McLeod links different attitudes toward mediation to differing cultural notions about the mutability of national identity. Some societies regard national identity as highly mutable and allow and indeed expect newcomers to become full-fledged members. At the other extreme are those societies which regard national identity as highly immutable and deny membership even to lifelong but nonindigenous residents. Between these two extremes are many societies that have a more flexible approach to the mutability of ethnic identity.

Since the mediating function implies the exchange of cultural manifestations and at the same time the preservation of the core identity of the participating cultures, McLeod concludes that mediators will be more effective in those societies which view national identity as partially mutable, but only up to a well-defined point. The mediating role is more likely to be accepted in societies maintaining an intermediate position regarding the mutability of national identity, and less likely to be accepted in societies at either extreme.

In their chapters, both Bochner and McLeod refer to heteroculturality as a characteristic of the mediating person. The next contribution in this section, by Ronald Taft, explores the concept of biculturality. Taft regards the bicultural person as one who is competent in more than one culture, captured by the phrase "two skills in one skull." These skills include knowing about the respective societies, being able to communicate with members of both groups, and possessing the technical and social accomplishments appropriate to the individual's status and role in each culture. Taft identifies the conditions under which these skills develop and the relationship of biculturality to the mediating function. Although there is an extensive literature on primary enculturation, there is sparse empirical evidence on how individuals respond to two or more socializing influences, either simultaneously, as in the case of bicultural childhoods, or successively, as in the case of adult culture-learners. Consequently, Taft draws on research in second-language learning for the bulk of his analysis, arguing that there are many parallels between learning another language and learning another culture. Taft's inquiry suggests that the following variables will be important in the acquisition of second-culture competence: the age at which learning occurs, the sequence of learning, the culture of the parents, the facilitative or inhibitory effect of one culture on the other, the role of cultural models, the stability or transitional nature of the family, continuity or discontinuity in cultural influences, and changes that occur in the culture during the person's lifetime.

Finally, Taft distinguishes between a person who is competent in more than one culture and a person who is competent in the mediating role itself. The conditions most likely to contribute to the mediator's competence include intelligence, cognitive flexibility, the ability to empathize, emotional stability, tolerance for ambiguity, high motivation, youth, education, and previous exposure to other cultures. Taft concludes that a person who functions competently in his own culture should also adapt more easily to a second set of cultural influences.

Taken together, the contributions in this section provide a general theoretical framework for the inquiry into cultural mediation, describe the main conceptual elements in the model, review the relevant empirical literature, and identify the major issues in the area. Later in this book, some of the specific implications of the concept of cultural mediation will be explored in more detail, including the experience of being a mediator, some of the practical consequences of mediation, and the mediating person's involvement in the process of cultural change.

S.B.

Stephen Bochner

The Social Psychology of Cultural Mediation

Introduction and Overview

This chapter analyzes cultural mediation and cultural mediators from a social-psychological perspective. Cultural mediators are men and women who function as links between diverse cultural systems. The chapter identifies the situational and institutional determinants of cultural mediation, and then develops an interpersonal model of the mediating individual. The approach to the problem is empirical and operational. Thus, all of the theoretical constructs in the model have a specific empirical referent, such as a test score, an operationally defined dimension, or some other observable object or event.

The chapter begins with a brief demonstration of the practical function of cultural mediation. The illustration draws on experience in the area of modernization and the diffusion of innovations. Two modes of technological development are distinguished and then contrasted: (1) the direct transfer of technology and (2) the less common but more desirable form, where the exogenous technology is modified and adapted to indigenous practices and institutions. Only the second form of modernization is consistent with the principles of cultural mediation. The worldwide shortage of mediating persons, coupled with an oversupply of "development-at-all-costs" technocrats, explains the relatively low incidence of the transfer of culturally appropriate technology.

In the next section, the concept of mediation is explored. Again, a pragmatic approach to the problem is adopted. In particular, the main empirical antecedents, correlates, and consequents of mediation in the interpersonal area are identified. The "between-skin" framework of the model leads to an analysis of the social interaction of individuals located at the interface between different cultures, and four broad behavior styles are distinguished. The section primarily consists of a conceptual and empirical analysis of mono/bi/multiculturality and of culture-learning. This is done by describing some of the tests, procedures, and experiments that have been used to define and explore the various concepts. A synthesis of these variables provides a working model of the mediating person as an individual who is multicultural, functions in a transnational role, has a transcultural reference group, obtains transcultural social support for his professional work, and has a social network spanning many cultures.

The discussion then turns to the problem of creating cultural mediators, identifying and contrasting various models that a transcultural training organization might adopt, and speculating about the ideal institution for training mediators.

The concluding section brings together the personal, interpersonal, structural, and institutional aspects of cultural mediation as an interrelated, mutually reinforcing system. Thus, mediating persons are most effective when they operate within a political and intellectual climate that supports and rewards multicultural individuals, values their social role, and maintains the institutions that produce them.

The Mediating Person and Modernization: An Illustration of the Mediating Function

The decades since the end of the Second World War have seen an unprecedented diffusion of Western technology. There is hardly any area of the world today which has not in some way been affected by "modern" techniques, practices, and ideas. Initially, most of the diffusion of innovations was the result of deliberate, planned action, jointly agreed to by both donor and recipient governments and often coordinated by some international or supranational agency. Subsequently, private enterprise has also played its part in exporting modern "amenities," and today the multinational companies are a fact of international life.

At the outset, I should make it clear that I am neither arguing against social change, nor opposing technology per se. Some of the advantages of technology are undeniable, and as Crocombe (1972) notes, it is doubtful whether there are many people in the world today who would wish to go back to the conditions of their great-grandfathers. In any case, social change is an inevitable process—the world is an interdependent, open social system (Berrien 1968; Emery 1969), with events in one part of the globe ineluctably affecting and being affected by happenings elsewhere. With the possible exception of ancient Australia (Elkin 1964), the earth system has always functioned in this way, but in contemporary times the impact is more immediate owing to the advent of instant worldwide communication (McLuhan 1964).

Thus, the intention is neither to stem the spreading tide of technology nor to preserve cultures in some pure state, like an anatomical specimen in a bottle of spirits. Rather, the focus here is on how to prevent cultures from being destroyed by industrialization. Unfortunately, there are many examples of societies which have lost their cultural integrity as the price for modernization. Too often, imported technologies are introduced in unmodified form, and the indigenous social system must adapt to the machines, procedures, and materials that the donors have assembled as an "aid project" (Boxer 1969). As Mortimer (1973) has written,

> Generally, we proceed upon the basis that Western technology
> cannot but be beneficial to a country which lacks it. But books
> could be written on the untoward results of technological interven
> tion upon the ecology, the society and the culture of poor countries.
> There have been literally tens of thousands of Aswan Dams, large
> and small, inflicted upon the people of the third world in the name
> of a technocratic rationality that is mindless in its appreciation of
> social consequences. (p. 3)

Although Mortimer has probably overstated the case, there is sufficient truth in his assertion to demonstrate the potential for harm of technical aid that is uninformed by considerations of cultural preservation.

Not all of the cultural damage, however, can be attributed to the direct actions of donor countries. Aiding and abetting the importation of inappropriate technology is what Alatas (1972, 1975) has called the captive-mind syndrome that characterizes many of the officials and administrators in the recipient countries. A captive mind "is the product of higher institutions of learning, either at home or abroad, whose way of thinking is dominated by Western thought in an imitative and uncritical manner" (Alatas 1975, p. 691). Thus, there are many Third World technocrats who perceive a development problem and its solution in terms of the academic training they received, which almost certainly will have taken place abroad, or at a local university dominated by Western ideas and foreign teachers. The evidence indicates that all too often, overseas-trained graduates become uncritical, imitative, and passive consumers of knowledge that was generated in other cultural settings and for other purposes (Faure et al. 1972). Finally, as Curle (1970) has pointed out, wealth and prestige reward those indigenes who collaborate with powerful outside interests in the exploitation of their own people. So, even when a culturally appropriate technological solution to a particular problem is available, it may be rejected from a mixture of psychological, political, and self-serving motives (Wade 1975).

Thus, a number of forces contribute to the needless degradation of indigenous cultures. However, a denominator common to all of these pressures is a shortage of people who have the skills and attitudes necessary to synthesize technological development and cultural growth. The majority of those who are professionally involved in developmental work appears to accept a definition of modernity patterned on the political and economic institutions of

Western industrialized societies. The underlying assumption, shared by many non-Westerners, is that most of the world's ills will be cured by a straight transfer of Western technology to the underdeveloped regions of the world. One of the most influential exponents of this view is Alex Inkeles (1975; Inkeles and Smith 1974), who has served notice on the "emerging nations" (Inkeles 1975, p. 323) that unless they dismantle their traditional kinship, political, educational, religious, agricultural, industrial, and economic infrastructures, they will be excluded from international economic and political participation in the twentieth century.

Why do we take particular exception to this doctrine? First, Inkeles and others like him exhibit the worst kind of cultural ethnocentrism in implying that the "modern" political and economic institutions of Western industrialized societies are superior to those of nations that do not fit some arbitrary definition of modernity. In fact, research on the psychological consequences of modernization suggests the contrary (Triandis 1973). Modernization appears to be associated with deindividuation, social disorganization, anomie, problems of identity, unrealistic levels of aspiration that lead to feelings of frustration, difficulty in maintaining high self-esteem, crime, suicide, and alcoholism.

Second, the destruction of cultures has negative global consequences that stretch well beyond the particular society being submerged (Bochner 1979). The variability in world cultures provides mankind with a range of alternative solutions to the future. Man's biological nature is pretty well fixed, and in any case he does not have enough time to evolve genetically to the rapidly changing conditions of the contemporary world. In point of biological fact, *Homo sapiens* is still adapted to a hunting and gathering life-style, even though these abilities are irrelevant to the survival of most people alive today. All man's adaptations have been in the realm of culture, that is, in institutions, social arrangements, and symbolic expressions. In recorded history, man has "evolved" not by adapting his biological nature, but by explicitly modifying his physical and social environment.

Thus, on a limited scale, *Homo sapiens*'s intraspecies variability in cultural adaptations mirrors the biologically based interspecies heterogeneity of the rest of nature. And just as nature does not put all of its evolutionary eggs in the one basket, it would be very foolish for the human species to stake its future on one single course, or even a limited number of alternatives. From this perspective, the preservation of individual cultures and the maintenance of global heterogeneity would appear to be one goal that all of mankind can share.

The successful diffusion of innovation, then, is a function of the presence or absence of qualified mediators in the social system undergoing change. If the individuals who implement technical assistance have a knowledge of and respect for both the donor and recipient cultures, then there is a greater chance that they will select, modify, or adapt technologies that are culturally appropriate and that have no, or few, negative side effects on the integrity of the receiving culture. However, if the diffusion of innovations is administered by individuals with little knowledge of and respect for the receiving society, it is likely that technological solutions will be given precedence over cultural considerations. This latter form of diffusion contributes to cultural erosion and to a reduction in worldwide heterogeneity. Thus, the modernization process takes on an entirely different aspect and has entirely different practical consequences, depending on whether it occurs within a mediating or a nonmediating context.

The mediating function is relevant to many other processes besides the diffusion of technical innovations, such as migration, international trade and relations, multi-cultural education, cross-cultural counseling, and tourism. These are treated elsewhere in this volume. Modernization is only one example of cultural mediation. The next section continues to focus on the modernization process to help generate some of the universally valid attributes of cultural mediation.

Attributes of the Concept of Cultural Mediation

In an earlier illustration, mediating innovators were referred to as possessing knowledge of and respect for both donor and recipient societies. Let us now extend and generalize this example into a paradigm of cultural mediation.

A survey of the literature and of experience with and observation of the mediating function indicates that three major sets of variables interact in the process of cultural mediation: (1) the *structural* context, or the nature, organization, and location of those institutions in a society that have a mediating function; (2) the *interpersonal* context, or the groups and interpersonal networks which define and sustain the social role of cultural mediation; and (3) the *personal* attributes of cultural mediators. The three conceptual domains of cultural mediation are presented here in a descending order of generality, drawing on the language of sociology, social psychology, and personality theory, respectively.

THE STRUCTURAL CONTEXT OF CULTURAL MEDIATION

Interface situations can range all the way from the macrolevel of Cold War ideologies splitting the world in half, through the intermediate level of different ethnic groups engaging in nonisomorphic interaction (Triandis 1975), as for example in a multiracial school (Gallimore et al. 1974), to the microlevel of cognitively "mismatched" individuals (Foa and Foa 1974)

not being able to communicate effectively with each other because of differences in their subjective cultures (Triandis 1973; Triandis et al. 1972). The
principle common to all these interface situations is that they represent the
intersection of the boundaries of two open social systems (Berrien 1968;
Emery 1969).

One implication of open-systems theory is that four alternative outcomes
exhaust all the possibilities when societies, groups, or individuals are locked
into an interdependent relationship: mutual profit, asymmetrical profit,
mutual loss, or the unlikely outcome of neither side being affected in any
substantial manner. Thus, the result of contact between two disparate cultural systems can be located on a theoretical continuum of cost or benefit
to either group. Cultural interaction can have mutually beneficial effects; or
the benefits can be asymmetrically distributed, favoring one system at the expense of the other; or both systems may emerge harmed from the encounter.

One advantage of the open-systems formulation of cultures in contact is
that at least in principle, ethnocentric value judgments about what constitutes
profit or loss can be avoided. Each culture can evaluate the outcome of the
contact in emic terms (Berry 1969), that is, from the internal perspective of
its indigenous value system. Let us take a hypothetical case to illustrate this
principle. The Kingdom of Nepal may decline the offer of a four-lane highway across the Himalayas on the grounds that the negative side effects on
Nepal's traditional culture, including an influx of tourists, pollution, ambiguous defense implications, and the diversion of scarce land from agriculture
would outweigh any benefits resulting from the provision of modern transportation facilities. On the other hand, the Commonwealth of Australia might
be grateful for assistance with which to build a four-lane highway from
Adelaide to Darwin. Such a road, in the government's view, would have many
benefits, not the least of which would be to open up the country to tourism
and other industry, attract population to a deserted but potentially productive
region, and make the Top End of Australia easier to defend against invasion.

Another structural aspect is the extent to which different cultures regard
mediation as a valid and desirable process. This is one of the main themes of
McLeod's chapter in this volume.

THE SOCIAL PSYCHOLOGY OF THE MEDIATING PERSON

This section concerns the social and interpersonal context of cultural mediation. The "between-skin" perspective of human behavior construes mediation
as a social activity, involving the creation and maintenance of certain relationships between culturally diverse people. The method of inquiry consists of an
exploration of the various social parameters of mediation, including the
nature of the mediating role, the social contingencies of mediation, and the

values and organizational structures of mediating institutions. Unfortunately, relatively little systematic research is available which specifically addresses itself to the interplay of these forces. The reason for the paucity of such data is that most of the cultures-in-contact research has described the unidirectional impact of one group on the other, rather than the mutually reverberating influences.

Two theoretical models have guided most of past research in transcultural relations: a linear model emphasizing assimilation and adjustment, and, to explain the failure of adjustment, an interaction model emphasizing confrontation. Most of the cultures-in-contact literature has been concerned with such issues as attitudes toward minority groups (Adorno et al. 1950), migrant assimilation (Doczy 1971), racism (Pettigrew 1964), attitudes of overseas students to their hosts (Selltiz et al. 1963), or the determinants of prejudice (Allport 1954). None of these studies focuses on the concept of mediation. It is only when the cultures-in-contact phenomenon is viewed as an open-systems interface problem that questions of genuine mediation arise.

The present treatment departs from most previous studies of transcultural relations by emphasizing mutual growth which also preserves the integrity of each participating culture. While this interaction model is not altogether new (Gullahorn and Gullahorn 1960; Useem and Useem 1967, 1968; Useem, Useem, and Donoghue 1963), it has not been developed in a systematic or comprehensive manner, and its impact has not been very visible either in the literature or in practice. The present chapter, and indeed this whole book, explores relatively uncharted territory.

As in previous sections, an operational definition of the theoretical construct provides the focus for the discussion of the social parameters of cultural mediation. We have placed both the theoretical language and the empirical findings within the framework of an operational definition of culture-learning. "Culture-learning" refers to changes in an individual during and after he has been immersed in an interface situation. Theoretically, four broad outcomes are possible: (1) A person may remain monocultural, by clinging to the culture of his origin and rejecting all alien influences. (2) An individual may reject his culture of origin and adopt a new culture. The result is still a monocultural person. (3) An individual can become bicultural, by retaining his culture of origin and also learning a second culture. (4) Finally, an individual may become multicultural, by retaining his culture of origin and also learning several other cultures.

Monocultural individuals are unlikely to make very effective mediators between different cultural systems. Bicultural and multicultural individuals do have the correct qualifications, but whether such people in fact become *mediating persons* depends on a complex set of determinants. Thus, knowing more than one culture is a necessary but not sufficient condition for cultural mediation. This entire book constitutes an attempt to identify and explore the nature of these determinants, and what is meant by learning another culture. In particular, the chapters by Taft and McLeod provide a detailed theoretical analysis of the circumstances under which men and women in interface situations can be expected to behave in a mediating style. Taft also speculates about the conditions that might facilitate or hinder the acquisition of another culture, through an extrapolation of research and theory from the field of second-language learning. Rather than duplicate the material covered elsewhere in this book, the present section is concerned with the theoretical and empirical explication of the concept of culture-learning and the relationship of this variable to mediation.

Culture-Learning as a Theoretical Construct

The model assumes that individuals can learn a second culture in the same way that they acquire a second language. However, this analogy should not be taken too far, as cultures are more complex than languages. Consequently, there are very few individuals who know all aspects of even their culture of origin, let alone all aspects of a second culture. Paradoxically, a person usually does not become aware of the gaps in his knowledge of his own society until he comes into contact with members of other cultures who, through their curiosity about his origins, push him into the role of cultural ambassador and explicator (Bochner 1972). Thus, it must be acknowledged that in practice, mediators will be able to act as links between only certain segments of the two societies they straddle: those segments that they are sufficiently familiar with and have entry to.

A further assumption of the model is that individuals do not merely acquire knowledge about and skill in performing second-culture practices— the "facts" of a new culture. They also develop feelings and attitudes toward those facts, and it does not necessarily follow that culture-learners will like what they have learned. It is therefore essential to distinguish between the cognitive, skill, and affective strands of culture-learning. It is reasonable to expect (although the question is ultimately an empirical one) that individuals who know, are competent in, and like their two intersecting cultures are going to be more effective mediators than individuals who know but disapprove of facets of one or more of the cultures concerned.

Since an individual can participate in a variety of interface situations during his lifetime, the same person can function as either a good or bad mediator, depending on his attitude to the cultures involved. For example, an American Peace Corps volunteer may have served for several years in Thailand and Fiji, developing an extensive knowledge of both societies. In the process, he may have developed a liking for Thai culture, but a dislike of some facets of the culture of the Pacific Islands. It is probable that he was a more effective mediator in Thailand than in Fiji. Again, the same volunteer would probably not be a very effective mediator in either location if he was alienated from his own American society. The relationship between culture-learning and mediation is greatly influenced by the affective responses of the person to the new knowledge, further modified by the person's feelings about his own culture.

One implication of the above is that effective cultural mediation is unlikely to be an unvarying characteristic of an individual's style, so that instead of speaking of mediating *persons*, it might be more accurate to think in terms of mediating *systems*. It is also possible that in the process of learning a second culture, an individual may acquire the attitude of cultural relativism (Herskovits 1948)—the doctrine that all practices are valid if they are sanctioned by the indigenous norms and traditions of their society. To the extent that a person does subscribe to a nonethnocentric value system, it would be appropriate to ascribe to him a general personality trait of mediation. However, cultural relativism can be expected to serve only as a limited guide to action in the practical world of affairs. For example, although it may just be possible for a Western layman (not an anthropologist) to accept cognitively that cannibalism was an integral part of the religious rituals of the Mundugumor (Mead 1935), it is another matter to approve of that practice or mourn its passing. Whether we like it or not, there exist individual and collective differences with respect to the affinity that persons from one group have for the cultural manifestations of alien societies. At the collective level, this is largely a function of the degree of similarity between the respective societies.

People vary in the strength of their commitment to a doctrine that avoids making value judgments about the cultural practices of other societies. Another assumption of our model is that the more cultures a person knows, the stronger will be his commitment to cultural relativism. This effect should flow from knowledge about the great diversity of human cultures, and the realization that there is no one right way of doing things. Allied to this is the assumption that persons who are familiar with several cultures have more variegated and richer inner experiences than bi- or monocultural individuals. The implication of both of these hypotheses for mediation is that multicultural individuals are likely to make better mediators and likely to function as mediators in a wider variety of interface situations than are bicultural individuals. Whatever the actual shape of an individual's progression from mono- to heteroculturality, the theory assumes the process to be correlated with the individual's capacity to mediate between different cultural systems and in part to account for this capacity.

It should be emphasized that the theory outlined above has not yet been adequately tested, and serves only as a working model. However, the theory has already generated a substantial amount of empirical research, some of which will now be reviewed. The main purpose of the next section is to flesh out with data and experimental procedures some of the more abstract features of the preceding discussion.

Empirical Studies of Culture-Learning

Post-sojourn research. In this section, a major study of returned scholars will be described. The study (Bochner 1973) consisted of an extended interview of sixty-nine returned Thai, Pakistani, and Filipino students. The interviews were conducted in Bangkok, Karachi, and Manila, respectively. Most of the interviews lasted about two hours. All of the respondents were professionals, and all had completed graduate work in the United States. Forty-two of the subjects were East-West Center alumni, and twenty-seven had studied abroad under Fulbright fellowships.

The interview explored the groups to which subjects referred themselves; the interdependencies and role relations that defined a respondent's location in his social network; the social comparisons he made and how these determined the degree of satisfaction which he derived from his interactions; the hierarchies and power relationships that circumscribed the amount of personal freedom he could exercise; and the norms, values, customs, and traditions of the formal and informal groups to which he belonged. In particular, the interview schedule contained questions about the subject's occupational history since reentry, whom he or she had married, whether he had traveled overseas since returning, what clubs or associations he belonged to, who his friends and associates were, who he corresponded with, who and what the significant people and events in his life were, and what his plans for the future were. Subjects were also asked to give a retrospective account of their sojourn, again emphasizing the nature of their interpersonal relationships while they were students.

The purpose of these questions was to determine broadly the subject's mono/bi/multiculturality. Thus, were his primary associates exclusively fellow nationals, exclusively Americans, a mixture of the two, or truly international in scope? How many close friends were, like himself, trained overseas? Did he work for an indigenous, foreign-dominated, or international (for example, the United Nations) organization? Did he belong to an international professional association? Did he attend international conferences? Did he express ethnocentric or culturally relativistic attitudes? Was he a nationalist, a potential expatriate, or an internationalist? What were his attitudes to technological development, modernization, and cultural preservation? Did he read international magazines, scientific journals, and foreign books? Did he listen to Radio Australia or the Voice of America? How many languages did he know? Whom did he eat and drink with, and how did he spend his leisure? How many letters did he receive and write, from whom and where?

The interview schedule and the results have been reported in detail elsewhere (Bochner 1973). In summary, the findings suggest that the modal sojourn experience, as measured by retrospective accounts, was bicultural. The main reason why graduate students go abroad to study is to get a degree. While overseas, their lives are structured around academic advancement. Usually, the people who control the resources that facilitate academic achievement are host-culture members. These significant host-country nationals, initially because of their instrumental value, loom very large in the participation, friendship, and interaction patterns of the sojourner.

A second powerful environmental pull comes from the compatriot peer group, which serves the important function of reinforcing the sojourner's national identity while abroad and provides a setting for self-expression in such areas as marriage, courtship, and childbirth.

The pressing needs of academic achievement, compatriot obligation, and personal concerns leave a limited scope for multicultural contact because of competing influences on the time, energy, and allegiance of the student.

Once the student has returned, the data suggest, his life-style reverts to being predominantly monocultural. His work environment is largley monocultural, or at best peopled by a minority of overseas-trained compatriots. Similarly, the modal personal and familial life-style of the respondents was monocultural, upper middle class, materialistic, and conservative and reflected the interaction among the pre-sojourn social background of the students, their during-sojourn professional training, and their post-sojourn occupational status. Education, law and order, and good government were highly regarded, partly because these values benefit the established middle class, but also because the respondents were genuinely convinced that this was the proper course toward national and international peace and prosperity.

The results of the study underline the importance of taking a systems approach to the problem of cultural mediation. The main elements of the system were the personal and social attributes of the students prior to their culture-learning phase; the culture-training experience; and the social, political, and occupational environment of the students after their return home. The dependent variable was the cultural and mediational style of the returned students. The investigation revealed that only a very small proportion of these returned students led lives that fitted the strict definition of multiculturality. There were no significant differences between the effects of the traditional Fulbright exchange program and the more innovative East-West Center scheme. The reason for this "failure" lies partly in the nature of the programs themselves, and we shall return to this point in a subsequent discussion of the structure of international training institutions. However, the data suggest that the main sources of the problem were the lack of social support for mediating functions and the as yet unclearly defined role of cultural mediation.

This raises the question of the relationship between the mediating person and the "marginal man" as originally described by Stonequist (1937). Unlike the mediating person, who can be thought of as *linking* two or more groups, the marginal person is someone who has *fallen between* the various social systems. His problem consists of a simultaneous identification with two conflicting or incompatible reference groups, with the result that he belongs to neither culture. In role-theory terms (Secord and Backman 1964), a marginal person undergoes role strain, since he is required to enact two incompatible or antagonistic social roles. This generally results in considerable personal anguish, although society frequently benefits, since many individuals who satisfy Stonequist's criterion of marginality have also functioned as mediators.

A poignant passage from Nehru's autobiography illustrates better than social scientists ever can the problem of the person who is marginal and who also wishes to serve as a cultural mediator:

> I have become a queer mixture of the East and the West, out of
> place everywhere, at home nowhere. Perhaps my thoughts and
> approach to life are more akin to what is called Western than
> Eastern, but India clings to me, as she does to all her children, in
> innumerable ways; and behind me lie, somewhere in the subcon-
> scious, racial memories of a hundred, or whatever the number may
> be, generations of Brahmans. I cannot get rid of either that past
> inheritance or my recent acquisitions. They are both part of me, and
> though they help me in both the East and the West, they also create
> in me a feeling of spiritual loneliness not only in public activities,
> but in life itself. I am a stranger and alien in the West. I cannot
> be of it. But in my own country also, sometimes, I have an exile's
> feeling. (Nehru 1936, p. 596)

Although individuals located at the interface between two cultural systems probably cannot avoid the marginal syndrome altogether, it is clearly desirable to minimize the risk of falling between the various groups. The essential difference between the marginal and the mediating syndrome is that whereas the marginal individual responds to different cultures as if they were mutually incompatible, the mediating person seeks ways of coordinating and reconciling them. Whereas the marginal person is passively buffeted hither and thither, the mediating person is an active agent—clarifying, communicating, persuading, even, as Ritchie and other contributors to this book have shown, wheeling and dealing. As will be expanded on later, it is the responsibility of international training institutions to ensure that their curricula do not contribute to the development of the marginal syndrome.

The concept of the mediator as a creative synthesizer comes sharply into focus when viewed against the contrasting attributes of the marginal man caught up in a double approach-avoidance conflict. However, it should be noted that some of the authors in this volume have been content with, and indeed have advocated, a less active role for the mediating person. In particular, Klineberg has repeatedly emphasized the communication function of mediators as a means of promoting international understanding. For Klineberg and others, the main contribution of mediating persons is to represent one culture to another faithfully, accurately, and sympathetically. The model that these authors favor is that of the translator who can make a body of literature accessible to individuals who are not familiar with the language in which the material was written. There is no question that this is an extremely valuable service, and in the cultural domain it has been provided by anthropologists, novelists, journalists, returned students, and others to the general benefit of mankind.

However, the analogy between linguistic mediation and the translation of cultures breaks down when the cultural mediator-as-translator is faced with two sets of incompatible demands which require an active response. In such a case, the neutral, faithful representation of one culture's stance to another is less likely to promote mutual understanding; such situations require creative reconciliation of the two opposing points of view.

This can be illustrated with a hypothetical example involving the transfer of technology from an industrial to an agrarian society, in which both parties employ indigenous but bicultural spokesmen in the mediator-as-translator role. The Western mediator has been instructed by his principals to install a Detroit-designed assembly line in rural Asia. Being bicultural, the mediator is aware that the proposed factory will violate most of the local cultural traditions, including the religious practices of the people, which do not permit them to handle the raw material unless it has undergone ritual purification; their extended family obligations, which require all able-bodied men, women, and children to bring in the harvest when the crops mature; the allocation of occupations to different castes, which is likely to lead to a shortage of local labor in certain critical segments of the manufacturing process; the lack of suitable supplies of fuel to drive the machines; and the lack of an infrastructure to support the factory. Being a conscientious mediator-translator, he provides his principals in Detroit with all this salient cultural information, but at that point his responsibilities cease; his job is to represent one culture to the other, but he considers it someone else's job to do something about the problems he has identified.

Conversely, the Eastern mediator has been instructed by his principals to travel to Detroit and there to place an order for an assembly line that must include a ritual purification unit; that can be operated intermittently in harmony with the seasons and the gathering of the various harvests; that provides a majority of the jobs for members of the most numerous caste in the region; that can be driven by a variety of fuels, preferably charcoal and cow dung; and that can be repaired by the village bicycle mechanic. The mediator, who did his degree at the Massachusetts Institute of Technology, knows that he is unlikely to find a machine-tool company in Detroit that would be willing and able to fill this order, and, being a conscientious cultural translator and educator, he explains the theory and practice of assembly-line technology to his principals. But that is as far as he is prepared to go; his job is done, once he has represented one culture to the other.

This hypothetical case study illustrates that a strict interpretation of mediation-as-translation cuts the process short at the very point where it might have the greatest real impact, that is, at the point where *action* could be informed by considerations of cultural mediation. But the mediator as mere cultural representative is excluded from action. On the other hand, the mediator-as-synthesizer is much more likely to perceive that his responsibilities extend to the action stage and beyond. In the present example, this might take the form of designing a factory which combines the best features of both cultures, drawing on the strengths of the existing social system and on appropriate elements of modern technology. In order to integrate the exogenous technical system and the indigenous social system, both the culture and the technology may have to undergo some modification. It will be the responsibility of the mediator-as-synthesizer to ensure that this mutual accommodation takes into account both the cultural and the material aspirations of the people in the region, and that the donor society sees the result as worthwhile.

Formally, the role of the mediator as synthesizer is to create a new concept out of the various elements that were previously parts of different worlds. The product will be a new configuration that incorporates and harmonizes these elements, but is different from the sum of its parts.

Multiculturality is associated with personal growth, the acquisition of a greater range of expressive options, and future-oriented creative work, values that are probably shared by most of mankind. However, it should be noted that at the present, there is a chicken-and-egg barrier that must be overcome before any inroads on the shortage of mediating persons can be made. The growth in the supply of mediators will depend on the emergence of a *culture* of multiculturality, or what the Useems (1967, 1968) have called the Third Culture. As Asch (1956) conclusively showed, being in a minority is very uncomfortable, particularly if the views that one is expressing deviate sharply from the majority position. In practical terms, international training organizations ought to be turning their attention to producing mediating *groups* rather than individuals—groups with shared norms and interpersonal and institutional supports for their emerging supranational roles.

Sojourn research. In the alumni study (Bochner 1973), subjects responded to a number of questions concerning their experiences while abroad, leading to the conclusion that most of these students had a bicultural sojourn. However, the retrospective nature of the data diminishes its validity. To correct this problem, a new research program directly explored the social psychology of the academic sojourn.

Much has been written on whom overseas students do *not* interact with. Thus, the sojourn literature contains many references to the lack of intimate personal contact between overseas students and host nationals (for a recent review, see Klineberg 1970 *a, b*). But with some exceptions (Klein, Miller, and Alexander 1974), there is relatively little direct information on whom foreign students do associate with, and there are hardly any data regarding how and why the students form friendships. Finally, a review of the literature revealed only a few studies (Eide 1970; Gullahorn and Gullahorn 1960) which explicitly explored the academic sojourn from the perspective of cultural mediation.

The studies have all been reported in full elsewhere and will therefore only be described in summary form here. The subjects were East-West Center participants. The East-West Center is an international educational institution located on the campus of the University of Hawaii in Honolulu. Center participants come to Hawaii from approximately forty different countries and territories and include established scholars, graduate and undergraduate students, and short-term, nondegree professional trainees. All four studies focused on graduate students, who typically spend between two and four years pursuing a master's or a doctoral degree. The subjects in three of the studies were students actually present at the Center. In the fourth study, the subjects were American alumni. Two of the studies employed friendship as the dependent variable, one study used helping behavior, and one study explored subjects' anticipations concerning their imminent reentry into the culture of origin.

Bochner, Buker, and McLeod (1976) adapted Milgram's (1967, 1969) "small-world" method to trace communication patterns in the East-West Center dormitory. The procedure is a variant of the chain-letter. In the present experiment, eighteen residents served as starters. Each of the starters was given a booklet and instructed to hand it personally to a "good friend" in the dormitory and to ask this friend to hand the booklet over to one of his or her good friends. The booklet had printed instructions carefully explaining the chain-letter requirements of the task. In addition, the booklet contained fifteen detachable postcards addressed to one of the investigators. Each time the booklet changed hands, the subject recorded the following information on one of the cards: his name and room number; the name and room number of the person to whom the booklet was being transferred; the date of the transaction; and a checklist of "the things that I and the person to whom I gave the booklet have in common." The subject then detached the card and mailed it to us.

The cards were consecutively numbered and marked with an idiosyncratic prefix which clearly identified the chain origin and sequential position of each transaction. From the eighty-six cards that were returned to us, we were able to infer some of the characteristic patterns of friendship in the multicultural setting under scrutiny. The major unit of analysis was the transaction, defined as the handing on of a booklet by one person to another. The transactions could then be tabulated and examined from the point of view of culture, gender, residential proximity, similarity in academic discipline, or any other category relevant to the aims of the investigation. From the perspective of culture similarity, a transaction could occur between two individuals from the same national group or between two persons from different countries. Similarly, a transaction could occur between two individuals of the same sex, or cut across sex lines.

The rather complex treatment of the data is fully described in the original report. The gist of the findings was that there is an extremely strong association between friendship choice and culture similarity. Out of the eighty-six transactions that were recorded, forty-four, or more than half, were between individuals of the same culture, a result that has a chance probability of one in a thousand. There was an even stronger effect for sex similarity—seventy-four out of the eighty-six transactions were between initiators and receivers of the same sex, with males just as reluctant as females to cross gender lines. Finally, there was a marked absence of the proximity effect usually found in research on how people get acquainted (Festinger, Schachter, and Back 1950). The modal transaction occurred between two persons who occupied the same building but lived on different floors. Thus, physical proximity played an unusually minor role in determining the social relations of the subjects, further confirming the importance of the bonds of culture and sex similarity for the respondents in our study.

At institutions such as the East-West Center, there are many official and unofficial pressures to "interculturate," that is, to form interpersonal bonds that cut across cultural boundaries. In such settings, conventional questionnaire studies run the risk of revealing little more than a reflection of the official institutional dogma (Bochner 1980). To overcome this methodological problem, we developed the chain-booklet technique, which reflects the behavioral sequence of the initiator seeking out another person, enlisting that person's help, motivating the receiver to keep the chain going, and filling out and mailing a postcard. Furthermore, the transaction constitutes an overt affirmation of friendship, since the phrase "good friend" appears in the printed instructions included in the booklet. Under these fairly stringent experimental conditions, the study revealed a predominantly monocultural pattern in the social relations of the dormitory residents, with respect to both ethnicity and sex. It appears that the majority of the respondents did not, for whatever reason, form multicultural associations, even though the social system that they lived in afforded them an excellent opportunity to do so.

Our interest in the mediating process led us to do a number of analyses of the forty-two transactions that had crossed cultural boundaries. Unfortunately, there was no systematic pattern in these data. Perhaps the most interesting negative result was that no single national group stood out as likely to form cross-cultural friendships, including the host group of Americans. The crossover friendships were distributed over a wide range of cultures, roughly in proportion to the concentration of their members in the dormitory. Thus, no single national group appeared to be playing the role of "cultural confidant," a finding relevant to the hypothesis that some cultures are more mediation-oriented than others. This hypothesis was not confirmed by our data.

The second study of friendship patterns employed a more conventional technique. Bochner, McLeod, and Lin (1977) asked East-West Center dormitory residents to identify their five best friends and the five persons with whom they spent most of their time. Great care was taken to avoid suggesting that having either compatriot or host-national friends was socially desirable. In the second half of the study, subjects were asked to indicate whom they would prefer as a companion for a variety of situations and activities.

The results of this investigation confirmed and extended the findings of the chain-booklet experiment. Once again, there was an overall preference for friends of the same culture. However, because the respondents were asked to identify not just one but five friends, and because the subjects were not restricted to listing dormitory residents, the procedure implied a less stringent definition of friendship. We were thus not surprised to find that host-culture members appeared as the second most frequent target for friendship.

The most significant outcome of this investigation was to confirm a hypothesis generated by the Bochner alumni study (1973), to the effect that sojourning students form associations with different categories of individuals for different and predictable reasons. We have called this the functional model of the academic sojourn. Our study showed that in accordance with expectations, foreign students typically tend to be members of three distinct interpersonal networks. Their primary network is monocultural and consists of bonds between compatriots. The main function of the conational network is to provide a setting in which ethnic and cultural values can be rehearsed and *expressed*. The secondary network of foreign students is bicultural and consists of bonds with host nationals. The main function of this network is *instrumentally* to facilitate the academic and professional aspirations of the sojourner. A third and much less salient network is the foreign student's multicultural circle of friends and acquaintances. The main function of this network is to provide companionship for *recreational*, nonculture- and nontask-oriented activities.

The functional model of the academic sojourn has put the problem of why some individuals become mediators and others do not in a new light, suggesting that the mediators will be those students who establish personal relationships with members of the host culture, while at the same time retaining close ties with their compatriots. It is clear to us that future research will specifically have to probe the personal needs that are fulfilled by friendship with a host national. Also, what are the needs that are gratified by association with compatriots, do these needs change over the period of the sojourn, and what cross-cultural differences exist with respect to these relationships? Such research may ultimately lead to an understanding of the functional value of mediation, that is, of the personal needs that are fulfilled by acting as a mediator between different cultures.

In the third study, Bochner, Lin, and McLeod (1980) administered a questionnaire to terminating students immediately prior to their departure for their homeland. One of the items asked students to list those activities that they were most looking forward to after reentry. Another item asked the subjects to anticipate those events about which they were most anxious. As we had predicted, the subjects eagerly looked forward to but were also extremely anxious about precisely the same set of events. The anticipated significant reentry situations could be classified into three categories: the immediate family, social relations in the job environment, and general sociocultural interactions in public and institutional settings such as the street, shops, schools, government departments, concert halls, and football grounds. The data indicate ambivalence toward the impending return to their own culture. In this sense, the students reveal that they have become bicultural individuals who are clearly aware of the nature of the two cultures they now represent and of the disparity between the two social systems claiming their allegiance. The data also suggest that the students had not been able to resolve, reconcile, or synthesize the disparity and were thus not in a position to function as synthesizing mediators between their two cultural systems.

The study supports the contention made earlier in this chapter that the mediator-as-translator model breaks down if the material being translated is mutually inconsistent. The earlier discussion was illustrated with a hypothetical example involving the transfer of technology, in which the mediator-translator served exclusively as a communication channel between two different cultural systems. In the present instance, the data are real and refer to the personal conflict that is generated by internalizing two sets of mutually incompatible guidelines to social conduct. Unless the individual can actively integrate these different rules into a new and internally coherent system, one of the following outcomes is highly likely: the student will become marginal to both cultures, vacillating between them; the student will revert to a monocultural style soon after reentry; or the student will develop negative attitudes toward his culture of origin and probably become an expatriate in due course. None of these outcomes is desirable, or consistent with the aims of international education.

In the fourth study, Bochner, Lin, and McLeod (1979) attempted to evaluate the impact of structured cross-cultural experiences on attitudes relevant to mediation. It is generally assumed that exposure to multicultural environments (such as the East-West Center) generates or expands inter-national-mindedness in its participants (Fulbright 1976). Indeed, that is one of the main claims made to justify the allocation of large amounts of public funds to subsidize educational exchange programs. However, the hypothesized link between cross-cultural experiences and international-mindedness (and, by implication, international understanding) is extremely difficult to measure because it is hard to point to empirical operations that unequivocally denote international-mindedness; and if it is put to subjects, everyone favors having an international perspective and claims that virtue for himself. For these reasons, the study that we are about to describe employed an indirect, operationally defined, and largely unobtrusive measure of inter-national-mindedness.

Bochner, Lin, and McLeod (1979) sent letters to American alumni of the East-West Center (EWC), and to a similar group of University of Hawaii (UH) alumni. (The East-West Center subjects were all, of course, also grad-uates of the University of Hawaii.) The experiment therefore contained two groups of subjects, a sample of Americans who were alumni of both the EWC and UH, and a sample of Americans who were alumni of UH only. Half of the letters apparently emanated from Ms. Beverly McLeod, "a grad-uate student from California, studying for a master's degree at the University of Hawaii." The rest of the letters were apparently sent by Ms. Anli Lin, "a graduate student from Taiwan, studying for a master's degree at the Univer-sity of Hawaii." All of the letters exhibited the same return address, a house in a Honolulu suburb. In the letter, the writer said that she was conducting research in the area of second-language acquisition and that she would be grateful if the recipient could help her by filling out and returning to her a questionnaire which was enclosed with the letter. The questionnaire was a genuine instrument and contained items regarding the number of languages the subjects knew; their level of reading, writing, and speaking competence in each language; the countries that the respondents had lived in; and so forth.

The dependent variable was the relative frequency of returned question-naires in each of the experimental conditions. The rather complex results have been reported elsewhere. Of interest to the present discussion was an overall greater willingness of East-West Center than non-East-West Center University of Hawaii alumni to participate in the research program "on second-language acquisition." The ethnic identity of the person making the appeal had no effect on the return rate. Neither the purported research nor its alleged originators were in any way identified with the East-West Center. Why, then, did EWC alumni respond more favorably than comparable non-EWC University of Hawaii graduates, as indeed we had expected?

Our prediction was based on the rationale that multicultural living experiences do have a significant impact, but that this effect is subtle, covert, and difficult to measure directly. If this is the case, then the appropriate research strategy consists of identifying those variables which are indirectly implied in the acquisition of multiculturality and then systematically exploring the relationship between these parameters and the experience of living in a multicultural setting. This reasoning led us to predict that alumni of the explicitly multicultural East-West Center would be more willing to participate in research with supranational implications than alumni of even such a culturally heterogeneous institution as the Univeristy of Hawaii. The substantive hypothesis was confirmed, but a more detailed analysis of the data and a second experiment revealed that the training effect (exposure to East-West Center programs) was confounded with prior residence in a foreign country. Specifically, the EWC alumni who responded to the appeal had also lived abroad before coming to the East-West Center. International-mindedness, therefore, as measured by willingness to participate in research on a topic with cross-cultural connotations, was the joint outcome of earlier international experience and subsequent exposure to an explicitly designed multicultural living program. This finding reveals two interconnected problems, the first in relation to evaluating cross-cultural living programs, and the second in relation to the question of what sorts of individuals would most benefit from participating in such programs.

The problems arise because a major criterion for selecting participants for explicitly designed multicultural living programs is prior cross-cultural experience. Thus, most of the American students at the East-West Center had previously lived abroad, and there is no reason to believe that the East-West Center program is atypical in this regard. This has two consequences. First, it makes gauging the impact of the training experience per se extremely difficult, since it is virtually impossible to rule out the alternative hypothesis that the effect (whatever it might be) was primarily a function of the participants' preprogram cross-cultural history. Second, it is likely that the main contribution of EWC-type programs is to maintain and expand the already existing cross-cultural orientation of its participants, rather than to create a new set of mediating attitudes in initially opposed or neutral individuals. Although there is nothing intrinsically wrong with such a goal, it does suggest that institutions such as the East-West Center are not making an impact where one is most needed—in the ethnocentric and chauvinistic sections of society.

THE PERSONAL ATTRIBUTES OF CULTURAL MEDIATORS

In the preceding sections, the structural and interpersonal attributes of mediation were presented. That discussion reflected the bias of social psychology, which emphasizes the situational determinants of behavior. Social psychologists are uncomfortable with the assertion that an individual possesses a set of enduring personality traits which somehow control and explain his actions and feelings. Consequently, when a social psychologist speaks of the personal attributes of cultural mediators, he is referring in a purely *descriptive* sense to those behaviors which mediators either exhibit or can theoretically be expected to exhibit by virtue of being located structurally at the interface between two cultures, and/or belonging to a mediating reference group, and/or coming under the influence of a mediating situation.

Most of these personal attributes have already been identified and refer to the necessary and sufficient responses of individuals in interface situations who would wish to translate one culture to the other, and/or who desire to produce positive effects in both systems. The formal descriptive categories can be derived from some of the traditional concepts of behavioral science. Thus, in considering the attributes which an individual might display in a mediating situation, we can refer to his knowledge, motives, attitudes, feelings, and skills—to his cognitive, conative, affective, and habit structures—and hypothesize that the mediating person should be familiar with the nature of both systems, able to use that knowledge to perform well in each culture, like and respect both life-styles, be a good communicator, and be equally at home or comfortable in either society.

At a slightly more complex level of analysis, we can use concepts that functionally relate the characteristics of the individual to his social environment, and this has been the approach adopted in the present chapter. Thus, we have been particularly interested in identifying the role requirements and role conflicts of cultural mediation, the societal forces that reinforce or extinguish (Guthrie 1975) mediating behavior, and the nature of the reference groups (Newcomb 1943) and influential people on whom mediating persons model their behavior and from whom they gather their social support.

This theoretical approach is based on the assumption that the "mediating personality" is predominantly the product of the individual's contemporary social context. The approach can be criticized for neglecting or underemphasizing the personal qualities that individuals bring to social situations, including their early childhood experiences and subsequent history. Nor is there any consideration of how these personal characteristics might interact with situational determinants to produce mediating behavior. The criticism is valid. However, as Taft has indicated in his chapter, there is very little direct empirical evidence regarding the enduring personality traits of cultural mediators; and as Guthrie has shown in his chapter, the evidence that is available speaks negatively to the proposition that cultural mediators can be described in terms of a set of personality characteristics that reliably distinguish them from other categories of persons. This does not mean that future research may not uncover a mediating-personality syndrome. At the present state of knowledge, though, "between-skin" explanations of cultural mediation tend to have greater utility than "within-skin" accounts.

The Empirical Definition of Cultural Mediation

The review of the empirical literature has revealed that the meaning of cultural mediation varies with the sorts of questions being asked, the level at which the analysis is conducted, and the conditions under which the phenomenon is measured.

The formal model of mediation utilized a three-tiered framework; at the structural level, the process was located at the interface between two or more cultural systems. An implication of the open-systems formulation of cultures in contact is that the outcome of an interaction can be evaluated in terms of emic cost-benefit analyses for each culture. The interface formulation brought out the need to distinguish between cultural marginality and cultural mediation. This in turn led to distinguishing between the mediator as translator and the mediator as synthesizer.

At the interpersonal level, mediation was treated as a group process, performed by persons in mediating roles and supported by mediating institutions, traditions, and norms. The concept of culture-learning was used to predict the cognitive, affective, and behavioral changes of individuals placed in interface situations, the possible outcomes being mono/bi/multiculturality. The empirical procedures used to define the social world of cultural mediators operationally were then described in some detail. This empirical program generated a functional model of the academic sojourn, which implied that foreign students would have three social networks—a conational network for culture rehearsal, a host-national network to facilitate adjustment, and a multicultural network for recreation.

At the personal level, mediation was treated as a descriptive category referring to the behaviors, feelings, and attitudes that persons in a mediating role exhibit.

Until further empirical evidence becomes available, the preceding set of propositions has the status of a working model only. The main value of the model lies in its ability to generate testable predictions about the antecedents, correlates, and outcomes of cultural mediation and thereby provide empirical and theoretical referents for a heretofore conceptually elusive phenomenon.

Training Mediators

An individual who wishes to enter an established profession or master an established trade usually has an obvious career path to follow. Entry into established occupational categories is based on the principle of acquiring the necessary qualifications from institutions that have the requisite legal and/or traditional status. All societies contain such institutions, and they tend to reflect the values of their respective cultures. For example, Thailand has relatively many monasteries, or training complexes for the contemplative life, and relatively few management training centers, or courses devoted to the maximizing of industrial output per worker. The opposite is true in Australia.

An individual who wishes to become a cultural mediator does not have an obvious path to follow. Cultural mediation is not a recognized profession, although throughout the world there are a great many individuals who, whether they know it or not, are practicing cultural mediators. The necessary qualifications for mediators are not properly understood, nor is there general agreement about the attributes of the ideal mediator. Finally, society is just beginning to concern itself with establishing institutions to train and certify mediating persons (for example, the East-West Center was only established in 1960, and is still in the process of crystallizing its functions and goals).

If and when cultural mediation becomes institutionalized, it will acquire the definition it now lacks. Since it is much easier to influence the shape of emerging institutions than it is to modify existing ones, the time to debate the professionalization of mediation is *now*, before the mediating role has become rigidly circumscribed.

EXISTING TRAINING MODELS

Probably the most common form of structured culture-learning is assumed to occur as a *by-product* of the academic sojourn. The chapter by Klineberg provides an account of this process. However, evidence has been presented in this chapter and throughout the book that casts doubt on these assumptions; many foreign scholars are primarily interested in obtaining a degree or furthering their professional goals, rather than in learning a new culture; many foreign scholars make only superficial contacts with host nationals; host nationals sometimes reject the overtures for contact made by sojourning scholars; and at times the academic sojourn has disastrous consequences for mutual understanding and goodwill (Tajfel and Dawson 1965).

This evidence has not deterred the architects and administrators of international educational exchange from continuing and even expanding their activities, and rightly so. Even if the programs do not produce the intended number of heterocultural persons, they at least provide higher education to many individuals who might otherwise have been denied this opportunity, and that is sufficient justification for the enterprise. However, there is enough evidence to indicate that the by-product model of culture-learning is not a very effective training procedure for mediating persons.

The second category of structured culture-learning provides specific information and skills in order to make a person's sojourn in an alien culture more effective and less stressful. The individuals who participate in these types of culture-learning programs are usually on an assignment to carry out a particular task in another culture. Well-known examples include Peace Corps volunteers (Guthrie, this volume), foreign service personnel (Dane, this volume), and technical experts (Seidel, this volume). Culture-training consists of predeparture orientation programs that give the learner systematic information which, in the opinion of the trainer, he will need in order to do his job effectively. This might be called the *instrumental* model of culture-training. The framework is task-oriented, and the learning is promoted and justified on the grounds that it will facilitate the primary aim of the sojourn, whatever that might be. It is claimed that individuals who have been through such a training course will be better at teaching English to Thai children, establishing cordial diplomatic relations with Brazilian officials, or installing a meat processing plant in Egypt than persons not exposed to a training experience.

However, evidence has been presented by various authors in this book that these task-oriented cross-cultural training programs have sometimes not had the intended effect of reducing culture shock and enhancing performance in the field. Guthrie is particularly scathing about the failure of the Peace Corps orientation programs; Dane and Sullivan both refer to the many American officials who experience personal and professional difficulties while representing their country abroad; and Seidel describes some of the problems surrounding the preparation of experts for service in foreign countries.

Why do these training efforts sometimes fail to meet expectations? An analysis of their structure and curriculum content provides a hint: the weakness of the instrumental model of culture-learning appears to be its task orientation. This is because culture tends to be presented as an obstacle that stands in the way of the real purpose of the assignment. Culture is something that has to be adjusted to, coped with, defended against, maybe even ignored; the job is the challenge, and task performance is the tangible measure of success. And because the intrinsic value of learning a second culture is understated, the trainee tends to remain essentially monocultural, with the exception of the few superficial cultural skills that he acquires to cope temporarily with his situation. Because of its task orientation, the instrumental model of culture-learning is limited in its effectiveness as a training procedure for mediating persons, either as translators or as synthesizers.

As has already been noted, both the by-product and the instrumental models refer to *structured* culture-learning experiences, that is, intervention programs deliberately introduced by sponsoring or training agencies to give selected participants a heterocultural perspective. In addition to these deliberately created instances of culture contact, there exist many unstructured and natural opportunities for culture-learning. Of greatest relevance to the issue of mediation are those individuals who by the accident of their birth were raised simultaneously in more than one culture. In particular, they include the children of persons working in foreign countries (such as diplomats, soldiers, businessmen, missionaries), the children of mixed marriages, and second-generation migrants. The evidence is equivocal regarding the relation between exposure to two cultures as a child and subsequently becoming a mediating person. On the one hand, many marginal persons seem to have had a bicultural childhood. On the other hand, as Taft has indicated in his chapter, there are instances of outstanding mediators who by the accident of their birth started life as biculturals.

Further research is needed to tease out those variables in the *accident-of-birth* syndrome which contribute to the development of mediating persons. At present, however, there is insufficient evidence to be able to assert that a bicultural childhood constitutes an effective training procedure for mediating persons.

A MEDIATION-CENTERED TRAINING MODEL

The preceding discussion drew attention to the limitations of existing training models. There is little doubt that the current training of mediators occurs under haphazard and unsystematic conditions. Some mediators are the by-product of international educational exchange. Some are alumni of job-related sojourns in other cultures. Some have had bicultural childhoods. However, too many individuals who were exposed to any one or all of these types of cross-cultural experiences fail to realize their potential as mediating persons. There is an urgent need to establish a more systematic and theoretical approach to the training of cultural mediators. The formal requirements of a training model can be derived from the premise that the mediating role should be professionalized and institutionalized. This implies a curriculum built around the theory and practice of cultural mediation. However, since both theory and practice in this field are still developing, a central aspect of the curriculum must be an explicit responsiveness to data about effectiveness of the curriculum. Such evaluation will clarify the objectives of training programs, monitor the correspondence between performance and intention, and suggest ways in which the program and/or its objectives should be modified to bring about their greater congruence. Training courses based on these principles should serve the dual aim of producing mediating persons while at the same time adding to the content and precision of the theoretical construct of cultural mediation.

The preferred means of implementing mediation-centered training programs would be for tertiary institutions to offer postgraduate degrees in cultural mediation. It is vital to their success that these courses conform to the highest possible standards. Established universities are probably the institutions most likely to possess the resources, traditions, status, and political independence required to develop academically and professionally excellent curricula in cultural mediation.

The proposal to establish degree courses in cultural mediation has ample precedents from other emerging professional fields, such as recently introduced programs in architectural psychology, community medicine, urban studies, environmental science, and foreign-student counseling. There is already a substantial body of theory, research, and practice that bears directly on the subject of cultural mediation. There is also the entire area of the behavioral sciences to draw on for the formulation of hypotheses and for collateral evidence that might have an indirect bearing on the subject.

In addition to general theoretical and empirical issues in culture-learning, it would be highly desirable for the curriculum to include segments specifically aimed at facilitating task-oriented achievement in alien cultures. However, departing from present practice, the cultural variable would not be treated as an obstacle to overcome or as a nuisance one must learn to live with. Rather, cultural differences would be presented in positive terms, and task achievement would be judged on whether the job was performed in a style consistent with the principles of cultural mediation. The content of these modules would be worked out in conjunction with organizations actually engaged in cross-cultural work. In return for this free training, these organizations would be asked to provide internships for on-the-job training and employment opportunities for graduates.

In the past, many students (both foreign and indigenous) have been reluctant to commit themselves to nondegree programs of culture-learning for fear of not obtaining qualifications leading to well-paying and highly regarded jobs. A degree course in cultural mediation would simultaneously satisfy the professional, status, and culture-learning aspirations of students, and should attract a high caliber of candidate to this area.

In summary, the proposed degree would consist of three components: a "pure" strand, aimed at theory appreciation and building; a research and evaluation strand that would monitor the effectiveness of the concepts and procedures, propose modifications to the model and the training curriculum, and generate hypotheses for further investigation; and an applied strand, aimed at introducing mediation at the work place, making an impact in the practical world of affairs, attracting able students, and creating career opportunities in cultural mediation.

Conclusion

In this chapter, the language and concepts of social psychology were used to present an empirically based working model of cultural mediation. Structurally, the mediating person is located at the interface between two or more cultural systems. Functionally, the mediating person links these systems either as a translator or as a synthesizer. The mediating person's general purpose is to contribute to international understanding. In the area of social change, he is concerned with cultural preservation. With respect to the diffusion of innovations, he recognizes that societies should absorb outside influences without losing their core identity. Cognitively and behaviorally, the mediating person is heterocultural rather than monocultural. A pitfall for the mediating person is the marginal syndrome. To avoid that syndrome, the mediating person must have social support, including a clearly defined professional role with a reasonable degree of status, and a reference group against which an individual mediating person can evaluate his performance. The most effective way of training mediators and concurrently legitimizing their professional role is through degree courses in the theory, research, and practice of cultural mediation.

In the area of intercultural transactions, two widespread practices seriously threaten the quality of life on this planet. The first is the tendency for the nations and cultures of the world to meet each other in a spirit of confrontation, mutual suspicion, and exploitation. The second is the tendency for heretofore nonindustrialized societies to modernize through the straight transfer of Western technology, disregarding any side effects this might have on the integrity of their culture. The first tendency, if unchecked, may lead to global war. The second tendency, if unchecked, will lead to the gradual disappearance and ultimate extinction of many of the cultures that presently give variety to the family of man. Is there anything that can be done to avert these disasters? Theoretically, mediators-as-translators should help to prevent intercultural transactions based on suspicion, mistrust, and misunderstanding, and mediators-as-synthesizers should help to prevent the diffusion of innovations based on fallacious assumptions about the superiority of Western technological practices.

Unfortunately, theory and practice do not always go hand in hand. However, an optimistic scenario of the future suggests that there will be a greater realization of the predicament that faces mankind in intercultural and international relations. That realization will be accompanied by an accelerated search for ways of improving the conduct of international affairs. Various solutions will be tried, including an attempt to replace the existing dysfunctional style of international intercourse with a form of dialogue that is more consistent with the principles of cultural mediation. The success of that attempt will depend in part on the availability of mediating persons to act as role models and agents of change and generally to provide leadership in the movement toward a healthier pattern of international interaction. The typical mediating person will be an organization man, since the business of the world tends to be conducted among institutions (governments, banks, universities, corporations) rather than among individuals in their private capacity; he will be highly trained in at least two professions, his substantive discipline (for instance, architecture, agronomy, physiology, psychology) and the profession of cultural mediation; he will be a heterocultural individual with systematic knowledge of at least two and probably more cultures; he will occupy a transnational professional role; and he will belong to a transcultural reference group whose norms transcend national and cultural barriers.

The rather clinically drawn picture of the mediating person of the future may cause some dismay, particularly among those who believe that the backbone of sound international relations is the natural mediator—the inspired amateur who instinctively adopts a mediating role when circumstances require it. Unfortunately, life in the twentieth century has become too complex for the world's predicaments to respond readily to the remedial efforts of amateurs, no matter how inspired. Only professionals can provide the sustained and informed thrust needed to overcome the acute difficulties inherent in international relations. The professional mediator cannot work effectively in a vacuum, isolated from the practical world of affairs. He needs a political and intellectual climate that values his achievements and approves of his goals. The active support of ordinary people in all walks of life is essential if the idea is to catch on that mediation is the preferred style for the conduct of intercultural transactions.

References

Adorno, T. W., Frenkel-Brunswik, E., Levinson, D. J., and Sanford, R. N. *The Authoritarian Personality*. New York: Harper, 1950.

Alatas, S. H. The Captive Mind in Development Studies: Some Neglected Problems and the Need for an Autonomous Social Science Tradition in Asia. *International Social Science Journal*, 1972, *24*, 9–25.

_____. The Captive Mind and Creative Development. *International Social Science Journal*, 1975, *27*, 691–700.

Allport, G. W. *The Nature of Prejudice*. Garden City, N.Y.: Doubleday Anchor, 1954.

Asch, S. E. Studies of Independence and Submission to Group Pressure: I. A Minority of One Against a Unanimous Majority. *Psychological Monographs*, 1956, *70* (9, whole No. 416).

Berrien, F. K. *General and Social Systems*. New Brunswick, N.J.: Rutgers University Press, 1968.

Berry, J. W. On Cross-cultural Comparability. *International Journal of Psychology,* 1969, *4*, 119–128.

Bochner, S. Problems in Culture Learning. In S. Bochner and P. Wicks (eds.), *Overseas Students in Australia.* Sydney: New South Wales University Press, 1972.

_____. *The Mediating Man: Cultural Interchange and Transnational Education.* Honolulu, Hawaii: East-West Center, 1973.

_____. Unobtrusive Methods in Cross-cultural Experimentation. In H. Triandis and J. W. Berry (eds.), *Handbook of Cross-cultural Psychology: Methodology. Vol. 2.* Boston, Mass.: Allyn and Bacon, 1980.

_____. Cultural Diversity: Implications for Modernization and International Education. In K. Kumar (ed.), *Bonds Without Bondage: Explorations in Transcultural Interactions.* Honolulu, Hawaii: The University Press of Hawaii, 1979.

Bochner, S., Buker, E. A., and McLeod, B. M. Communication Patterns in an International Student Dormitory: A Modification of the "Small World" Method. *Journal of Applied Social Psychology*, 1976, *6*, 275–290.

Bochner, S., Lin, A., and McLeod, B. M. Cross-Cultural Contact and the Development of an International Perspective. *Journal of Social Psychology*, 1979, *107*, 29–41.

_____. Anticipated Role Conflict of Returning Overseas Students. *Journal of Social Psychology*, 1980, *110*, 265–272.

Bochner, S., McLeod, B. M., and Lin, A. Friendship Patterns of Overseas Students: A Functional Model. *International Journal of Psychology*, 1977, *12*, 277–294.

Boxer, A. H. *Experts in Asia: An Inquiry into Australian Technical Assistance.* Canberra: Australian National University Press, 1969.

Crocombe, R. Preserving Which Tradition? The Future of Pacific Cultures. *Pacific Perspective*, 1972, *1*, 1–15.

Curle, A. *Educational Strategy for Developing Societies.* 2nd ed. London: Tavistock, 1970.

Doczy, A. G. Minority Groups and Problems of Adjustment. In F. S. Stevens (ed.), *Racism: The Australian Experience. Vol. 1: Prejudice and Xenophobia.* Sydney: Australia and New Zealand Book Company, 1971.

Eide, I. (ed.). *Students as Links Between Cultures.* Paris: UNESCO, 1970.

Elkin, A. *The Australian Aborigines.* Garden City, N.Y.: Doubleday Anchor, 1964.

Emery, F. E. (ed.). *Systems Thinking.* Harmondsworth, England: Penguin Books, 1969.

Faure, E., Herrara, F., Kaddoura, A., Lopes, H., Petrovsky, A. V., Rahnema, M., and Ward, F. C. *Learning to Be: The World of Education Today and Tomorrow.* Paris: UNESCO, 1972.

Festinger, L., Schachter, S., and Back, K. *Social Pressures in Informal Groups: A Study of a Housing Community.* New York: Harper, 1950.

Foa, U. G., and Foa, E. B. *Societal Structures of the Mind.* Springfield, Ill.: Charles C. Thomas, 1974.

Fulbright, J. W. The most significant and important activity I have been privileged to engage in during my years in the Senate. *The Annals of the American Academy of Political and Social Science*, 1976, *424*, 1–5.

Gallimore, R., Boggs, J. W., and Jordan, C. *Culture, Behavior and Education: A Study of Hawaiian-Americans*. Beverly Hills, Calif.: Sage, 1974.

Gullahorn, J. T., and Gullahorn, J. E. The Role of the Academic Man as a Cross-cultural Mediator. *American Sociological Review*, 1960, *25*, 414–417.

Guthrie, G. M. A behavioral analysis of culture learning. In R. W. Brislin, S. Bochner, and W. J. Lonner (eds.), *Cross-cultural Perspectives on Learning*. New York: Wiley, 1975.

Herskovits, M. J. *Man and His Works*. New York: Knopf, 1948.

Inkeles, A. Becoming Modern: Individual Change in Six Developing Countries. *Ethos*, 1975, *3*, 323–342.

Inkeles, A., and Smith, D. H. *Becoming Modern*. Cambridge, Mass.: Harvard University Press, 1974.

Klein, M. H., Miller, M. H., and Alexander, A. A. When Young People Go Out in the World. In W. P. Lebra (ed.), *Youth, Socialization, and Mental Health*. Honolulu, Hawaii: University Press of Hawaii, 1974.

Klineberg, O. Psychological Aspects of Student Exchange. In I. Eide (ed.), *Students as Links Between Cultures*. Paris: UNESCO, 1970*a*.

―――. Research in the Field of Educational Exchange. In I. Eide (ed.), *Students as Links Between Cultures*. Paris: UNESCO, 1970*b*.

McLuhan, M. *Understanding Media: The Extensions of Man*. London: Routledge and Kegan Paul, 1964.

Mead, M. *Sex and Temperament in Three Primitive Societies*. New York: Morrow, 1935.

Milgram, S. The Small World Problem. *Psychology Today*, 1967, *1*, 61–67.

―――. Interdisciplinary Thinking and the Small World Problem. In M. Sherif and C. W. Sherif (eds.), *Interdisciplinary Relationships in the Social Sciences*. Chicago, Ill.: Aldine, 1969.

Mortimer, R. Aiding the "Underdeveloped" Countries. *Australia's Neighbours*, 1973, *4* (85), 1–5.

Nehru, J. *An Autobiography*. London: Bodley Head, 1936 (rpt. 1958).

Newcomb, T. M. *Personality and Social Change*. New York: Holt, Rinehart and Winston, 1943.

Pettigrew, T. F. *A Profile of the Negro American*. Princeton, N.J.: Van Nostrand, 1964.

Secord, P. F., and Backman, C. W. *Social Psychology*. New York: McGraw-Hill, 1964.

Selltiz, C., Christ, J. R., Havel, J., and Cook, S. W. *Attitudes and Social Relations of Foreign Students in the United States*. Minneapolis, Minn.: University of Minnesota Press, 1963.

Stonequist, E. V. *The Marginal Man*. New York: Scribner, 1937.

Tajfel, H., and Dawson, J. L. (eds.). *Disappointed Guests*. London: Oxford University Press, 1965.

Triandis, H. C. Subjective Culture and Economic Development. *International Journal of Psychology*, 1973, *8*, 163–180.

_____. Culture Training, Cognitive Complexity and Interpersonal Attitudes. In R. W. Brislin, S. Bochner, and W. J. Lonner (eds.), *Cross-cultural Perspectives on Learning*. New York: Wiley, 1975.

Triandis, H. C., Vassiliou, V., Vassiliou, G., Tanaka, Y., and Shanmugam, A. V. *The Analysis of Subjective Culture*. New York: Wiley, 1972.

Useem, J., and Useem, R. H. The Interfaces of a Binational Third Culture: A Study of the American Community in India. *Journal of Social Issues*, 1967, *23*(1), 130–143.

_____. American-educated Indians and Americans in India: A Comparison of Two Modernizing Roles. *Journal of Social Issues*, 1968, *24*(4), 143–158.

Useem, J., Useem, R. H., and Donoghue, J. Men in the Middle of the Third Culture: The Roles of American and Non-Western People in Cross-cultural Administration. *Human Organization*, 1963, *22*, 169–179.

Wade, N. Third World: Science and Technology Contribute Feebly to Development. *Science*, 1975, *189*, 770–776.

Beverly McLeod

The Mediating Person and Cultural Identity

Introduction

This chapter will focus on some of the barriers to becoming a successful mediating person, as a first step in developing solutions to these difficulties. The chapter opens with an attempt to formulate a tentative definition of mediation and the mediating person, as a point of reference for the subsequent discussion. Then, examples of different types of mediation and their possible effects will be given. Next, the problem of the acceptance of the mediator by the cultural groups concerned will be discussed. This will be followed by a treatment of the inner conflicts and problems which a mediating person may experience. Finally, an attempt will be made to expand and delineate more clearly the role and characteristics of the "ideal mediator."

Definitions

A conceptual analysis of the term "mediating person" suggests that the construct refers to at least three distinguishable domains of discourse: the mediating person can be thought of in terms of who he is, what he does, or where he fits into two or more cultures. Table 1 illustrates some of the perspectives from which the mediating person can be viewed.

How can we define the mediating person? Is he a person who has some knowledge of more than one culture? Is he, beyond that, someone who has incorporated in his own personality the values and behavior patterns of more than one culture? Or rather, is he someone with whom the people of more than one culture feel comfortable? Is he a member of a group which historically has played the role of cultural mediator? Is he a person who has a secure identity in one culture, or one who floats among cultures but belongs to none? Or is he the cultural counterpart of a bilingual, belonging fully to more than one culture? Is he someone who has special personality characteristics, or one who just happens to be in the the right place at the right time? Is he likely to be more task-oriented or more socially oriented?

Table 1. The Mediating Person: Personal, Functional, and Ascribed Attributes

Who He Is: Personal Attributes	What He Does: Functions	How He Is Regarded: Socially Defined Roles
1. Knowledge and experience 2. Cultural identity; personal security 3. Task or social orientation	1. Bridges; transmits 2. Floats between cultures 3. Profession; purpose	1. Acceptance or rejection 2. Categorization by culture 3. Point in time: historical relations between cultures

Purposes of Mediation

These questions illustrate the difficulty of providing a simple characterization of the mediating person. In addition, consideration must be given to the purpose of mediation; is it for business, diplomacy, education, technical interchange, world peace, or something else? Perhaps a different type of mediating person is needed for each of these purposes. In any case, the purposes of the individuals located at the conjunction of two or more cultures interact with their personal, functional, and ascribed attributes. The product of this interaction, from the point of view of who benefits from the process, can be the improvement of the home culture, the host culture, both cultures, or mankind in general. As Bochner has indicated in his chapter in this part, only the latter two outcomes can be considered to fulfill the requirements of cultural mediation; that is, a person located at the conjunction of two or more cultures is performing a mediating function only if his presence or activities result in some measure of benefit for both of the cultures he is straddling. Table 2 presents a schematic summary of this analysis.

We will look at several examples of types of people who, by profession or experience, are active at the point of conjunction of two or more cultures and therefore have an opportunity to be mediators. Perhaps the most ancient and persistent form of mediation between cultures has been carried on by traders, or their modern counterparts, international businessmen. Traders deal in objects and money, and they must possess at least rudimentary communication skills in addition to the objects desired by their clients. A deeper knowledge of the clients' culture is often not necessary, but may enhance the trader's sales by making him aware of the preferences of his customers. His vested interest in the process of mediation is himself, and his success can easily be measured in terms of his wealth. In theory, the activities of a trader

Table 2. The Process and Outcomes of Cultural Conjunction

Process		Outcome	Mediator Function
The Mediating Person	x Purpose	Benefit to:	
Identity	Political, ideological,	Home Culture	No
Function	and doctrin- al influence	Host Culture	No
Ascription		Both Cultures	Yes
	Exchange of goods and services	Mankind	Yes
	Welfare and quality of life		
	Education		

or businessman could confer benefits on both the home and the host cultures, as well as on the individual himself. However, in practice, the benefits tend to be asymmetrically arrayed in favor of the home culture, especially if the trader or businessman is sponsored by the government or stockholders of the home culture.

A second type of mediator may be termed the diplomat, and includes all those individuals who are official or unofficial representatives of governments. The diplomat deals with other people as representatives of their own government. He must himself possess, or have access to, communication skills of a somewhat more sophisticated nature than must the trader, although occurrences of international "incidents" arising from mistranslations indicate that in practice, communication is not always as good as it could or should be. The diplomat must also possess objects, power, or concessions with which to bargain. A deeper knowledge of the other culture may be beneficial in terms of gaining greater power, but this aspect has been deemed of little importance in the conduct of diplomacy, with the possible exception of spying and other undercover activities. The vested interest of the diplomat is in the greater power, prestige, and security of the government which he represents, and his success can be measured in these terms. Theoretically, the activities of the diplomat can result in mutual benefit for the two cultures with which he deals, in terms of preventing war and launching joint ventures. However, the diplomat is constrained even more firmly than the trader is by the sponsorship of his own government, and this usually results in an asymmetrical balance of benefit in favor of the home culture. This is especially true if, as is often the case, international politics is seen as a zero-sum game, that is, where one party can "win" only if the other side "loses."

A third type of mediator may be termed the missionary, and this category includes those persons who "have a mission," either as individuals or as representatives of groups such as religious organizations, businesses, governments, health and educational organizations, and so on. They deal with the people and the culture of the society, and their mission is to change some aspect of the society and the behavior of its members. In order to be successful, they must have good communication skills and/or power to force compliance. Their success in persuading people to accept change will usually be enhanced by a deeper knowledge of the culture. Their vested interest is in their own mission, and success can be measured in terms of numbers of people baptized, churches, roads, and hospitals built, diseases conquered, telephones installed, and so forth. This type of mediator is more likely than the trader or the diplomat to confer benefits on the people of the host culture. However, this is not an inevitable result. The crucial factor here is the mission, the nature of which has most likely been determined in and by the home culture. As such, this type of activity lacks the mutuality necessary for true mediation.

The bicultural individual is being included in this typology not so much for what he does as for what he is. His characteristics afford him the opportunity of being a mediating person, but they are not a sufficient guarantee that he will actually play a mediating role. By virtue of his birth and childhood or adult experience, the bicultural individual is able to participate as a member of more than one cultural group. He is competent to a greater or lesser degree in the language, customs, and values of more than one culture. Whether the bicultural individual remains only a potential mediator or becomes an actual mediator depends on what he does with his competence and how he is received by members of both cultures. (These aspects will be discussed later in the chapter.) The bicultural individual has the choice of being a nonmediator or becoming a true mediator, whose characteristics will be discussed next.

I use the word *teacher* to refer to the true mediator, because his success can be measured in terms of what is learned by those with whom he has contact. The teacher may be a bicultural person, but does not necessarily have to be. But he must possess good communication skills and, above all, an extensive and intensive knowledge and understanding of more than one culture, on both the cognitive and affective levels. He must use this knowledge to educate members of each culture about the other. Thus, the criteria for success are the mutually increased knowledge, respect, and empathy of the members of the two cultures. The true mediator's vested interest may come from a variety of sources, including dedication to world peace, personal interest in other cultures, or ambition for fame, but his success must be measured in terms of the extent to which the members of the two cultures have gained a greater knowledge of and respect for each other as a result of his actions. Thus, true mediation is being defined as a two-way process. (The four categories of culture conjunction and their respective mediational styles are summarized in Table 3.)

The actions of the true mediator should result in some mutual benefit to the two cultures involved. More particularly, the presence and actions of a true mediator should have some positive influence on the general populations, or significant sectors of the populations, of the two cultures between which he is mediating. This influence should be measurable in terms of increased knowledge, respect, and empathy on the part of members of the two cultures for each other. The true mediator has been termed a teacher not because teachers are best equipped to be mediators, but because people in a wide variety of professional and nonprofessional roles who are true mediators take on a teaching role—acting as a channel of information and an aid in the development of humanitarian attitudes. With this tentative definition of the mediating person as teacher in mind, we can proceed to discuss the problem of acceptance.

Acceptance

In order to be a successful mediator, it is not enough for a person just to have the necessary characteristics, background, motivation, or training and to be in the right place at the right time. Probably the most crucial determinant of the success of a mediator is his acceptance or rejection in his role by both of the cultures concerned. This leads us to the question of whether a mediating person can "mediate" between any two cultures of which he might possess

Table 3. Four Types of Cultural Conjunction

Category	Vested Interest	Criterion of Success	Culture Likely to Benefit
Trader	Himself	Profit	Home
Diplomat	Home government	Power	Home
Missionary	The mission	Innovations	Depends on mission
Teacher	Variable	Mutual understanding	Host and home

sufficient knowledge, or whether the success of a mediator is contingent upon the particular cultures involved and their attitudes toward and degree of acceptance of mediation. There may be quite a different reaction to the concept of mediating person by various cultures.

For example, countries such as the United States and Australia, which were founded by immigrants and have continued to accept immigrants, view foreigners as potential citizens. In law as well as in ideology, anyone can become an American. American culture views nationality and cultural identity as mutable; one can change one's cultural identity consciously and without a great deal of difficulty. On the other hand, cultures which have had a long history without extensive immigration may view cultural identity differently. While anyone in the world can become American, no one can become Japanese. The immigration laws of Japan reflect the attitude of the Japanese that cultural identity is determined both by one's parentage and by childhood experiences; neither non-Japanese who have been raised in Japan nor Japanese-Americans who are racially Japanese but have been raised outside Japan can ever be considered truly Japanese.

There have been several non-Japanese who have tried to "become Japanese." Most notable among them was the writer Lafcadio Hearn. After years of diligent striving to master the language, customs, and soul of Japan, he had to admit to complete failure, not because *he* could not "feel" Japanese, but because the Japanese people would not accept him as one of their own. In an essay titled "A Glimpse of Tendencies," Hearn had this to say about the attitude of the Japanese to foreigners:

> The barriers of racial feeling, of emotional differentiation, of language, of manners and beliefs, are likely to remain insurmountable for centuries. Though instances of warm friendship, due to the mutual attraction of exceptional natures able to divine each other intuitively, might be cited, the foreigner, as a general rule, understands the Japanese quite as little as the Japanese understands him. What is worse for the alien than miscomprehension is the simple fact that he is in the position of an invader. Under no ordinary circumstances need he expect to be treated like a Japanese; and this not merely because he has more money at his command, but because of his race. (Hearn 1910, pp. 134-135)

What Hearn describes has been a common experience for many non-Japanese who have lived most of their lives in Japan—they feel that they are not completely accepted by the Japanese. Thus, although by virtue of their biculturality such individuals would be in an advantageous position to become mediators, their task is made very difficult owing to the nonacceptance of the mediator role in one of the two cultures.

The Japanese view of the immutability of cultural identity applies in only one direction, however. Thus, while it is impossible for a non-Japanese to become Japanese, it is not impossible for a Japanese to lose his cultural identity by becoming something else (Bennett, Passin, and McKnight 1958; Caudill 1952; Caudill and DeVos 1956; Caudill and Scarr 1962; Lebra 1972; Mandelbaum 1956; Silberman 1962). Both Japanese and Americans share the notion that cultural identity is an all-or-nothing proposition. This attitude is reflected in America's prevalent "melting-pot" philosophy and the desire of immigrants to show themselves to be "100 percent American." Mainstream American culture still has great difficulty in knowing where to place hyphenated Americans. The Japanese, too, tend to feel that cultural identity is unidimensional, and that becoming more of something else automatically means becoming less Japanese. This psychological preconception is reflected in language difficulties. Both Japanese and Americans are notoriously poor at foreign languages, but when Japanese begin to master a foreign language, their ability in their native language often declines. It is as if there is room enough for only one identity and one language at a time in their consciousness (McLeod 1976). For these reasons, perhaps both the American and the Japanese cultures contain elements which are not conducive to the development of mediating persons. Indeed, in recent history, neither the Americans nor the Japanese have been viewed as sensitive middlemen by the peoples of other countries.

Furthermore, and perhaps for the same reasons, neither the American nor the Japanese cultures, with their ideas of an all-or-nothing identity, are very receptive toward mediating persons. American culture, instead of utilizing its wealth of immigrants as potential mediators, has been intent on turning them into 100 percent Americans. This is an example of pseudo- or one-way mediation. There are numerous ethnic groups in the United States, representing the cultures of every country of the world. One would imagine that, consequently, Americans would be well-informed about the world, but in actuality they are woefully ignorant. Why is this so? If we take, for example, the Greek-American community in the United States, we can see that it possesses the characteristics necessary for mediation. Greek music, food, dance, religion, language, and other customs and values are kept alive by the community. In addition, there are many bicultural Greek-Americans who fully participate in mainstream American culture as well. The community keeps in contact with and visits friends and relatives in Greece periodically, so that Greek-Americans—at least the older ones—are well acquainted with Greek culture. Also, the Greeks in Greece with whom they have contact are given some idea of what life in America is like. But the chain of communication stops there, for the majority of non-Greek Americans know very little about Greece or Greek culture. If they live in a city with a sizable population of Greek-Americans, they may have tasted Greek pastry or watched Greek dancing at an annual festival, but that is the extent of their knowledge and involvement. The prevailing philosophy of American culture, at least until recently, has not encouraged the maintenance of Old Country culture by immigrant groups. This has had the simultaneous effects of making immigrants hide their own culture from outsiders and of making Americans in general uninterested in any culture but American.

Another example of one-way mediation is the situation of foreign students in the United States. Although most of them return to their own countries after finishing their studies, they are treated by many Americans as potential immigrants, and they are thus urged to learn as much as possible about American culture. Most of the studies of foreign students in the United States focus on their "adjustment"—in other words, on the extent to which they have adopted the "American way of life" (Bailyn and Kelman 1962; Becker 1968; Chu et al. 1971; Deutsch and Won 1963; Gezi 1965; Ibrahim 1970; Lysgaard 1955; Schild 1962; Selltiz and Cook 1962; Shattuck 1965). These students, who are bilingual and who are urged to become bicultural, are in a position to become mediators. But in most cases, their mediating activities extend in only one direction, toward their homeland. Americans learn very little about other cultures from foreign students. They enjoy seeing a show of foreign songs and dances and tasting exotic food once in a while, but few learn how to do those dances or prepare that food themselves, or inquire into the background and meaning of these customs. These are examples of the failure of qualified mediators to mediate successfully, that is, to teach something beyond the superficial about each culture to the other, and this failure can be explained in terms of the nonacceptance of the mediating role by American culture.

The Japanese also are not very receptive to those in mediating roles. They are distinctly uncomfortable with Japanese-Americans or with foreigners who speak Japanese too well or behave as the Japanese do. I have witnessed several encounters between Japanese and Westerners raised in Japan who act Japanese and speak Japanese with native fluency. This type of person makes the Japanese nervous, and one Japanese friend told me that he felt as if there must be a tape recorder inside the American's head, because he could not believe that perfect Japanese could issue from a non-Japanese mouth. The Japanese would rather not relate to a person whose cultural identity is in between, and they prefer individuals whose ethnic role is clearly defined and predictable (Caudill 1962; De Vos 1973; Doi 1973; Lebra and Lebra 1974; Nakane 1970).

Another example of the failure of mediation in the Japanese case is that of Japanese students who lived abroad as children. There were quite a number of such students at the International Christian University in Tokyo, which I attended for one year, and they formed their own clique, finding themselves rejected by the other Japanese students. Their experience in the United States and their nativelike ability in English made these individuals potential mediators, but the other Japanese viewed them with an attitude of distance and ambivalence. Although the monocultural Japanese respected and rather envied the bicultural experience of these people, they also feared them, found them strange, and consequently resorted to accusing them of not being "real Japanese." This is the dilemma which is faced to some extent by every returnee from a foreign sojourn; the stay-at-homes are reluctant to be shown up by someone who has had broader experience than they have had, and so they devise ways of putting the returnee down.

The Japanese bicultural individuals were also rejected in the role in which they could have been most useful, as English tutors. There is a great demand for tutoring in conversational English in Japan, and most foreigners spend some of their time teaching English, often quite profitably. But the bicultural Japanese, whose English had been acquired in childhood and was therefore accentless and perfect, and who in addition could speak Japanese and thus explain grammatical structures and clear up misunderstandings, nevertheless were not able to command as much money for tutoring English as were the monolingual Westerners. Thus, both American and Japanese society put constraints upon those individuals who are potential mediators, forcing them to choose one identity and abandon the other.

The all-or-nothing attitude of the Japanese and the Americans concerning cultural identity and its effects on mediation may be contrasted with the Chinese view. The Chinese attitude toward cultural identity is "once a Chinese, always a Chinese," or, more accurately, "once a Wong, always a Wong." The basic security which the Chinese find in their family and clan membership gives them the psychological freedom to migrate to distant places and adopt foreign patterns without feeling that their basic cultural identity is threatened (Hsu 1963). Even now, any Chinese, though his family may not have lived in China for generations and though he may not even speak Chinese, is given a special status by the Chinese government and may visit China without the usual restrictions placed on non-Chinese. No such special consideration is given by the Japanese government to Japanese immigrants. There is no Japanese equivalent of the term "overseas Chinese." Moreover, many Chinese speak several different Chinese dialects as well as the language of their country of residence, and do not have the same degree of difficulty in learning foreign languages as the Japanese or Americans do. Nor do they tend to lose their native language when learning a foreign language, as some Japanese do (McLeod 1976). This indicates that the Chinese view of cultural identity is multidimensional rather than unidimensional; they feel psychologically free to take on more than one identity simultaneously. This attitude has implications for the ability of the Chinese as mediating persons. Historically, the Chinese have proven themselves to be successful mediators, a good example being the modification of Chinese food to local tastes, so that Chinese restaurants can be found in every part of the world.

Although there have always been people who could be identified as mediating persons, the concept of mediation as something with definite characteristics is rather new. Most people are not accustomed to thinking about mediators in positive terms; rather, mediators have more often been considered to be marginal (Stonequist 1937) or otherwise unusual. They have tended to be located at the fringes rather than at the heart of a society. They may have had special powers ascribed to them, as do shamans; or special qualities, as do the mixed-race popular entertainers of Japan; or special experiences, as do foreign students—all of which tend to set them apart from the general populace and make them seem strange. No culture readily accepts the unusual into its midst, and thus the problem of acceptance remains a formidable one. It is necessary for the mediator to convince people that the unusual is not inherently threatening, and may even be interesting and beneficial. Some ways in which the mediator can accomplish this will be discussed in the final section of the chapter, but first we will focus on the internal conflicts which a mediator himself may experience.

Internal Conflicts

The problem of acceptance is a formidable one for the mediating person, but in addition, he often faces internal conflicts. First, in a world where mono-culturality is the norm, the mediating person cannot help but feel strange, an outsider to both of the cultures he knows. Thus, he may lack a certain basic psychological security which others gain from an unambiguous cultural identity. There are other sources of internal conflict as well. Some examples in the areas of social custom, language, and values will now be described.

Having a natural familiarity with the customs of more than one culture may cause confusion in the mediating person. For example, I was raised in the United States, which is a "noncontact" culture, in that it discourages physical contact of any kind among members of the same sex. I then spent a year in Japan, which more or less observes the same cultural rule. Subsequently, I spent two years in Thailand, where there is a great deal of touching among same-sex friends. This was initially disturbing to me, but I soon found it pleasurable, and it seemed natural to act in this way. When I returned to the United States, I "naturally" embraced a Japanese friend whom I had known in Japan, and she was obviously surprised by my strange behavior.

This example raises two points. First of all, it may be difficult for the mediating person to switch his cultural hat appropriately in accordance with changing contexts. He may find himself unthinkingly kissing Englishmen on both cheeks and shaking hands with Frenchmen, not out of ignorance, but because the patterns of the other culture have become natural to him. The difficulty increases with the number of cultures one has to deal with.

Although greetings may seem a trivial matter, this difficulty extends to more fundamental issues than customs. Being a successful mediator may require a good deal of cognitive juggling and perhaps a certain amount of abstraction from, or objectivity of perspective on, one's activities and habits.

Inner conflicts may also arise in the area of language. An example of this difficulty are the very different acceptable styles of speaking and writing in English and in Japanese (Ervin-Tripp 1964; Goldstein and Tamura 1975; Higa 1970). The preferred English style is direct, logical, rational, and chronological, while the proper style in Japanese is circumlocutious, emotional, and veiled. Members of each culture learn the style of the other only with great difficulty, for to the English-speaker, the Japanese style seems vague, wasteful, and weak, whereas to the Japanese-speaker, the English style is crass and impolite. Thus, even Japanese who know English well find it difficult to use forms which for them signify behaving in an impolite manner.

Culture is what seems natural and right to the members of a group, and it must be highly dissonant (Festinger 1957) to be expected to regard the contradictory aspects of two different cultures both as natural and right. Each culture defines not only what is natural and right, but also what is interesting, exciting, and important; in other words, the values of the culture. The mediator may experience conflict when one culture defines an educated man as one who has read a great deal, and the other culture characterizes an educated man as one who disdains academic knowledge but can track and kill a kangaroo. Or one culture may consider it important to spend one's time and energies primarily with friends and relatives, while the other culture may consider work to be more important. The bicultural individual is pressed not only by the two societies in which he participates, but also by his own conscience, to decide what is natural, right, and important. Instead of being freed by his knowledge of more than one culture, the mediating person may in fact be bound by the norms of two cultures instead of just one. People are willing to forgive outrageous behavior by "ignorant foreigners," but not by persons who have some knowledge of and claim some affinity with the culture. This dilemma is felt by groups such as Peace Corps volunteers, whose purpose is to "change archaic and unproductive practices" and at the same time to "be adaptive and culturally sensitive." Often this conflict seems unresolvable.

Ideal Mediator

In spite of the external and internal constraints on the role of the mediating person, success is not impossible. What, then, are the qualities or situations which would facilitate the success of a mediating person? First, although it seems reasonable to assume that a bicultural individual would be the best mediator, perhaps this is not so. The bicultural person knows his cultures implicitly, or subjectively, in that he can always speak and behave appropriately. However, like the anthropologist's native informant, he may not possess the explicit or objective perspective which is necessary in order to explain aspects of one culture to members of the other. A measure of both kinds of knowledge is necessary for those who would take on a mediating role. To some extent, the mediator must be able to behave naturally and appropriately in both cultures, but he must also be able to objectify his knowledge and experience. And ideally, he should have an affective relationship with as well as a cognitive understanding of both cultures.

Perhaps the ideal mediator is one who is less than perfect, just as the ideal teacher is one who appears not to be teaching at all. The problem of acceptance has already been discussed; perhaps people would be more willing to accept a mediator who acts as a learner rather than as a teacher. Most peoples (with the possible exception of Americans) would reject the notion that an outsider could learn their culture easily and completely. In other words, since most cultures will not accept an outsider as one of their members, the mediator should not strive for this futile goal. There have been many Japanophiles, for example, who become "more Japanese than the Japanese" in their love for the traditional arts (in which, incidentally, many young Japanese have no interest), but this self-identification with Japanese culture does not make them any more Japanese in the eyes of the Japanese.

Another reason why the mediator should not be perfect is that perfection may actually impede his mediating role. Which is the better mediator, one who knows about the other culture and is continually sensitive to cultural differences, thereby insulating those with whom he comes into contact from cultural shock, or the ignorant but good-hearted bumbler whose behavior may surprise people but may also delight them and teach them something new? A Japanese father who receives a farewell kiss from an American friend's daughter, something his own daughter could never do as it is contrary to Japanese custom, may treasure this "culturally insensitive" experience all his life. Everyone has heard stories about the foreigner who did everything "wrong" and yet was loved by the people. This evidence is, of course, of an anecdotal nature, and awaits empirical research for confirmation.

I would suggest that the ideal mediator should know enough about both cultures so that he does not make any drastic mistakes which will alienate him from the people; in other words, that he be familiar enough to be non-threatening. But it is also important that he be novel enough to catch the interest of people and teach them something about his other culture. The mediator should be like a poet, who takes familiar words and allows the reader to see them in a new and different manner. If a foreign student masters American culture to the extent that he can act exactly as an American with other Americans, then learning has taken place in only one direction, and the Americans have gained nothing from the presence of the foreign student in their country in terms of expanding their knowledge of his country. Would people rather have a knowledgeable but boringly familiar guest, or one whose differences make him interesting and give them a wealth of anecdotes with which to entertain their friends and relatives for years to come?

This discussion illustrates two points. First, in order to be a successful mediator, one must not appear to be an expert, even if one actually is. And second, the true mediator's goal should be not to demonstrate his cleverness in mastering a second culture and language, but to teach something about each culture to the other.

How can the mediator best achieve this result? As all good teachers know, a successful educator must be to some extent also an entertainer. This is not to say that he makes dull topics artificially interesting, but that he brings out the inherent interest of the subject. Thus, the mediator should convey to those with whom he has contact that they ought to learn about other cultures, not because it is good for them, like medicine, or because it is the Christian or humanitarian thing to do, but rather because it is inherently interesting and enriching and will confer ultimate benefits on the learner. The mediator should serve as an example of these benefits, rather than as an expert who has a monopoly on special knowledge and experiences.

A related issue in this connection is that of authenticity. In teaching about another culture, is it better to present authentic artifacts, or is it wiser to utilize modifications? It may be that a small sacrifice in authenticity is the better course. For example, should Americans be introduced to Chinese or Thai culture by taking them to authentic Chinese opera or an authentic Thai dinner? Should a Korean get his first exposure to English culture at an authentic Shakespearean play? Most likely, the reaction in all three cases would be negative, preventing any further interest in the subject. Would it not be better to allow minor alterations in culture presentations so as not to lose the audience, and as a means of leading the neophyte toward a subsequent appreciation of the authentic product? Perhaps, as with the ideal mediating person, the ideal mediating culture product should be familiar enough to be readily appreciated, but novel enough to teach something new.

How useful are artifacts and other cultural products to the mediator? They can be very useful in catching people's interest, but they must be put into context by their relation to actual people. An illustration will make this point clear. Many schoolchildren in the United States study about the American Indians, mostly by means of reading about them and viewing artifacts. Most children are quite fascinated by Indian lore and eagerly play at being Indians. But they soon forget whatever superficial knowledge they may have gained, because most of them have no opportunity to meet an actual Indian as a person. They thus develop either a romanticized view of Indian culture or the derogatory opinion of the adult world. Thus, it is important for the mediator to be personally involved with the two cultures, to be able to convey the essential humanity of each to the other, rather than to relate their exotic customs. Involvement usually means some kind of long-term commitment. Outsiders will be trusted only if they demonstrate continued interest in and loyalty to the group. An example of such a mediator is a former U. S. ambassador to Japan, Edwin O. Reischauer, who, as a professional diplomat, writer, and teacher, had a lifelong involvement with Japanese culture and acted as a channel of information between Japan and the United States (Reischauer 1964).

Conclusion

The attempt to characterize the mediating person is of rather recent origin, and thus definitions tend to be rather broad in scope. As we saw in the first section of this chapter, the mediating person can be viewed from several perspectives, among them his personality, his functions, and his socially defined role. We then looked at several different roles played by people who cross cultural boundaries, and examined the conditions under which such individuals can become mediators. One of the most important factors is the purpose for which people go outside their own culture. Another important variable is the reaction of a host culture to a foreigner. We saw that acceptance of a foreigner may be significantly influenced by the values and philosophical outlook of the particular culture involved. Thus, persons who wish to or are in a position to take on mediating roles are often impeded by a rejection on the part of one or both of the cultures. In addition, the mediating person may face internal conflicts which arise from being competent in more than one set of social customs, values, and languages.

Taking into account the internal and external obstacles faced by mediating persons, an attempt was made to characterize the ideal mediator. It was concluded that although bicultural persons have a unique opportunity to play mediating roles, they may not be the best mediators unless they have resolved their internal conflicts and have the desire and ability to teach each culture about the other. The ideal mediator must not appear to be an expert, and need not be accorded complete acceptance in order to accomplish something. In whatever field he works, his mediating activities should result in some kind of benefit for the two cultures between which he is mediating. The success of the mediating person must be measured in terms of his effect on the people of the two or more cultures with which he is familiar. As a result of his presence or actions, members of the cultures should have a greater knowledge of, respect for, and empathy with each other. In addition, they should be able to realize that culture is learned behavior and therefore relative rather than absolute. They should be able to say, "Other people's customs are different, not strange, and if I had been raised in another culture, I would act as those people do." If such a relativistic outlook were common, a continued diversity of life-styles, values, and approaches to human problems would be guaranteed.

References

Bailyn, L., and Kelman, H. C. The Effects of a Year's Experience in America on the Self-image of Scandinavians: A Preliminary Analysis of Reactions to a New Environment. *Journal of Social Issues*, 1962, *18* (1), 30–40.

Becker, T. Patterns of Attitudinal Changes Among Foreign Students. *American Journal of Sociology*, 1968, *73*, 431–442.

Bennett, J. W., Passin, H., and McKnight, R. K. *In Search of Identity: The Japanese Overseas Scholar in America and Japan*. Minneapolis, Minn.: University of Minnesota Press, 1958.

Caudill, W. Japanese-American Personality and Acculturation. *Genetic Psychology Monographs*, 1952, *45*, 3–102.

Caudill, W. Patterns of Emotion in Modern Japan. In R. J. Smith and R. K. Beardsley (eds.), *Japanese Culture: Its Development and Characteristics*. Chicago, Ill.: Aldine, 1962.

Caudill, W., and De Vos, G. Achievement, Culture and Personality: The Case of Japanese Americans. *American Anthropologist*, 1956, *58*, 1102–1126.

Caudill, W., and Scarr, H. Japanese Value Orientations and Culture Change. *Ethnology*, 1962, *1*, 53–91.

Chu, H. M., Yeh, E. K., Klein, M. H., Alexander, A. A., and Miller, M. H. A Study of Chinese Students' Adjustment in the U.S.A. *Acta Psychologica Taiwanica*, 1971, *13*, 206–218.

Deutsch, S. E., and Won, G. Y. M. Some Factors in the Adjustment of Foreign Nationals in the United States. *Journal of Social Issues*, 1963, *19* (3), 115–122.

De Vos, G. *Socialization for Achievement: Essay on the Cultural Psychology of the Japanese*. Berkeley, Calif.: University of California Press, 1973.

Doi, L. T. *The Anatomy of Dependence*. Tokyo: Kodansha International, 1973.

Ervin-Tripp, S. An Analysis of the Interaction of Language, Topic, and Listener. *American Anthropologist*, 1964, *55* (6), 86–102.

Festinger, L. *A Theory of Cognitive Dissonance*. Evanston, Ill.: Row, Peterson, 1957.

Gezi, K. Factors Associated with Student Adjustment in Cross-cultural Contact. *California Journal of Educational Research*, 1965, *16* (3), 129–136.

Goldstein, B., and Tamura, K. *Japan and America: A Comparative Study in Language and Culture*. Rutland, Vt.: Charles Tuttle, 1975.

Hearn, L. *Kokoro: Hints and Echoes of Japanese Inner Life*. London: Gay and Hancock, 1910.

Higa, M. The Sociolinguistic Significance of Borrowed Words in the Japanese Spoken in Hawaii. University of Hawaii, Department of Linguistics: *Working Papers in Linguistics*, 1970, *2* (no. 9).

Hsu, F. L. K. *Clan, Caste and Club*. Princeton, N. J.: Van Nostrand, 1963.

Ibrahim, S. Interaction, Perception, and Attitudes of Arab Students Towards Americans. *Sociology and Social Research*, 1970, *55*, 29–46.

Lebra, T. Acculturation Dilemma: The Function of Japanese Moral Values for Americanization. *Council on Anthropology and Education Newsletter*, 1972, *3* (1), 6–13.

Lebra, T., and Lebra, W. P. (eds.). *Japanese Culture and Behavior*. Honolulu, Hawaii: University Press of Hawaii, 1974.

Lysgaard, S. Adjustment in a Foreign Society: Norwegian Fulbright Grantees Visiting the United States. *International Social Science Bulletin*, 1955, *7*, 45–51.

Mandelbaum, D. Comments. *Journal of Social Issues*, 1956, *12* (1), 45–51.

McLeod, B. Intercultural Education: Japanese and Singaporean Students in the United States. Unpublished Master's Thesis, University of Hawaii, 1976.

Nakane, C. *Japanese Society*. Berkeley, Calif.: University of California Press, 1970.

Reischauer, E. O. *Japan Past and Present*. 3rd ed., rev. London: Duckworth, 1964.

Schild, E. O. The Foreign Student, as Stranger, Learning the Norms of the Host Culture. *Journal of Social Issues*, 1962, *18* (1), 41–54.

Selltiz, C., and Cook, S. W. Factors Influencing Attitudes of Foreign Students Toward the Host Country. *Journal of Social Issues*, 1962, *18* (1), 7–23.

Shattuck, G. M. *Between Two Cultures: A Study of the Social Adaptation of Foreign Students to an American Academic Community*. Ithaca, N.Y.: Department of Rural Sociology, Cornell University, 1965.

Silberman, B. *Japanese Character and Culture*. Tucson, Ariz.: University of Arizona Press, 1962.

Stonequist, E. V. *The Marginal Man*. New York: Scribner, 1937.

Ronald Taft

The Role and Personality of the Mediator

Introduction and Overview

A cultural mediator is a person who *facilitates communication, understanding, and action between persons or groups who differ with respect to language and culture*. The role of the mediator is performed by interpreting the expressions, intentions, perceptions, and expectations of each cultural group to the other, that is, by establishing and balancing the communication between them. In order to serve as a link in this sense, the mediator must be able to participate to some extent in both cultures. Thus, a mediator must be to some extent bicultural.

It will be argued in this chapter that biculturality involves the possession of competencies that are relevant to each of the two cultures; that is, there should be "two skills in one skull." This chapter opens with an analysis of the social-psychological role of the cultural mediator as a communicator and of the relationship to mediation of cultural marginality and biculturalism and multiculturalism. An analysis is then made of the process of enculturation and how this may affect the personality of the mediator and the competence with which he carries out his role. Finally, a review is made of the characteristics of mediators that influence this competence.

The previous literature on these topics is quite sparse, and what does exist is devoted more to aspects of biculturalism and multiculturalism than to the cultural mediating process and the characteristics of mediators. A beginning has been made by Bochner (1973*a, b*), with special reference to the overseas student as a mediator between cultures. Bochner writes: "Some attributes of the mediating man are a belief in the common unity of mankind, cultural relativism of values, cognitive flexibility, membership in international and trans-national social networks, and supra-national groups" (1973*b*, p. 35).

Without calling their multicultural subjects mediators, other scholars have dealt with similar topics, particularly with reference to foreign students (Bennett, Passin, and McKnight 1958) and technologically trained experts in transitional societies (Cleveland, Mangone, and Adams 1960; Useem and Useem 1955). Much of the literature on methodology in anthropological research (Kimball and Watson 1972; Naroll and Cohen 1970) is concerned with mediation between cultures, in this case mostly between social scientists in technologically advanced countries (such as anthropologists) and the cultures of traditional societies. The literature on language translation and interpretation is also highly relevant to mediation between cultures (Hymes 1964; Nida 1964; Werner and Campbell 1970). Useful psychological approaches to translation are to be found in Barik (1972, 1973), Brislin (1976), Goldman-Eisler (1972), and Jakobovits (1970). Basic work on the psychology of bilingualism (Ervin and Osgood 1954; Imedadze 1960; Kolers 1968; Macnamara 1966; Peal and Lambert 1962) has prepared the ground for the study of language translation, but there seems to have been a strange dearth of psychological analyses of the process of translating and of factors related to skill in it, other than those mentioned above. Even the study of loose interpretation from one language to another has been neglected.

The Role of the Mediator

There are many formally defined social roles in which persons are required to mediate between cultures or aspects of cultures, but few of these are assigned the formal title of "mediator." Situations in which a person's role leads him to act as a mediator between cultures and subcultures are not confined just to mediation between nations and peoples. Here is a diverse set of examples of social roles in which mediation is a central requirement: language interpreter, tourist guide, industrial relations conciliator, marriage counselor, ombudsman, student counselor, native welfare officer, representative of ethnic communities on a government board, factory foreman, representative of workers on a management committee, technical aid expert, manager of touring sportsmen or entertainers, business agent for a foreign company.

There are a number of other roles that are likely to lead to biculturalism and mediation but in which these are not an essential requirement of the role. There are many situations in which a person is brought into contact with another culture by reason of his role and as a result of which he learns some aspects of that culture. The circumstances that can bring about the exposure of people to new cultures have been categorized (Taft 1977) as *sojourning* (foreign students and technical aid experts), *settling* (immigrants, captives), *subcultural mobility* (entrants into a profession), *segregation* (hospital patients, prisoners), and *changes in society* (modernization, military occupation). Each of these situations requires the person to cope with an unfamiliar culture, and in most cases involves some degree of culture learning and behavioral adaptation as a result of which the person becomes increasingly multicultural. This may apply to members of an ethnic minority, or to new settlers who learn some of the majority culture in addition to their own original culture. It also may apply to temporary sojourners such as foreign students and tourists, who are likely to learn about the new culture if they stay long enough and to develop culturally relevant competencies that will enable them to play the role of mediator.

This listing includes only a fraction of all of the possible mediation roles that have a formal existence in modern societies. These roles are mediating to the extent that they require that at least two cultures are brought together, so that an exchange or negotiation can take place effectively. For example, when a local person acts as an agent for a foreign company, his post requires him to participate to some extent in the business aspects of the culture of the company headquarters, as well as of the general local culture and, preferably, some of the local subcultures. Or, to take another example, the representative of an ethnic community on a public affairs committee must participate in the wider culture of the region, his own ethnic subculture, and the narrower subculture of the committee. If he appears on the committee only as a spokesman for his ethnic community, another person will still be needed to act as mediator between this and the wider culture.

One occupation that deserves special mention in the context of mediation is that of writer. Even a novelist writing in his own language about his own country may be communicating about a subculture with which he is quite familiar and his readers are not. The mediation role of a writer is more obvious when he comes from a foreign background or grew up as a member of a minority group, especially when he writes a book that is frankly autobiographical. The role of a writer as mediator is impressive when he or she writes in a language that was acquired as an adult. Samuel Beckett, an Irish-born Nobel Prize-winner for literature, has written largely in an acquired language, French. So did Vladimir Nabokov. One of the most remarkable multicultural, multilingual writers is Arthur Koestler, who was educated in Hungary and Austria and subsequently lived in Germany, Palestine, Russia, France, Spain, and Britain. Koestler's first book in English (*Arrival and Departure*) was written at the age of thirty-five in 1943, only three years after he had arrived in England, and subsequently Koestler has been a prolific writer of quality material in this language. Each one of these writers represents a striking example of two (or more) skills in one skull, and illustrates the process of mediating between languages and cultures.

COMMUNICATION AND MEDIATION

The definition of the function of a mediator given above stresses the communication aspects. In order to carry out his role, the mediator must be able to transcend the cultures concerned, and yet he must also be able to comprehend the signals used in the expression of each culture. To be able to do this adequately requires some knowledge of the languages and also of the roles employed by members of the cultures.

When an explorer or other pioneer into unexplored territory makes contact with a people whose ways and language are unknown, mediation is impossible until some common basis for communication has been established by trial and error. Effective communication requires not only a commonly understood set of symbols to represent experience and meaning—that is, a common verbal language—but also some agreement on the conventions concerning the tactics of conversations, the nonverbal language, the what, when, and how of the exchange of information, and the complex interaction among all of these. An error in respect to these conventions can set up impenetrable barriers and may lead to violence. Even when some common language is used or an interpreter is available to provide a translation, the communication will not lead to effective social intercourse unless there is some agreement on what behavior may be expected and what may be treated as socially appropriate in the given circumstances. In other words, a common understanding about role behavior must exist before social interaction may take place, and this is where the cultural mediator comes in. Through his knowledge of both cultures, he may be able to perceive, and even anticipate, possible areas of futile and frustrating attempts to communicate, where differing conceptions of the object at hand leave a gap that can only be bridged with the help of an intermediary. An example of a situation where such help was needed is presented by Triandis (1975), based on research conducted by Vassiliou in Greece. An American manager tried to gain the cooperation of a Greek worker by inviting him to collaborate in a decision about when a task should be completed, whereas the worker expected the boss to *tell* him, not *ask* him. The result was mutual irritation and led to the resignation of the worker, which possibly could have been prevented by an intercultural mediator.

Ideally, a mediator should be thoroughly steeped in the two cultures which he is bridging, but he can still perform a useful role if he has only partial knowledge of one or both of them. For example, a Japanese who has been brought up in Germany but has no knowledge of English would be able to mediate between Japanese and Americans better than if he had had only Japanese experience. At least he would be likely to have some appreciation of the styles of address and the tactics of exchanging information that are fairly universal throughout European-derived cultures. This principle is used when first contact is being made with a tribal group in remote territory; wherever possible, a mediator is employed who has some familiarity with a related or regional language and who has a general understanding of the larger culture of which this particular one is a special instance.

It should be mentioned parenthetically that communication and social exchange are possible between completely strange groups even without a mediator. The most obvious examples are such primitive exchanges as the provision of food and drink and the discharge of weapons. These exchanges are readily possible because they are based on the common biological structure of the participants. Gestural behavior in these contexts can also easily be understood without any need for linguistic and cultural mediation. Donald Campbell (1964) dealt with the question of how people can communicate and understand each other across cultures. He used the analogy of a color-blind person who can learn to discriminate colors by inference from the secondary characteristics that are perceived in a similar fashion by both the color-sighted and the color-blind. In the same way, an individual can construct the meanings attributed to events by persons in another culture from the way those persons react to events that they perceive in common. To some extent, cultural mediators operate in a similar way: they may not have a complete understanding of the two cultures, but, by inference from what they observe and what they know, they can still link the cultures together. Even members of the same culture have to indulge in such inferences to some degree in order to interact effectively with each other, since there is rarely full congruency between two people in their perception and construction of events.

MEDIATION AND TRANSLATION

Is a mediator a translator? Probably this is one of the things he is, but he is more than that. A machine can be programmed with two dictionaries and grammar books so that it can apply a set of formal rules to decode into a target language a communication which was originally encoded in a different language. Machines can carry out this task fairly effectively when the content consists of concrete information, and to the extent that the decoding is comprehensible, the machine acts as a mediator; but translation machines are notably stupid. That is, they pay insufficient regard to the context in which words and phrases are embedded to determine which of two or more optional meanings is the correct one. The weakness of machine translation becomes obvious when the machine is programmed for back translation. Thus, "out of sight, out of mind," when translated into another language and then translated back, becomes "the invisible idiot." Some of us may have met moderate versions of this confusion in the simultaneous translations at international conferences in which the rendition of the sentences translated into English are completely plausible but utterly devoid of any connected meaning.

The process of mediating between linguistic communication (interpretation) is of interest to the psychologist because it involves complex cognitive processing at the level of both surface and deep meaning, including judgments relating to the emotional connotation and aesthetic balance of the language.

Unlike the translation machine, a bilingual mediating person involves his personality in the communication by using his knowledge of the nature of human functioning in general and of the two cultures in particular. With the help of this knowledge, he can choose the most likely of two possible interpretations of the communicator's meaning, and can rule out virtually impossible meanings. Such decisions are usually so automatic that the human translator is not aware of having made them. In practice, a person playing a mediating role may never be called upon to engage in the exact *translation* of words; rather, he will communicate the ideas in terms that are meaningful to the members of the target culture. A most important problem in mediating between messages in different languages is that of translating the network of connotations and associations that accompany the actual words. An elegant translation will convey the cultural equivalents of these to the fullest extent possible, conjuring up equivalent phonetic sounds and symbols, images, emotionally charged associations, metaphors, puns, and witty transpositions. It is a tall order for a mediator to be able to achieve such a translation, and to do so, especially in the case of poetry, requires a broad and deep knowledge of the two languages and cultures.

It would be impossible to convey the full meaning of metaphors, myths, and literature in general from one language to another by simply translating the words. It could be only achieved through a radical interpretation of the superficial contents by a mediator who is so conversant with the traditions, the ways of thinking, and the current preoccupations of the second culture that he can find phrases that are semantically equivalent; but even then, they would not be a true translation. These issues have been given further treatment by Brislin (1976) in his introductory chapter, and by Lila Ray and Rudolf Kassuehlke in their chapters in the same volume on the translation of poetry and of the Bible, respectively.

Le Vine (1973) has presented an interesting account of the translator role of mediation in anthropology. He describes the process by which a Western ethnographer learns to understand a non-Western culture as analogous to language translation. First, the translator constructs a "grammar of interpersonal communication" for encoding the behavior of the people in the culture, and then he uses it to become aware of his own automatic cultural interpretations. Le Vine points out an interesting analogy between cultural translation and the functioning of the ego of a psychoanalytic patient. "Translation can only occur through a process akin to that preliminary aspect of psychoanalysis in which the ego of the patient is 'split' into its *experiencing* and *observing* functional components, so that the latter can report on the former" (1973, p. 222, italics supplied). In order to achieve this translation, Le Vine advocates a "learning alliance" between an outside Western ethnographer and a Westernized indigenous behavioral scientist. He points out that the latter is more suitable than the former to take on the major responsibility for the translation, since he is more likely to have acquired the indigenous culture in childhood and the Western one soon afterward. In other words, the total bicultural competence of the indigenous mediator is probably considerably greater than that of the Western scientist. The same argument probably also applies when the mediation is in connection with a collaborative effort between a foreign technical expert and a local counterpart: the chances are that the latter possesses relatively greater competence in the two cultures than the former, although, of course, this may not always be the case.

To sum up this section, mediation between cultures requires the communication of ideas and information from one cultural context to the other. This is analogous to the process involved in linguistic translation, even though there is more to mediation than mere translation.

The pursuit of the analogy between translation in the narrow sense and cultural mediation could be valuable to an understanding of both processes. For example, Goldman-Eisler (1972) divides translation into two processes, *decoding* the original and *encoding* the result into the target language, which to some extent corresponds to Le Vine's "observing ego" and "experiencing ego," respectively. The former requires distance and the effort of attention, while the latter is more directly felt in an automatic way. Probably the most satisfactory translations are achieved in a way that is similar to Le Vine's recommendation for cultural mediation—through a collaborative relationship between persons who know something of the two cultures and are steeped in at least one of them.

In our analysis of the characteristics of the mediator, we will have occasion in this chapter to return continually to the analogy between cultural mediation and linguistic translation. We shall now consider cultural mediation in relation to another social role—that of marginality, which is quite different from that of translation.

SOCIAL MARGINALITY AND MEDIATION

The term *marginal* applies to several different possible relationships between a person and two relevant groups (Taft 1974). The common element in all marginal situations is that the person is in contact with two (or more) distinguishable groups (or societies), and this, of course, is one of the prerequisites for playing the role of mediator. Figure 1 illustrates three different ways in which marginality can occur (I, II, and III). Diagram A describes a fourth situation which is not truly a marginal position: that of alienation, in which the person does not participate in either of the groups. Life in such an isolated state would be very difficult, if not impossible, and the person

Key: X person
     A the original group, or minority
     B the new host group, or majority
     C a new, marginal group

A.   *Isolation*

I   Peripheral membership (assimilation or pluralistic separation)

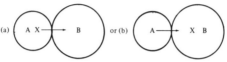

II   Dual membership (True mediation)

III Marginal group (Pluralistic integration)

Figure 1. Descriptions of marginal situations.

would be unable to act as a mediator between the groups with which he is out of contact.

Diagram I (a) describes the situation where a person is oriented toward joining the majority group but has not yet crossed the formal boundary to become a member, and may not in fact be able to do so because of barriers. In diagram I (b), he has already crossed into group B and in the process has shed the former membership. This is the position that is implied by the concept of assimilation, especially in its extreme sense of complete loss of the former identity. Situation I (b) also, paradoxically, describes the form of cultural and structural pluralism (apartheid) in which communities are in physical contact with each other but psychologically separate, so that a person may be a member of either one or the other, but not both. Clearly, this situation limits the possibility of the person's acting as a mediator, although it does not completely preclude it.

In both I (a) and I (b), the person is at the periphery (margin) of his group but has contact with the other. In diagram II, the person is already located in an area which participates in both groups. This represents the true bicultural person, who has dual membership and little difficulty in moving freely in either group, but still retains his membership in group A when he is participating in group B, and vice versa. Simon Herman (1970) places the foreign student in Israel in this type of situation: "He is located within the common part of two or more psychological situations which exist simultaneously for him. . . . While maintaining his ties with the home culture, he cannot, and often does not wish to, ignore the demands of the host culture in which he is a sojourner" (pp. 15-16).

Diagram III is in some ways a combination of the two previous situations. The person has moved into the majority group, but he has also become a member of a subgroup within it consisting of persons with a similar background to his own. This situation is sometimes described as "integration" (Sommerlad and Berry 1970), in which diverse ethnic groups are encouraged to retain their cultural and structural continuity but are integrated into the larger group through a common political loyalty, occupational interconnections, some social intermingling, and a considerable degree of learning of the prevailing language and culture. Examples of marginal groups of this nature are recently arrived immigrants in Canada or Australia, *Gastarbeiter* in Germany, and "coloureds" in South Africa (the latter group is specifically studied as a marginal group par excellence by Dickie-Clark 1966 and Mann 1958).

In diagram III, group C represents a substructure within the larger group B consisting of people with the same background, i.e., former members of group A. The formation of this marginal group is typical of social mobility situations. For example, Bochner (1973*a*) found that foreign students at the East-West Center in Honolulu tend to form groups of their own national background among the total body of students, and when they return home, still express a preference for fellow workers who, like themselves, have had foreign experience. In other words, biculturals tend to form subcultural groups of their own kind, especially with those who have shared the same cultural experiences, but also with others who merely share biculturality itself. Situation III enables the marginal person to act as a mediator between cultures, but he is not as well placed to perform this role as the type II marginal, who moves more fully between the groups.

Mention should be made of the meaning of *membership* in these situations. This may be interpreted either as being objectively accepted by the group according to some criterion such as registration as a citizen, or in a subjective sense as the person's perception of his own position as a member. In both the objective and the subjective sense, the term *membership* refers to a complicated relationship between the individual and the social group, embracing his self, his knowledge and skills, his social relations, and other socially relevant behavior. This relationship will be explored in more detail later.

The Development of Multiculturality

ENCULTURATION

This section deals with how individuals learn in the course of their lives to participate in one, two, or more main cultures and many subcultures. Every person is multicultural in the sense that he participates in more than one subculture, even the members of relatively simple and homogeneous societies. In complex societies, such as all modern industrialized ones, individuals are differentiated into subcultures on such dimensions as age cohorts, family and kinship membership, social class, place of residence, religion, education, occupation, and so on.

To provide a background for the analysis of personality factors related to the multicultural state of mediators, a brief treatment will be given of the process through which a person acquires his cultures, i.e., becomes enculturated, and especially how a child learns to become a member of a human society. This process involves the learning of basic human social skills such as how to engage in social relationships, how to control one's behavior and to use emotions appropriately, how to satisfy basic urges, how to perceive the world, how to communicate with others both verbally and nonverbally, what to expect from others and what roles are appropriate for oneself, how to carry out these roles, and what to value positively and what negatively. The form which these trained skills take is peculiar to the child's own culture, and through the process of enculturation he learns the specific knowledge and skills that are required to live in that culture. This provides him with the rules that guide his cognitions, his evaluations, and his behavior and trains him in the necessary skills to cope with social living.

A foundation is laid in early childhood for a person's role performance as a member of specific societies and subsocieties and as a representative of specific cultures and subcultures. The acquisition of these role repertoires is not a mechanical imposition by society on the individual, since the socialization process represents an interaction between the society and the peculiar characteristics of the individual. There is thus an interplay between an individual's biologically given temperament and drives and the unique combination of socialization processes that impinge on him. These external factors include the characteristics of his parents and other socializing agents; accidental circumstances in his life such as illness, social change, natural disasters; and the time of their occurrence in relation to the individual's level of maturity. The development of individual personalities is a complex subject, and it is not intended to go into it here in detail, other than to repeat that any individual personality reflects the continuous sequence of interactions among the person, his social environment, and his personal experience.

The preferred theory of socialization and personality growth adopted here for the understanding of the development of mediating persons is a sociologically oriented one, based to a considerable extent on the work of Baldwin, Cooley and Mead, but, as Brim (1966) puts it, "It is more a point of view than a theory." The central theme of this orientation is that a child develops a sense of self by incorporating the teaching, both intended and unintended, which is imparted by "significant others," who act as idiosyncratic transmitters of the common culture and of the society. These teachings provide a setting for the acquisition of cognitive structures and styles and strategies for coping with problems. The socializing agents also help to shape the other aspects of individual behavior that make up personality such as habits, goals, values, performance skills, expressive behavior, and the use and control of emotions. The role of enculturation in shaping the psychological functions necessary for coping with society is dealt with in more detail in Taft (1977) through an analysis of the cognitive, dynamic, and performance aspects of behavior.

EARLY AND LATER ENCULTURATION

In order to play the role of mediator, an individual has to be flexible in switching his cultural orientation. Writers on socialization and enculturation, ranging from Ignatius of Loyola through Freud and G. H. Mead to Berger and Luckmann, have stressed the dominant and perseverant role played by the experiences in the first few years of life.

Parsons (1951) and Berger and Luckmann (1967) refer to primary socialization, in which the family teaches the child a strong and well-internalized concept of the real and only conceivable world. The products of the primary socialization stage provide programs for the person's everyday life and form the core of his feeling of identity and sense of worth. This early learning is the child's "home world," the familiar, safe, and fundamentally meaningful world. Cognitive and performance functions that are acquired in this early phase have a flow and automaticity about them which provide a base on which competent social behavior can be built.

From the enculturation point of view, what happens in the period from two to six years (Mead's "play period"; Piaget's "preoperational stage") is basic, and implies the growth of a primitive sense of self through the child's identification with his parents and other important agents (Mead's "significant others"). The child learns to use these agents as models for his own behavior, and through them to receive messages that teach him what is approved by and appropriate to his social environment.

The primitive concept of what is appropriate tends to persist even after considerable exposure to other ways. Berger and Luckmann (1967) point out that the conditions under which primary socialization occurs induce no doubt in the child about the correctness of the choices made by the signifi- cant other. They describe this process as "the most important confidence trick that society plays on an individual—to make appear as necessity what is in fact a bundle of contingencies" (1967, p. 135). It is only later that the child has a chance to learn the truth about the selectivity of the rules of behavior, as a result of exposure to other models of behavior from outside his home. The effectiveness of this experience is partly dependent on the child's having developed sufficient cognitive maturity to be able to separate self and not-self, so that he can become an observer as well as a participator in the experience (see the references above to the roles of the observing and the experiencing selves in learning about other cultures).

Because of the break from the well-practiced responses learned in the primary socialization, later-life learning is likely in the first instance to be dominated by the application of cognitive rules, although it too can eventu- ally be assimilated into the self and become internalized, automatic, and absolute, but not as readily as what is learned in primary socialization. The new discovery that another world is possible terminates an innocence that existed in the monistic world of the young child. Foote (1951) contrasts the absoluteness of the concept of personal identity that is instilled in the primary stage with the relativity of the later development of the self-concept: "Of course, as soon as he encounters alternatives, he (the child) is released from such pre-conscious bondage to any particular conception of himself. Thenceforth his identities accrue from conscious choice and pursuit of the values he has discovered" (p. 19).

There are limits, however, to the flexibility of the person in the face of later-life influences. Socialization in adulthood is dependent on the nature of the primary socialization and may be considerably limited by it. Some skills, for example the ability to pronounce phones correctly, may require learning before the age of twelve in order to be fully attained (Lenneberg 1966). As Brim (1966) points out, sometimes the absence of early training in skills prevents later training, and sometimes the presence of early training inter- feres with the acquisition and performance of different skills later. Both cases provide obstacles to becoming a mediator between cultures in later life. The effects of early emotional conditioning to objects and events are especially hard to eradicate or change; so are the associations with events. Thus, a person will tend to respond either positively or negatively to ex- periences, including sensory ones, in accordance with the responses estab- lished in primary socialization. These automatic cognitive and emotional responses are not easily extinguished, even when the circumstances that gave rise to them in the first place no longer apply. Immigrants often mourn the absence of certain familiar sounds (such as music), smells (perfume of flowers), tastes (food), and sights (natural scenery), and even long-standing immigrants can become excited at the renewed experience of these childhood memories (Schuetz 1964). Where the new culture attaches different connotations to the same symbols or different symbols to the same connotations, it may be difficult, if not impossible, for a stranger to make the emotional change. Thus, while he may achieve the necessary cognitive adaptations and may appear outwardly to have acquired the new culture, he may inwardly feel quite alienated from it.

This provides a serious limitation to his possible effectiveness as a mediator, especially where his emotional response to a situation in the second culture is strongly at variance with that of the native members. A striking example is that of an anthropologist who mediates between a government and a community which has carried out a brutal institutionalized killing of a person who has accidentally violated a sacred prohibition of that community. The anthropologist may find it repulsive to participate emotionally in the attitudes of the community which are at variance with his own. Exposure to a second culture later in life is one of the most striking instances in which a person's accepted social reality is cast into doubt. Most persons who play the role of mediator have had to contend with a constant awareness that other cultural models exist beside the one or ones to which they were socialized. In benign form, this realization can be enriching and liberating; in pathological form, alienating and destructive. In practice, we would argue that most normally socialized persons are quite able to handle the existence of a pluralism of cultures and their participation in them, and thus, multiculturalism is more likely to be positive than negative (Taft 1977).

THE MAKING OF A MULTICULTURAL

The treatment of the enculturation process has so far failed to distinguish between those mediating persons who acquire their multiculturality simultaneously in their childhood and those who acquire it after the foundation for the first has been laid in their initial enculturation. The differences between these two situations are of considerable importance to the competence with which the person is likely to be able to handle the second culture.

Before examining the effect of individual personality differences on the acculturation process in mediators, we should first examine the different ways in which a person can become bi- or multicultural, each one of which is likely to have somewhat different effects on the possible role of the individual as a mediator. An understanding of the role of the mediating person requires an analysis of the varieties of circumstances that can produce a mediator. This involves, in particular, a consideration of the age at which the individual has been exposed to the cultures involved, the circumstances of the exposure, and the attitudes toward the cultures involved in that exposure. These factors may be expected to play an important role in the development of the person's ability and inclination to play the role of mediator. The basic question is whether more than one culture was involved in the primary socialization stage, or whether the child was monocultural until further cultures were acquired in later life. It also is likely to be important whether the biculturality was acquired simultaneously or sequentially, and whether the two cultures were both modeled from the same person or from different ones, or acquired sequentially from different models.

Little reference has so far been made to these matters when the characteristics of multicultural people have been considered by scholars, but one area of cultural competence where some attempt has been made to do so is in connection with bilingualism. Koestler (1954) has argued very cogently that language can act as a symbol for a culture. When he discusses his gradual conversion to being able to express his thoughts in English and his eventual adoption of it as his language, he comments that he acquired "not only a new mode of communication but a new cultural background" (1954, p. 425). In this chapter, I frequently have occasion to use the literature from social linguistics to support arguments in the cultural field generally, since studies of language are relatively objective, and quite a few have been reported.

Haugen writes: "A crucial factor in the kind and extent of bilingualism is the *age* at which the second language is learned. The aptitudes, opportunities, and motivations for learning are so different at various ages that it is of the greatest importance to distinguish them" (1956, p. 72). Thus, infant bilingualism essentially means the simultaneous learning of two languages, and, according to Leopold (1939–49), they may not even be distinguished at first as separate languages. The acquisition of a second language at the age of seven years or later, after the first is well established, is seen by Haugen as much more favorable for learning, since there is less confusion between the two languages.

Ervin and Osgood (1954) made a distinction between two types of bilinguals, "coordinate" and "compound" (or "fixed"), in terms of the way in which the languages were acquired. In coordinate bilinguals, the learning of the two languages occurs independently in different environmental settings, while in compound, the second language is learned sequentially in the same setting as the first, using the latter as the starting point. Even though the conceptualization of the distinction is ambiguous (Diller 1970) and the concepts are now being phased out from the terminology of linguists, the understanding of cultural mediation in biculturals may be helped by the study of the relationship between how two languages are acquired and the ability to translate from one to the other. Jakobovits (1970, pp. 165–179) presents a theoretical analysis of these two systems which suggests that the compound bilingual is more competent at translating than is the coordinate. Unfortunately, the empirical studies on ability to translate do not clearly point to an advantage for compound bilinguals (see the review by Diller 1970), but it is possible that the way in which a compound bilingual has learned the second language provides him with a training in translation which the coordinate bilingual has not received. In an analogous way, a bicultural person may be better trained to function as a mediator when he acquires the two cultures in a manner that trains him to compare one with the other.

We shall now deal with the various possibilities with respect to stage of life and circumstances in which people can become multicultural (or multilingual), and we shall consider the ways in which these may differentially affect the person's functioning as a mediator.

Primary Familiogenic Multiculturalism

This represents the situation where the child's primary socialization simultaneously includes more than one culture. (To paraphrase Merrill Swain [1972], these children have biculturalism as their first culture. Ruth Useem [1971] calls this their third culture.) Primary multiculturalism may occur simultaneously in three different ways, each of which may have its own significance for the individual's personality. These ways will be illustrated in terms of bilingualism, as it is convenient to use language as an index of culture, although it does not necessarily follow that a bilingual person has a deep knowledge of other aspects of the two cultures.

1. Each parent has a different cultural background and contributes a different element to the enculturation of the child. A variant on this occurs when, even though the parents have a similar background, there is another member of the household, usually a grandparent, who carries a second culture. Many bilingual immigrants in English-speaking countries report that they spoke English as a child with their locally born parents, but spoke only the native tongue with their grandparents.

One interesting variant on this was a four-year-old Thai girl of mixed Australian and Thai parentage, who spoke English to those who addressed her or her parents in English and Thai to those who spoke Thai to her. When a Thai friend first addressed her in English, the child answered in English, and refused to answer in Thai when the friend subsequently spoke Thai to her. Apparently the language first used determined the category in which the speaker was placed by the child.

Some writers on bilingual training advocate the principle "one person, one language" which was first suggested by Grammont (1902) as the optimal method of acquiring two languages. In Ronjak's classic study (1913) of the language development of his child, he describes how the latter learned to recognize French and German as different languages by the age of sixteen months, as a result of speaking French exclusively with his father and German with his mother. This method of learning is supposed to avoid conflict, but the experimental literature on the validity of this argument is very limited—"hardly explored," according to Weinreich (1964, p. 74). The effect of these mixed but separate situations on the competence, values, and personal identity of a child, in terms of the primary socialization process described above, is a potentially important subject that remains yet to be fully researched. Examples of questions to be asked are the effect of the cross pressures on the self-concept, on the relationship between identification of the person with each of the significant socializers and his competence in the respective cultural skills (to be measured mainly by language), and on his attitude toward the societies or nations that are identified with each culture.

One important question is whether the bilingual child's skills in the two languages are as good as the monolingual's. There is much literature on this question based on studies conducted on schoolchildren, but little evidence on preschool infants (Kovac 1969; Lambert 1975; Mackey 1970; Macnamara 1966). The results are conflicting on the relative competence of bilinguals, but resolution is not likely until more attention is given to the conditions under which two languages are acquired, and especially whether this occurs simultaneously or sequentially.

2. One or both of the parents may be bicultural, and the child is brought up with biculturality as part of his self-concept. In this sense, the child's "home culture" may itself be bicultural, and he may be equally competent in both cultures.

On the assumption that "one person, one culture" has the same advantage as "one person, one language" is alleged to have, it could be that situation 1 leads to greater competency in both cultures than situation 2, but situation 2 may be more favorable for creating a mediator between the cultures, since the two have been taught as one system (see the discussion above of coordinate and compound bilinguals). Whether this is so needs to be investigated. On the theory that primary socialization occurs through the internalization of models, situation 1 should lead to more proficiency but is more likely to interfere with the development of a clear self-concept than is 2, especially if there is conflict between the two parents over their cultural stances. On the other hand, in situation 2, the bicultural parent may transfer his own cultural ambivalence to the child. Case studies are needed in order to look further at these questions.

One possible advantage in becoming bicultural through situation 2 is that a bicultural background may facilitate the acquisition of later cultures. It is interesting to note that two prominent political leaders in Papua New Guinea who have written their autobiographies both stem from a mixed cultural background. Sir Maori Kiki, whose book is called, with some justification,

Ten Thousand Years in a Lifetime (1963), had a freakish background for a person brought up in a traditional, relatively isolated Papuan village, in that his parents were members of traditionally inimical and culturally quite diverse communities. It is significant, however, that his father was the village constable, who had to make regular visits to officials in the regional center and thus had contact with various cultures, including that of the Australian administration. Although Kiki himself was brought up in the unsophisticated environment of his parents' two villages and was initiated into a clan, he was eventually "dragged" to a school and became a medical aide and qualified pathologist and the founder of a national political party. Kiki is primary multicultural in senses both 1 and 2; his parents came from diverse backgrounds, and his father was himself multicultural.

Michael Somare, the first chief minister of Papua New Guinea, was also the son of a multicultural police official who was a village chief, and his relatives had worked at various times for the German, Australian, and Japanese administrations in New Guinea. Somare was a primary bilingual; his family spoke pidgin at home, and he spoke the regional language with his playmates. He learned "his own language" (his parents' native village tongue) only at the age of six. Somare writes: "In such a situation it is a distinct advantage to have been exposed to two cultures in one's childhood. I always thought of myself as having two homes, I grew up understanding that, in spite of so many superficial differences, there are many similarities between us" (1975, p. 1). To cap this, Somare, like Kiki, underwent a traditional initiation but had schooling in both Japanese and English. With such backgrounds, neither Kiki nor Somare could adhere to cultural absolutes, even though both of them make it clear that they identify with one or more of their primary cultures—as well as (presumably) with the cultures of modern society.

3. A third situation where primary socialization involves multicultural learning occurs when the child lives in a mixed community and is subject simultaneously to diverse learning between his home and the outside of it. This was Somare's situation, and it is also typical of a child whose parents belong to a minority culture. In such cases, it is difficult to evaluate the relative influences of the two environments (minority and majority) on the child's culture learning; the home might be expected to be the most influential, but much could depend on the interpretation that the parents transfer to the child of their own culture and that of the surrounding community.

Family in Transition

A second type of familiogenic acquisition of more than one culture is the family-in-transition condition, in which the family is in the course of change during the person's childhood. In these cases, the acquisition of the cultures is better described as "transitional," rather than either "simultaneous" or "sequential." A typical example would be an upwardly mobile immigrant family which moves from an area of first settlement in an inner slum district of a city to a middle-class area. This is well-illustrated by accounts of upwardly mobile Jews (Goldstein and Goldscheider 1968; Wirth 1928). As a result of the change that is occurring to the whole family, there need be little break between the culture of the parents and that of the child, and the child will eventually become enculturated to the middle-class majority culture of the host community, rather than to the working-class (or peasant) culture of the community of origin.

A person who has this type of family-in-transition enculturation may have some defects in fulfilling the role of mediator between the two cultures, even though members of both cultures may make the mistake of believing that he represents a mediator par excellence. Such a person may, in the long run, be the object of quite ambivalent attitudes on the part of members of the original group, and where the groups are in conflict, he may even be accused of being a traitor to his origins.

The remainder of the types of multiculturalism are *idiogenic* rather than *familiogenic*, that is, they arise sequentially after the basic social patterns and concept of self have been established.

Primary Idiogenic Biculturality

Movement from one culture to another by an individual child can occur during the primary socialization period, and, provided that the transition of parental models can be achieved smoothly, this is likely to lead to the replacement of the first culture by the second. But if the changeover is traumatic—for example, where the new parents reject or maltreat the child—there is likely to be a severe personality disturbance because of an unsatisfactory primary socialization period. Such disturbances are not necessarily due to culture conflict, but rather to the unfavorable circumstances for the growth of a healthy ego. However, the abrupt change in cultural environment is likely to be blamed.

A not uncommon case of idiogenic movement between cultures during primary socialization occurs when a rejected infant or child is adopted by members of another culture; an example is the adoption of an aboriginal child, a Japanese child of mixed parentage, an orphan from Korea, or a Vietnamese or Timorese refugee by a white Australian family. An important aspect of this example is that no matter how Australian the child may be by culture and environment, his physical characteristics lead to frequent reminders of his origin. Consequently, the child is more likely to have to contend with his mixed identity and periodic rejection by his environment than an adopted child of the same racial background as his foster parents. Alienation and conflict are thereby likely to occur, but it would not necessarily follow that this is due to imperfect primary socialization. In such cases as these, the person when fully matured may not be able to act as an effective mediator between the two cultures without special training, since he would have little connection with his original one. The effect of perceived rejection by the Australian culture may drive him to try to recapture the culture associated with his racial origins, but little of it will actually still remain within him. What often happens in these cases is that a group of persons with a similar history get together and try to create a synthetic culture which has some associations with the traditional one (see marginal situation III, above). For example, some Australian aborigines in Sydney who were born of detribalized parents completely cut off from tribal traditions are attempting to learn an aboriginal language and to associate themselves with some generalized rituals and sacred objects. This will, however, do little to increase their ability to mediate between Australian society and any particular traditional aboriginal culture.

Secondary Idiogenic Biculturality

Finally, we come to secondary idiogenic biculturality. This is the most common circumstance that creates mediators between cultures. This is the typical situation with immigrants, foreign students, and technical aid officers —the person has a primary enculturation in one or more home cultures, and other cultures are added later. These secondary cultural acquisitions occur as a result of exposure to the new culture after the primary socialization has run much of its course, say, after the age of seven years. The exposure can range from indirect contact through the written or spoken word, including academic study, to an all-encompassing engulfment in which the person emigrates and is virtually cut off from his home culture other than in his memories, the possession of a few personal effects, and perhaps an occasional contact. However, even in this latter situation of isolation from the original culture, it is unlikely that his feelings of identity and his basic values and cognitive style will completely change, although his language and the other skills that are relevant to the original culture may fade.

Primary resocialization does not occur easily, and in most cases a return to the original cultural environment will restore the emotional attachments and the cultural competencies to the full, although it should be noted that these may have become anachronisms, since the culture may have changed so much that the social reality does not fit the one to which the individual is attached. For example, the nostalgia for the simple, traditional village life may be completely inappropriate for a society that has in the meantime become urbanized. One of the senses of the phrase "you can't go home again" is that *you* have changed too much; but another is that *home* has changed beyond the person's expectations (Schuetz 1964).

The incongruity that may exist between the outlook of a person who has developed new acculturations in later life and the current state of his original culture has implications for his ability to mediate between the old and the new cultures. If he has been out of touch with the original culture, he may not know it sufficiently well currently to act as a mediator, and he may or may not be aware of this deficiency in his knowledge. The situation of the secondary idiogenic bicultural is not unlike that of the primary in that his competence as a mediator is likely to be misjudged, especially if his physical characteristics mark him off for continual reminder of his alien origins. This point is made by Bochner and Wicks (1972) in connection with foreign students. Even if a foreign student becomes a citizen of his adopted home and marries a local person, he is still likely to be called on for the rest of his life to act as a mediator, although he is no longer competent to do so.

Enculturation and Competence

Ultimately, enculturation is all about the acquisition of competence, the ability to cope with the demands placed upon the individual by society. A satisfactory training in culturally relevant knowledge and skills is one of the bases on which competence rests, although this is not the full story, since the person must also possess suitable abilities and temperament so that the knowledge and skills can be applied effectively. Competence has been defined variously, but the most relevant to the present purpose is that of Brewster Smith (1968) as "the capacities for role performance." As the techniques adopted by a child through learning and maturation lead to success and reward, so a sense of mastery is achieved. There is a mutually reinforcing interaction among actual competence, perceived competence, and the development of further competence, in which the teaching and encouragement by the significant others play an important part. Ultimately, the child's sense of identity comes from his perception of what he should do and of how well he does it.

Not many empirical studies have been made on the acquisition of the ability to cope in the early socialization period. Some exceptions are the Coping Project carried out by Lois Murphy and her associates at Topeka (Murphy 1962); Burton White's studies at Harvard on competence (maturity) in young children (White et al. 1973); and Bruner's studies of the acquisition of skills in infants and children (1972). These studies deal not only with how a child is taught to cope with the task posed by the environment, but also with how he teaches himself by learning from experience and practice. These studies, together with a personality theory such as Erikson's model of ego development

(1959), can provide a working basis for describing the type of competence that is needed to cope effectively with the task of mediating between cultures.

One question that arises in connection with ideogenic biculturals is whether it is necessary for the person to become identified (in a subjective sense) with the new culture in order for him to be able to act as a mediator between it and his old one. A mediator can perform his role competently without having any loyalty to the second culture, but this does not necessarily provide the optimum conditions. The ideal situation for mediation between cultures would almost certainly require the bicultural person to be highly identified with each one. When the cultures are acquired sequentially, as is the typical case with sojourners and settlers, this means that the ideal mediator should retain his identification with his original culture but develop an involvement in the new one. As I have demonstrated in connection with the loyalties of Jews in Australia (Taft 1973), there is no essential reason why an increase in identification with one culture should necessarily lead to a reduction in the other—provided that the cultures are not incompatible. The same point holds for cultural skills. Just as there seems to be no limit to the number of languages a person can know, although any person's ability to learn languages would impose its own practical limits, likewise it may be that there are no limits to the number of other cultural skills that can be acquired. Thus, there is also no limit, in theory, to the number of cultures a person can mediate.

To serve as a mediator between cultures, a person must possess competencies that are relevant to each culture. These may refer to at least four different aspects of either culture:

1. *Knowledge about the society*, such as its history, folklore, traditions, and customs; its values and its prohibitions; the natural environment and its importance to the society; the neighboring peoples; the important persons in the society, and so on.
2. *Communication skills*, which include at least the gestural and spoken language or languages (and in some societies, the written). Also, the ability to orate or to use graphic skills other than writing for communication may be important.
3. *Technical skills* that are required by the person's status in the society, such as hunting, athletics, crafts, academic skills, and the ability to perform rituals. Some of these skills are taken for granted and not viewed as skills except by foreigners—for example, being able to use the required eating instruments (such as chopsticks) or to don conventional apparel (such as a sari).
4. *Social skills* needed in order to perform effectively in appropriate social roles. These skills require a knowledge of the rules that govern social relations within the society. At the same time, the individual

also needs sufficient self-control to be able to perform the roles. The relationship between the latter and social skills came out clearly in a study of competence in schoolgirls carried out by Tait (1976), in which a high correlation was found between measures of "emotional competence" and "social competence." Emotional competence was also found to provide a basis for the ability to plan and carry out a complex task.

Each of these clusters of skills must be transmitted to children during the course of their socialization, and various types of socializing agencies participate in this process. In modern societies, the formal educational institutions play a major part. The field of pedagogical science—the study of how people learn and how they can be taught—is concerned largely with the enculturation of members of the society with the knowledge and skills that are considered to be necessary for them to fulfill their roles. In fact, a teacher may be thought of as a mediator between the cultures of the educated and the uneducated. Thus, the curriculum includes language and computational skills, history, geography, "high" culture (the arts), knowledge about the functioning of society, and vocational and craft skills. There are also some aspects of socialization that are taught in schools largely unofficially. These are usually related to personality development and cover such areas as how to control one's emotional expression, what to value in life, and how to interact with other people in an effective and acceptable manner—that is, the "hidden curriculum," in which the children are implicitly prepared to take particular roles in society that are considered to be appropriate to their background, interests, and abilities.

Different types of competency are required by different cultures, and a person who is competent in one may be incompetent in another. The competency requirements even differ between subcultures within the one society. Thus, among middle-class Jews, for example, academic competence may be regarded as a prerequisite for being esteemed, whereas among rural workers, physical prowess may be more relevant. These differences alone could partly explain the notoriously poor mediation between these two subcultures in Eastern European countries. Effective performance as a mediator between any two cultures would require differing emphasis on the various types of competence required, depending on the type of mediator and the particular cultures involved. Since training courses in cultural adaptation—for example, courses for foreign specialists and voluntary helpers such as Peace Corps personnel—are primarily aimed at training the students in cultural competencies, careful consideration needs to be given to which ones are the most relevant.

Not all of the competencies relevant to a culture are required for a person to act as a mediator with another one. Often it is sufficient to be able to handle only a segment of a culture. For example, a foreign businessman can be a mediator with just some knowledge of the culture of the customers, some knowledge of their social rules, and perhaps some of their language. The aspects of acculturation that are considered to be important can be illustrated by the various tests that have been devised to measure the degree to which people are competent in a second culture. Some examples are measures of language skills used, for example, in the studies of bilinguals in Canada by Jakobovits (1970); the use of Australian slang expressions by British immigrants (Richardson 1974); Knowledge of local heroes by adolescent immigrants in Australia (Doczy 1966); awareness among immigrants of the attitudes held by the local population on social questions (Taft 1961); and role-performance expectations, embodied in the various "culture assimilator" training-program tests developed by Stolurow, Fiedler, Triandis, and their associates for the training of foreign specialists (Fiedler, Mitchell, and Triandis 1971).

KNOWLEDGE OF A CULTURE AS A SKILL

Since most of the skills that are required by a culture are usually imparted in childhood and early adolescence through semiformal and fully formal institutions, a special problem is posed for an adult newcomer who wishes to become a mediator with that culture, because his knowledge of the new culture is likely to be thin, and his mastery of technical skills and the language somewhat weak. For some mediating purposes the superficiality of this competence may not matter, but for more reliable and lasting mediation a deeper level of skill is desirable.

A deeper level of competence involves some subtler aspects of psychological functioning. It requires that the mediator possess the necessary cognitive structures in order to be able to perceive the culture in the same way as other participants are able to do; he also must know when it is culturally appropriate for him to do so. Part of culture learning is to learn to construct the environment in the culturally appropriate way. A Westerner who undergoes a typical vigorous massage in Japan would probably be making an error if he constructed this as a hostile act on the part of the masseuse, and would betray his inadequate knowledge of the culture if he reacted to it as if it were. The cultural sensitivity training program at the Peace Corps Training Center at Hilo (Downs 1969) aimed to develop in the learner insight into the cultural idiosyncracies of his own cognitive structures, employing a confrontation technique.

An understanding of the culture further implies that the perception of events will be accompanied by appropriate emotional reactions. Unless an integration is achieved between the cognitive and the dynamic aspects of the culture as they coexist within a person, enculturation has not occurred, that is, the person is not able to perform the necessary social skills. Competence in performing culturally defined roles implies an ability to empathize with the participants in the culture, and without this facility, a person remains alien to the culture. Empathizing with the attitudinal set of other persons involves not only a knowledge of what to expect in their overt behavior, but also the capacity to simulate the covert affective aspects of the behavior, including muscle tonus and readiness for action and the emotional states. If we have this capacity, a new culture is no longer alien to us.

The need for congruence between the verbal and gestural aspects of language is brought out when we observe a dubbed film on television and are puzzled by the expressions of the character, until we realize that the gestures are, say, Japanese, but the words are perfect English. It is even more puzzling when the language and the motor behavior of a person interacting across cultural lines communicate conflicting messages. For example, an American businessman's words to a Javanese counterpart may communicate friendliness and flattery, but (according to Hall and Whyte 1960) his putting his arm on the latter's shoulder communicates an attempt to humiliate him. Hall and Whyte point out that social skills require appropriate behavior with respect to many more things than choice of words—for example, dress, emotional expression, use of time and space, physical contact, selection of channels for communicating, degree of forthrightness, and so on. Without knowledge of these norms regarding communication behavior, one is not culturally competent.

A word should be said about the use of rules as a guide to cultural competence. In secondary idiogenic biculturality, the deliberate use of rules is likely to be more prominent as a guide to behavior in the later-learned culture than in the original one. Thus, in the learning of a new language, vocabulary and grammatical rules are stressed in a way that is almost irrelevant to primary acquisition. In the same way, simple cultural rules (usually of etiquette) are adopted; for instance, "always shake hands with a Frenchman on arrival and departure," "Never point your feet at a Thai," and so forth (see Hall and Whyte 1960 for some simple rules). In practice, a strict adherence to these rules may reflect incompetence rather than competence in the culture, since most rules have their limits and exceptions, a knowledge of which is necessary for a skilled role performance.

A person who is skilled in a culture seldom consciously employs rules in his performance. The rules are embedded in the behavior, which occurs automatically in response to the cues that trip it off and to the situation in which it occurs. Social skills, like other skills, represent sequences of behavior which proceed according to their program unless there is feedback that it is inappropriate to the anticipated behavior. Cultural competence implies not only that the person should possess the knowledge and basic skills that are needed in order to carry out the required sequences of behavior, but also that he should be able to recognize when the feedback indicates that his behavior is inappropriate. In these cases, a competent person will know enough to suggest what adjustment to make, or at least, what behavior to try out tentatively for its effectiveness.

This analysis of the skill requirements for competent cultural performance provides a basis for considering the qualities needed by a mediator, and this will be taken up in the next section.

DETERMINANTS OF COMPETENCE AS A MEDIATOR

A competent mediator between cultures must be skilled in the relevant aspects of the two cultures so that he is able to carry out automatically the normally required performances in either of them but to resort to rule-governed behavior when the circumstances call for it. He must also be skilled in a performance that goes beyond that, in the actual carrying out of the role of mediator itself. As was pointed out earlier, being competent in the cultures concerned is a necessary but not sufficient requirement for being a mediator, and competence in performing the role of mediator is a further requirement. It is to these topics that we now turn.

The relevant variables that might determine an individual's competence in cultural mediation can be grouped under the following headings:

> Abilities
> Training
> Personality variables and, in particular, personal competence
> Interests, identification, and other intrinsic motives
> Instrumental or extrinsic motives
> Background factors, including age and parental influences

These will be considered in relation to both the ability to learn new cultures and the ability to mediate between cultures. The literature on lingual aspects of cultures will be included but treated separately.

The Ability To Learn New Languages and Cultures

Languages. Jakobovits (1970) has summarized the studies on factors that have been shown to relate to ability to learn foreign languages. These include:

Abilities. General verbal intelligence has been found to be predictive of ability to learn languages, and there probably also exists a special talent for languages, defined operationally by performance on such tasks as those in the Modern Language Aptitude Test (MLAT) (Carroll and Sapon 1967). Apart from the fact that this aptitude consists of certain verbal skills, little is known of its origins (Lambert 1975, pp. 60-61).

Training. Jacobovits reports that there are indications that learning a foreign language at secondary-school level facilitates the learning of a different one at the postsecondary stage (1970, p. 248), but he presents no evidence on whether primary bilinguals are better or worse at learning a new language than are primary monolinguals or secondary bilinguals. It is possible that the advantage applies only to primary bilinguals, since Lambert and Tucker (1972) report that secondary "bilinguals" (English-speaking children who were being instructed in French at school) were not advantaged in learning Russian phonetics. However, this latter task is a limited test of language skills. The findings are conflicting and the evidence weak on whether bilinguals are better than monolinguals at learning a third language. As Weinreich puts it: "This point, too, awaits clarification by research" (1964, p. 73). The required experimental controls are difficult to impose to permit a convincing test of the effect on further language learning of a person who is already multilingual. There is probably an interaction between the degree of competence in a language and the interference between it and another language. Thus, there is interference in the early stages of learning a foreign language between the two imperfectly known languages, but when a second language has been learned well, this learning may facilitate the acquisition of a third one. Only further investigation will tell.

Personality. The work of Guiora and colleagues (1975) indicates that the ability to empathize with others is a positive indicator for learning a foreign language, although this has to date been demonstrated for phonetic skill only. Apparently being able to put oneself "in the skin" of the speaker helps. Jakobovits claims that perseverance is the important consideration, but this might simply be an expression of a strong interest in learning languages, and may not be a personality trait at all. Jakobovits (1970, pp. 265–266) also tentatively suggests that ethnocentrism and authoritarianism are negative indicators, and this would tend to support the argument that empathy is helpful.

Intrinsic and extrinsic motivation. One of the most important determinants of ability to learn is the learner's interest in the language and his own personal involvement in the language and its culture. Studies of the ease with which immigrants in Australia acquire English indicate that identification with the new country is an important factor (Taft 1966). However, the evidence (see summary in Jakobovits 1970, pp. 243 ff.) is equivocal of the importance of these variables. The work of Lambert and his colleagues at McGill University (Gardner and Lambert 1972) clearly suggests that an orientation toward "integration" with the culture helps language learning more than does an "instrumental" orientation, but Carroll (1960) argues that whatever will make students persevere in learning will be effective, whether it be interest, material reward, or ulterior motive.

Later studies by the McGill workers on the learning of English as a second language by students in the Philippines (Lambert 1975, pp. 63-64) provide support for the contention that the strength of motivation is probably more important than its nature. Thus, the instrumental need for the students to acquire English in connection with their studies influenced their proficiency— but so also did an integrative outlook toward speaking English.

Motivational factors play a much less important role, if any at all, in the learning of a second language by young children. Marian Bodi (1977) studied factors that related to both the relative and the absolute competence in oral and written English and Russian of primary-school children in Australia. Since they started school as virtual monolingual Russians and then learned English in the regular classroom, their knowledge of English bore no relationship to their motivation to learn it. Measures of verbal ability, general intelligence, and language-learning ability were highly related to their competence in English, and there was a positive correlation between their competence in English and in Russian. The role played in new-language learning by intrinsic and extrinsic motivation is dependent on the circumstances under which the learning takes place, and in any case, its influence is likely to be far less than that of ability.

Background factors. The literature on background and ability to learn languages is deficient. There is evidence, however, as has already been suggested, that those with a bilingual background may have certain cognitive advantages over monolinguals. One background factor whose relevance to ability to learn languages has been well demonstrated is age of learning. Clearly, older persons are handicapped and children are advantaged, but there is some controversy about whether or not learning is maximal during the ten-to-twelve age period or earlier (Weinreich 1964). Studies in Australia of English language skills in immigrants (Taft 1966) show a high correlation between the number of years of education and fluency in the use of English, but it is difficult to separate out the contributions made by innate ability, the general effect of education, and specific training in English.

Bodi's study of Russian children (1977) showed that the competence of the bilingual children in the two languages reflected the influences of the home and, in particular, the parents' knowledge of English and the degree to which they used it. However, again, several variables are involved together.

Cultures. Most of the characteristics that relate to the ability to learn a new language probably apply, with appropriate modification, to learning a new culture. Thus, youth, intelligence, education, previous contacts with other cultures, empathy, identification, parental pressure, and high motivation all seem to be relevant.

It has already been suggested in the discussion on secondary enculturation that experience with more than one culture makes it easier to acquire a further one. A multicultural person is less likely than a monocultural individual to suffer culture shock when exposed to unfamiliar cultural mores, since he probably has already learned to accept the relativity of cultures. Because of this experience, a multicultural person is able to deal with an unfamiliar culture in a relaxed manner which may aid learning. The multicultural person is also more likely than a monocultural to possess cognitive structures that are relevant to the new culture, and is thus able to learn it more quickly.

It is assumed that bi- or multiculturality helps in the learning of a new culture irrespective of whether it was acquired in a primary or secondary manner, but it seems likely that the latter situation would teach a person more about learning new cultures than would primary biculturality. This question, however, cannot be answered on the evidence so far available, since the two types of biculturality are seldom treated separately in the literature.

Life histories, such as those of Maori Kiki and Michael Somare which were described earlier, suggest that a multicultural family background is one of the factors that help in adapting to modern societies, but these accounts do not differentiate between types of multiculturality. There is evidence in their biographies that cross-cultural contacts later in life assist in developing a general cultural adaptation. Thus, Somare (1975) characteristically titles one of his chapters in his autobiography "Broadening Horizons—Overseas Travel." In a recently opened primary school in the eastern highlands of New Guinea, a handful of the children indicated to me that they would like to go on to high school. In all cases, the occupation of these children's fathers was one that brought them into contact with the government administration and frequently took them beyond their own village area. This demonstrates the possible effect of a bicultural background in facilitating the acquisition of a further culture—in this case, that of the modern, literate society. Empirical evidence to that effect is reported in a study of O'Brien, Fiedler, and Hewett (1971), which found that U.S. Peace Corps trainees in "culture assimilation" in preparation for service in Honduras gained more from the course when they had previously had experience in other cultures.

Lambert (1975, p. 64 ff.) summarizes several recent studies conducted in a variety of multicultural societies, such as those of Singapore, Switzerland, South Africa, and Canada, that find very distinct advantages for bilingual children—presumably also bicultural children—over those who are monolingual (monocultural). On the basis of these findings, it would seem that biculturality (mainly, it seems, primary) leads to markedly increased cognitive flexibility. This, of course, would greatly aid the learning of new cultures.

There is evidence that apart from the effect of intercultural experience, personality characteristics related to general flexibility and competence in life are predictive of the ability to adapt to new cultures. There may be personality factors that are specific to being able to adapt to particular cultures and not others, but so far we know too little about this subject to make this type of differentiation.

A review was carried out by the author (Taft 1967) of various studies that had been conducted on personality factors related to the ease with which foreign students in the United States adapt. The findings consistently support the overriding importance of emotional stability. Other characteristics mentioned in the studies seem to relate to tolerance for ambiguity. Thus, the following traits have been found in those who adapt easily: a relaxed, trusting attitude to people (versus cynicism, mistrust, and authoritarian attitudes), and flexibility. Together with Jan Daw, I conducted a study on a sample of Dutch male immigrants in Australia, and obtained low correlations between an overall index that measures adjustment to Australia and measures of emotional stability, personal trust, autonomy, and low alienation. Intelligence and education correlated moderately highly with an index of acculturation, and especially with the speed of acquisition of the English language. On the other hand, flexibility, authoritarianism, and extraversion were unrelated to the measures of adjustment and acculturation to Australia (Taft 1967).

Doczy (1966) studied the characteristics that relate to how well immigrant adolescent boys adapted to life in Australia, using as his criterion a mixture of measures of adjustment, satisfaction, acculturation, and feelings of identification. Those who adapted most easily were more intelligent and better emotionally adjusted. In a different type of study conducted by the present author (Taft 1970), an "experience" questionnaire was filled in by several hundred adults in Australia, together with other self-descriptive personality measures. The respondents who scored high on items in which they described their ability to adapt to unfamiliar situations, including different cultures, tended to be emotionally mature, competent, stable, and humanistic.

In general, although not in all cases, the characteristics that aid the learning of and adapting to new cultures boil down to competence in all of its manifestations: intellectual, emotional, social and organizational. Thus, a person whose general personality functioning in his own culture is competent also seems to be more capable of adapting to another one.

The studies reported here refer only to persons brought up in developed societies, and the question must still be asked whether their findings apply to the ability of members of traditional cultures to cope with technologically developed cultures. Some of the literature on modernization is relevant to this question (see reviews in Berry 1980 and Inkeles and Smith 1974). The studies suggest that the people from a traditional background who are best fitted for this type of change are those who have had formal education. They are found to be more open to information and new experiences in general and to have more initiative, drive for achievement, independence, and emotional detachment; in other words, they are more "competent" in the modern sense. In the studies reported, however, it is difficult to separate cause and effect with respect to modernization, since the studies tend to be conducted *ex post facto*. Also, as Berry (1980) points out, little effort has been made so far to consider the significance of these qualities in terms of the traditional cultures concerned, rather than from the point of view of the technologically advanced ones.

In summary, the ease with which a person can learn a new language or culture is a function of a number of variables. These include previous intercultural experience, age and other background factors, ability and personality characteristics related to flexibility, tolerance of the unknown, general competence, high motivation to learn, and acceptance of the new culture. There also are relevant situational determinants, such as opportunities and relations with members of the new culture. The most important immediate general factors are probably motivation, opportunity, and general competence.

The Ability To Perform the Role of Mediator

We shall now move on from the determinants of the ability to learn a new culture to factors related to being a good mediator once the relevant cultural competencies have been acquired.

Language Mediators. In this case, the relevant mediating role is that of translator. A literature search for data on the characteristics of a good translator failed to reveal anything other than the obvious: they must know both languages, and they must be able to read or listen in one language and express themselves in the other. The review by Caillé (1974), which is a typical example, refers to the training of translators, but not to their required personal qualities. Gerver (1976, pp. 189-191) reports two studies of the personality characteristics of simultaneous interpreters that indicate that they are intelligent and resourceful and that the best performers under noisy (stressful) conditions are those with low neuroticism scores on the Eysenck Personality Inventory (EPI). On the whole, however, the very sparse literature on the ability to translate adds nothing to the earlier conclusion that translators need to be competent.

Cultural Mediators. First and foremost, the quality needed to act as a bridge between members of diverse cultures is sensitivity to the feelings of people and the ability to put oneself in their position, to construct the world as they do and to experience the action tendencies and emotions that they do: in other words, the ability to empathize with others.

An outlook that extends beyond one's own culture also seems to be relevant. Thus, ethnocentrism would be a handicap in a person acting as a mediator, and a broad "world-mindedness" an advantage. Sampson and Smith (1957) defined the latter as a value orientation in a person "whose primary reference group is mankind, rather than Americans, English, Chinese, etc."

(p. 99). A world-minded person in this sense would seem likely to make a more competent mediator than a non-world-minded one, although this is not yet well established. On a Likert-type scale of this dimension, it was found that a summer trip to Europe increased the scores of U.S. students, and that the more highly world-minded ones were more likely to carry on correspondence with people that they had met on the trip. To understand the further significance of world-mindedness for developing mediators, we would need to know what are the characteristics that lead to this quality in a person brought up in a society such as the United States and what it means for members of other societies.

Most of the empirical studies reported on cultural mediators have concerned the efficacy of U.S. Peace Corps volunteers. The typical finding is that the volunteers who function best have generally competent personalities and are also well-motivated toward their work and technically competent in it. Studies of the characteristics of successful U.S. Peace Corps volunteers (see the review by Harris 1975) suggest that apart from the need for technical competence, the required characteristics are adaptation, perseverance, dependability, and tolerance for frustration, all of which are characteristics that relate to emotional stability. Similar results were reported by Brewster Smith (1966), who found that what he called "self-confident maturity" was the main cluster of qualities needed. However, Guthrie in this volume reports disappointing results in attempts to predict the performance of Peace Corps workers in the Philippines. Tests of interests and abilities did not predict at all the judgments made of the workers by local Filipino colleagues, and Guthrie even reports that some "high-risk" volunteers (risks on psychiatric grounds) seem to have adapted well.

Reports of other studies are also puzzling. Jones and Popper (1972) found marked differences in relevant variables for males and females. For example, the more effective females were better educated, younger, and had poorer language proficiency, while the opposite was the case for the males. There are many such confusions in this area. The review by David (1972) of the adaptation of American sojourners (mainly Peace Corps workers) in more traditional societies concludes that the evidence is ambiguous on the value for effective adaptation of such factors as level of education, intelligence, language skills, and personality adjustment.

Guthrie (this volume) makes the point that the success of Peace Corps volunteers is determined more by accidental factors that occur early in their experience in the field assignment and which could not have been predicted in the selection procedures. Nevertheless, the overall evidence of all of the studies does suggest that intellectual, social, and emotional competence are relevant to performance. A defect in many of the studies regarding the success of Peace Corps volunteers is some confusion concerning the criteria for success. For example, if the volunteer is working as a schoolteacher, as many of them are, the ratings may refer to their ability as a teacher in general rather than to their cross-cultural competence, and still less to their competence as a mediator.

There is little or no empirical evidence available that analyzes the qualities that make one bicultural person an effective mediator and another one not, and until this evidence is available, we can rely only on the relatively meager findings on the characteristics of those who are able to learn unfamiliar cultures to provide hints. Presumably such qualities as intelligence, general competence, self-confidence, sensitivity to other people, emotional stability, and tolerance of differences all play their part. So also, presumably, does love of humanity. In fact, since biculturality is part of the characteristics of a mediator, acceptance, if not love, of both aspects of oneself should be important.

In view of the contribution of experience with second cultures to the adaptability of a person to further cultures, it may turn out that intercultural training and guided experience is far more important in producing mediators than is an analysis of their personal qualities. For this reason, scholars who are interested in the development of mediators should be paying more attention to such questions as: What are the characteristics of primary bi- and multiculturals, and how does their enculturation occur? What is the effect of intercultural experiences in adult life on further adaptability? How can children be educated to be more appreciative of other cultures and to seek links with them? What are the best ways in which to motivate and to train people to act as cultural mediators? This chapter has merely touched on aspects of these questions, and further answers must wait on a much more extensive examination of them.

References

Barik, H. C. Interpreters Talk A Lot, Among Other Things. *Babel, Revue Internationale de la Traduction*, 1972, *18*, 3–10.

_____. Simultaneous Interpretation: Temporal and Quantitative Data. *Language and Speech*, 1973, *16*, 237–270.

Bennett, J. W., Passin, H., and McKnight, R. K. *In Search of Identity: The Japanese Overseas Scholar in America and Japan*. Minneapolis, Minn.: University of Minnesota Press, 1958.

Berger, P. L., and Luckmann, T. *The Social Construction of Reality*. New York: Doubleday Anchor, 1967.

Berry, J. W. *The Psychology of Social Change*. In H. Triandis (ed.), *Handbook of Cross-cultural Psychology*. Vol. 3. Boston, Mass.: Allyn and Bacon, 1980.

Bochner, S. *The Mediating Man: Cultural Interchange and Transnational Education*. Honolulu, Hawaii: East-West Center, 1973*a*.

____. The Mediating Man and Cultural Diversity. In R. Brislin (ed.), *Topics in Culture Learning*. Vol. 1. Honolulu, Hawaii: East-West Center, 1973*b*, pp. 23–37.

Bochner, S., and Wicks, P. (eds.). *Overseas Students in Australia*. Sydney: New South Wales University Press, 1972.

Bodi, M. The Effect on Language Acculturation of the Attitudes of Pre-adolescent Immigrant Children. Unpublished master's thesis, Monash University, Melbourne, Australia, 1977.

Brim, O. G. Socialization Through the Life Cycle. In O. G. Brim and S. Wheeler (eds.), *Socialization After Childhood*. New York: Wiley, 1966.

Brislin, R. W. (ed.). *Translation: Application and Research*. New York: Gardner, 1976.

Bruner, J. S. Nature and Uses of Immaturity. *American Psychologist*, 1972, *27*, 687–708.

Caillé, P. F. Translators and Translation: 1974 Survey. *Babel, Revue Internationale de la Traduction*, 1974, *20*, 130–141.

Campbell, D. T. Distinguishing Differences of Perception from Failures of Communication in Cross-cultural Studies. In F. S. C. Northrop and H. H. Livingston (eds.), *Cross-cultural Understanding: Epistemology in Anthropology*. New York: Harper, 1964, pp. 308–338.

Carroll, J. B. Foreign Languages for Children: What Research Says. *National Elementary Principal*, 1960, *39*, 12–15.

Carroll, J. B., and Sapon, S. M. *Elementary Modern Language Aptitude Test*. New York: Psychological Corporation, 1967.

Cleveland, H., Mangone, G., and Adams, J. *The Overseas Americans*. New York: McGraw-Hill, 1960.

David, K. H. Intercultural Adjustment and Applications of Reinforcement Theory to Problems of "Culture Shock." *Trends*, 1972, *4*, (whole no. 3).

Dickie-Clark, M. F. *The Marginal Situation*. London: Routledge and Kegan Paul, 1966.

Diller, K. C. "Compound" and "Coordinate" Bilingualism: A Conceptual Artifact. *Word*, 1970, *26*, 254–261.

Doczy, A. G. The Social Assimilation of Adolescent Boys of European Parentage in the Metropolitan Area of Western Australia. Unpublished doctoral dissertation, University of Western Australia, 1966.

Downs, J. F. Fables, Fancies and Failures in Cross-cultural Training. *Trends*, 1969, *2*, (whole no. 3).

Erikson, E. H. Identity and the Life Cycle. *Psychological Issues*, 1959, *1*, monograph 1.

Ervin, S. M., and Osgood, C. E. Second Language Learning and Bilingualism. In C. E. Osgood and T. Sebeok (eds.), *Psycholinguistics*, suppl. to *Journal of Abnormal and Social Psychology*, 1954, 139–146.

Fiedler, F. E., Mitchell, T., and Triandis, H. C. The Culture Assimilator: An Approach to Cross-cultural Training. *Journal of Applied Psychology*, 1971, *55*, 95–102.

Foote, N. N. Identification as the Basis for a Theory of Motivation. *American Sociological Review*, 1951, *16*, 14–21.

Gardner, R. C., and Lambert, W. E. *Attitudes and Motivation in Second-Language Learning.* Rowley, Mass.: Newbury House, 1972.

Gerver, D. Empirical Studies of Simultaneous Interpretation: A Review and a Model. In R. W. Brislin (ed.), *Translation: Application and Research.* New York: Gardner, 1976, pp. 165–207.

Goldman-Eisler, F. Segmentation of Input in Simultaneous Translation. *Journal of Psycholinguistic Research*, 1972, *1*, 127–140.

Goldstein, S., and Goldscheider, C. *Jewish Americans: Three Generations in a Jewish Community.* Englewood Cliffs, N.J.: Prentice-Hall, 1968.

Grammont, M. *Observations sur le Langue des Enfants.* Paris: Mélanges Meillet, 1902.

Guiora, A. Z., Paluszny, M., Beit-Hallahmi, B., Catford, J. C., Cooley, R. E., and Dull, C. Y. Language and Person Studies in Language Behavior. *Language Learning*, 1975, *25*, 43–61.

Hall, E. T., and Whyte, W. F. Intercultural Communication: A Guide to Men of Action. *Human Organization*, 1960, *19*, 5–12.

Harris, J. Identification of Cross-cultural Talent. In R. Brislin (ed.), *Topics in Culture Learning.* Vol. 3. Honolulu, Hawaii: East-West Center, 1975, pp. 66–78.

Haugen, E. I. *Bilingualism in the Americas: A Bibliography and Research Guide.* American Dialect Society Publication No. 26, 1956.

Herman, S. N. *American Students in Israel.* Ithaca, N.Y.: Cornell University Press, 1970.

Hymes, D. H. (ed.). *Language in Culture and Society: A Reader in Linguistics and Anthropology.* New York: Harper, 1964.

Imedadze, N. V. Kpsikhologikoskoy Prirode Rannego Dvuyazyikiya. (On the Psychological Nature of Early Bilingualism.) *Voprosy Psikhologii,* 1960, *6*, 60–68.

Inkeles, A., and Smith, D. H. *Becoming Modern.* Cambridge, Mass.: Harvard University Press, 1974.

Jakobovits, L. A. *Foreign Language Learning: A Psycholinguistic Analysis of the Issues.* Rowley, Mass.: Newbury House, 1970.

Jones, R. R., and Popper, R. Characteristics of Peace Corps Host Countries and the Behavior of Volunteers. *Journal of Cross-cultural Psychology,* 1972, *3*, 233–245.

Kassuehlke, R. Linguistic and Cultural Implications of Bible Translation. In R. W. Brislin (ed.), *Translation: Application and Research.* New York: Gardner, 1976, pp. 279–304.

Kiki, A. M. *Ten Thousand Years in a Lifetime: A New Guinea Autobiography.* Melbourne: Cheshire, 1963.

Kimball, S. T., and Watson, J. B. *Crossing Cultural Boundaries: The Anthropological Experience.* San Francisco: Chandler, 1972.

Koestler, A. *The Invisible Writing.* Boston, Mass.: Beacon, 1954.

Kolers, P. Bilingualism and Information Processing. *Scientific American,* 1968, *218*, 78–85.

Kovac, D. Command of Several Languages as a Psychological Problem. *Studia Psychologica*, 1969, *11*, 249–257.

Lambert, W. E. Culture and Language as Factors in Learning and Education. In A. Wolfgang (ed.), *Education of Immigrant Students: Issues and Answers*. Ontario: Ontario Institute for Studies in Education, 1975, pp. 55–83.

Lambert, W. E., and Tucker, G. R. *Bilingual Education of Children: The St. Lambert Experiment*. Rowley, Mass.: Newbury House, 1972.

Lenneberg, E. H. The Natural History of Language. In F. Smith and G. A. Miller (eds.), *The Genesis of Language*. Cambridge, Mass.: MIT Press, 1966, pp. 219–252.

Leopold, W. F. *Speech Development of a Bilingual Child* (4 vols.). Evanston, Ill.: Northwestern University Press, 1939–49.

Le Vine, R. A. *Culture, Behavior and Personality*. Chicago, Ill.: Aldine, 1973.

Mackey, W. F. The Description of Bilingualism. In J. Fishman (ed.), *Readings in the Sociology of Language*. The Hague: Mouton, 1970, pp. 554–584.

Macnamara, J. *Bilingualism and Primary Education: A Study of Irish Experience*. Edinburgh: University of Edinburgh Press, 1966.

Mann, J. W. Group Relations and the Marginal Personality. *Human Relations*, 1958, *11*, 77–92.

Murphy, L. B. *The Widening World of Childhood*. New York: Basic Books, 1962.

Naroll, R., and Cohen, R. (eds.). *A Handbook of Method in Cultural Anthropology*. New York: American Museum of Natural History, 1970.

Nida, E. *Toward a Scientific Theory of Translation*. New York: Brill, 1964.

O'Brien, G. E., Fiedler, F. E., and Hewett, T. The Effects of Programmed Culture Training Upon the Performance of Volunteer Medical Teams in Central America. *Human Relations*, 1971, *24*, 209–231.

Parsons, T. *The Social System*. Glencoe, Ill.: Free Press, 1951.

Peal, E., and Lambert, W. E. The Relation of Bilingualism to Intelligence. *Psychological Monographs*, 1962, *27*, (whole no. 546).

Ray, L. Multidimensional Translation: Poetry. In R. W. Brislin (ed.), *Translation: Application and Research*. New York: Gardner, 1976, pp. 261–278.

Richardson, A. *British Immigrants and Australia: A Psycho-social Inquiry*. Canberra: Australian National University Press, 1974.

Ronjak, J. *Le Développement du Langage Observé Chez un Enfant Bilingue*. Paris: Librairie Ancienne H. Champion, 1913.

Sampson, D. L., and Smith, H. P. A Scale to Measure World-minded Attitudes. *Journal of Social Psychology*, 1957, *45*, 99–106.

Schuetz, A. *The Homecomer*. Collected Papers, vol. 2, A. Brodersen (ed.). The Hague: Nijhoff, 1964.

Smith, M. B. Exploration in Competence: A Study of Peace Corps Teachers in Ghana. *American Psychologist*, 1966, *21*, 555–566.

Smith, M. B. Competence and Socialization. In J. A. Clausen (ed.), *Socialization and Society*. Boston, Mass.: Little, Brown, 1968.

Somare, M. T. *Sana: An Autobiography of Michael Somare*. Port Moresby: Niugini Press, 1975.

Sommerlad, E., and Berry, J. W. The Role of Ethnic Identification in Distinguishing Between Attitudes Towards Assimilation and Integration of a Minority Racial Group. *Human Relations*, 1970, *23*, 23–29.

Swain, M. Bilingualism As a First Language. Unpublished doctoral dissertation, University of California at Irvine, 1972.

Taft, R. The Assimilation of Dutch Male Immigrants in a Western Australian Community. *Human Relations*, 1961, *14*, 265–281.

———. *From Stranger to Citizen*. London: Tavistock, 1966.

———. The Role of Personality Traits in the Social Assimilation of Immigrants. *Australian and New Zealand Journal of Sociology*, 1967, *3*, 19–31.

———. The Measurement of the Dimensions of Ego Permissiveness. *Personality: An International Journal*, 1970, *1*, 163–184.

———. Jewish Identification of Melbourne Jewry. In P. Medding (ed.), *Jews in Australian Society*. Melbourne: Macmillan, 1973, pp. 61–102.

———. Ethnically Marginal Youth and Culture Conflict: A Problem in Cross-cultural Sciences. In J. L. M. Dawson and W. Lonner (eds.), *Readings in Cross-cultural Psychology*. Hong Kong: University of Hong Kong Press, 1974, pp. 268–276.

———. Coping With Unfamiliar Cultures. In N. Warren (ed.), *Studies in Cross-Cultural Psychology*. Vol. 1. London: Academic Press, 1977.

Tait, A. M. A Broadened Construct of Intelligence: Measures of Emotional, Task and Social Competencies as Non-intellective Factors of Intelligence Using the California Personality Inventory. Unpublished master's thesis, Monash University, Melbourne, Australia, 1976.

Triandis, H. C. Culture Training, Cognitive Complexity and Interpersonal Attitudes. In R. W. Brislin, S. Bochner, and W. J. Lonner (eds.), *Cross-cultural Perspectives on Learning*. New York: Wiley, 1975, pp. 39–77.

———. (ed.). *Handbook of Cross-cultural Psychology*. Boston, Mass.: Allyn and Bacon, 1980.

Useem, J., and Useem, R. H. *The Western-Educated Man in India: A Study of His Social Roles and Influence*. New York: Dryden, 1955.

Useem, R. H. *Education of Third Culture Children: An Annotated Bibliography*. Studies of Third Cultures: A Continuing Series, no. 1. Michigan State University: Institute for International Studies in Education, 1971.

Weinreich, U. *Languages in Contact: Findings and Problems*. The Hague: Mouton, 1964.

Werner, D., and Campbell, D. T. Translating, Working Through Interpreters and the Problem of Decentering. In R. Naroll and R. Cohen (eds.), *A Handbook of Method in Cultural Anthropology*. New York: American Museum of Natural History, 1970, pp. 398–420.

White, B. L., Watts, J. C., Kaban, B., Marmor, J., Shapiro, B., and Barnett, I. *Experience and Environment: Major Influence on the Development of the Young Child*. Vol. 1. Englewood Cliffs, N. J.: Prentice-Hall, 1973.

Wirth, L. *The Ghetto*. Chicago, Ill.: University of Chicago Press, 1928.

Part II

Being a Mediator:
Cross-Cultural Stress
and Its Alleviation

Introduction

The previous section established a broad theoretical base for the treatment of the mediating function. In this section, contributors describe what it is like being a mediator, the stresses that mediating persons encounter, and the adaptive strategies they can employ to reduce cross-cultural stress.

The first chapter, by Guthrie, provides an overview of the mediating experience from the particular perspective of social learning theory, which states that much of human behavior is learned and maintained by its consequences. In general, responses that are rewarded by the social environment tend to persist and become habitual, whereas acts that are ignored or punished tend to be carried out with diminishing frequency and ultimately disappear from the repertoire of the individual.

When a person moves into a new and alien environment, the contingencies that previously controlled his behavior may no longer apply, or may perhaps even change in significance. For example, responses that would have normally been rewarded in the person's own culture may now be ignored or even attract social disapproval, and behaviors that were treated with indifference or disdain previously may now be the very actions that are necessary to achieve the good opinion of his new colleagues. In the language of learning theory, well-established habits may no longer attract the customary reinforcement; previously punished behavior may no longer have the expected aversive consequences; and, in extreme cases, previously reinforced behavior may be punished and previously punished behavior reinforced.

The obvious implication of the social learning model is that exposure to an alien society can be a very stressful and confusing experience. The stress will persist until the sojourner has mastered the new set of reinforcement contingencies, a very precise formulation of the culture-learning process referred to in more general terms by some of the other contributors. Guthrie reviews the pertinent literature on the effect of sudden and massive changes in an individual's matrix of reinforcement schedules. He refers to studies carried out in natural settings as well as experiments conducted in the laboratory, and concludes that lack of continuity in the cultural context is the main source of stress for mediators. A corollary, supported by empirical data, is that situational factors are more important than enduring aspects of the sojourner's personality in determining the success or failure of the mediating experience. In turn, this proposition has consequences for the selection, training, and evaluation of mediators, implying that rather than trying to recruit individuals with special character traits, teachers of mediators should devote more attention to giving structure to the mediating situation. In particular, there is a need to specify the goals of the program clearly, so that mediators can get direct and immediate feedback on their rate of success.

In the next chapter, Otto Klineberg reviews the literature on international educational exchange from the perspective of cultural mediation. In theory, those who go abroad to teach or study should be mediators par excellence, in the sense of bringing nations closer together and contributing to better mutual understanding. However, in practice, many of the participants in educational exchange do not fulfill this function. It is therefore important to identify the conditions that prevent foreign students from becoming mediators. High on the list is the disparity between the goals of exchange programs and the reasons that students actually have for going abroad; the evidence indicates that students tend to rank as their first objective academic success and professional development, whereas the sponsors of the programs have broader aims in mind. Another problem relates to the student's role as a carrier of culture. To be effective, the student must possess extensive and accurate knowledge about his own society, and his hosts must be interested in what he has to offer. Neither condition may necessarily obtain in any particular instance. Finally, there is the related problem of what the student does with his experience when he gets home and how receptive his own social milieu is to the information that he has brought back with him.

Klineberg's main practical concern is how to reduce the number of academic sojourners who fail to adopt the mediating role. The analysis follows the life history of the typical overseas scholar and includes recommendations about improving the process of selecting persons for exchange programs, providing adequate predeparture orientation, easing entrance into the new university, supervising and contributing to the successful academic and/or professional progress of the scholar, facilitating the establishment of positive social relations with members of the host culture, providing specialized counseling services for the prevention and early treatment of mental health problems, and making explicit provisions to facilitate reentry into the home culture.

Klineberg notes that the concept of international understanding has two components. The first is cognitive, and refers to the knowledge and beliefs that people have about each other's societies. The second is affective, and refers to how people feel about each other's cultures. The evidence suggests that participation in international education does lead to greater accurate knowledge of other cultures; but research regarding the affective consequences of university exchanges is inconclusive, neither confirming nor denying the predicted increase in mutual goodwill.

Klineberg's general treatment of academic exchanges is followed by an intensive analysis of one particular group of overseas students. Using a psychiatric framework, Yeh and his colleagues describe the social adaptations of Chinese students in the United States. A special feature of the study is its longitudinal perspective. Many of the students were interviewed prior to leaving Taiwan, later participated in a survey during their sojourn, were treated by one of the authors if they underwent psychiatric repatriation, and were subsequently followed up after the termination of the sojourn and/or therapy. The most prevalent form of mental illness found among the Chinese students was paranoia, which Yeh and his colleagues attribute to two main determinants: conflict between traditional Chinese and American values, and the status loss to which this particular group of students seems specially susceptible.

The psychiatric literature contains many references to the tendency for overseas students to manifest paranoid symptoms. From their case studies, the authors conclude that the so-called paranoid behavior of foreign scholars has a considerable basis in reality and can best be understood as an overreaction to some of the circumstances inevitably associated with the academic sojourn. A major underlying cause is the very real loss of self-esteem and self-confidence that many foreign students experience and the tendency to blame other people for this loss. In trying to compensate for their actual or imagined reduction in status, sojourners often behave in ways that are misunderstood and rejected by their hosts, thereby further exacerbating the problem. It is therefore not surprising to find a high incidence of paranoid symptoms among foreign students, including extreme suspicion, feelings of persecution, projection, and the attribution of general hostility to the social environment.

Yeh and his colleagues draw the further conclusion that since culture conflict is the main determinant of psychiatric disturbance in foreign students, when a sojourner breaks down he should be treated by a therapist from the patient's own culture; if such a therapist is not available, the student should be repatriated for treatment. These are contentious recommendations.

The problem is that with the large number of cultures represented on the campuses of most major universities throughout the world, it may not always be possible to secure the services of a conational therapist. The alternative proposed by Yeh, psychiatric repatriation, has obvious undesirable consequences, such as the stigma attached to being sent home for treatment, the expense involved, and the interruption to the student's attendance at university. One solution is to design psychological services that are specially tailored to the needs of foreign students and that take into account quite explicitly the cultural component in the etiology and treatment of the disturbance.

The contribution by Yeh describes the stresses encountered by non-Westerners in the United States. The next chapter, by Dane, looks at the other side of the coin, and considers the difficulties that Americans experience when they go abroad for extended periods of time. In particular, Dane writes about Foreign Service personnel and their adaptation to the peripatetic nature of their lives. Dane's analysis suggests that the major source of stress is the change and discontinuity that mark the existence of diplomats and their families, thereby supporting Guthrie's contention about the aversive effects of novel environments. The stress is more acute for the dependents than for the head of the household, which in practice means that the adjustment is easier for the men than for their wives and children. This is because the breadwinner's job will have many elements in common with his previous work setting and hence supply the needed continuity in his life. On the other hand, the day-to-day activities of the wives and children may bear little resemblance to their customary existence at home.

The primary aim of Dane's chapter is to draw attention to the utility of paraprofessional methods in the reduction of cross-cultural conflict. Paraprofessional resources can complement traditional counseling procedures or provide an alternative approach under appropriate circumstances. Paraprofessional methods are highly practical in that they are readily available, are not costly, do not depend on highly trained experts, use local resources, and are acceptable to the client. The techniques include consciousness-raising, folk therapy, and the use of mediating paraprofessionals in cotherapy, where a disturbed expatriate is treated by a local professional with the assistance of a paraprofessional therapist who is a cultural cohort of the client.

The final chapter in this section deals with the topic of cross-cultural training. There has been a growing realization that people whose occupations take them to foreign lands will do their jobs more effectively if they receive some systematic orientation about the cultures in which they earn their living. Courses for a wide range of professional groups are becoming available, but perhaps the most comprehensive and sophisticated training schemes are those directed at technical experts. It is recognized that experts have a special need for cross-cultural training, since they are usually required to work very closely with indigenous counterparts. In his chapter, Seidel presents a brief history of the training movement and describes the rationale, methods, aims, limitations, criteria of success, and achievements of current cross-cultural orientation programs for technical experts. The overall aim is to improve interpersonal relations between foreign experts and their indigenous counterparts. The training procedures also have mediating goals, expressed with varying degrees of explicitness. Thus, the successful expert does not merely install and maintain technological equipment, but also teaches the local people how to become self-sufficient in the area of his expertise; and the successful expert respects the values, beliefs, and customs of the people with whom he is working.

The five chapters in this section address two themes. The first is the stress that various categories of mediating persons experience, or the perils of mediation. The second theme concerns the countermeasures employed to reduce cross-cultural stress, and these might be called the cautionary tales of mediation. A later section will deal with some of the achievements of cultural mediators.

S.B.

George M. Guthrie

What You Need Is Continuity

The title I have used is a reversal of the usual prescription, "What you need is a change." It is the lack of continuity that makes life difficult for the mediating person. While a change of scenery, diet, and friends can be exhilarating at first, a new society poses sooner or later a set of problems which the mediator must deal with. Our physical being, which we share with all other peoples, is concealed by such a thick layer of culturally determined practices that we rarely experience the elements which are common to all of us. Immersion in an alien cultural setting is the most profoundly convincing evidence we can have of the extent to which our humanity, our qualities as human beings are acquired and, because they are learned, subject to great variations.

While I agree that in a sense, we are alike, I assert that it is our differences that matter and that give us trouble. Looking for differences, therefore, is essential, even though some people have trouble talking about cultural differences without implying that some patterns, and the peoples who hold them, are superior to others. To deny differences out of some sense of equality is to imply that others are like the one who denies differences, an assertion which is hazardous and ethnocentric.

Differences in cultural patterns constitute the great challenge which a mediator faces. His problem is, in a sense, twofold: analyzing the nature of the differences, and understanding the effect of the differences on his own behavior and experience. As an illustration of the former problem, consider an episode reported in a biography of Adlai Stevenson. The story is that when Stevenson was U.S. ambassador to the United Nations, he entertained at his official residence the chief of state of an African country and his wife. The guests arrived in the colorful attire of their homeland at the appointed time and place. They had accepted American cultural patterns about punctuality. But it also happened to be Halloween, and the butler met them at the door, congratulated them on how interesting they looked, handed each an apple and some candy, and closed the door.

In this chapter, I shall be more concerned with the effect of the differences on the mediator than with the differences in cultural patterns which mediators may encounter. This, it seems to me, is a productive area of study for both theoretical and practical reasons. Other societies can impose variations in the cultural context of behavior much more profound and of much greater duration than are possible in laboratory settings—or most laboratory settings, at least, if we omit those which have been used to study obedience or to simulate prisons. On the practical side, the study of the impact of alien cultures on mediators may help mediators to prepare better and in a more general way may help us to develop ingenious techniques to modify behavior.

Going to live in an alien society can be a profound emotional experience, the more so if one goes alone and lives among people on the terms of the new host society. Most tourists who go abroad stay at international hotels, eating the same food they would enjoy at home, sleeping and traveling under similar circumstances, and associating only with other tourists and guides who speak the tourists' language. Under these circumstances they experience an exhilaration that comes from new sights and acquaintances, but they never let go of the supports and controls which guide their lives at home. Men and women who are sent abroad on diplomatic or commercial assignments may be able to preserve many of the familiar materials and social processes of home. Concerted efforts at such preservation are made on American military bases abroad, where self-contained American communities are established. On the other hand, the sojourner who "goes native" has a profoundly different experience.

Living on the terms of the host society not only means changes in one's food and other aspects of the physical environment, but also involves profound modifications in interpersonal behavior. One has to learn to be controlled by *their* expectations and to live by *their* norms. This means that actions valued by the newcomer may not be considered important by one's hosts, and vice versa. It is this profound change in sources of satisfaction and feelings of personal worth that leads to culture fatigue (Guthrie 1967).

Living in an alien culture setting is also a profoundly revealing experience in which one can gain insights into one's own sources of satisfaction and control and into the unrecognized and implicit assumptions of one's society. For example, in our society there are widely held beliefs about child-rearing, but these beliefs are violated by members of other societies. Dependency, for instance, is encouraged much more in some other societies than in our own; the others call it respect. Different ways of treating children can be experienced as morally reprehensible behavior because we have held our beliefs since childhood and because we have acquired a profound sense, a moral obligation, of how we should treat children. Because immersion in an alien society affects many of our values and because the effects appear only after weeks and months of immersion, it is difficult, indeed impossible, completely to simulate this process in a laboratory situation, where greater controls and better measurement may be possible.

In this chapter, I propose to examine some aspects of the effects of changes in cultural context on mediators and to try to interpret these changes in terms of some experiments which psychologists have carried out in laboratories. This may not sound like a very novel undertaking, and it should not be. But it is, because behavioral scientists have tended to work in one of two settings and traditions, either the laboratory or the field, and they have not paid much attention to one another. Those who are intrigued by experiments read and publish in certain journals, while those who tackle social problems share their ideas elsewhere. In a sense, then, I am trying to be a mediator between the cultures of experimental social and applied social psychology.

Specifically, I propose to review a series of rather diverse studies and try to draw implications which bear on the experiences of a culture mediator. These will include predictions of performance of Peace Corps volunteers, studies of the causes we attribute to others' actions, experiments in which individuals are subjected to marked changes of social controls, laboratory studies in which human beings and other animals are subjected to shifts in reinforcement schedules, and studies of alienation. I also want to review a study concerned with the process of group formation in a multicultural situation. The problem of evaluation of performance warrants some attention. Finally, I want to draw attention to an interesting emerging area of medical research on the role of psychosocial factors in changes in the body's reactions to infections and neoplasms, reactions which are subsumed under the category of immune reactions. This appears to be what Filipinos might call a *halo-halo*, or mixed dish, of laboratory analogues; we will try to show the relevance of each to the very complex process of cultural mediation.

Predicting Performance in the Peace Corps

Pennsylvania State University was asked to train the first four groups of Peace Corps volunteers who went to the Philippines. Because our project was among the first two or three undertaken by the new organization in 1961, we had an opportunity to develop a training program and an assessment project with little interference (and no support, I might add) from the central offices of the organization. They had little experience to go on, as did we. We were able to incorporate into the selection process an extensive psychological testing and evaluation program in the hope and expectation that we would be able to predict who would perform well in the Philippines setting. Tests, interviews, peer ratings, and staff ratings were collected carefully during the training program, and predictions were made about anticipated performance. Fewer than 10 percent of the trainees were dropped during training or at final selection, and the remainder proceeded to Manila for their two-year assignment.

We were able to obtain ratings on their performance in the Philippines of all 278 whom we had trained from supervising American staff members, and on some 70 of the volunteers from Filipinos in the communities where the volunteers had worked. We have reported the results (Guthrie and Zektick 1967). Briefly summarized, we found that while there was a correlation of .32 between ratings of the final selection board and the performance ratings of American supervisors, the correlation dropped to .004 when Filipinos' ratings rather than Americans' ratings of performance in the field were used as the final criterion. Tests of interests and abilities showed no appreciable predictive power, nor did peer ratings of the volunteers obtained during training. While selection and prediction programs for Americans who are going into assignments in the United States are not completely successful, they do score a little better than chance. Inasmuch as no one has come up with a selection and prediction program for Peace Corps volunteers which is successful against the criterion of host nationals' judgments, we conclude that it is not possible to predict the performance of Americans in an alien cultural setting.

Interviews with volunteers and with Americans who had served abroad in technical assistance programs (Guthrie and Spencer 1965) led us to the impression that there is a marked discontinuity in how a person functions at home and how he functions abroad when the usual controls and supports of behavior and self-esteem are absent or greatly different. In describing their fellow Americans, members of both groups frequently said, in essence, "He acted differently here than in the United States. He did not seem to be the same person." Sometimes the differences were viewed as favorable, such as greater patience, more willingness to listen to others, and greater effort; while changes in other people were seen as unfortunate, such as irritability, demandingness, secretiveness, or depression. It should also be noted that respondents tended to report fewer changes in themselves. In various ways, the volunteers expressed the idea that events early in their experience in the Philippines tended to set a pattern for later behavior. If a newcomer had a good first month, his chances of success were much greater. On the other hand, if the newcomer was exposed initially to other Americans who were resentful and annoyed and who had generally negative attitudes toward living in the Philippines, the newcomer would learn those patterns and retain them. Our data from the prediction study and the reports of volunteers convinced us that the factors of greatest importance in determining the quality of experience in the field lay in what the person learned early in his stay in the new setting rather than in personality, attitude, and interest variables which were present in the individual prior to his departure from the United States.

This represents an extreme position in the controversy between those who emphasize characterological antecedents and those who, like Mischel (1973), emphasize situational determinants of behavior. Ours is not a new emphasis, however; it is simply another manifestation of the principle that attitudes are acquired from attitude-holders and not from direct experience with the objects of the attitudes.

Faced with similar problems of the adjustment of Americans in an alien setting, American oil companies in the Arabian Gulf have worked out an effective program designed to help new American employees achieve a satisfactory relationship with the social life of the Arab world. They rely on good models for their in-country orientation, virtually quarantining new arrivals with employees who hold positive attitudes toward life and work in the Middle East.

In our experience with Peace Corps training, we collaborated with a team of psychiatrists who were responsible for identifying trainees who might develop disabling psychiatric symptoms during their period of service. We identified a half-dozen individuals whom we considered at high risk. They all went to the Philippines and completed their tours without serious diffi-culties. Three others who showed no indications of emotional problems during training did return prematurely. Even an examination of their files after their symptoms appeared failed to show indications which, in retro-spect, should have led us to question their stability. These limited data suggest that the emotional disorders which occur in unfamiliar environments are as unpredictable as other aspects of performance.

Situation or Character

In mediating situations, as in social situations within one's own society, an individual must constantly make judgments about the causes of or reasons for the behavior of others. Our behavior is modified from moment to moment by our perception of the behavior of others with whom we are in contact and, more particularly, by the inferences we draw concerning the determinants of what others are saying or doing. It would be most reasonable in a relationship with someone from a different society to conclude that one does not understand why the other person is acting as he is. But our lifelong habits prevent us from suspending judgments and cause us to make inferences and to proceed on those inferences whether they are right or wrong. In a summary of a series of experiments, Jones (1976) has shown that within our own society, one explains his own (actor's) behavior primarily in terms of the demands of the situation, but explains the behavior of others (as an observer) in terms of their character or other personality and dispositional characteris-tics. If this is true within our own society, where we can presume that social processes are somewhat similar for participants in a social encounter, it becomes a very important source of difficulty in mediating encounters where participants have much less understanding of the social pressures operating on others. Jones's research suggests that in mediating encounters, each participant sees himself as responding to external social factors, while the member of a second society is governed by inner dispositions. Support for this extrapolation is suggested in Jones's experiments in which inner determinants or character are attributed maximum significance when the observed person is seen as acting under free choice in an unexpected way.

We can see anecdotal support for Jones's principle in the statements of people distressed in cross-cultural encounters when they perceive deceit or lack of candor in members of the other society. Our newspaper reports habitually picture foreign leaders who are hostile to us as driven by evil motives and rarely as responsive to social pressures. It would be desirable, however, to replicate some of the experiments which Jones has conducted or cited on pairs of subjects who are from different societies. Our guess is that the tendency of the actor to see his own behavior as determined by external social factors and of the observer to see the other's behavior as determined by character and even national character would be even greater than Jones has found.

The Process of Deindividuation

For the past decade, Zimbardo has been studying the loss of control over their behavior which individuals experience when they become anonymous and indistinguishable from others. In experiments, subjects who are hooded or nameless or alone in booths will inflict more harm on other subjects, or at least press buttons which supposedly inflict more harm, than they will if they know one another (Zimbardo 1969). In field situations, people in groups commit acts of vandalism which they would never contemplate if alone and individually identifiable. Deindividuated behavior, as Zimbardo calls it, tends to be of high intensity, emotional, impulsive, irrational, and atypical.

Zimbardo has demonstrated the deindividuation process in the activities of those who dismantle and destroy cars abandoned by owners on the streets of New York. After removing the license plates, he parked a car on a street where he could observe it continuously. Within the first ten minutes, ordinary citizens appeared and removed valuable parts. After adults had stolen all they could disconnect, younger people proceeded to break the windows, slash the tires, and demolish the vehicle, completing the task in three days, with the theft and destruction carried out in daylight hours.

Zimbardo placed a similar vehicle on the campus at Stanford University and no one touched it. But when his accomplices began to strike the car with a sledgehammer, others joined in and reduced it to a heap similar to that of the car in New York. Zimbardo inferred that a model might be necessary for initiation, but the activity, once begun, was exciting and self-sustaining.

Less attention has been given to the socially desirable state of individuation in which the individual feels an identity separate from others, a sense of personal responsibility for his own behavior, and a time perspective beyond the immediate present. Zimbardo has inferred from previous research and from his formulations that people seek individual identity when the environment is positive, but seek anonymity under threat. Maslach (1974) has demonstrated in an experimental situation that when subjects anticipated the possibility of positive rewards, they made many more attempts to individuate themselves than when they expected that negative consequences were forthcoming.

Zimbardo's research bears on the behavior of sojourners in at least two interesting ways. American military personnel and tourists, both in groups and anonymous—especially those in uniforms—engage in a variety of deindividuated behavior which they would never do at home. Military personnel in Vietnam, for instance, are said to have used drugs extensively and to have violated the Vietnamese people in many ways, My Lai being the most distressing example. Tourists intrude on others with their cameras and their stares in ways they would not among their own people. Cultural mediators need to examine ways of reducing the deindividuation which leads to such disastrous consequences.

By contrast, extremes of individuation, which Zimbardo has not examined, are more frequently the experience of such mediators as Peace Corps volunteers and those engaged in technical assistance. Peace Corps volunteers in the Philippines, for instance, reported that they had a great deal of difficulty, after the initial pleasure had passed, in being the center of attention. They said that they felt they were living in a goldfish bowl, that they had lost their privacy, and that they could not be themselves. The pleasures of being the object of attention faded and were replaced by an irritation at having everything they said and did noted by others. Too much individuation robbed them of their spontaneity. Because they were not Filipinos and because they were in a special role with unique resources, they could not fade into the background. Being in the company of other Americans under these circumstances was especially relaxing, but it also prompted feelings of guilt among those committed to merging with the Philippine community.

The concepts of individuation and deindividuation appear to be very useful when applied to the behavior changes and experiences of exhilaration and despair encountered by culture mediators.

Schedule Changes

The heading of this section suggests a harangue on cultural differences in punctuality. But, just as in many other aspects of cultural matters, appearances are deceptive. We propose to examine some of the effects obtained in laboratory studies when schedules of reinforcement are changed.

The experiences of sojourners have been examined from a number of perspectives, depending on the school of thought of the examiner. We propose to look at some of the experiences and behavior of the cultural mediator from the perspective of an experimental analysis of behavior, an approach commonly identified with B. F. Skinner. From this perspective, there is an emphasis on the degree to which behavior is learned and is maintained by its consequences. In human beings, with their capacity for symbolic activities, much is learned through imitation and is maintained by self-reinforcing responses or self-approval. One's satisfaction with or approval of his own behavior is, of course, deeply rooted in the approval which others communicate. While pellets of food are used to strengthen behavior in such animals as pigeons, praise and acknowledgment are powerful determiners of behavior in human beings. The matter becomes more complicated in human beings than in pigeons, unfortunately, because while pigeons in their cages cannot provide pellets for themselves, human beings can and do continue to approve their own acts after approval from external agents has been terminated.

In an earlier paper (Guthrie 1975), I attempted a behavioral analysis of culture learning, applying concepts from an experimental analysis of behavior to the experiences people encounter living in a new society. The term "social learning theory" is often applied to this approach to the analysis of human behavior because people have so much more influence on one another than pigeons do on other pigeons.

From this perspective, much of human behavior is learned and maintained by its consequences. In an alien society, the consequences change so that activities which have been reinforced at home are treated as less important abroad, and new activities are approved in the new settings. The activities which are no longer approved undergo extinction, a phenomenon which often induces aggressive behavior. For example, the cultural mediator may have set certain goals for himself, or have been sent abroad to try to achieve certain goals. Examples might be an American Peace Corps volunteer whose mission is to teach English as a second language, or a Filipino physician in North America who wants to learn about the treatment of nutritional disorders. If these sojourners encounter some initial success and then find that none of their goals is being achieved, they may develop strong feelings of resentment, impatience, and anger. In other terms, many of the activities which a sojourner brings with him are put on an extinction schedule because they are no longer being reinforced. Other animals, and probably human beings as well, often react with anger and aggression for no apparent reason when reinforcement for a previously effective activity is terminated.

In addition to withdrawal of reinforcement for some activities, the sojourner is likely to experience reinforcement or approval for activities which he does not consider meritorious, and he may even receive reinforcement in the form of approval and attention without knowing why. These forms of noncontingent reinforcement in laboratory situations produce superstitious and ritualized behaviors. In human beings, noncontingent reinforcement, rather than making an individual feel good because he got something for nothing, tends to produce feelings of powerlessness.

Another aspect of operant conditioning which suggests some insights into the sojourner's experience is manipulation of the interresponse time (IRT), or the interval which elapses between a reinforcement and the availability of another reinforcement. When IRT is short, high stable rates of responding are possible, but a long IRT generates an interval of no responding (because it won't be reinforced anyway). Someone who wants to accomplish a great deal encounters a good deal of difficulty with a long IRT. The cultural mediator wants a DRH (differential reinforcement for a high rate of responding), while the host society may impose a DRL (differential reinforcement for a low rate of responding).

In one of the few studies of the effect of changes in reinforcement schedules on human behavior that we have been able to locate, Weiner (1965, 1970) found that people who had learned a high rate of responding tended not to slow down when they were reinforced equally for much lower rates of response. Conditioned initially on an FR 40 schedule (reinforced for every fortieth response), subjects developed consistently high rates of button-pressing which persisted when they were switched to FI 10-sec schedules (reinforced only for responding after ten seconds had elapsed following the latest reinforcement). This meant that with the initial training to respond rapidly, they continued to respond rapidly when a slower rate would have been as productive. Introduction of a penalty system for rapid responding (FI 10-sec cost), in which responses during the ten-second interval resulted in a loss of one percent of the reinforcement, did not reduce the high rate of responding of someone who had been trained initially on an FR 40 schedule. Intermittent reinforcement apparently overrode the cost imposed on inappropriately rapid responses. If, however, subjects received DRL 20-sec training (reinforced only when they waited twenty seconds after a reinforcement before responding again and with inappropriate responses restoring the twenty-second delay requirement) either before or after the FR 40 training, they quickly adopted low, efficient rates of responding when placed on a FI 10-sec schedule. In Weiner's terms, DRL 20-sec training gave to the FR 40 individual a greater repertoire of responses, so that he no longer remained a one-game individual.

Weiner concluded:

> One-game individuals can be changed and taught new games but not by an environment that pussy-foots around. As we have seen, the behavior of one-game individuals may tend to persist despite changes in stimulus conditions, despite reductions in reinforcement frequency, and despite the fact that it produces preventable withdrawals (cost) of different types of reinforcement.
>
> In order to change one-game individuals, the environment may need to make all reinforcement contingent upon such change. After the acquisition of critically needed alternative behavioral repertoires, the environment can loosen the constraints and change can be produced by merely providing greater reinforcement for change than for persistence. (Weiner 1970, p. 456)

Alienation

There is a vast literature in the social sciences which in one way or another speaks of *alienation*, a word that has many definitions. More order has been brought to studies of alienation by Seeman than by anyone else, with his suggestion that there are six forms of alienation: powerlessness, meaninglessness, normlessness, cultural estrangement, self-estrangement, and social isolation (Seeman 1975). Alienation has a long history in the social sciences, going back at least to Marx and to Durkheim. It is commonly used to refer to the disillusionment and rebellion of some members of a society, members who do not share all of the values of the majority or do not have access to the good things enjoyed by or at least accessible in theory to the majority. As defined and described, the alienated are a minority within a society—the poor, the young, the aged, or ethnic minorities. Some of the theory and research on alienation may be relevant to the problems of the cultural mediator who does not share fully the value system of those around him. He may experience frequently the powerlessness, meaninglessness, and isolation from self and society which are part of the phenomena subsumed under alienation.

There is a serious problem with much of the research on alienation which makes it relatively useless for our concerns with cultural mediators. Alienation is defined in terms of a number of responses, often to a questionnaire, and not in terms of antecedent conditions. The result is that we are no further ahead if we find that a mediator is or is not alienated.

In a review of cross-cultural studies of alienation (Guthrie and Tanco, 1980), we found that people who preserved significant interpersonal patterns with friends and relatives and retained familiar living styles showed few symptoms of alienation in spite of marked changes in place of abode. Primary group relationships could be preserved even in factories by those with rural backgrounds. Furthermore, the benefits of urban life reinforced the transition from rural living and made it impossible to return to the countryside.

There are some testable implications in these observations for culture mediators. It would appear that if one wants someone to introduce alien ideas, to perform some of the functions of a mediator, one must pay attention to the mediator's needs for reinforcement, for some control over his life, and for continued help in maintaining a definition of his purpose. Because his hosts will often not approve and reinforce his mediating activities, the culture-broker needs acknowledgement from his sponsoring agency.

The role of symbolic support from home was demonstrated dramatically in the experience of the Peace Corps. In the early 1960s when the program began, those who volunteered were dedicated to their work, so that voluntary resignations during training were low—less than 2 percent in our program—and similarly low percentages resigned prior to the completion of their field assignments. By 1970 there had been a remarkable change, with as many as 50 percent or more dropping out during training abroad and during their period of service. This change coincided with the war in Vietnam and the realization by many Americans that they had been deceived by high officials of their government, and that the idealism and sense of purpose of a decade earlier had been perverted by those who earlier had been sources of inspiration. When reinforcement for idealism no longer came from one's reference group back home, behavior changed in the field. There was no measurable change in the talents or cultural background of volunteers over the span of fifteen years, nor in the need for the help they might give; only a change in the social climate of approval and support for the mediators' activities.

Perils of Mediation

Many mediating persons are in teaching activities in programs which are of brief duration and with specialized purposes. Examples of such programs might be a three-week seminar on Hindu philosophy, a business management seminar, or a workshop on community nutrition. Later we shall use as an example a four-month session on cross-cultural research for social and behavioral scientists.

In 1967, as part of a coordinated research project by Ateneo de Manila University and the Pennsylvania State University, Barbara Mann Franck studied social processes in a Rice Production Training Program (RPTP) at the International Rice Research Institute (IRRI) at Los Banos, Philippines.

Franck's work was directed by Paul Hare of Haverford College. She prepared an extended report (Franck 1972) which we will summarize.

New strains of high-yielding varieties of rice had been developed by IRRI, but these strains required special cultivation practices, including regulated irrigation and addition of fertilizer and pesticides. Without improved farming practices, the improved strains did not yield well. IRRI had brought together thirty-six rice-production technicians from six countries for the RPTP. The program was directed by four Filipinos. Instruction involved three hours of work and practice in the institute's rice fields each morning and four hours of reports and lectures in a classroom each afternoon.

Franck joined the RPTP for its second and third months. She was identified as a social scientist, but she joined in all field and classroom activities. During the two-month period, she observed a remarkable transition which had many implications for the amount which trainees might learn. Initially, the trainees were profoundly impressed by the instructors' special knowledge, but this was followed by an interval in which there was considerable pairing of participants and, finally, a stage of fight-flight. In her analysis and especially in her interpretations, Franck drew extensively on the work of Slater (1966). Slater's discussions deal with training groups, or t-groups, set up for training in interpersonal sensitivity and personal growth; his theoretical orientation is psychoanalytic. We will restrict our summary of Franck's work to her observations, which can be interpreted from a social learning perspective.

During phase I, she reported that the trainers were sought out as specialists, listened to, and respected. There was a considerable level of uncertainty about who was to do what and how much. The participants were optimistic, cooperative, and accepting of almost everything they were told.

Phase II brought resentment of the trainers and disillusionment with the scientific approach to rice culture. Dependent attitudes toward the trainers disappeared, to be replaced by critical attitudes and questions whether the trainers really had a program or were simply improvising. Another rumor that spread was that participants were all part of some vaguely defined experiment. Franck's presence may have prompted the rumor, but the participants showed no resentment toward her.

In phase III, which appeared in the third month, the trainees settled into a pattern of sullen resentment, questioning the value of the RPTP. The instructors responded with resentment toward the trainees. In this phase, the dependency on the leaders of the trainees was replaced by an attitude of complete independence. They regarded the trainers as unnecessary and considered their opinions no more valid than those of their fellow trainees. At this point, Franck had to leave to return to the United States. The project carried on to its scheduled completion, and spirits picked up as the end approached.

The significance of Franck's paper lies in the fact that the pattern of dependency, pairing, and resentful independence with positive feelings

restored at the end is repeated in many settings. We witnessed it in four succeeding Peace Corps training projects. The same pattern appeared in a project
for training social and behavioral scientists for cross-cultural research, a
project conducted by the Culture Learning Institute of the East-West Center
from November 1975 to February 1976.

In the Peace Corps projects, we came to expect a midterm slump; we
warned trainees to expect it, we told ourselves as staff members that it was
inevitable and that it would pass. Peace Corps staff members from Washington developed favorable or unfavorable views of our efforts depending on
whether they visited us during the slump. We made a variety of moves to try
to reduce the lethargy and resentment, including field trips, parties, and
lightened schedules, but we did not feel that we were successful. As staff
members we were able to inhibit in part our hostile reactions to the resentment of the trainees.

In the Peace Corps, only one cultural group was being trained; where
members of several cultural groups are involved, the situation becomes
quite confusing. Members of different societies have learned to express and
to inhibit expression of annoyance in different ways. Some people fall
silent, others speak up; some smile, others frown. It is difficult under the
best of circumstances to deal with strong emotions in members of one's
own society; it is a greater task still to cope with members of several societies,
each of whom is experiencing and manifesting stress in different ways. A
cultural mediator, given these sources of difficulties, may be well advised
to keep his programs short.

Because of the vagueness of the cultural mediator's activities, the process of
dependency, pairing, and resentment seems almost inevitable; at least, we do
not know how to prevent it. Knowing that it is likely to occur may make it
possible for the mediator to avoid responding in ways which are permanently
damaging to him and to his successors. One preventive step that might be considered would be to keep all programs very brief. A two-week program will
be over before the first positive phase has passed, and may accomplish as
much as a much longer effort.

Mediators and Life Change Units

Holmes, Rahe, and colleagues (Holmes and Masuda 1974) have presented
evidence that individuals who have experienced many changes in their lives
in the recent past are more likely to become ill. The nature of the illness can
vary across almost all of the conditions which would prompt one to seek a
physician's help. Differentially weighted changes called Life Change Units can
occur in many aspects of an individual's life, including finances, family,
employment, marriage, and legal status. The relationships between total Life

Change Units and illnesses are low but statistically significant and replicable. The matter may have consequences for cultural mediators because they, more than most others, undergo great life changes. Mental health, too, has been considered vulnerable to extensive changes of social environment. The mental health problems of mediators receive detailed attention elsewhere in this book, particularly in the chapters by Yeh and Dane.

There is also an active area of research which deals with the physiological basis of the clinical phenomena described by Holmes and Rahe. The influence of the brain and behavior on the immune system has been reviewed by Stein, Schiavi, and Camerino (1976). Experimental studies with animals indicate that psychosocial factors such as stressful situations alter resistance to various infections. The authors also assert that psychosocial factors appear to play a role in the development, course, and outcome of neoplastic disorders and to some aspects of humoral and cell-mediated immune responses.

Much of this physiological research is beyond the scope of this chapter. It is important, however, that mediating persons be reminded that they are physiological as well as cultural beings. We can acquire a few immunities through inoculations prior to going abroad, but there remain a vast array of infectious agents to which one has no acquired immunities, which can disable the mediator. Furthermore, it seems reasonable that resistance to alien infections will be lowered if the mediator is experiencing difficulties in his work. The role of infection in cultural contacts was demonstrated most tragically in Polynesia, where European traders and adventurers brought diseases which wiped out more than half of many island populations. Some islands only now, 150 years later, are back to precontact population levels. We may not like to think of it this way, but we should not lose sight of the fact that mediators not only exchange ideas, art forms, material objects, and other products of scholarship, but diseases and changes in the body's immune processes as well.

Measuring Mediation

A psychologist who discusses the mediating person from a social-behaviorist perspective must include some consideration of measuring the effects of mediating efforts, not just to maintain a pretense of being scientific but to indicate steps by which successful practices may be strengthened and unsuccessful activities modified or eliminated. In addition, persons involved in mediating activities have an obligation to show their sponsors that their activities have led to demonstrable results.

We believe that all social action programs, including cultural mediation, should be presumed ineffective unless proven otherwise. Programs can be proven effective if their stated goals are met, provided that the goals are stated in such a manner that they can be said to have been achieved or not achieved. This poses a problem, because many cultural exchange programs have such vague goals that no one can assert that these have or have not been achieved. Consider a program that is dedicated to promoting peace through increased mutual understanding. Who can disagree, and who can say it is not worthwhile? We can. There is no evidence that the likelihood of peace is enhanced through understanding. The English-speaking world and the Germans have had great mutual understanding for a century, yet they have fought two of the worst wars in history. India and Pakistan certainly understood one another quite well, but they have had some bitter armed conflicts. Furthermore, mutual understanding has never been defined in a way that would enable one to determine whether a given program made a difference.

That worthy culture-mediating institution, the East-West Center, was established to "promote better relations and understanding between the United States and the nations of Asia and the Pacific through cooperative study, training, and research." No one can doubt that this is a worthy objective, but it is so vaguely stated that it suggests no indices by which some programs can be chosen from among all those that are possible, nor are any indices deducible which would indicate whether or not a program that was chosen did in fact "promote better relations," etc.

Culture-mediating efforts are not alone in this matter. The discipline of clinical psychology with which I identify was quite disturbed a decade ago when a rebellious psychologist organized evidence that people improved as much without psychotherapy as with it, at least as treatment was offered at that time. Those who have promoted special programs for schoolchildren who are not doing well by conventional criteria have had only limited success demonstrating that their efforts have made a difference. Foreign assistance programs of our own government, of other nations, and of the United Nations can produce innumerable success stories, but little systematic evidence of effectiveness. The Peace Corps, to which we have referred several times, has survived on anecdotes. There are no data that would indicate that the $10,000 a year it costs to keep a volunteer in the field produces a level of results which warrants that expenditure.

It must also be acknowledged that some evaluation efforts are ill-conceived and inappropriate to the program being examined. Those who develop social action programs are constantly harassed by fly-by-night evaluators. There is an escape, however, and that is to define the purposes of a program in terms of concrete objectives which can be achieved to differing but specifiable degrees. The goal of an educational program should be not to enhance the integrity of the whole child, but to raise his reading level from grade 3 to grade 5. By the same token, mediators can summarize their objectives as enhanced mutual understanding, but they have to spell out what this implies in behavior which can be observed. Such specific criteria might be knowing more facts about another country, being able to report accurately the other country's leaders' views on specified issues, maintaining personal correspondence with colleagues in that country, and so forth.

Evaluation of social programs is a complex matter with few firmly established principles. There are excellent reviews of applied social research and education policy by Cohen and Garet (1975) and of evaluation of social action programs at the U.S. federal government level by Rivlin (1971). It should be noted that the State of Colorado has just passed a bill that all state regulatory agencies will be limited to a six-year life unless extended, and that extension will depend on their demonstrated usefulness. If the policy finds favor among legislators, we can expect that culture mediators will also have to demonstrate their effectiveness and worth.

Summary

In this chapter, we tried to improve our understanding of some aspects of the process of cultural mediation by drawing on social-psychological experiments and field studies. It would appear that someone who undertakes to live in an alien society and to mediate is subjected to changes in the reinforcements or rewards which he receives, and that these changes can disrupt his habitual patterns of behavior. While he sees his own behavior as a response to social environmental factors, he is likely to interpret the unexpected in a foreigner as an expression of the foreigner's deep-rooted character traits. Given these circumstances, it would seem to be important that the mediator receive approval and reinforcement from those whom he understands, especially his supervisors, because he cannot be sure that he will derive predictable approval from those who participate in a different cultural tradition. Finally, the present state of the art of evaluation of mediation efforts is most *underdeveloped*, to use an international term. We must learn to specify as explicitly as possible all of the goals which we hope to achieve in a mediating effort, because it is only when we know for sure where we are succeeding and where we are failing that we can take steps to do a better job.

References

Cohen, D. K., and Garet, M. S. Reforming Educational Policy With Applied Social Research. *Harvard Educational Review*, 1975, *45*, 17–43.

Franck, B. M. Phases of Development of Multinational Training Group. *Comparative Group Studies*, 1972, *3*, 3–50.

Guthrie, G. M. Cultural Preparation for the Philippines. In R. B. Textor (ed.), *Cultural Frontiers of the Peace Corps*. Cambridge, Mass.: MIT Press, 1967.

_____. A Behavioral Analysis of Culture Learning. In R. W. Brislin, S. Bochner, and W. J. Lonner (eds.), *Cross-Cultural Perspectives on Learning*. New York: Wiley, 1975.

Guthrie, G. M., and Spencer, R. *American Professions and Overseas Technical Assistance*. University Park, Penn.: Pennsylvania State University, Institute of Public Administration, 1965.

Guthrie, G. M., and Tanco, P. P. Alienation. In H. C. Triandis (ed.), *Handbook of Cross-Cultural Psychology*. Boston, Mass.: Allyn and Bacon, 1980.

Guthrie, G. M., and Zektick, I. Predicting Performance in the Peace Corps. *Journal of Social Psychology*, 1967, *71*, 11-21.

Holmes, T. H., and Masuda, M. Life Change and Illness Susceptibility. In B. S. Dohrenwend and B. P. Dohrenwend (eds.), *Stressful Life Events: Their Nature and Effects*. New York: Wiley, 1974.

Jones, E. E. How Do People Perceive the Causes of Behavior? *American Scientist*, 1976, *64*, 300-305.

Maslach, C. Social and Personal Bases of Individuation. *Journal of Personality and Social Psychology*, 1974, *29*, 411-425.

Mischel, W. Toward a Cognitive Social Learning Reconceptualization of Social Psychology. *Psychological Review*, 1973, *80*, 252-283.

Rivlin, A. M. *Systematic Thinking for Social Action*. Washington, D.C.: Brookings Institution, 1971.

Seeman, M. Alienation Studies. *Annual Review of Sociology*, 1975, *1*, 91-123.

Slater, P. E. *Microcosm*. New York: Wiley, 1966.

Stein, M., Schiavi, R. C., and Camerino, M. Influence on Brain and Behavior of the Immune System. *Science*, 1976, *191*, 435-440.

Weiner, H. Conditioning History and Maladaptive Human Behavior. *Psychological Reports*, 1965, *17*, 934-942.

_____. Human Behavioral Persistence. *Psychological Record*, 1970, *20*, 445-456.

Zimbardo, P. G. The Human Choice: Individuation, Reason, and Order Versus Deindividuation, Impulse, and Chaos. In W. J. Arnold and D. Levine (eds.), *Nebraska Symposium on Motivation*. Lincoln, Neb.: University of Nebraska Press, 1969.

Otto Klineberg

The Role of International University Exchanges

Introduction

Theoretically, those who go abroad to teach or to study should be mediators par excellence. They are identified with one culture but live for a time in another. They ought to be able to interpret their own ways of life to residents of the country of sojourn; to learn about that country's culture; and, on their return home, to describe that culture to their fellow nationals. They may be expected to constitute what has been called "bridges to understanding," in the sense of contributing to both better mutual knowledge and increased friendliness and acceptance.

When one reflects on the length of time during which this particular variety of "exchange of persons" has been going on, it seems reasonable to assume that such a contribution has been substantial. Breitenbach (1970) has found material indicating that as early as the fourth century B.C. there were groups of foreign students in the schools of philosophy and rhetoric in Greece; in the fourth century A.D., special provisions were made for dealing with the large numbers of foreign students flocking to Rome; in the seventh century, there were more than eight thousand students in China described as coming from the "barbarian peoples." With regard to India, Ganguli (1975) reports that exchanges between India and China started as far back as the third century B.C. When the first European universities were founded around the twelfth century A.D., they were truly "universal," with foreign students as the rule rather than the exception.

Even though universities are somewhat more limited and restrictive in their acceptance of foreign students today, the number of people affected by the exchange process has increased in recent years, and if they fulfilled their role as mediators, their impact could be expected to be enormous. In 1960, a UNESCO report indicated that foreign students made up approximately 10 percent of the French student population, 12 percent in the United Kingdom, and over 30 percent in Switzerland. The United States had the largest absolute number of foreign students found in any country, although they constituted only 1.4 percent of the American student population (Marshall 1970).

A more recent survey, in which seven nations participated, included the following figures (Klineberg 1976): UNESCO estimated that in 1968 there were about 430,000 students at foreign universities; the Federal Republic of Germany has about 22,000; the United Kingdom, about 19,000; France, approximately 110,000 attending courses, with 30,000 enrolled in state universities; the United States, about 135,000 in 1969; Japan, about 4260 in 1971; India, 7200 in 1970. In most countries, the number of foreign students is increasing. It is difficult to obtain comparable figures for those who go abroad to teach or conduct research, but their number is by no means negligible.

Has the impact really been enormous? Have foreign students and professors taken their role as culture-carriers seriously? Have they contributed to better mutual understanding? Have they brought the nations concerned closer together? In an earlier publication (Klineberg 1964), I referred to a discussion on this topic at UNESCO with a group of social scientists from various countries. An Australian expert volunteered a personal observation. In Australia, he said, the leaders of organizations and activities devoted to strengthening the bonds among members of the British Commonwealth and encouraging friendly attitudes toward the United Kingdom were all returned Rhodes scholars who, after spending two years or more at Oxford, came home full of enthusiasm for the mother country. He then added that the leaders of the movement for more complete independence for Australia and withdrawal from the Commonwealth were also all returned Rhodes scholars.

If this judgment is correct, it may mean that what looks at first glance like a similar experience for participants—a Rhodes scholarship for an Australian at Oxford—may turn out to be very different indeed for each. As will be indicated below, there are many aspects of the foreign sojourn which may have an influence on the outcome. It may also be that the sojourn has had little or no influence whatsoever. No one has expressed this possibility more elegantly than Omar Khayyam, in Fitzgerald's translation of the Rubaiyat:

> Myself when young did eagerly frequent
> Doctor and Saint, and heard great argument
> About it and about: and evermore
> Came out by the same door wherein I went.

In the present context, I would suggest a slight amendment to this judgment. It is extremely unlikely that a foreign sojourn has had no impact whatsoever on the individuals concerned. It is possible, however, that it may have had no impact on the role of the foreign student as a mediator, as a link between cultures, as a contributor to better mutual understanding. He may be uninterested in or feel himself to be incapable of playing the part of cultural ambassador, or he may have little or no opportunity to do so. This was not, at least in most cases, his motive for going abroad. It may have been the goal of those responsible for the student exchange program, but (again, in most cases) it certainly was not his. Being a mediator must therefore often be seen as of secondary importance; it may not even occur to the student or teacher as having any importance whatsoever. As we shall see below, however, many do accept this role and find it palatable.

The Goals of Exchange Programs

In the case of students, there have been a number of attempts to define these goals. Abrams (1960), for example, listed (1) the intellectual and professional development of the student in his specialized field of study, (2) the general education of the student, and (3) the furthering of international understanding. Another approach, discussed more fully below, would place the emphasis on the (one hopes, positive) changes which these programs are designed to produce in the individual student, in the universities involved, in the country as a whole, and in international relations. It is not surprising that students tend to rank first, as their important objective, success in academic undertakings and professional development, whereas the sponsors of the programs may be much more interested in broader goals (Coelho 1962). These latter goals may include various forms of technical assistance (now euphemistically called "technical cooperation") designed to aid in the development of universities or more broadly to help a country's production, train its administrators, raise the standard of living, facilitate certain types of research, and win friends for the sponsor's country or organization. Only in programs under truly international auspices (such as the UNESCO or United Nations fellowships) does international—as distinguished from bilateral—friendship or understanding become the main goal of the exchange process. It may, however, be included in other programs as part of the total picture. In the seven-nation survey to which reference has already been made (Klineberg 1976), the reports from Japan and Yugoslavia made frequent mention of the goal of international understanding. It is perhaps more specifically in the bilateral programs that the foreign student is expected to fill the role of cultural ambassador or mediator.

The available research gives us some insight into the degree of readiness with which this role is recognized and accepted by the students themselves. Marshall (1970) supplies a useful summary which suggests that such readiness may vary greatly depending upon the specific situation and on the individuals and sponsors concerned. He refers to the study by Lambert and Bressler (1956) of Indian students at the University of Pennsylvania, which found that they arrived with the intention of being students and tourists but also unofficial ambassadors. On the other hand, the report by Useem and Useem (1955) of Indians who had studied abroad found this role to be of negligible importance; in an account of the sojourn of colonial students in the United Kingdom in 1955, only 20 percent mentioned the opportunity to get to know British people as an advantage. Marshall concludes his account of the role of foreign students as culture-carriers as follows: "Some students have, while abroad, erected impenetrable barriers against foreign influences for fear of being assimilated or denationalised. They return home embittered, with nothing to communicate. Others run to the opposite extreme and accept too much, including ideas and practices which cannot possibly be applied in their home country. When they return, they feel they have left a part of themselves behind. The aim of those who plan and execute programs of international exchange must be to broaden the middle path between these two extremes, in order that as many as possible may be able to find it and walk in it" (p. 22).

Students as Links Between Cultures

This is the title of a book edited by Eide (1970) which represents the most direct investigation into the issue under consideration here. She reports the results of an ingenious research design which compared the reactions of students from three different "developing" countries (Egypt, India, and Iran) who had studied abroad in three different technically "advanced" countries (the German Federal Republic, the United Kingdom, and the United States). The data were collected by local social scientists: in Egypt by M. K. Barakat, in India by B. Kuppuswamy, in Iran by M. Nassefat. The 3 by 3 design permitted a large number of interesting comparisons, only a small sample of which will be presented here.

In a final chapter entitled "Students as Culture Carriers," Eide gives a summary of what she regards as the most important conclusions to which the study leads, and at the same time raises a number of issues which in her judgment have not received the attention they deserve. One such issue refers to the relation between the student and his home culture. To what extent is he its representative, accepting and internalizing its values? Perhaps even more important, how much does he know about it? Should he be taken seriously as an informant about his own country?

This is an old but still significant problem in terms of the communication between cultures. As far back as 1938, Edward Sapir, in an important article entitled "Why Cultural Anthropology Needs the Psychiatrist," remarks on the fact that in a report on Omaha Indian culture by Dorsey, he found the phrase "Two Crows denies that." He then raises the question as to why two different informants, equally responsible and honest, should give different versions of a particular item of behavior or belief in the same community. This may be due to a difference in values or in information or both. As far as information is concerned, a chemistry student from Italy may not be in a position to explain the role of the various political parties in his country; an American specializing in French literature may know little about the detailed functioning of the primaries or of the electoral college, and he may have difficulty in "explaining" Watergate. (A few years ago, American students and other visitors were all asked to "explain" McCarthy.) Obviously, no one can know everything about his own complex society, but the fact remains that foreign students can, and frequently do, convey to their hosts significant information about the home culture. The question as to whether they should be encouraged to do so more often and more effectively will be discussed more fully below.

If the foreign student is to convey anything to his hosts, he presumably must believe that his hosts are interested in what he has to offer. One question asked of the foreign students in Eide's study was the following: "On the whole, how much were the people of your former host country interested in your country?" The percentage answering "very much interested" varied from a high of 74 percent, given by Egyptian students who had been in the German Federal Republic, to a low of 25 percent for Iranians in the United Kingdom. In general, all three groups found most interest among the Germans and least among Britons; Egyptians were most apt to report interest in their country, then come the Indians, and last, the Iranians.

Without attempting the difficult task of deciding to what extent these judgments were accurate, we are certainly justified in concluding that the role of culture-carrier will not arouse much enthusiasm among those—substantial in number—who find little or no interest in their potential audience. There remains the fact that about half of these foreign students do perceive such interest in their hosts. The question then arises, did the students have the opportunity to inform their hosts about their home country? Those who said they had "many opportunities" to do so varied from 70 percent for Egyptians in the United States down to only 12 percent for Iranians in the United Kingdom. Usually, but not consistently, high interest goes with many opportunities (correlation coefficient of 0.65). As to the media used, it is clear that for all groups, wherever they have been, "informal communications ranks first or second among reported efforts at 'culture carrying' . . . a high proportion mention the informal conversations to be one of the main forms . . ." (Eide 1970, p. 178).

The most important "cultural link" refers to the reverse form of communication, that is to say, the impact of the host culture on the foreign student. To a certain extent, this variety of impact is inevitable. The surrounding culture must affect students who live in the host country and who must make some adjustment to it if they are to succeed. This appears to be true not only for adjustment to the university, since more than 50 percent in all three visiting groups felt that they had become better informed regarding the mentality, customs, and life of the people in the host countries. This majority also indicated that the principal sources of information (together with books and special studies) were social contacts, leisure-time activities, and informal conversation.

The further question arises as to what the returned student sees as his role in bringing to the attention of people back home what he has acquired as cultural values during his foreign sojourn. Within the area of technical training, a majority in all three countries did suggest innovations in their respective specialities. In Eide's words, "This is indeed a very active, although restricted, kind of culture carrying" (p. 183). She goes on to say that when it comes to recommending for acceptance more fundamental cultural values of the West, particularly those that affect personal primary relations (for example, the status of women, family life and child-rearing, individual freedom and rights), there is less willingness to "carry culture." There is, however, an indication that a substantial number of foreign students do make an attempt to introduce some of the newly acquired cultural values when they return home. This is particularly true for the Egyptians, somewhat less for the Iranians, and considerably less in the case of the Indians. Eide believes that this is to be expected, in view of the feeling on the part of the many Indian students that theirs is an old and established culture that deserves to be preserved rather than modified. Many Egyptians and Iranians might be expected, however, to have a similar attitude.

Eide has described the role of foreign students as falling into four major categories, obviously interrelated but sufficiently distinct to warrant separate consideration. There is (1) the relation of the student to his home culture, his degree of acquaintance with it in detail, his understanding of its nature and its complexities; (2) the degree to which he is able, willing, and active in communicating this knowledge to the people in his country of sojourn; (3) the impact upon him of the culture of the host country, the extent to which he understands it, the changes which it introduces into his own values and attitudes; and finally (4) what he does with this experience when he returns home. These four aspects are all important in the mediation process, and the results of Eide's analysis do throw light on the problems which arise at various stages. At the same time, while on the whole the study is positive with regard to the success with which the role of culture-carrier is being realized in a substantial number of cases, it makes it clear that a large number of students are uninterested in, unwilling to, or incapable of performing this function. Eide quotes, for example, a statement by A. K. Singh who speaks of Indian students in the following terms: "With great embarrassment they discovered their ignorance and even their previous indifference when they met inquisitive people in the West who seemed to know more about

India than they did themselves" (Eide 1970, p. 194). Knowledge is clearly a part of the picture, but the attitudes toward the role of culture-carrier may be influenced by a number of other experiences during the foreign sojourn.

In the following section, an attempt will be made to look at the foreign sojourn as a kind of "life history," in which many factors may enter to affect the student's satisfaction with the sojourn, his judgment regarding the value of his experience, and his interest in becoming a mediator between the two cultures.

The Foreign Sojourn as a Life History

Earlier we spoke of the goals of exchange programs. Another way of looking at these goals is to raise the question of the impact of the foreign sojourn in terms of the targets to which the programs are directed. We may then distinguish among the impacts (1) on the individual student, his development, his career, the changes which have occurred in his attitudes and values, his degree of satisfaction with his experience abroad; (2) on the university or institution which receives or sends students in the hope that either during their sojourn or after their return home, they will perform a useful function; (3) on the countries involved, particularly those looking for trained personnel to aid the process of development, but also those which welcome an improved communication regarding the nature of other cultures and societies; and finally (4) as a contribution to international understanding.

This classification, although helpful in setting up research on evaluation or on the impact of exchanges, may create the false impression that the four targets listed are separate and independent. On the contrary, what happens to the individual during his experience abroad will determine what he will do later to help his institution or his country and what he will try to do to improve the relations between peoples. In the present context, it seems clear that his experience abroad, his success or failure, his degree of satisfaction, his contact with the local community, and the extent to which he is accepted or rejected by his hosts, as well as his own level of competence, will all play a part in his success as culture-carrier. This justifies, in my opinion, the life-history approach in what follows. If the accent appears to be placed on what can go wrong, this is not to be interpreted as indicating that failure is common. On the contrary, the goal here is to identify the factors which may lead *either* to success *or* to failure, in the hope that this may aid in facilitating the mediating role in the future and in reducing the proportion of those who for one reason or another fail to perform this important function. The various stages in the life history may be conveniently listed as follows.

THE PROCESS OF SELECTION

We know too little about how foreign students are selected and about their motivations for going abroad. In some programs, as in the Junior Year Abroad of many American universities, academic criteria, including competence in the field of specialization to be pursued, presumably play a dominant role. When scholarships are available, there is usually a selection committee which evaluates the students' credentials, although various degrees and varieties of nepotism may enter where government scholarships are concerned. There is, of course, a substantial proportion of students who select themselves, their expenses paid by their families or themselves or they hope through jobs obtained abroad. Undoubtedly, a certain number of students decide to go abroad because of a genuine interest in foreign cultures and a desire to know more about them; these are presumably the ones who, at this early stage in the life history, have already developed an interest in being mediators between cultures. As far as I know, however, no present selection process explicitly recognizes such an attitude as an important criterion, and the question arises as to whether those responsible for selection might be persuaded to give it greater attention.

In the seven-nation study to which reference has been made (Klineberg 1976), the relatively haphazard process of selection was mentioned with some frequency. To the extent that the "wrong" people go abroad, failure and dissatisfaction may be expected to occur relatively often, and all subsequent development, including the role as culture-carriers, may suffer as a consequence. The American report indicates that a certain proportion of students—a small minority, it is hoped—use study abroad as an escape from their difficulties at home. This is hardly a promising introduction to the exchange experience.

THE PROCESS OF PREPARATION

Such preparation has many aspects, the most important of which can perhaps best be stated in the form of the following four questions.

Does the foreign student have enough academic preparation in the field of his proposed study abroad? This will include not only the requisite technical training, but also adequate command of the language of instruction. The relation of this kind of preparation to cultural mediation may seem somewhat indirect, but it is still significant, since failure or excessive difficulty in university work (an issue which will be discussed below) will hardly develop in the student the motivation to bring the two cultures closer together.

Does the foreign student know enough about the nature of the university which he is planning to enter—its rules and regulations, what is expected of him as a student, the relations between students and faculty, and so forth? As Bochner (1972) points out, the informality characteristic of most American universities, for example, may be confusing and disturbing to foreign students accustomed to a more "respectful" attitude toward the professor; similarly, Asian students in Australia may rely on authority rather than attempt to develop their own critical approach. Both the German and the French reports in our study indicate that orientation in this area is haphazard in nature, with the necessary information available, but often without the student knowing where and to whom he must go to obtain it. This, like inadequate preparation in general, may lead to frustration and failure, and again reduce the likelihood that the student will be happy in the role of mediator.

The remaining two questions regarding preparation are more directly related to the present issue. Has the foreign student learned enough about the culture of the country of sojourn to adapt to it successfully? Orientation programs directed at culture learning are common, but they vary in extent and quality, and students frequently express disappointment with what they have to offer. Our Japanese colleagues urged that greater use be made of alumni associations made up of students who had visited the same country on a previous occasion; it was also thought that cultural affairs officers in Japanese embassies abroad might play a more useful role. The German report also indicates that the needed information is not always easily available. There can be no doubt about the importance of this kind of orientation. The trauma of cultural shock could certainly be reduced if the foreign student on arrival knew more about general norms or standards of behavior. Sometimes the relevant information is gained by the student during his foreign sojourn, but without some preparation, some guidance as to what to look for, he may remain puzzled and confused. To be anecdotal for a moment, a colleague from the Netherlands reported to me his great disillusionment because the Americans who called him by his first name during his sojourn turned out not to be close friends after all; he had apparently not learned that first names do not have the same connotation of intimacy in the United States as they do in Holland. There is almost no limit to the number of examples of cultural misinterpretation that could be given. The consequences for the role of mediator are obvious, but what is not at all clear is what kind of orientation program will supply the kind of knowledge needed.

Does the foreign student know enough about his own culture to serve as mediator; if not, what kind of preparation is needed? Reference has already been made to this issue, but its importance is so rarely recognized that it bears repetition. Eide's investigation showed that many foreign students did undertake the role, but there is unfortunately no indication as to their effectiveness or as to the accuracy with which they described their own culture to their hosts. If students could be convinced in advance of the importance of the mediating function, they might also be persuaded to regard a fuller knowledge of their own society as an essential part of their preparation for the foreign sojourn. This may seem to be rather a forlorn hope at the present time, but if foreign students are indeed to become cultural ambassadors, they must accept the need to obtain the necessary training.

THE ENTRANCE INTO THE NEW UNIVERSITY

Requirements for the admission of foreign students vary greatly from one country to another, and even between different universities in the same country. The question of admission is, of course, closely linked to the credits given for work done before arrival. French and German university authorities have established a set of equivalences which may in time take care of this problem as far as these two countries are concerned. On the other hand, German students usually do not know until their return to their own university how much their foreign study counts toward the degree or diploma for which they are working. This whole issue of equivalences may cause frustration and even heartbreak to many students, consequently affecting their degree of satisfaction with their foreign sojourn and contributing to their sense of success or failure. In the latter case, the role of culture-carrier will hardly be facilitated.

THE ACADEMIC EXPERIENCE: SUCCESS OR FAILURE

All the factors mentioned in this section—selection, preparation (including language facility), equivalences or credits for previous work—may contribute to the student's success or failure in the university of the host country. As has already been indicated more than once, if the foreign student is unsuccessful, he is less likely to adopt or relish the role of link between cultures, since failure can hardly make him feel especially sympathetic toward the people or the culture symbolic of his frustration. The question then arises, is failure more frequent among foreign students than among students in general?

The available data are somewhat contradictory. In Eide's study, 88 percent of the Egyptian students and 97 percent of the Iranians obtained a degree from the host country before they went home. The figure dropped to 71 percent in the case of the Indians, but this is interpreted as due to the level of education the students had achieved before leaving home. An earlier study in Germany by Aich (1962), however, reported that about 80 percent of Asian and African students fail in intermediate and 40 percent in final examinations. This high proportion of failures may be due, in Aich's opinion, to the fact that these foreign students have limited qualifications, since many of them came to Germany because they could not gain admission to universities in their own country. More recent information reported by von Alemann (see Klineberg 1976) indicates that Aich's data may not be typical, since results obtained in 1968 and 1969 show that German and foreign students differ only very slightly as far as general success or failure in examinations is concerned. Bochner (1972) makes a similar point with regard to foreign students in Australia. Kapur (1972) found a higher failure or drop-out rate ("wastage") among foreign than among British students at the University of Edinburgh, but at the University of Sussex, the failure rate among foreign students is low, probably because of the careful selection process and the guidance supplied by university tutors. It is difficult to draw definite conclusions from this scattered evidence, but it is probable that the failure rate is indeed a little higher among foreign students.

In an investigation of students from the Third World attending various European universities (Klineberg and Ben Brika 1972), an attempt was made to test the hypothesis that the degree of satisfaction with the foreign sojourn would be closely related to the success or failure which the students experienced in their examinations. The results showed no clear relationship of this nature, although logically it might have been expected. Unfortunately, however, this finding was based on the students' own reports as to their results. Although they may all have been telling the truth, it would certainly have been better to use more objective indicators, but in this study these were not available. It is to be hoped that further research on this relationship will soon be forthcoming.

GENERAL ADAPTATION TO THE NEW ENVIRONMENT

This issue was initially raised in connection with preparation for the foreign sojourn, but it has important implications throughout the whole experience. A major aspect of the adaptation process, and one which is significant for the mediating role, is the relation with people in the host country. A substantial proportion of the research which has been conducted on student exchanges indicates over and over again that satisfaction is expressed with the foreign experience when the student has made friends in the host country (Klineberg 1965). Of course, it could be argued that if the student starts out with positive feelings toward his hosts, he is more likely to make friends. It may be that the causal relation obtains in both directions; in any case, it seems clear that whatever stimulates the development of friendship between visitors and hosts will have a favorable impact on the reactions of the visitors to the total experience.

The students in Eide's study reported a considerable degree of contact with the local population, with frequent mention of the development of friendly relations. Other investigations are less optimistic, with foreign students indicating that they have experienced great difficulty in achieving even a moderate degree of familiarity with their hosts. Many of them establish friendships only with their conationals or with other foreigners. My own study with Ben Brika (1972) indicated that students from the Third World attending universities in Austria, France, and the Netherlands had many contacts in about 50 percent of the cases; a majority said they had made some local friends among their hosts. A more thorough analysis of the French data showed that those who had more money and who lived outside the university in lodgings were more likely to have many local contacts. The majority of students, however, reported frequent feelings of isolation and loneliness. Detailed interviews indicated that a great many students would have liked to have more friendly contacts, but made few specific suggestions as to how this might be accomplished. The same desire for more contact is expressed with some frequency in the report by Tajfel and Dawson (1965), who analyzed essays written by African, Asian, and West Indian students in the United Kingdom; their book bears the significant title *Disappointed Guests*.

Many factors contribute to this personal disappointment: lack of knowledge on the part of foreign students regarding the etiquette of interpersonal relations and of the behavioral cues involved, race prejudice or the expectation that one will be met by prejudice, stereotypes about the inaccessibility of the host population, the conviction that one's home country is looked down upon or ignored by the hosts, differences in the sense of humor, the feeling that one is being treated as an exotic specimen rather than as an individual, and so on. On the part of the hosts there may be indifference, if not animosity (many dark-skinned students have trouble finding adequate housing), and unwillingness to make any special effort in this direction, particularly in those university cities with a large proportion of students from abroad.

A number of questions appear to be worth raising in this connection. If friendships are as important as the research appears to indicate, could not more be done to discover the friendship patterns which prevail, to inform foreign students of the behavior which they are likely to encounter, and to acquaint them with its meaning? Could the local student populations be made aware of the misunderstandings to which their behavior may give rise? In more general terms, would increased knowledge on both sides of the cultures which come into contact aid the process of adaptation and friendship formation? It would be helpful to have an account of what is actually done in various countries to make foreign students feel at home socially, of what provisions are made by governments, universities, religious groups, and other private agencies to create the possibilities for such students to make friends.

Personal contacts, though important, represent only one of many factors which contribute to the relative satisfaction or dissatisfaction with the foreign experience. Many things *can* go wrong, but in the majority of cases, students look back with pleasure on the period they have spent abroad.

MENTAL HEALTH ASPECTS

There are two additional reported characteristics of the sojourn taken as a whole which should be considered at this point. The first refers to the frequently mentioned "U-curve," first described and investigated by Du Bois (1953) and Lysgaard (1955) and referred to repeatedly in subsequent publications. To oversimplify considerably, the U-curve begins with a relatively happy first phase, experienced as an exciting adventure; then there is a trough in the curve, as the student becomes involved in difficulties of various kinds and as he has to face his problems in the university and the society in general; and finally, a relatively high point again as he succeeds in this process before he prepares for his departure.

One important implication of the U-curve, to the extent that it applies, is that the interviews of foreign students designed to determine their reactions to the sojourn abroad may be greatly influenced by the precise point on the curve at which the respondent happens to be when he is being questioned. This represents a research hazard that is very difficult to control, since the curve will vary in shape from one individual and one situation to another, and from intensity to nonexistence. The later rise in the curve of satisfaction may be steep or shallow, or may not occur until the student's return home, as a kind of retrospective "sleeper effect." The extensive literature on the U-curve still leaves a number of important questions unanswered.

A second major issue relates to what may be called the mental health of the foreign student. Mention has already been made of feelings of isolation and homesickness reported by a substantial number of the visitors. At a more serious level, the general impression appears to prevail that cases of psychological maladjustment occur more frequently among foreign than among native students. This whole issue is the subject of a recent review by Alexander and colleagues (1976) which touches on many of the issues already considered in this chapter, such as the feelings of isolation and loneliness. The authors, on the basis of their own investigation of Asian and African students in the United States, suggest that such feelings are much more widespread than is usually assumed. They write: "Our research has shown that the vast majority of non-Western or Third World students . . . feel vulnerable and at risk during much of their time in the United States" (p. 83). They go on to speak of the "painful social vulnerability" of the students, their lack of contact with Americans, and the fact that they are "fearful and pessimistic" about the possibility of establishing such contact. Their general conclusions are as follows:

1. foreign students are a high risk group, under considerable stress.
2. this stress is more likely to be experienced in the form of physical complaints than psychological complaints.
3. the foreign student is more likely to seek medical than psychological help, with the latter sought only after all other resources have been exhausted.
4. there is considerable commonality to foreign student psychosomatic and emotional problems. (Alexander et al. 1976, pp. 87–88)

The authors make another important point, namely, that as clinicians, they are convinced that when foreign students ask for help with emotional problems, they are in greater need of help than their American counterparts. This is because foreign students are more reluctant to ask for professional help, since such resources are usually not easily available in the home country, and because the admission of such a need would constitute a loss of status. This would imply that statistics comparing the proportion of appeals for help would underestimate the frequency of such needs in the case of foreign students.

If these conclusions are verified by further research, they would lead to a very pessimistic view indeed as to the adjustment of foreign students and consequently as to their role as mediators. Our own studies and those of our colleagues suggest that maladjustment is a minority reaction, that most students are on the whole satisfied with their foreign experience, and that severe emotional problems, while they do occur, are relatively infrequent. This does not mean that we should be complacent regarding the unhappiness of that minority. The previous discussion of the various problems that arise during the course of the life history at least should have the virtue of pointing to what *may* go wrong, and directing our attention to measures that might be taken to reduce the likelihood that these factors will contribute to maladjustment.

THE RETURN HOME

Reference has already been made to the important mediating role of the foreign student when he returns home and is able to interpret to his fellow nationals what he has learned about another culture. Eide's results indicate that such a role is more frequently assumed in connection with technical innovations or university activities than with proposed changes related to the cultural values of the former host society. Even the latter, however, are not completely neglected. In this case also, too much appears to be left to chance. Some returned students perform this role with enthusiasm; others remain indifferent, or at the most answer questions only when they are raised by their conationals. It is encouraging to note that many of Eide's students do remain in touch with friends and colleagues in the host country. More would probably do so, and would also play a more important role as cultural ambassadors, if it were brought to their attention that this was expected of them; those reponsible for administering exchange programs might be encouraged to include this in their briefing.

Another significant issue refers to the length of time during which the mediating role is assumed. Is it for a year, or two years, or throughout the remainder of the student's career and his subsequent professional life? The answer to this question requires a retrospective, long-term study, interviewing the former foreign student ten or fifteen years after his sojourn abroad. Such a study would shed light on what (if any) are the lasting consequences of that sojourn as far as mediation is concerned, and would identify the factors which may affect the length of time during which the student continues to be a link between cultures and the strength of his long-term commitment to fulfill that role.

Not all students return home, and the consequent "brain drain" constitutes a great worry to those responsible for exchange programs. Most foreign students do return, but the fairly large minority which takes up residence abroad is often considered to demonstrate the weakness and wastage in the programs concerned. This issue cannot be adequately explored at this point, since so many complex factors enter both in the foreign country and at home, but a brief comment with regard to the mediating role may be helpful.

Obviously, if the foreign student does not return home, he cannot function with regard to what Eide describes as the fourth "communication line," which consists of disseminating to his home country upon his return those cultural elements which have been implanted in him by the host country. This is clearly a loss. May there not be a compensating gain, however, in the fact that the student who becomes an immigrant may continue to function throughout his life in connection with the second communication line, namely, from the student (now a professional) to the host culture?

We know too little about the extent to which these immigrants fulfill this role. It has been said, for example, that there are in the United Kingdom so many doctors and nurses of Indian, Pakistani, and West Indian origin that without their presence, the British medical service would collapse. Are these doctors and nurses also culture-carriers? Is their relation to their British colleagues and patients a purely professional one, or do they transmit to them some knowledge of the culture in which they themselves were raised? In the social sciences, I know personally a number of Indian professors in Canadian and American universities; a German and a Pole teaching in Scotland; many British and French scholars in the former African colonies; and several Americans, black Africans, one Egyptian, and one Pole in Paris universities. Even in terms of my own acquaintances, this list could be considerably extended. What I do not know is how many of them function as mediators, to what extent, and how successfully. Research along these lines, as far as I know, has as yet never been undertaken; it might help us decide whether in this particular context the brain drain is really a sign of failure.

Exchanges at the Faculty Level

So far I have dealt with foreign *students* as links between cultures; many of the issues recur in the case of visiting *faculty members*—professors and research scholars—who may also be presumed to fulfill a similar function. It is in fact impossible to draw a sharp line between the two. An advanced graduate (or postgraduate) student may also be a university instructor; a professor from a developing country may go abroad to obtain an advanced degree; a faculty member who enjoys status and prestige in his own university may wish to spend some time sitting at the feet of a distinguished foreign colleague who is a recognized expert in the same field, or he may find it desirable to learn what has been happening in a neighboring discipline which has close links with his own. In some cases, the year abroad may represent a combination of teaching and study for the same individual.

For the most part, the foreign student's life history described above would also apply reasonably well to faculty, and the problems which present themselves—selection, preparation, language difficulties, differences in university folkways, contacts with the home population—will occur at both levels. There are, however, certain issues which apply more specifically to exchanges at the faculty level.

Striking variations, for example, are to be noted among different universities (which in many cases means variations among governments whose universities function under control of national ministries of education or their equivalent) in their policy regarding exchanges at the professorial level. Such policy applies both to the acceptance of foreigners as professors and to the ease or difficulty experienced by their own professors to obtain leave of absence to teach in another country.

With regard to the acceptance of foreigners as professors, the differences relate primarily to the willingness or legal right of universities to accept foreigners as regular members of their faculties. In the national universities of many countries, such acceptance is impossible. This is the case in Japan, Italy, and Brazil, for example, and only recently has it become possible in

France; in others, including the United Kingdom, the United States, the German Federal Republic, Canada, and Australia, there is no such restriction. Since this interdiction exists only in the case of regular professors (there appear to be no restrictions on the appointment of visiting professors), it might be regarded as a kind of barrier against a certain variety of brain drain. It is at the same time a barrier against a form of cultural contact which is relatively permanent in character and which, as has already been indicated, is at least potentially able to make a contribution toward cultural mediation.

There are equally striking variations in the conditions under which universities permit their professors to obtain a leave of absence to teach or to conduct research abroad. In the case of a large number of American universities, such leaves are greatly facilitated by the institution of the sabbatical year, which permits members of the faculty above a certain level to absent themselves for a year with at least half of their total yearly salary paid by the university. It is not possible to estimate what proportion of professors who are given this opportunity actually use it to go abroad. The practice of the sabbatical was supposedly introduced in order to help those who were teaching in the relatively isolated New World to go back briefly to the fountains of culture in Europe to rebuild their stock of knowledge, and even though this attitude of inferiority among Americans is not very widespread today, the institution has persisted.

Automatic sabbaticals are rare in other parts of the world, but government policy frequently has a positive impact on this variety of exchange. Programs of technical aid or cooperation frequently involve sending professors abroad for extensive periods. Both the British and the French governments are particularly generous in this respect, with the relevant programs directed mainly, but not exclusively, to the former colonies. Mediation may again be a valuable side effect, but little is known about the consequences in cultural terms of a form of "exchange" which comes mainly from a technically advanced society and is directed to one in the process of industrial development.

There is one problem which our research has identified as occurring with some frequency among professors at a foreign university and which may have very unfavorable consequences for the sojourn as a whole. Too often, the foreign professor on arrival receives inadequate information as to what is expected of him and no clear indication of the slot into which he can fit. He must therefore spend a considerable portion of his year abroad creating a satisfying role for himself. Sometimes he may fail in this attempt and spend an unhappy year; sometimes he may become so disturbed by this experience as to leave before the year is over. I can testify from my own observations that these reactions do occur, although I am convinced that such cases are in the minority. There are, unfortunately, very few investigations of these subjective aspects of the foreign experience at the professorial level.

There is, however, one recent study relevant to this whole issue and also to the role of the foreign professor as mediator. The report by Róse (1976) is entitled *Academic Sojourners* and deals with senior Fulbright programs in East Asia and the Pacific. Over one hundred former Fulbright scholars and a number of administrative officers of binational programs were interviewed, and mail surveys were conducted with a large sample of Fulbright alumni. There is a striking parallel between the problems raised in Rose's report and many of those previously dealt with in this chapter.

The executive secretary of a binational commission is quoted as saying: "People-to-people understanding begins on a person-to-person basis. That is what this program is really all about" (p. 34). The detailed interviews with individual scholars, together with the questionnaires, indicate that many of them accepted this goal as a valid one. Rose concludes that the "Fulbright program in East Asia and the Pacific has well served its participants, *having clearly enhanced their mutual understanding*, their academic achievement, and their personal honor. It has been a model for interpersonal, intercultural relations" (p. 2, italics supplied).

One of his recommendations, namely, that "the roles and expectations of the various agencies of the exchange process be clarified, and common orientations be adopted" (p. 4), is very similar to what has been said above. Many grantees express a willingness to reach wider audiences and to serve as more effective cultural interpreters, and it is suggested that "the use of senior grantees as 'occasional Fulbright scholars' should be more fully institutionalized in order to allow those willing to serve in such roles greater opportunities to do so" (p. 6).

Many of the respondents speak of enhanced mutual understanding and of the cultural benefits of living and working in another country. On the negative side, many refer to inadequate advanced preparation, *lack of adequate guidance in settling into their new duties*, frustrations on the job, and feelings of inadequacy in the role of cultural ambassador. An American who had been in Japan to teach in Tokyo in the field of American literature stated: "While I tried to understand the complexities of Japanese social and political life, I'm afraid I hardly scratched the surface. Yet, lo and behold, I come back and I'm considered some sort of expert . . . . I was an English professor, I told them, not a goddam political sociologist" (p. 29).

Some Aspects of the Dynamics of Cultural Contact

When a member of one cultural group undertakes a foreign sojourn, a number of complex relationships are involved and include problems of adaptation which are difficult to resolve. Some of these problems may be related only indirectly to cultural aspects of the sojourn. In the case of the foreign student, for example, Bochner (1972) points out that there are four categories of problems which may have important consequences. There is, first, the overseas student's status as a foreigner living in an unfamiliar environment—a situation which he shares with other foreigners. Second, the overseas student faces problems by virtue of simply being a university student, and may in that respect not differ markedly from all other students. Third, the student from abroad, again like all others, must face the problems of all adolescents in the process of becoming adults. Finally, he finds himself serving, because either he is expected to or he wants to, as a representative of his country. The problems to be faced can be related to these four social roles. The first and the fourth of these apply equally well to the foreign professor; the other two are clearly less relevant.

The specific nature of the contact with another culture may vary enormously, depending on how the foreign sojourner interprets his role, the expectations which he brings with him, the situations and the people he encounters, his goals, and—most elusive but not least important—his own personality characteristics. As a consequence of these and perhaps other factors, a whole gamut of reactions to the new culture is possible. The foreign student or professor may in certain cases maintain an almost complete indifference to the surrounding culture. This occurs when the student comes with the overriding impulse to become a specialist in a technical field and to obtain the degree requisite to advancement in his own country, or when the researcher immerses himself in the library or laboratory in order to complete an investigation for which the facilities or guidance is lacking at home. This kind of person may remain uninterested in his cultural surroundings and indifferent as to whether or not he makes friends among the host population. There is another group of foreigners who are not indifferent but antagonistic to the surrounding culture, and who make every effort to keep the folkways typical of home alive in a distant setting. Examples which have always aroused amusement are those of the Englishman who wears formal dress for dinner in the jungle and of the American who orders a hamburger at a three-star restaurant in Paris. At the other extreme are those who attempt to "go native," to adopt in toto (as far as they can) the way of life of the new culture, complete with clothes, food, social relations,and all other aspects which they are able to absorb and to practice. This attitude may be due to the conviction that this will lead to greater success in the assigned role (evidently the motivation of a number of Peace Corps volunteers), or may indicate a genuine conversion to the new system of values. It is clear that none of these reactions is likely to lead with success to the role of mediator.

Between these extremes, there are all possible degrees of assimilation—a whole range of potential combinations of the folkways of the two cultures. This may be limited to the borrowing of specific items, such as the appreciation of artistic contributions, for example, or of the values inherent in the pattern of personal relations in the surrounding community. In some cases, this will lead to a simple arithmetic summation, with some of the new cultural acquisitions regarded as sufficiently interesting or valuable to add to one's original cultural possessions. In other cases, the result may be a true integration between the two cultures in the life of the person concerned.

A number of writers have referred in this context to the formation of new, binational, third cultures through a process identified as *interculturation*. The third culture is described by Useem, Useem, and Donoghue (1963) as a web of "patterns generic to the intersections of societies" and as "the behavior patterns created, shared, and learned by men of different societies who are in the process of relating their societies, or sections thereof, to each other" (p. 169). The individuals concerned may be said to have "interculturated" new perceptions and actions into a more or less congruent third pattern, gaining membership in the binational third culture as a consequence.

There will, of course, be diffferent third cultures depending on the two original societies involved. This binational third culture will include standards of interpersonal behavior, work norms, styles of life, and new types of personality. It has been suggested that the individuals concerned may begin to lose resemblance to any particular culture, but may tend to resemble each other. One may be witnessing the emergence of a third culture equivalent to a kind of internationalism among those who have had the same kind of experience (Ventura 1977).

It is in my judgment impossible to decide at this point how important this concept of a third culture will turn out to be in the context of mediation. Is it a help or a hindrance to transmute one's own values in the manner indicated? Could perhaps a greater contribution be made by those who retain their own cultural identity, even though they may borrow those aspects of the new culture which they find palatable? Do not an understanding of and respect for another culture make mediation possible without belonging to a third culture? This important problem I shall have to leave to future investigation.

Mediation and International Understanding

At various points throughout this chapter, reference has been made to the relationship, actual and potential, between the foreign sojourn and international understanding. This is the explicit goal in many of the foreign exchange programs undertaken by private institutions or functioning under governmental and intergovernmental auspices. It seems logical that the success of the programs in realizing this goal should have a bearing on the mediation process. The foreign scholar is unlikely to be a successful mediator unless he has a positive attitude toward the new culture which he is called upon to bring into relation with his own. We must therefore raise more directly the question of the impact of the foreign sojourn on international understanding.

It has been pointed out on many occasions that one of the major difficulties in answering this question is due to the ambiguity in the concept of international understanding and to the fact that it is rarely, if ever, defined clearly enough to permit an answer based on solid and acceptable data. Without going into all the possible complexities of the concept, we must at least distinguish two aspects of "understanding," both of which are important. The first refers to its cognitive content: What do we know (or think we know) about the new culture; what have we learned? The second aspect is emotional or affective in tone: How do we feel about the other group; have our feelings become friendlier as a consequence of our foreign sojourn? The two aspects are frequently, but not necessarily, related. Greater knowledge of the character of Nazism in Germany would not, in most cases, lead the foreigner to react to it with increased warmth or appreciation. It could still be argued, however, that in the long run, it is safer to base our attitudes toward another people on accurate knowledge rather than on hearsay or anecdote.

Both of these aspects—the cognitive and affective, knowledge and feeling—have been of concern to investigators in this field. Very recently, Flack (1976), writing on the basis of an extensive review and evaluation of research on foreign students in the United States since 1967, conducted in association with S. Spaulding and others, concludes as follows: "The sojourn and educational experience tends to engender a more sophisticated, differentiated, personalized, and concretized knowledge and perception of the host society, its achievements and problems, its peoples and policies, and of its 'ways of life,' as compared to 'knowledge' and images held before" (p. 111). This is usually reflected in a reduction of ethnocentric stereotypes, greater understanding of the functioning of the host society, and a heightened awareness of its diversity. "The result is a soberer appraisal of some of its features, values, and practices and of their relevance to one's own role, one's field of activity, and one's own country" (Flack 1976, p. 111). These conclusions are clearly positive with regard to the knowledge aspects of international understanding.

When he turns to the area of attitudes and relationships, Flack is less certain of the consequences on foreign scholars in the United States. "The realm of international relations is probably the most difficult and most complex of the effect areas considered. Seldom . . . was 'international understanding' operationally defined and then tested and followed up in action" (p. 115). He goes on to say that although the attitudes toward the whole experience abroad were on the whole positive, and Americans were generally liked, there was frequent criticism of specific United States foreign policies and of features of the society such as discrimination, level of cultural life, ignorance of other societies, and so forth.

A note of uncertainty is also sounded by Wicks and Bochner (1972), who write with regard to the presence of foreign students in Australia: "Whether Australia has attracted much international goodwill by providing places for students from other countries is an open question, since evidence on this issue is scarce indeed" (p. 228). It is a source of some discouragement to be obliged to say once again that we need more research on this problem, but this very fact may serve as a stimulus to do something about it.

A Concluding Note

This chapter has shown some of the complexities as well as some of the hopes associated with the role of the foreign scholar as a cultural mediator. One factor emerges which needs to be accentuated. Students and professors visiting another country can serve as cultural ambassadors, as links between cultures, but they will usually be successful in this role only if they are informed in advance that this is expected of them and given the preparation and training which the role requires.

References

Abrams, I. *Study Abroad*. Washington, D. C.: U. S. Government Printing Office, 1960.

Aich, P. *Farbige unter Weissen*. Cologne: Kipenheuer and Witsch, 1962.

Alexander, A. A., Workneh, F., Klein, M. H., and Miller, M. H. Psychotherapy and the Foreign Student. In P. Pedersen, W. J. Lonner, and J. G. Draguns (eds.), *Counseling Across Cultures*. Honolulu: University Press of Hawaii, 1976.

Bochner, S. Problems in Culture Learning. In S. Bochner and P. Wicks (eds.), *Overseas Students in Australia*. Sydney: New South Wales University Press, 1972.

Bochner, S., and Wicks, P. (eds.). *Overseas Students in Australia*. Sydney: New South Wales University Press, 1972.

Breitenbach, D. The Evaluation of Study Abroad. In I. Eide (ed.), *Students As Links Between Cultures*. Oslo: Universitetsforlaget, 1970.

Coelho, G. V. Personal Growth and Educational Development Through Working and Studying Abroad. *Journal of Social Issues*, 1962, *18* (1), 55–67.

Du Bois, C. Research in Cross-cultural Education. *News Bulletin of the Institute for International Education*, 1953, *28* (9), 5–9, 60–64.

Eide, I. (ed.). *Students As Links Between Cultures*. Oslo: Universitetsforlaget, 1970.

Flack, M. J. Results and Effects of Study Abroad. *The Annals of the American Academy of Political and Social Science*, 1976, *424*, 107–117.

Ganguli, H. C. *Foreign Students: The Indian Experience*. New Delhi: Sterling, 1975.

Kapur, R. L. Student Wastage at Edinburgh University. *Edinburgh University Quarterly*, 1972 (Summer), 353–377.

Klineberg, O. *The Human Dimension in International Relations*. New York: Holt, Rinehart and Winston, 1964.

_____. Research in the Field of International Exchanges in Education, Science and Culture. *Social Sciences Information*, 1965, *4* (4), 97–138.

_____. Psychological Aspects of Student Exchange. In I. Eide (ed.), *Students As Links Between Cultures*. Oslo: Universitetsforlaget, 1970.

_____. *International Educational Exchange: An Assessment of its Nature and Its Prospects*. Paris: Mouton, 1976.

Klineberg, O., and Ben Brika, J. *Etudiants du Tiers-monde en Europe*. Paris: Mouton, 1972.

Lambert, R. D., and Bressler, M. *Indian Students on an American Campus*. Minneapolis: University of Minnesota Press, 1956.

Lysgaard, S. Adjustment in a Foreign Society: Norwegian Fulbright Grantees Visiting the United States. *International Social Science Bulletin*, 1955, *7*, 45–51.

Marshall, T. The Strategy of International Exchange. In I. Eide (ed.), *Students As Links Between Cultures*. Oslo: Universitetsforlaget, 1970.

Rose, P. I. Academic Sojourners: A Report on the senior Fulbright Programs in East Asia and the Pacific. Washington, D. C.: U. S. Department of State, 1976 (mimeo).

Sapir, E. Why Cultural Anthropology Needs the Psychiatrist. *Psychiatry*, 1938, *1*, 7–12.

Tajfel, H., and Dawson, J. L. (eds.). *Disappointed Guests*. London: Oxford University Press, 1965.

Useem, J., and Useem, R. H. *The Western-Educated Man in India*. New York: Dryden, 1955.

Useem, J., Useem, R. H., and Donoghue, J. Men in the Middle of the Third Culture: The Roles of American and Non-Western People in Cross-cultural Administration. *Human Organization*, 1963, *22*, 169–179.

Ventura, P. Interculturation and the "Been-To": The Dynamics of Communication Between Cultures. Unpublished master's dissertation, University of Pittsburgh, Department of Speech and Theatre Arts, 1977.

Wicks, P., and Bochner, S. A Continuing Inquiry. In S. Bochner and P. Wicks (eds.), *Overseas Students in Australia*. Sydney: New South Wales University Press, 1972.

Eng-kung Yeh, Hung-ming Chu, Marjorie H. Klein, A. A. Alexander, and Milton H. Miller

Psychiatric Implications of Cross-Cultural Education: Chinese Students in the United States

Historical Background

The year 1860 marked a turning point in Chinese history. Before that time, tradition reigned supreme, and all foreigners were considered distant and uncivilized people, fit only for becoming vassals of the Middle Kingdom. A preliminary sign of change occurred in the years from 1839 through 1842, when China was defeated in the Opium War by Great Britain. This was followed by the Taiping Rebellion in 1853 and a new war with Britain and France in 1856. The wound to China from these events was too deep to be ignored, and the way was prepared for reform.

When one day in 1862 the shrewd Governor Hu lin-I saw a fast-moving steamer on the Yangtze River, he realized at once the immense difficulties China would have to face in coping with the West. Another scholar-general, Li Hung-chang, was no less impressed by the might of Western weapons. In his memoranda to the throne, he repeatedly emphasized that Western artillery and steamships had caused an unprecedented change in China's situation in the world. He and his enlightened colleagues were convinced that in order to survive, China had to obtain knowledge of these weapons from the West. It was largely because of the efforts of these officials that China began to adopt Western technology.

From the last two decades of the nineteenth century, hundreds and later thousands of young men and women broke away from the confines of their own culture and immersed themselves for years of study in the technologically developed and modernized world of Japan, the United States, Western Europe, and Russia. This was one of the most striking phenomena in the modern history of China. Most of the nation's leaders during the twentieth century studied abroad, or at least learned from teachers who had had this experience. This group became the driving force in nearly every aspect of the nation's modernization. Studying abroad was also a part of the process through which the Chinese began to adjust to the realities of the world outside the Middle Kingdom. Unless one takes into account the influence of Western education, modern China is incomprehensible. The whole history of this phenomenon has been well documented by Y. C. Wang in his excellent work, *Chinese Intellectuals and the West: 1872-1947* (Wang, 1966).

Among the countries receiving students, the United States has absorbed the largest number and thus is the nation which has had the single most powerful influence on the modernization of China. The first group of students sent to the United States sailed in 1872. But it was not until the beginning of this century that the influx of Chinese students into the United States started. Before the end of World War II, the number of Chinese students who went to the United States was relatively small. But they were highly selected, and most of them were supported by state funds. These students often attended prestigious American universities, and most of them returned home when they completed their studies.

This level of exchange program lasted for half a century, until the 1950s, when the number of Chinese students started to increase dramatically. Several factors contributed to this increase, the most important perhaps being the political transformation on the China mainland in 1949. Since 1950, there has been a trend for mainland Chinese in Taiwan to migrate to other countries. The large influx of Chinese students into the United States represented this movement, at least partially. According to the statistics of the Ministry of Education of the Republic of China, over 2000 students came to the United States from Taiwan every year since 1963. This movement reached its peak in 1969, with 3015 students.[1] During 1969-1970, there were about 19,000 Chinese students in the United States: approximately 8000 from Taiwan, 7000 from Hong Kong, and 4000 from unidentified origins. They constituted the third largest group of foreign students in the United States, after the Canadians and the Indians.[2]

Even though these Chinese students tend to stay in the United States for a long time after the completion of their studies, they have been playing a significant role in the economic development and construction of their home country. Nevertheless, to encourage further both the recent graduates as well as the more established scholars to return home has become an important policy of the nation.

The Problems

As the world gets smaller and cross-cultural experiences became more common to modern men and women, psychologists, sociologists, and other behavioral scientists have become increasingly concerned about the stress aspects of foreign education. Research has revealed that many problems arise during sojourn. These include the effects of cross-cultural adaptation on the student's image of self and host nationals, value systems, social attitudes, personal growth, and the capacity of adjustment after returning home.

Psychiatrists have been more concerned about the psychological difficulties that students may encounter and the nature and extent of any psychopathology that they may experience during sojourn. In addition, there has been an attempt to find measures to predict psychopathology and to devise interventions that can be used before the sojourn to maximize the student's ability to deal with any problems that he might encounter.

What are the problems that face Chinese students in the United States? The present authors have for several years been investigating the social adaptation of Chinese students from Taiwan attending the University of Wisconsin, by means of specifically designed questionnaires and intensive interviews. We were interested in finding out (1) the students' psychosocial background and the motivation for sojourn; (2) their social adaptation, especially their relationship with host nationals; (3) how Chinese students perceive themselves, their fellow countrymen, their own cultural norms, and their host nationals before going abroad and having cross-cultural contact; and (4) how any discrepancy between this perception and subsequent reality might have affected their adaptation to the host culture. Some findings have been reported elsewhere (Alexander et al. 1976; Klein et al. 1971a and b; Yeh and Chu 1969, 1974). For comparative purposes, American students in Taiwan were studied by the same authors (Yeh et al. 1973). The present authors also had an opportunity to study a group of Chinese students and faculty members at the University of Hawaii (Chu et al. 1971).

One of the present authors, Yeh, has for many years had clinical experience in treating numerous Chinese students who had to return home because of psychotic breakdown or some other psychiatric disorder which emerged during their sojourn. These experiences have added to our understanding of the psychiatric problems that arise in cross-cultural adaptation, and of the personality problems, role conflicts, and identity crises that students experience in new cultural settings (Yeh 1972). More recently, Yeh (1976) investigated a group of Chinese students who had returned home after years of study in the United States. The present chapter draws on the findings from these studies to arrive at some of the psychiatric implications of cross-cultural adaptation. Three aspects, in particular, will receive special emphasis: the influence of cross-cultural experiences on the students' psychopathology, and conversely on their psychosocial growth, and the detection of high-risk students before sojourn.

The Living Style and Social Adjustment of Chinese Students in the United States

During 1966 and 1967, a total of 580 foreign students from 35 countries were given a background questionnaire as they passed through the Foreign

Student Reception Center at the University of Wisconsin. The questionnaire was designed to assess variables related to the students' adaptive capacity, to the specific stresses that they might encounter, and to their general life-style. Over the two years, approximately one hundred students from the Far East and forty students from Taiwan and Hong Kong were studied, by intensive interviews and/or questionnaires about social adaptation. Most students saw themselves as functioning well. Only two had psychiatric problems, although there were some psychosomatic complaints, mostly gastrointestinal, which brought them to the student health service.

While most respondents were functioning adequately, few had made close, warm contacts with the host culture. Social isolation from Americans was a fact of life for the Chinese students. They associated almost exclusively with their fellow nationals. Their relationship with host nationals rarely went beyond superficial pleasantries. Thus, they formed a strong subculture within a university subculture. This isolation becomes so accepted by the Chinese subculture that there is a great resistance to changing the pattern. These facts, which are quite opposite to what is expected of international students, may come as a surprise.

However, not all the evidence unequivocally supports this conclusion. Thus, in a study of 109 Chinese students returned from the United States, Wei (1971) found that (1) 34.6 percent indicated that they had problems of adjustment; (2) 94 percent reported that they made friends with Americans while they were in the United States; and (3) 47 percent declared that half of their friends were Americans. Wei emphasized that these Chinese student returnees had adjusted well to the host country and had established satisfactory friendships with Americans.

Two questions might be raised at this point. One concerns the criteria for "adjustment" used in this study; the other, the stage of the sojourn at which the students were studied. It is quite likely that students may be experiencing different degrees of stress at different stages of the sojourn, resulting in different attitudinal patterns. These changes in adjustment have been described as a U-curve by some investigators and as a W-curve by others (Gullahorn and Gullahorn 1963; Lundstedt 1963; Lysgaard 1955). The inconsistencies between the Wisconsin findings and Wei's (1971) results are not irreconcilable, and may be explained by noting that data collection in the two studies occurred at different temporal stages of the sojourn. The former study was conducted during the early phase of the sojourn, while the latter soon after return home. Any evaluation of cross-cultural adaptation and its effects on the student must be longitudinal in scope. Whether the style of social adaptation as observed in the University of Wisconsin investigation is the more or less fixed pattern of behavior of Chinese students throughout their entire time overseas or just represents one phase of the sojourn can only be proved by further follow-up study.

The other point which calls for special attention is that the evaluation of the adaptation of foreign students requires multiple criteria. Many studies have simply focused either on superficial indices of academic adjustment or on the development of positive attitudes toward the United States. Though such criteria are valid from the standpoint of the goals for international exchange, they do not tell the whole story. What is also important is the personal and social adaptation that occurs underneath the surface and that meets educational needs, career goals, and situational demands. To reflect this complexity adequately, evaluation research designs will need to address at least the following aspects of adaptation: completion of educational goals, successful career placement, development of positive and friendly contacts with Americans, a continued sense of confidence, health, and well-being, and the emergence of differentiated and detailed perspectives on American life.

There are two other important themes which have to be considered in understanding the nature of the barriers that exist between Asians and Americans. First, there is the need by the sojourner to adjust to the differences in social behavior, that is, the need to relearn the rules and patterns of social conduct. Second, but perhaps more important, are the emotional risks inherent in such an adaptation. What is feared most is the loss of familiar structure and social anchorage and the absence of a familiar, supportive social peer network to fulfill dependency needs. This fear seems to emerge as a direct function of the discrepancy between Chinese and American culture.

The functions of the conational subgroup contribute toward perpetuating this social isolation. This group provides structure in a world where manners and morals are different from patterns valued at home. It provides mutual support and approval in a familiar frame of reference when academic stresses are at an all-time peak. It may provide suitable marriage partners, and substitute peers for parents in the complex mechanism of mate selection. It provides relief from the stresses of coping with new situations in a strange tongue, where ignorance is equal to inferiority and where embarrassment and loss of face are strongly negative experiences. Social isolation from the Americans and formation of a closely knit conational subculture are perhaps the most efficient resolution of the "psychoeconomics" of Chinese students' situation.

Negative attitudes and experiences of foreign students are often difficult to assess reliably. There is a tendency to give socially desirable, "feeling obliged," or "showing politeness" kinds of answers, particularly in studies using questionnaires. Perhaps the best way of reducing such a cultural bias is via a nonstructured interview conducted by a member of the students' own culture. Questionnaires may then be used to cross-validate the findings.

The style of adjustment of the Chinese students has also been observed among the other Asian students at the University of Wisconsin (Klein et al.

1971). When we turn our eyes to the opposite side of the world, it is interesting to note a parallel phenomenon. Thus, approximately half of a group of American students in Taiwan experienced similar difficulties (Yeh et al. 1973). Living in the Orient appears to be as difficult for American students as living in the United States is for Chinese students. Difficulty in adjustment and negative feelings and prejudice toward host nationals have been openly expressed by many American students. "Stick to your own kind" is thus not only a message sung in *West Side Story*, but a watchword for everyone faced with the problem of adapting to a foreign culture (Miller et al. 1971).

Who Goes to Study Overseas; Their Psychosocial Backgrounds

The social isolation of Chinese students abroad does not mean that they are poorly selected or mentally unhealthy. On the contrary, our study of 132 students prior to their departure for graduate study in the United States showed them to be significantly better prepared than a group of 108 control students in graduate schools at home. The prospective sojourners (1) were from families with higher socioeconomic and educational status; (2) had more family members, relatives, and close friends who had studied or were studying in the United States; (3) were more confident about their physical and mental health; (4) were more willing to meet members of the host culture and more open to new experiences; and (5) showed greater appreciation of and identification with positive aspects of the American people (Yeh and Chu, 1969, 1974).

The focal students were highly task-oriented in their motivation for overseas study. Nearly all or a great majority of our going-out sample rated "getting a degree" (95 percent), "getting training in my field" (93 percent), "having different experiences" (93 percent), and "finding out more what I am like" (84 percent) as the main goals for their overseas study. They were less interested in "knowing the new country, government, and people" and "living with people in another country." Though the students were generally confident and optimistic about their overseas study, their task-oriented attitudes were also reflected in the difficulties that they anticipated, such as "not have enough time for study" (37 percent), "not enough money" (35 percent), "getting a job if I want one" (35 percent), and "finding schoolwork too difficult" (34 percent). They anticipated much less difficulty in "making friends with Americans" (6 percent), "getting to meet Americans outside the university" (12 percent), or "making friends with the opposite sex" (13 percent) (Yeh and Chu 1974). These findings may indicate that sojourning Chinese students are primarilty study-oriented and are less interested in building close friendships with American people. This is clearly consistent with the study of adaptation described above.

Psychiatric Disturbances in Cross-Cultural Adaptation

Psychopathology resulting from cross-cultural adaptation is a subject which has received increasing attention in recent years. The studies that will now be reviewed are drawn from a wide range of subjects, so that the findings may not be directly applicable to overseas students. However, the research provides a perspective against which the special case of the sojourning student may be reviewed.

Kojak (1974), in a study of the American community in Bangkok, reported a high prevalence of psychopathology as measured by incidence of marital problems (21 percent of the 3260 American officials affiliated with the United States government) and incidence of emotional problems in adolescents, such as heroin abuse and other behavior problems (19 percent and 14 percent, respectively). Kojak compared these findings with the American community in Japan, where the prevalence of psychopathology was found to be strikingly low, and concluded that the higher incidence of psychopathology in the Bangkok sample was related to the state of social disintegration among the American community there. The main problem areas seemed to be poor leadership, lack of supportiveness in interpersonal relationships, secularization, lack of social organization, and the negative influences of the predominant Thai culture values of *sanuk* (fun-loving or pleasure-seaking), and *mai-pen-rai* ("it does not matter").

Yap (1972), studying one hundred Western expatriates in Hong Kong, found significantly more alcoholic disorders and sexual deviations, but fewer functional psychoses such as schizophrenia and severe depression, among the Westerners than in a control group of Chinese patients. Analysis of symptoms of sexual disorders revealed an interesting contrast. There were four cases of homosexuality, three of hyposexuality including impotence, one of hypersexuality, two cases of masturbatory excess, and one instance of male masochism among the expatriates. Among the Chinese patients, by contrast, not only was sexual deviation absent, but there were only two men with masturbatory worries and two with a fear of sexual exhaustion due to what they believed to be excessive coitus. One of these four also had a fear of penis shrinkage or *koro*, a culture-bound depersonalization syndrome (Yap 1965). Yap speculated that the prevalence of mental illness among colonial expatriates may be higher than that of the home population because of stress related to culture shock, but also because some susceptible persons troubled at home tend to seek relief abroad, where they in due course succumb.

King (1975) found in a four-year follow-up study of 130 American professional personnel working in 12 countries in Asia, Africa, and Latin America that the depressive syndrome was the most common psychiatric disorder diagnosed, but that this syndrome had a good prognosis. No subject in these samples met the criteria for a diagnosis of schizophrenia, organic brain syndrome, antisocial personality, alcoholism, drug dependence, or neurosis.

Two factors in particular enter into an analysis of the psychopathology in cross-cultural adaptation. One is the motivation for the sojourn, and the other is the nature of the sojourn. Those who go out voluntarily (such as students) may be more adaptable than those who have been assigned to their posts (such as the military personnel in King's study). Again, those leaving developed Western countries for developing non-Western regions may differ in motivation, style of going out, emotional preparation, and attitudes toward host nationals from those going in the opposite direction. Westerners go out primarily to travel, to work, to serve, to explore, and less to learn or study. Their style of going out seems to be more aggressive and confident than that of the Easterners (Klein, Miller, and Alexander 1974). Most Americans who travel to other countries are convinced of the superiority of their culture. They are less motivated to learn from the host cultures. Instead, they may be motivated by the desire to spread American virtue, as seen in the Peace Corps program, which attracted thousands of American youth. Most Americans who go abroad express confidence and optimism about making satisfying friendships with host nationals and being able to adjust to the new environment. These hopes, unfortunately, often turn out later to be quite unrealistic and lead to disillusionment. In the case of East-West sojourners, taking young Asian students as an example, the primary motivation may be more for study, training, and to learn something from the host culture. They are by and large positively selected in terms of language ability, academic achievement, confidence in health, financial resources, and attitudes to host nationals. They are probably more cautious and better prepared psychologically than the West-East traveler. Psychopathology in cross-cultural adaptation may thus be different depending on the combination of the various factors reviewed, including the direction of the sojourn (from East to West or from West to East), the reason for the sojourn, and who the sojourners are.

As far as can be ascertained, a well-designed epidemiological study of the psychopathology of Chinese students before, during, and after their overseas study has not yet been reported. We do not at present have exact data about the prevalence of psychiatric disorders, the extent of disturbances, or the relation of disturbances to the different stages of adjustment as hypothesized by the U-curve or W-curve. However, our clinical experiences with Chinese students who have had to return home because of psychiatric disorders seem to demonstrate some characteristic features. In particular, there is a connection among some psychiatric disorders, premorbid personality problems, and the impact of certain cross-cultural experiences. These findings will now be presented and discussed.

PARANOID FEATURES

Altogether, seventy-seven Chinese students from Taiwan who had to return prematurely from overseas study because of psychiatric disorders were treated by one of the authors (Yeh). The diagnoses are shown in Table 1. The majority of cases were schizophrenias or paranoid psychoses (85.7 percent). The paranoid manifestations were the most conspicuous symptoms among these psychotic Chinese students, and this finding confirms the results of a previous study (Yeh 1972). The paranoid symptoms were significantly more prevalent among males than females. There were only five affective disorders, including two manias and three depressions.

Delusions and hallucinations were mostly persecutory in nature and were usually verbalized as "being investigated," "being watched," "being poisoned," and "mind being read." The delusions of reference and persecution related to failure in studies, lack of job opportunity, and problems with professors or employers were quite common. Political references, such as being investigated by the FBI or by the Chinese government, or of being suspected by the Americans as a Communist, were frequently observed among the male patients. Frequently the "persecutors" were fellow countrymen rather than host nationals. Neurotic competition and frustrated dependency needs seemed to create a sense of failure, which in turn led to denial and projection onto fellow countrymen. For example, student A, a physics major, suddenly

Table 1. Diagnostic Classification of Chinese Students Repatriated from the United States on Psychiatric Grounds

	Male		Female		Total	
	N	%	N	%	N	%
Paranoid Psychosis or Paranoid Schizophrenia	39	83.0	15	50.0	54	70.1
Other types of Schizophrenia	4	8.6	8	26.7	12	15.6
Mania	1		1		2	
Psychotic Depression	2		1		3	
Psychophysiologic Reactions			1		1	
Neurosis	1		3		4	
Epilepsy			1		1	
TOTAL	47		30		77	

developed the idea that a slow-acting poison had been put into his soft drink after a ping-pong game with another Chinese, student B. Student A thought that the poison was administered by B to dull his mind, to disturb his memory, and to paralyse him. A's persecution complex was supposedly initiated by another Chinese, student C, who hated A. Student C had entered the department two years before A as a teaching assistant. He once graded A lower than A thought was fair. A in turn put some provocative notes on the blackboard in C's laboratory. Then, just before the episode, C had failed in a subject in the Ph.D. qualification examination given by A's professor. Therefore, A suspected that C was retaliating through B.

Suspicion of poison in tea or food was manifested in twelve cases. One such patient recalled after recovery that his fantastic ideas about poisoning may have come from Chinese novels about ancient chivalry, which he had read during his high-school days.

In some female students, the psychotic breakdown was precipitated by failure in a love affair—real or imagined—and by sexual frustration. For instance, a twenty-six-year-old female student majoring in library science became acutely disturbed, with crying spells, delusions of being poisoned, and the hearing of voices accusing her of misconduct with boys and threatening to kill her. The episode was precipitated after she received a threatening letter from the Chinese girlfriend of a Chinese physician whom she was also dating. The patient was an intelligent, highly sociable person and a frequent participant in various student activities. She had represented her college on an International Student Conference and was a very popular figure at home. In the United States, however, she was kept at some distance by the Chinese students, especially those from Taiwan. After several unsuccessful affairs with different Chinese students, all of whom eventually left her, and an American student who was strongly opposed by her family, she got acquainted with a young Chinese physician from Taiwan. He had the reputation of being a Don Juan and had many girlfriends, regardless of nationality. The patent recovered quickly from her psychosis after she was sent home. She remained well and taught English at a girl's high school in her hometown for a year, until her second psychotic breakdown, which was precipitated by an unexpected telephone call from the physician, who happened to be in Taiwan for a short visit.

For Chinese students studying abroad, especially females, marrying or even just dating foreigners may create considerable anxiety and a sense of shame. The student may be disparaged by her fellow nationals, and she may have to sacrifice the emotional ties with other members of her culture. Four female students developed delusions that their American professor was interested in them as a prospective marriage partner. They became acutely disturbed when they were directly rejected. A twenty-six-year-old Chinese girl had a delusion that the dean of the college, a man of German descent in his fifties, was interested in her and was always watching her through a magic mirror. She believed that her blood was being exchanged with another person's, and that two-thirds of her uterus was taken away, and she hallucinated that electric charges were being applied to her body by jealous male Chinese students. This young lady, known to be a shy, modest, and quiet person at home, was openly sexual toward males and aggressive to the female ward staff during her hospitalization in the United States.

Three male students who had been preoccupied with their sexual inadequacy at home developed delusions of being castrated by American girls when they were embarrassed by their sexual impotence. A thirty-three-year-old married Taiwanese male, the father of two children, and a passive, dependent, and submissive person, had for a long time suspected the infidelity of his active and domineering wife, whom he had acquired through an arranged marriage. He had, however, never expressed his suspicions at home. He left for the United States at the age of thirty-two, against the wife's wishes. But the trip was justified on the grounds that overseas study would bring him better job opportunities in the future. In fact, the sojourn was his escape from the psychological difficulties he faced at home and probably his single acting-out of the hostility he bore toward his wife. While in the United States, he became intimate with a female Chinese student. When he received a letter from his wife accusing him of infidelity, deserting his family, and leaving his wife in conflict with her parents-in-law, he became acutely disturbed and replied with a long letter full of anger and jealousy. Paranoid notions of being castrated followed this episode.

A dramatic illustration of the development of paranoid delusions during cross-cultural adaptation was the case of three brothers who shared the same or mutually related delusions of persecution. The sharing of the same delusions by two or more persons who are connected by close emotional ties, such as husband-wife, parents-children, or siblings, is a rare but documented phenomenon referred to in the literature under the term *folie â deux* (psychoses of two persons) or, less commonly, *folie â trois* (psychoses of three persons) (Lehmann 1967). The following case illustrates how conflict between basic, traditional Chinese values and American values and the inability of the sojourners to assume new social roles resulted in psychological threat which the sojourners had to deny and which they finally projected on the outside world.

A thirty-year-old single Chinese student with an M.S. in civil engineering from the University of Missouri began to think that the Americans at his office, especially his immediate boss, were looking down upon him and intended to harm him. This followed an argument with an American colleague three months after the Chinese started in a job as a junior civil engineer at a private company in Chicago. Upon receiving a telephone call, his youngest brother came from the East Coast to Chicago to see the patient and took the whole story to be true. This brother then called a second brother in Los Angeles and asked him to come. The second brother recognized that the patient was mentally ill, but believed that the patient's illness was the result of being persecuted by a group of people who originally aimed to harm the second brother himself. Believing that the patient was the scapegoat for himself, and being overwhelmed by sympathy and guilt feelings and anger against the "persecutor," the second brother took the patient to Los Angeles in order to avoid further persecution. In Los Angeles, the patient became even more disturbed and was suspicious of and antagonistic toward the second brother. Finally he had to be hospitalized and ultimately repatriated after eight months under medical care in the state hospital.

Family history revealed that the father was a college-graduated mining engineer. He was a self-righteous, strict disciplinarian, who expected high achievement and absolute obedience from his children. He was the absolute authority figure in the home and revered by all four children. Though the family was not very wealthy, the father's hard work and sacrifices enabled his children (all boys) to complete a college education. When the eldest son graduated from college, he provided financial assistance to his three younger brothers for their college education at home and graduate study abroad.

The second brother was the first one to come to the United States, in 1960. As soon as he completed his degree in mechanical engineering, he married and took a job in order to assist his two younger brothers to come to the United States for their graduate study. He also regularly supported his mother at home out of his limited income. In addition, he invited his mother from Taiwan to live with his family after the death of his father. His wife was a Chinese born and educated in the United States, and she could not get along with her mother-in-law. All these things had resulted in marital discord between the second brother and his wife, who accused him of supporting his "old" family at the expense of herself and her children.

In order to increase his income, he moved from Los Angeles to Springfield, Illinois, to take a job in the state government. This move was initiated by his wife, through the arrangement of her brother. The Chinese husband was not happy in Springfield and became neurotic, especially sensitive about racial discrimination, and competitive with his American colleagues. After an episode of open and hostile argument with an American colleague about the Chinese government in Taiwan, he became paranoid and was overwhelmed by a fear of being watched and investigated by American people. He suspected that the salesmen who visited his house were secret agents sent by his American employer to kill him. Finally, he came to believe that it was all a conspiracy planned by his wife's brother and his wife, together with their American friends, to harm him and to keep him away from his own people. His delusions were taken for truth for a period of time by the fourth brother and his mother.

Mutual dependency and support, particularly within the family, and filial piety are virtues and obligatory in traditional Chinese culture. In this case, we see the conflict between the values of traditional Chinese culture and the values of modern American culture, in which independence of each individual is highly emphasized. Such conflicts between traditional cultural values and new values represented by the host culture may be construed in terms of role conflict. The psychiatric disturbance was the result of the sojourner's inability to integrate the new values into his existing ones and to assume new social roles. This kind of role conflict was not only seen among the students, but also observed among their parents. One of the present authors, Yeh, has treated many Chinese patients who developed depression after a period of living with their children in the United States, and who finally had to return home because of the increasing conflicts between the two generations and their respective in-laws.

IDENTITY CRISIS

Cross-cultural adaptation often brings about situations in which the sojourner's ability, personality, and capacity for dealing with problems comes under test. This may result in a kind of psychological turmoil characterized by identity crisis. For those who are predisposed to be vulnerable to such stress, the turmoil may provoke psychiatric disorder, neurosis, or psychosis. A case of this kind of psychotic depression is reported here.

The patient was a twenty-seven-year-old female graduate student in psychology, who during her five years in the United States, became deeply depressed, with strong feelings of guilt, condemnation, and unworthiness, to the extent that she had to return home for treatment. She was the eldest child, with one sister and a brother. The father was an architect, an admirer of Western technology but an old-fashioned disciplinarian who expected his children to study overseas for their higher degrees. After serving as a teaching assistant for two years at the department of psychology of the prestigious national university from which she had graduated, the patient came to the United States for graduate study, with high recommendations from her professor. She felt, however, that she was not prepared for overseas study. It was in this state of anxiety and uncertainty that she left for the United States. In the first year, she had difficulty with language and had to take supplementary English courses. It took her three years to get an M.A. in psychology. She was anxious that her supervisor might expect too much from her and look down on her if she could not meet his expectations. She often wondered whether she should have come abroad and whether psychology was a good choice. She thought of giving up psychology and becoming a missionary, and then her interest shifted to nursing.

Before coming to the United States she had had a steady boyfriend, but he was opposed by her father. The boy was passive, submissive, and was never able to mount a courtship. It was in this state of frustration and disappointment that she left him to study abroad.

Her sister, two years her junior, also came to the United States, two years later. She successfully obtained an M.S. degree in civil engineering with straight-A records. Soon after this, the sister married a Chinese boy. For the first two years, the couple lived with this patient. Subsequently the patient moved out at the request of her brother-in-law. It was at this time that she started to suffer from isolation, loneliness, a sense of insecurity, lack of confidence, and depression, with strong feelings of inferiority and unworthiness. She began to examine her relationship with the sister since childhood, and wondered whether her sister had been depending on her as the capable elder sister or whether she was emotionally dependent on her sister.

Her psychotic depression interrupted her study, and she was forced to return home for treatment. She recovered completely from her depression after two months of hospitalization, and returned to the college from which she had graduated, where she was appointed as an instructor. She did well there and was promoted to full professor eight years later. In the meantime, she married her previous boyfriend despite opposition from her father. She has been happy as a housewife, a mother of two children, and a college professor. What her colleagues observed during the years following her return home seem to support what she told Yeh during the regular follow-up interviews: "I became more aware of myself, the ability as well as the limitations, the assets as well as the shortcomings. I know what I should and should not do. Though it was really a painful experience, perhaps it was worthwhile in the long run in terms of having an opportunity to be confronted with my personality problems. After all, I am confident in myself and with others."

Another example is a patient who was a depressed, hypochondriacal thirty-two-year-old medical doctor who came to the United States in 1968 with her husband, immediately after graduating from medical college. She took residency training in anaesthesia, but she gave this up after two years, as she was not sure whether she really wanted to be an anaesthetist. She was in continuous conflict regarding whether she should stay at home as a full-time housewife, as her husband wanted her to be, or remain a professional person—a medical doctor. One of the reasons she wanted to be a medical practitioner was in order to be able to earn money of her own to support her parents at home and to assist her brother to come to the United States for graduate study. Her husband was responsible for supporting his own people at home (Taiwan), and had become increasingly critical of her supporting her parents.

This emotional conflict had made this patient neurotic, hypochondriacal, and depressed from time to time, and finally she decided to return home for treatment. Returning home and meeting her parents was a relief from neurotic depression for her. During two months of psychotherapy, she was able to see more clearly and objectively her personality problems, neurotic motivation for overseas study, and emotional conflicts with her husband.

Personality Problems and Adjustment Difficulties
Before Sojourn

Eight out of the fifty-four repatriated paranoid cases treated by Yeh—six males and two females—already had paranoid breakdowns resulting in hospitalization prior to their sojourn. Twelve other cases had manifested a series of behavior problems suggestive of either paranoid disorders or personality-pattern disturbances. The high rate of previous breakdowns in our sample deserves attention and explanation. Paranoid symptoms are mental disturbances that usually show little personality disintegration or intellectual deterioration. Those cases might, therefore, have been in their remission state at the time of departure, and the symptoms were not recognized. Paranoid behavior patterns are easily overlooked in present-day Chinese society because among the Chinese, projection seems to be the most frequently used defense mechanism, and the current social environment is one in which paranoid tendencies are realistically warranted.

For example, in a study of a large group of students at a major urban university in Taipei, about half of the students (54.8 percent) said "yes" to the question "Do you feel that the outside world is full of traps, so you must be very cautious to be free from plots that somebody may have against you?"; 21 percent agreed with the statement "Somebody was deliberately making trouble for you so you hate them very much"; and nearly one-fifth of the students felt that people were often criticizing them.[3] For those students with previous adjustment problems, going abroad appeared to be motivated by neurotic competition with others, or by parents who attempted to satisfy their own neurotic need vicariously, regardless of the students' psychological readiness for overseas study. This will be discussed in more detail later. Other students wanted to escape from difficult situations at home, or were making a blind effort to redeem failure at home by seeking better opportunities abroad.

OUTCOME OF TREATMENT

The immediate outcome of treatment of the returned Chinese students with nervous breakdowns was generally promising. About one-third of the psychotic cases showed remission or marked improvement, with satisfactory social adjustment in their professions—which included college teaching, research, and government employment. In half of the cases, mild to moderate improvement was observed. Only the remaining one-sixth, all schizophrenics, remained unchanged. Poor prognosis or relapse of the symptoms was significantly related to premorbid personality problems and to psychopathology in the family. By and large, returning home of itself seemed to release the students from emotional tensions, and in some cases greatly enhanced their capacity for reality-testing. The persecutory delusions involving school personnel, immigration officers, or security officers in the host country generally disappeared or became less intensive upon return home. The contents of delusions or hallucinations changed. A male student had a visual hallucination of Buddha instead of Jesus Christ, whom he had hallucinated in the United States, as soon as he arrived in Japan en route to Taiwan.

During the course of treatment, it was observed in some cases that subsidence of paranoid features was followed by depression as patients began to respond to therapy and as they became aware of their psychological difficulties. Depression usually improved as the students became able to cope with emotional difficulties under the therapist's support, but recurred when they were faced with new reality stress, such as a job, marriage, schooling, or going abroad again.

PARANOIA AND DEPRESSION

Paranoia and depression are generally considered to be based on different psychological mechanisms. The clinical experiences of the authors in Taiwan support Yap's findings in Hong Kong that depressive disorders among Chinese are by no means as rare as Westerners think, and that Western nosology is also valid in the symptomatology of Chinese depressive patients (Yap 1967). From the present study, it can be speculated that paranoia and depression could occur in the same person at different times, depending on changes in the social environment. Denial and projection mechanisms seemed to be more frequently used as defenses against anxiety in a foreign culture, where the individual was psychologically isolated and the outside world was regarded as potentially dangerous. In the home culture, where the environment is not dangerous, these mechanisms are no longer necessary and are replaced by other defense mechanisms, such as introjection, which leads to depression.

Predeparture Phase Study

As pointed out by Du Bois (1956), the predeparture phase should be considered as an important aspect of the student's sojourn experience and is in need of more detailed study. The clinical experiences of the authors with a group of Chinese students who developed major psychiatric disorders during their overseas sojourn, as described above, fully support Du Bois's statement.

During the predeparture phase, the student may be in the process of making what is often a very difficult decision and a major personal commitment. He may be in a state of conflict about leaving his family and feel considerable ambiguity regarding his future. Another study showing that foreign students come to the United States with an initial high level of positive attitudes suggests that the predeparture period may also be a time when important impressions of the host culture and its nationals are formed (Walton 1967). Klein and others (1971) hypothesized that adequacy of coping with decision-making stress and anxiety expressed during the predeparture period would be predictive of one's adaptational adequacy in the United States, and also of the nature of specific problems students may encounter.

SOME PSYCHIATRIC AND GENERAL HEALTH FINDINGS

One hundred and thirty-two Chinese students who were about to go to the United States for graduate work were studied by means of a specifically designed questionnaire. One hundred and eight students who were studying at the local graduate school with no intention of going overseas in the foreseeable future served as the control group. Eighty-six students of the going-out group were interviewed to cross-validate the findings of the questionnaire. In the interview, the subjects were rated on any psychiatric symptoms which they might manifest. The aim was to obtain a more dynamic picture of the students' personality, and, if possible, to predict any psychopathology they might develop and any psychiatric help they might need during sojourn.

Some preliminary findings from the questionnaire have been reported elsewhere (Yeh 1976; Yeh and Chu 1969, 1974). The findings on the interviewed cases are reported here. A few case histories are presented in some detail to illustrate the students' personalities, the problems manifested, and their significance in later cross-cultural adaptation.

Out of the eighty-six students interviewed, eleven presented neurotic symptoms and nine manifested psychophysiologic symptoms. There were also three personality-trait disturbances which could be regarded as psychiatric cases according to the objectively defined criteria used in the study of college students in Taiwan (Yeh et al. 1972). Four students were manifesting some physical health problems which needed medical attention. Fifty-nine cases, or 68.6 percent of the subjects interviewed, were free from psychiatric and physical symptoms. The proportion of psychiatric and physical symptoms found in this sample was about the same as among senior college students in a university in Taiwan (Yeh et al. 1972).

Distribution of symptoms according to sex and years elapsed after graduating is shown in Table 2. Significantly more psychiatric and physical symptoms were found among females (46.2 percent) than males (25 percent). Though statistically not significant, the years elapsed after graduation seemed to affect the rates for male and female psychiatric and physical symptom manifestation differently. In males, there were fewer symptoms among those students who spent one year or longer after graduation from college (15.4 percent) than at graduation (32.3 percent), while this tendency was opposite in females (63.6 percent versus 33.3 percent). It can be speculated that the year or two after graduation may provide males with opportunities to work through their problems in relation to the decision to proceed overseas, and thus this group of students is theoretically more positively selected than those who do not undergo this experience.

The opposite tendency in female students is difficult to understand at this time, but may be explained with reference to the different social role of the female overseas-trained student. There is some reason to believe that female students attend college or go overseas to study not primarily to prepare for a professional career, but rather for the social prestige attached to a degree. For those females who are not motivated, parental pressure is often the only significant driving force for a decision to go overseas to study. Parental expectation regarding their children's achievement could, however, be unrealistic and even neurotic, and thus the virtue of filial piety could easily become an anxiety-laden emotional burden for the students. The turmoil in decision-making for overseas study during the predeparture phase, on the other hand, provides students with the opportunity to confront reality and to reevaluate their own personality and their capability for cross-cultural adaptation. The following case, of an unmotivated female student under her mother's neurotic pressure for overseas study, illustrates this theme.

A twenty-two-year-old graduate from a small Catholic university was referred to one of the authors by the University of Wisconsin, where she had applied for admission. She failed to keep the appointment three times, and when she finally showed up on the fourth occasion, she was accompanied by her mother, who dominated most of the interview. This student was the third of five siblings, and came from a well-to-do physician's family. She had two elder sisters who were both prettier than she and academically superior to her. The eldest sister was a pharmacist with an M.S. degree, married to a Chinese student with a Ph.D., and living in New York. The second sister was a medical graduate and taking her internship, also in New York.

This girl, in contrast to the outgoing and extroverted personalities of the two sisters, was a quiet, introverted, and dependent person, with an inferiority complex resulting from her lower school achievement in comparison with the two sisters. She was dissatisfied with the college from which she had

Table 2. Number of Prospective Sojourners with Psychiatric Symptoms or Physical Health Problems, by Sex and Time Elapsed at Departure after Award of First Degree

Elapsed Time After Graduation

Symptoms	At Graduation		One Year or More		Completed Graduate School		Total		
	Males	Females	Males	Females	Males	Females	Males	Females	Combined
None	23	10	14	3	8	1	45	14	59
Neurotic	5	1	3	2	—	—	8	3	11
Psychophysiological	4	2	—	3	—	—	4	5	9
Personality Problems	2	1	—	—	—	—	2	1	3
Physical Health Problems	—	1	—	2	1	—	1	3	4
TOTAL	34	15	17	10	9	1	60	26	86

graduated and with the major she had taken. Her overseas study was entirely the scheme of her mother and two sisters, who arranged everything for her, including the selection of her major subject and the university where she would study. She was not prepared for the sojourn and openly expressed hostility to her mother, who was forcing her to go. She anticipated a great deal of difficulty in the United States, particularly in English and in mixing with American women, as she had had an unhappy episode with an American female teacher in college.

Information obtained later revealed a very interesting outcome. This student finally went to the United States a year later, under strong maternal pressure, but stayed only for three months in California instead of New York, where her mother wished her to stay with her sisters. She returned home without entering any college in the United States, and married a boy her mother opposed. The marriage was allegedly happy. The mother migrated to New York to live with her son, a medical doctor who was taking his internship there. After years of continuous frustration in getting a job and conflict with her son and the son's wife, the mother developed paranoid psychosis and finally had to be sent back home for treatment, as hospitalization in the United States apparently made her symptoms worse. There were language difficulties and consequent misunderstanding between the staff and the mother. She later openly criticized how badly she had been treated in the United States by those "immoral" and "cruel" American doctors.

To have to decide whether to study overseas under maternal pressure gave this student an opportunity to learn about herself in terms of her suitability for a sojourn and her ability and personality. It proved to be right that she decided, after a year of working through her psychological problems, to settle down in Taiwan instead of staying in the United States. This experience also enabled her to be free from her mother's domination and to be more independent in deciding about her own life.

Klein and colleagues (1974) found that many American students went overseas simply to escape their own system for awhile, or to continue a moratorium, often sanctioned by their parents, in adopting adult responsibility and commitment. Thus, going overseas is a way of postponing psychosocial or psychosexual maturity. This phenomenon was also found in our Chinese students.

Another example illustrates a student whose sojourn is motivated not for study, but to escape from parental domination, to avoid adult commitment, and to postpone psychosocial maturity. This client was an unhappy medical graduate from a most prestigious national university, to which he had gained admittance on the third attempt at the entrance examination. He was the eldest son of four siblings, and studied medicine under the pressure of his physician father. His class attendance was poor and his school records were marginal through his college years. As soon as he completed one year of compulsory military service after graduation from medical college, he applied for an internship to a small general hospital near New York and was accepted. During the interview, it was found that going to the United States was the only way sanctioned by his parents in which he could avoid the marriage which they had arranged for him. He expected to spend a couple of easy years, after which he hoped to be able to do what he wanted.

Going out is sometimes used by an individual to solve his psychological difficulties at home, especially in regard to becoming independent. By going abroad, the person may be able to escape from a rather dependent family situation into what he perceives as an independent way of life. This has been pointed out in studies of Peace Corps volunteers and of missionary candidates who request overseas service (Smith 1966; Paluszny and Zrull 1971). This mechanism was also observed in our Chinese students. The following case, of a neurotic student, is an illustration.

This was a twenty-five-year-old single male, a graduate in agricultural chemistry from a provincial university. He was one of twenty-five students who volunteered to serve as subjects in our study of the orientation program arranged by the USIS in Taipei for Chinese students about to go to the United States. After filling out the questionnaires, he requested one of the authors to see him privately, in order to talk about his problems, for which he thought he might be in need of psychiatric help.

Since his high-school days he had been suffering from headaches, dizziness, difficulty in concentration, and "impaired memory." The symptoms were aggravated during the examination period, when he had to concentrate and memorize. In considering his plan to go overseas, he was worried that these symptoms might affect his study. He also had a series of psychophysiological symptoms and a history of consulting several eye and ear, nose, and throat specialists, and finally psychiatrists, during his four years of college.

The development of his symptoms can be traced to his family environment and parental attitudes toward his study. The parents both came from a lower socioeconomic background, had only sixth-grade educations, and both had to work very hard to raise the socioeconomic status of the family. The mother was the dominant figure of the family and had high expectations for the patient, the eldest of four siblings, to succeed. This high expectation was greatly intensified when his father's small business prospered and the family financial situation improved.

Though the patient was near the top of his class throughout his three years of junior high school, he was neurotic about and afraid of failure in examinations and thus was driven to study very hard. This hard study and exhaustion of mental energy resulted in a duodenal ulcer in the final year of junior high school. From then on, his school records started to decline, and the above-mentioned neurotic and physiological symptoms began to appear. Worst of all, he failed the entrance examination to the prestigious high school which his parents wanted him to attend, and had to get into another one. He studied even harder in order to get into medical college. What frustrated him and his parents most was his failure in getting into medical college, and he ascribed all this failure to his physiological and mental symptoms.

The patient would stay at the university dormitory during his summer and winter vacations, as he wanted to be away from home and parental pressure. He seldom participated in extracurricular activities and associated with only a few selected friends. Through four years of college, he suffered from mental and physical symptoms and became quite hypochondriacal. His excessive concern about his physical health appeared to serve as a defense mechanism against anxiety over his academic failure and guilt feelings toward his parents. In connection with his sojourn, he anticipated a great deal of difficulty in regard to his health, study, and adjustment to a new living environment, but on the other hand, he wanted to be free from parental pressure and family dependency and to be able to stand on his own feet. It was predicted that this student would be in need of psychological or psychiatric consultation in the United States.

There seemed to be more neurotic symptoms among the male students than the females, while more psychophysiological symptoms and physical health problems were found among female students than males. The explanation for this finding might be that females are more vulnerable to physical stresses and tend to somatize their emotional difficulties, while in males, psychological defense mechanisms are more used against anxiety. Very similar findings have been found among Chinese college students at home. Alexander and colleagues (1976) and Yeh and colleagues (1972) found that the stress of Asian students was more likely to be experienced in the form of physical complaints, which led them to seek medical rather than psychological help. The following is an illustration of psychophysiological symptoms that emerged in a female student prior to going on sojourn.

This applicant was a twenty-one-year-old female, a graduate in plant pathology from a prestigious national university. While filling out the questionnaires, her face suddenly got pale. She complained of dizziness, nausea, and headache, and finally had to lie down for an hour before she could continue with her questionnaires. A brief interview with her revealed that she was the third of five siblings, the oldest of whom was studying in the United States. The patient had been suffering from a series of physical symptoms which seemed to be emotional in origin. The onset had been two years previously, following an appendectomy. Two weeks after the operation, while she was still in the hospital, she suddenly developed a gait disturbance for which no neurological sign was found, and conversion hysteria was highly suspected. Since then she had been suffering from poor appetite, anorexia, dizziness, occasional fainting episodes, and premenstrual tension with severe abdominal pain which needed analgesics. She recognized that these symptoms were associated with emotional factors, but failed to explain what these were. She anticipated a great deal of difficulty with American food and her physical health in the United States.

Personality disorder was suspected in three of the students in our sample. Careful study of these cases showed that they were in trouble at home mainly because of unsolved parent-child conflicts, and that they might do better abroad where they would be shielded from direct conflict. The following case history illustrates this theme.

This person, a twenty-five-year-old single male graduate in economics from a provincial university, suffered from a suspected personality disorder and had been in trouble with family members, but was predicted to do better abroad with or without professional help. The interview with him had to be brief as he showed much anxiety, open suspicion, and reluctance while filling in the questionnaire. He refused to write his name but wrote in English, "I am sorry I can't give you satisfactory answers, my mind has been inactive and sluggish recently." He told me with anger that he did not like to be investigated on private matters, quoting an episode in which he almost got into a fight with a security officer during his military service, when he thought the officer was investigating his private affairs.

This student had been seen by one of the authors, Yeh, several times, at the request of the patient's father, while the boy was still in high school. This patient indicated that he participated in the study only out of courtesy because of the previous association. The reason for the previous consultations was hostility and antagonistic behavior to his father. He would openly criticize his father and even interfere with his father's practice as a dentist. He also tried to discipline and dominate his brothers, behaving like a father-substitute. When things did not go as he wished, he would throw a big temper tantrum, and sometimes was even violent toward his father. On one occasion he shut himself in his room, would not come out to dine with the family, and threatened to kill anybody who tried to get into his room. In spite of his behavior problems at home, he appeared to be an outgoing and highly sociable young man outside of the family setting. He had always been interested in English and associated with several Americans, to whom he gave an impression of "an active, frank, but could be a little rude young guide." Once, in his college days, he represented his college in the English speech contest, which he won.

His father stressed that this boy would be a great problem and even a threat to him if he were to stay at home after graduating from college. So his father encouraged or even pushed the subject to go to the United States for study, hoping that he might do better by being away from his family and from Taiwan. The diagnostic impression of this case was personality disorder, though he had once been suspected of schizophrenia. This patient may have some problems in his adjustment in the United States, and may need professional help. But with this support, he may do better in the United States than he would have at home, where he would be exposed to continuing conflict with his father.

General Discussion

As reported in this chapter and earlier papers, paranoid manifestations appeared to be the most prevalent of the psychiatric symptoms of Chinese students who broke down during study in the United States (Yeh 1972, 1976). This finding was explained by Yeh (1972) on the basis of some of the characteristics of traditional Chinese culture and the contemporary social environment at home. Paranoid symptoms have, however, been also prevalent among other psychotic foreign students in the United States, particularly those from non-Western countries (Alexander et al. 1976; Zunin and Rubin 1967). These findings suggest that paranoid formations are more common among sojourners from non-Western developing countries in developed Western countries than among those who travel in the opposite direction, such as Westerners in Hong Kong, Bangkok, or Peace Corps personnel in Southeast Asia. The greater the cultural distance, the greater the difficulties in adaptation and psychological adjustment. The sojourners who travel to the West may be regarded as deprived, while those who travel in the opposite direction may be regarded as privileged. In the former case, sojourners are more subject to pressures to conform to the host culture, while in the latter case, the culture of the host countries may be more or less aspiring to conform to the traveler's culture. Depression, neurosis, alcoholism, and sexual disorders among Western expatriates in Hong Kong, as reported by Yap (1972), and marital problems and drug addiction among the adolescents of the United States government-affiliated officials in Bangkok, as reported by Kojak (1974), seem to be the prevalent psychiatric disorders among sojourners of the latter type.

ROLE CONFLICT, SELF-CONFIDENCE, ADULT ACCULTURATION, AND PERSONALITY

In studies of cross-cultural adaptation, focusing on a special array of problems unique to foreign students, such as culture shock, may be potentially misleading. The more experiences we have with our Chinese students, the more we come to recognize that role conflicts and loss of self-confidence and self-esteem seem to be the main contributors to their maladaptation.

"Role conflict" refers to the degree of correspondence versus dissimilarity between home and host values and expectations. It defines the amount of change required for adaptation, and can be regarded as a social-psychological redefinition of the concept of cultural distance. Academic and social adjustment should be easier when role conflict is minimal and more difficult when role conflict is severe. This was supported by Bochner (1972) in his study of foreign students attending universities in Australia. He emphasized that the learning of a new culture was contingent on the student's acquiring expectation patterns that were compatible with his new social system.

In regard to the role conflicts facing foreign students, Bochner (1972) stressed the importance of the transitional role of a young adult, besides the role of a foreigner and the role of a student. This aspect of role conflict in the developmental history of the student's personality seems to be overlooked or less emphasized in the study of cross-cultural student adaptation. The great majority of student sojourners are in the stage of early adulthood, which is a time for establishing and testing one's identity as a grown-up and mature person. The overseas students are not immune to the problems of psychosocial development during this stage of the life cycle. This psychosocial turmoil takes on a distinct character when a young person is maturing in an alien culture. When a young adult is suddenly transplanted from one cultural milieu to a different one, his existing socialization—his values, social attitudes, religious beliefs, political identity, and behavioral norms—may be of limited use in his new cultural context, and this may lead to serious adjustment difficulties and, in the case of vulnerable individuals, to psychiatric disorders.

One particularly acute problem that foreign students face is the loss of status and esteem. At home, recognition and status are usually high, but abroad such students' special appeal is at best only temporary and much too bound up with the "foreign" role. This status loss has been conceptualized as role shock (Higbee 1969). The condition is acute, and leads visitors to be hypersensitive about their status and to find ways of coping or compensating that are often misunderstood or that lead to out-and-out rejections by host nationals. In this regard, we are in agreement with Walton (1967) and others who concluded that "the foreign student's problems are more student's than foreign."

An individual's response and vulnerability to role shock and loss of self-confidence are very much determined by his personality. Those who adjust well at home are able to cope effectively with changes of social role, continue to maintain self-confidence and self-esteem, and adjust well during overseas study. The ideal adaptation of a foreign student would involve only minimal changes in behavior and attitudes, in those areas essential for the student to achieve his goals. This would allow the student to establish friendly, positive, and mutually supportive relationships with host nationals, but would not lead to permanent alienation from the home culture.

This kind of time-limited adaptation and rapid behavior change requires certain mediating capacities in the student's personality, such as tolerance of ambiguity, flexibility, willingness to experiment with the new, sensitivity to oneself and to social cues (especially to implicit assumptions and expectations in social situations), ability to take roles, and readiness to integrate changed behavior into personal value systems (Kelman 1965). These adaptational strengths will be positively or negatively reinforced by interpersonal experiences and opportunities abroad and by the availability of satisfying anchorages within the home culture. But these adaptational strengths are also largely determined by the personalities of the sojourners. Among those who are vulnerable to role shock and loss of self-esteem and those who develop psychiatric disorders, some may be constitutionally predisposed; for some, overseas study is a way of solving psychological difficulties at home; and for some, overseas study is the blind effort to solve unconscious neurotic conflicts. However, in all instances, the student's personality is a fundamental determining factor of pathology.

IDENTIFYING THE HIGH-RISK STUDENT

The rather high incidence of students in our sample who either broke down while overseas or presented psychiatric symptoms during the predeparture phase indicates the importance of identifying high-risk cases before or at the beginning of their sojourn. Yeh (1972) has emphasized the value of semistructured interviews conducted by experienced psychiatrists or psychologists before the sojourn. These explore the student's sociopsychological background, life experiences, interpersonal relationships, school and occupational history, health history, and ways of coping with emotional difficulties, and are used to predict risks for psychiatric disorders and adjustmental difficulties during sojourn. In the case of major psychiatric disturbance, such as psychosis, prediction by this method should have relatively high validity; but in the case of minor emotional and behavior disorders, such as neurosis, depression, or transient situational maladjustment, the predictive validity may be lower.

In studies of Peace Corps volunteers, unstructured interviews conducted by psychiatrists have not been of value in predicting the development of psychopathology during service overseas (Fisher, Epstein, and Haris 1967; Smith 1966). Some investigators suggest, however, that validity may be increased if the interviews are structured with precisely defined criteria for the diagnosis and the outcome variables to be predicted (Endicott and Spitzer 1972; Murphy and Woodruff 1974; Robins 1969). Thus, in examining fifty missionary candidates, Paluszny and Zrull (1971) were able to recommend accurately that five of them not be sent overseas. Two of those five had depressive symptoms. In the initial interviews with 104 candidates for professional service overseas, King (1975) found, however, that depression was the most common psychiatric syndrome. In a four-year follow-up study of 130 professionals working overseas, the same author found that depressive syndrome was the most common diagnosable psychiatric illness and usually had a good prognosis. She advised, therefore, not to exclude those who showed diagnosable depression from assignment abroad, but rather to identify the syndrome and recommend necessary treatment.

In the predeparture study of eighty-six Chinese students, we established tentative predictions concerning the kind and degree of professional care that students may need during sojourn. These predictions were made not on presence or absence of the manifested symptoms at the time of the study, but rather on the analysis of the student's past developmental and adjustmental history, the way he made the decision to proceed overseas, anticipated difficulties, and adequacy and willingness in emotional preparation to take a new social role and to meet with host nationals. These data are shown in Table 3. The validity of these predictions has not been confirmed.

UNIVERSITY OF WISCONSIN PROJECT

The University of Wisconsin Project is one of the most intensive and systematic longitudinal attempts to identify the high-risk student (Klein et al. 1971). At the time of admission, foreign students were given questionnaires carefully designed to assess variables that might be related to the student's adaptive capacity, to specific stresses that he may encounter, and to his general life-style. This included personal and family history, goals for study, intimacy of contact desired with Americans, adjustment problems anticipated, self-image, image of Americans and of fellow nationals, and two subscales from the MMPI that relate to adaptive capacity in Americans. This questionnaire was given as early as possible, so that it could serve as a predictive index of various patterns of subsequent adaptation and maladaptation. All questionnaire responses were correlated with the following objective indices of adjustment: (1) academic achievement, (2) student's health-service visits, (3) contacts with the counseling center, the psychiatric outpatient department, and hospitalization, (4) contacts with the foreign student office, and (5) follow-up questionnaires given at various time points.

The preliminary analysis of data on Asian students has shown that during the first year of study in the United States, there are seasonal differences in the incidence of health problems, and that the rate of illness at critical times in the academic year, such as Christmas holidays, is predictable from the amount of anticipated homesickness. Those most motivated to reach out to

Table 3. Number of Students at Departure Predicted to Need Professional Help During Their Sojourn and the Kind of Help They Will Require, by Sex and Time Elapsed after Award of First Degree.

Elapsed Time After Graduation

Kind of Help	At Graduation		One Year or More		Completed Graduate School		Total		
	Males	Females	Males	Females	Males	Females	Males	Females	Combined
None	23	7	11	3	7	1	41	11	52
Nonmedical	3	3	4	—	—	—	7	3	10
General Medical	3	3	1	4	1	—	5	7	12
Psychiatric: Mild	1	1	—	3	1	—	2	4	6
Psychiatric: Intensive	4	1	1	—	—	—	5	1	6
TOTAL	34	15	17	10	9	1	60	26	86

Americans are the more vulnerable; they expect more adaptational problems and score relatively low on the personality measures of adaptive capacity. Conversely, this suggests that students with the more favorable adaptive potential are less interested in contacts with host nationals. Over a three-year period, more than forty students out of the sixty studied have visited a psychiatric outpatient department or became inpatients. Complaints have ranged from severe psychotic episodes (usually paranoid in nature) and severe depressions to mild anxiety and neurotic states.

Once language and problems of communication are solved, there seems to be nothing unique about psychiatric illness in the foreign student population. There was a notable absence of cases of drug abuse or aggressive acting-out. Stresses varied at different points in the sojourn. Some students showed symptomatology (usually paranoid manifestations) almost immediately upon their departure from home. Early in the stay, depression was experienced, as students faced loss of family and went through the initial, somewhat lonely, getting-settled-in period. Problems during the middle phase of study were more often precipitated by academic stresses, such as academic failure or dissatisfaction with the chosen field. Later came problems associated with the necessity of resolving emotional or sexual relations with Americans and conflicts about the impending return home. Acute disturbances seemed to be most easily resolved by helping the student deal with situational stresses. Foreign students were found to be especially prone to experience psychological problems in physical terms. Typically, they visited the student health services with psychosomatic and anxiety-based complaints and denied that their problems stemmed from psychological stress (Alexander et al. 1976).

TREATMENT

Foreign students, particularly from Asia, are by and large not open to verbal, insight-oriented methods of treatment by American therapists because of language and cultural differences between student and therapist. They may be better helped by medication, changes of environment, and direct advice or instruction about what they should or should not do. They are generally poor candidates for attempts to expand their range of emotional self-awareness. Klein and colleagues (1971) stress that in order to retain foreign students in treatment, one has to develop very flexible methods, such as accepting irregular attendance, parrying threats to drop out, using short-term supportive psychotherapy, and sometimes even acting as intermediaries with professors and foundation officials. An active involvement of the patient with the conational network was emphasized by Alexander and colleagues (1976).

Yeh (1972) has recommended that Chinese students who have a serious breakdown during their overseas sojourn should be treated by a therapist of the student's own culture, and if such a therapist is not available, the student should be sent back home for treatment. In the case of mild or moderate psychiatric disturbances, however, the question of whether the patient should be advised to return home before completing his studies is one of the most agonizing issues a therapist may have to confront with a foreign-student patient. Returning home may raise in the student fears of being considered a failure or of abrogating a promise to be a special person, and the possibility of being disqualified from progress within the home country's professional or governmental system. The therapist should discuss these matters openly from both the practical and psychological points of view. Some practical measures to smooth the return home were discussed by Alexander and his colleagues (1976).

CROSS-CULTURAL ADAPTATION, PSYCHOPATHOLOGY, AND PERSONAL GROWTH

What do all these findings mean to the student's personal growth? To live in and to adapt to a foreign culture is not easy. Though cross-cultural adaptation often provokes a student's underlying psychopathology, for most sojourners studying abroad provides an opportunity for self-realization and actualization. Interviews with students who returned home after successfully completing their studies revealed that the experiences of working through these crises seemed to prompt personal growth in terms of more objective self-realization and more self-confidence. Even for some psychotic breakdown cases, such as those who were treated intensively at home, Yeh (1976) found that working through their emotional conflicts not only brought about clinical improvement, but also served to strengthen their ego functions. Ten such patients went back to the United States to continue their studies after they completely recovered from their psychoses. Follow-up studies with these patients and their families revealed that they have been doing even better than before with their studies. They seemed to be more confident, independent, and objective, with regard to both themselves and others, and more tolerant of frustration.

Preliminary studies of thirty-eight returned Chinese students revealed some changes in their images of host nationals, of themselves, and of fellow nationals, and also in their social attitudes and values (Yeh 1976). The comparison was made against students who had never had cross-cultural experiences. The changes in the images of Americans and fellow nationals were generally in a negative direction, while the changes in the images of themselves were all positive. These returnees became more confident, identifying themselves more with positive aspects of both the Chinese and the American character, and also became more objective and critical in their perception of Chinese and American people. The changes in social attitudes and values were complex. While they approved of some American and modern values, there were also some areas in which they were more reserved and conservative. For instance, they were more cautious and reserved about enjoying life and skeptical about friendship and equality between the sexes; they admired the values of the traditional Chinese extended, large family, and did not think that females should pursue advanced education "as it may sacrifice their family life." One striking change of attitudes was that the vast majority of the returnees (95 percent) became more cautious and reserved in their striving for westernization, and more aware of and sensitive to the conational's critical eyes. Years of experiences in cross-cultural living seem to make Chinese students more confident, realistic, selective, and objective in evaluating their own culture and appreciating the host culture.

Successful and satisfying adaptation for the cross-cultural student, who is exposed to multiple role crises in addition to the student role that he has to carry, is not easy and cannot be achieved without the risks of pain and loss. As a majority of our returnees put it, the experiences are, however, in the long run worthwhile for young people to try, no matter how hard and painful they may be.

Notes

1. Educational Statistics of the Republic of China, Ministry of Education, Annual Reports.
2. Institute of International Education, Open Doors: A Report on International Exchange, Annual Volumes.
3. From an epidemiological study of mental health problems of college students conducted by Yeh in Taipei during 1963–1967.

References

Alexander, A. A. Workneh, F., Klein, M. H., and Miller, M. H. Psychotherapy and the Foreign Student. In P. Pedersen, W. J. Lonner, and J. G. Draguns (eds.), *Counseling Across Cultures*. Honolulu, Hawaii: University Press of Hawaii, 1976.

Bochner, S. Problems in Culture Learning. In S. Bochner and P. Wicks (eds.), *Overseas Students in Australia*. Sydney: New South Wales University Press, 1972.

Chu, H. M., Yeh, E. K., Klein, M. H., Alexander, A. A., and Miller, M. H. A Study of Chinese Students' Adjustment in the U.S.A. *Acta Psychologica Taiwanica*, 1971, *13*, 206–218.

Du Bois, C. *Foreign Students and Higher Education in the United States.* Washington, D.C.: American Council on Education, 1956.

Endicott, J., and Spitzer, R. C. Current and Past Psychotherapy Scales (CAPPS). *Archives of General Psychiatry*, 1972, *27*, 678–687.

Fisher, J., Epstein, L. J., and Haris, M. R. Validity of the Psychiatric Interview. *Archives of General Psychiatry*, 1967, *17*, 744–750.

Gullahorn, J. T., and Gullahorn, J. E. An Extension of the U-Curve Hypothesis. *Journal of Social Issues*, 1963, *19* (3), 33–47.

Higbee, H. Role Shock: A New Concept. *International Educational and Cultural Exchange*, 1969 (Spring), 71.

Kelman, H. C. The Effects of Participation in a Foreign Specialists' Seminar on Images of Host Country and the Professional Field. *Journal of Applied Behavioral Science*, 1965, *1*, 149–166.

King, L. J. The Depressive Syndrome: A Follow-up Study of 130 Professionals Working Overseas. *American Journal of Psychiatry*, 1975, *132*, 636–640.

Klein, M. H., Alexander, A. A., Tseng, K. H., Miller, M. H., Yeh, E. K., and Chu, H. M. Far Eastern Students in a Big University: Subcultures Within a Subculture. *Bulletin of the Atomic Scientists*, 1971a, *27*, 10–19.

Klein, M. H., Alexander, A. A., Tseng, K. H., Miller, M. H., Yeh, E. K., Chu, H. M., and Workneh, F. The Foreign Student Adaptation Project: Social Experiences of Asian Students in the U.S. *Exchange*, 1971b, *6*, 77–90.

Klein, M. H., Miller, M. H., and Alexander, A. A. When Young People Go Out in the World. In W. P. Lebra (ed.), *Youth, Socialization, and Mental Health.* Honolulu, Hawaii: University Press of Hawaii, 1974.

Kojak, G. The American Community in Bangkok, Thailand: A Model of Social Disintegration. *American Journal of Psychiatry*, 1974, *131*, 1229–1233.

Lehmann, H. E. Unusual Psychiatric Disorders and Atypical Psychoses. In A. M. Freedman and H. I. Kaplan (eds.), *Comprehensive Textbook of Psychiatry.* Baltimore, Md.: Williams and Wilkins, 1967.

Lundstedt, S. An Introduction to Some Evolving Problems in Cross-Cultural Research. *Journal of Social Issues*, 1963, *19* (3), 1–9.

Lysgaard, S. Adjustment in a Foreign Society: Norwegian Fulbright Grantees Visiting the United States. *International Social Science Bulletin*, 1955, *7*, 45–51.

Miller, M. H., Yeh, E. K., Alexander, A. A., Klein, M. H., Tseng, K. H., Workneh, F., and Chu, H. M. The Cross-Cultural Student: Lessons in Human Nature. *Bulletin of the Menninger Clinic*, 1971, *35*, 128–131.

Murphy, G. E., and Woodruff, R. A. Primary Affective Disorders: Selection Efficiency of Two Sets of Diagnostic Criteria. *Archives of General Psychiatry*, 1974, *31*, 181–184.

Paluszny, M., and Zrull, J. P. The New Missionary. *Archives of General Psychiatry*, 1971, *24*, 363–366.

Robins, L. N. Social Correlates of Psychiatric Disorders: Can We Tell Causes From Consequences? *Journal of Health and Social Behavior*, 1969, *10*, 95–104.

Smith, M. B., Explorations in Competence: A Study of Peace Corps Teachers in Ghana. *American Journal of Psychology*, 1966, *21*, 555–566.

Walton, B. *Foreign Student Exchange in Perspective*. Washington, D. C.: Department of State Publication No. 8873, 1967.

Wang, Y. C. *Chinese Intellectuals and the West: 1872–1947*. Chapel Hill, N. C.: University of North Carolina Press, 1966.

Wei, Y. Sociopsychological Variables and Inter-nation Migration: Findings From Interviewing Returnees in the Republic of China. *Bulletin of the Sun Yat-sen Cultural Foundation*, 1971, *7*, 1–17.

Yap, P. M. Koro, a Culture-Bound Depersonalization Syndrome. *British Journal of Psychiatry*, 1965, *111*, 43–50.

_____. Phenomenology of Affective Disorders in Chinese and Other Cultures. In A. V. DeReuck and R. Porter (eds.), *Transcultural Psychiatry*. Boston, Mass.: Little, Brown, 1967.

_____. Mental Illness Among Western Expatriates in a Plural Society: An Exploratory Study. In W. P. Lebra (ed.), *Transcultural Research in Mental Health*. Honolulu, Hawaii: University Press of Hawaii, 1972.

Yeh, E. K. Paranoid Manifestations Among Chinese Students Studying Abroad: Some Preliminary Findings. In W. P. Lebra (ed.), *Transcultural Research in Mental Health*. Honolulu, Hawaii: University Press of Hawaii, 1972.

_____. Cross-Cultural Adaptation and Personal Growth: The Case of Chinese Students. *Acta Psychologica Taiwanica*, 1976, *18*, 95–104.

Yeh, E. K., and Chu, H. M. Who Go and Who Stay? Psychosocial Background of Chinese Students Going for Overseas Study. Paper presented at the Annual Meeting of the Formosan Medical Association, November 1969.

Yeh, E. K., and Chu, H. M. The Images of Chinese and American Character: Cross-Cultural Adaptation by Chinese Students. In W. P. Lebra (ed.), *Youth, Socialization, and Mental Health*. Honolulu, Hawaii: University Press of Hawaii, 1974.

Yeh, E. K., Chu, H. M., Ko, Y. H., Lin, T. Y., and Lee, S. P. Student Mental Health: An Epidemiological Study in Taiwan. *Acta Psychologica Taiwanica*, 1972, *14*, 1–26.

Yeh, E. K., Miller, M. H., Alexander, A. A., Klein, M. H., Tseng, K. H., Workneh, F., and Chu, H. M. The American Student in Taiwan. *International Studies Quarterly*, 1973, *17*, 359–372.

Zunin, L. M., and Rubin, R. T. Paranoid Psychotic Reactions in Foreign Students from Non-Western Countries. *Journal of the American College Health Association*, 1967, *15*, 220–226.

Leila F. Dane

The Use of the Paraprofessional for Treatment of Americans Abroad: A Survey of Theory and Practice

Introduction

This chapter is concerned with some of the problems that Americans face when they live abroad as expatriates. A central assumption of the chapter is that expatriate Americans are likely to encounter more stressful situations than their stateside counterparts, with less recourse for alleviating the stress. The stress of change, even without climatic and cultural differences, implies a shedding of old behavior patterns and an adoption of new ones. For example, it is necessary to acquire information about many mundane but nevertheless vital matters usually taken for granted in one's own culture, such as the location of city streets and neighboring highways, shopping practices, and recreational and educational facilities. Furthermore, the effectiveness of these facilities has to be evaluated, often without sufficient information on which to arrive at a confident judgment.

By borrowing a term widely used in city planning, *infrastructure*, we can get a quick mind's-eye view of the stress imposed upon the psyche during a move: the old personal infrastructure must be eradicated, and a new one built. Culture shock, along with its accompanying confusions of social integration, is a syndrome familiar to psychologists and sociologists; reverse culture shock, or the reentry phenomenon, is currently gaining wide recognition. The added changes of cross-cultural adjustment may in many cases be the straw that breaks the camel's back in terms of personality integration for the expatriate American. This further burden may precipitate even more stress-provoking events, such as marital rupture or major illness, which in turn often lead to depression or alcoholism and years of concerted effort toward recovery. In this chapter, I plan to delve briefly into the realities of life of those Americans who settle in a foreign environment for a prolonged but nevertheless temporary duration, review current countermeasures, and suggest a few new possibilities for preventive therapy for those Americans who recognize their problems and wish to seek help while abroad.

The General Need for Preventive Therapy Abroad

The mobile nature of American society has prompted much study of the effects of changes in life-style. Among the many specialists exploring this phenomenon are organizational psychologists, behavioral scientists, management experts, epidemiologists, and medical sociologists, and there is general agreement that the effectiveness of a man at his new job is directly related to his family's adjustment to the move. Our Western concern for efficiency has led to further interest in revealing the underlying elements in this common-sense causal relationship.

Holmes and Rahe (1967) have studied what they call Life Change Units and their effect on the body. Their research suggests that individuals who have experienced change in established patterns are more likely to become ill than individuals following a stable life sequence. Furthermore, both happy events, such as marriage or the birth of a wanted child, and unhappy events, such as divorce or the death of a loved one, seem to be equally capable of producing medical or psychiatric symptoms. Thus, there appears to be something about change per se which is distressful to the human organism.

Based on their research, Holmes and Rahe (1967) took a number of life events and arranged them into a rank order according to the magnitude of change implied in each set of circumstances. Then each event was given a weight, reflecting the hypothesized negative impact on the individual of that particular experience. The accompanying table (Table 1) sets out some of the life events, their rank order on the magnitude-of-change dimension, and the weight computed for each event, expressed as a mean value on a hundred-point scale. This table can be used to determine the sum of Life Change Units, or LCUs, that a person has just undergone. Thus, if a person has just been divorced and simultaneously commenced a jail sentence, his LCU score would be 73 + 63, or 136.

An implication of the Holmes and Rahe theory is that an individual's vulnerability to physical and mental disorder will increase with greater life changes, that is, that the magnitude of an individual's LCU score will reflect the magnitude of stress he is experiencing. This hypothesis has obvious consequences for persons who go to live in an alien culture. In applying the LCU scale to Americans moving abroad or back home, ranks 15, 16, often 18, 20, 22, 28, 29, 31, 32, 34, 35, 36, 38, 39, and 40 are appropriate to each head of household, totaling at least 280 LCUs; ranks 26, 28, 29, 31, 32, 34, 35, 36, often 38, 39, and 40 are appropriate to wives, totaling at least 200 LCUs; ranks 28, 29, 32, 33, 34, 35, 36, often 38, 39, and 40 are appropriate to children, totaling at least 175 LCUs.

However, to compute accurate cross-cultural change units from the Holmes and Masuda approach would be relatively complicated. For example, language change would have to be measured according to language-learning

Table 1. Social Readjustment Rating Scale: Life Change Units

Rank	Life Event	Mean Value	Rank	Life Event	Mean Value
1	Death of spouse	100	23	Son or daughter leaving home	29
2	Divorce	73	24	Trouble with in-laws	29
3	Marital separation	65	25	Outstanding personal achievement	28
4	Jail term	63			
5	Death of close family member	63	26	Wife begins or stops work	26
6	Personal injury or illness	53	27	Begin or end school	26
7	Marriage	50	28	Change in living conditions	25
8	Fired at work	47			
9	Marital reconciliation	45	29	Revision of personal habits	24
10	Retirement	45	30	Trouble with boss	23
11	Change in health of family member	44	31	Change in work hours or conditions	20
12	Pregnancy	40	32	Change in residence	20
13	Sex difficulties	39	33	Change in schools	20
14	Gain of new family member	39	34	Change in recreation	19
15	Business readjustment	39	35	Change in church activities	19
16	Change in financial state	38	36	Change in social activities	18
17	Death of close friend	37	37	Mortgage or loan less than $10,000	17
18	Change to different line of work	36	38	Change in sleeping habits	16
19	Change in number of arguments with spouse	35	39	Change in number of family get-togethers	15
20	Mortgage over $10,000	31	40	Change in eating habits	15
21	Foreclosure of mortgage or loan	30	41	Vacation	13
22	Change in responsibilities at work	29	42	Christmas	12
			43	Minor violations of the law	11

SOURCE: Holmes and Rahe 1967, p. 216.

facility, percentage of meaningful communication in the foreign language, and—for children—current cognitive development level; for instance, an American dyslexic first or second grader attending a French school in an Arab country would rate quite high. Similarly, assessing the cultural effects of the host country would require a complicated scale comprising values for deviance of local social patterns—overt and covert—from country of origin. Climatic change would lend itself to a similar treatment.

Nevertheless, despite some of the obvious measurement problems, there is little doubt that many expatriates score well in excess of 200 LCUs, simply because of change in the cultural environment. This by itself places them in the category of 50 percent risk of contracting a major illness, suffering an injury, or developing severe depression, schizophrenia, or alcoholism within the next two years. Add to the aforementioned totals the possibility of divorce, death of a spouse, or marital separation or reconciliation, and the expatriate is almost unerringly projected into the major risk category (over 300 LCUs), where he has more than an 85 percent chance of major illness within two years.

In another research project correlating LCUs with illness, Wyler, Masuda, and Holmes (1971)

> asked two groups of physicians to rate the graveness of 125 illnesses: we gave the seriousness of a peptic ulcer an arbitrary score of 500. Using the physician's ratings, we scored 42 diseases experienced by 232 patients. We also computed life change scores for these patients. There was a highly significant correlation between life change scores and chronic disease (leukemia, cancer, heart attack, schizophrenia, menstrual difficulties and warts). Patients who experienced the more serious life crises were also more likely to get the serious chronic diseases. (Holmes and Masuda 1972, p. 106)

Despite all of these hazards, government foreign services do function, and with a reasonable degree of efficiency and productivity. This suggests that the people in the foreign service may have special talents, probably in the area of being able to adapt to unusual social situations. Foreign service families move more often and more intercontinentally than do families who move for business, pleasure, or academic reasons. When discussing therapeutic countermeasures, I shall focus on what foreign service families do. A clear distinction has to be made between the job incumbent and his or her dependents. The person in the job is much more likely to function well than are spouses and children. This is almost certainly due to the continuity provided by the job itself, a continuity absent in the lives of the dependents.

The head of household is career-oriented, and his or her decision to move is clearly related to that psychological reality; the dependents go along with the decision and adapt or play out defiances at various levels of understanding. Thomas Szasz (1972) addresses this problem by clarifying the psychology of hinting and the protective function of indirect communication:

> Whenever language is used to transmit information, direct communication will predominate. . . . On the other hand, when the relationship between two people is emotionally significant but uncertain—or when either feels dependent or threatened or inhibited by the other—then the stage is set for the exchange of indirect messages between them. There is good reason for this—namely, that indirect messages serve two useful functions—firstly, to transmit information, and secondly, to *explore and modify the relationship* between the communicants. This explanatory function of indirect communications may include the aim of attempting, however subtly, to change the other person's attitude to make him more receptive to our needs and desires. . . . (p. 143, italics supplied)

> Whether a person considers bodily diseases and personal problems acceptable or unacceptable will depend upon his system of values. In today's health-conscious atmosphere, bodily diseases are acceptable, but problems in living—lip-service to the contrary notwithstanding—are not. Indeed, they are *especially unacceptable in a medical setting*. Hence, people—patients and physicians alike—are inclined to deny personal problems and to communicate in terms of bodily illnesses: for example, a man worried about his job or marriage may seek medical attention for hyperacidity and insomnia; and his physician is likely to treat him with antacids and tranquillizers. (p. 147, italics supplied)

If Szasz were a member of the Department of State Medical Division, perhaps he would have written ". . . a patient worried about the effect of too many LCUs on his or her job, school grades, health, or family relations. . . ." The thirty doctors and fifty nurses throughout the world attending to U.S. government foreign service families report that 50 to 65 percent of the symptoms presented are psychosomatic ailments, and that aside from the many who manage through administrative channels to transfer out of a difficult situation, three families per week are medically evacuated back to the United States for reasons of health or failure to adjust. Likewise, business statistics reveal that one-fourth of the Americans abroad fail to complete their assignments.

If funds were available, a computer-assisted investigation could relate the incidence of maladjustment to Life Change Units, using large samples covering specific geographic and cultural domains. Unfortunately, present management sophistication is not yet that advanced. The U.S. Foreign Trade Council and the Department of State have recently started meeting periodically to identify common goals and approaches. Perhaps they will one day address this possibility.

Over the last decade we have seen in the United States a rapid increase in community health clinics as well as concerted efforts among large business firms to ease the process of moving within the United States. For those Americans abroad, the establishment of specifically designated therapeutic agencies offering preventive programs and crisis-oriented treatment (in the sense of support systems) is a much more complicated problem. Business and government agencies tend to respond to the adjustment problem by refining personnel selection procedures. But this tends to miss the point, since the pressures on the dependents are dissimilar to those impinging on the employee-head of household. Furthermore, the employee at the time of hiring will almost certainly be naive about the job-related family mental health picture and, upon confronting the stresses involved in a move, is likely to immerse himself in his work—a reaction guaranteed to compound rather than compensate for the adjustment problem.

Recognition of the situation and consciousness-raising are two strategies that could provide a partial answer to the problem, and there are already concerted efforts along these lines. However, it is my understanding that for the most part these efforts are not satisfactory, in that they are directed toward the wives, thus communicating the message that though the career is for the husband, the problem is solely for the wife. The correction of this detail is clearly the responsibility of management. Large-corporation and government families preparing to move abroad are given literature on culture shock, on cross-cultural communication techniques, on education and child-rearing abroad, and on reverse culture shock upon return to the States. This literature highlights specifics such as the change in family valences, exposure to special sexual practices, and the vague but pervasive sense of alienation.

Sidney L. Werkman, formerly lecturer at the Foreign Service Institute of the State Department and senior psychiatric consultant for the Peace Corps, has made a significant contribution in his 1972 paper, "Hazards of Rearing Children in Foreign Countries." Through the use of case reports, Dr. Werkman points out that inhibitions, depression, dependency and fearfulness, confusion in sexual identity, and cultural value conflicts are recurrent pitfalls for children of Americans abroad.

Dr. Jerome V. Holland, child psychiatrist, has further stated that children who move more than twice after the age of three constitute a special risk group for emotional disturbances. According to Holland (1971), change of residence of a child is analogous to a change in parent. It involves a complete change of environment—established securities, friendships, and social patterns—possibly resulting in learning problems, underachievement, fighting, disruption in class, refusal to conform to class standards, truancy, overt anger and rage, lethargic attitudes, wandering off, and arguing in class.

The Limited Value of Folk Therapy

Folk therapy is a term that describes nonanalytical group acting-out sessions in which emotional release is triggered through the use of ritual. Gypsy campfire evenings are an extreme example and reveal the deep historical roots of this process. Ari Kiev (1972), in his discussion of cultural responses to social change, points out that "folk therapies may be viewed as culture-specific techniques and strategies for assisting troubled individuals to cope with conflict and stress. . . . Many disturbed people are able to adjust . . . because of their involvement in a sect or movement. In such cases personal problems mesh with sectarian ideologies and with group behavior patterns or rituals, which are often indistinguishable from idiosyncratic behavior patterns. . . . Folk therapies thus contain many elements for conflict resolution, corrective emotional experience, and the prevention of emotional illness" (pp. 13-14).

The process of folk therapy is at work in one form or another in many corners of the world among American wives, who get together over daytime card games or Christmas bazaar handwork sessions and exchange anecdotes relating to the difficulties of the local servants, schools, traffic, or cocktail-party practices. American children get together and dwell upon memories of milkshakes and hamburgers and TV back home.

Folk therapy need not be confined to contact with fellow expatriates. The cross-culturally comfortable individual whose ego identity is not jeopardized by differentiating himself from his fellow Americans can involve himself in local movements that reflect his own philosophical or political propensities. This is a more intellectual approach, nevertheless allowing emotional release through group identification. An example of this approach to folk therapy was the number of Americans abroad who joined local demonstrations against U.S. involvement in Vietnam. However, cross-cultural group identification through politically sensitive issues is generally not condoned among Americans representing their government abroad, and the backlash is likely to be even greater than the emotional release.

An Approach to Cross-Cultural Conflicts

Folk therapy is not the only answer to cross-cultural adjustment; more studied approaches have been devised. One example of a systematic, theory-derived approach is the work of Stewart (1971). Stewart conceives of a cultural pattern as an integrated whole with five distinct components: perception of the self and the individual, perception of the world, motivation, form of relation to others, and form of activity. Every cultural assumption or value falls into at least one of these categories.

These elements of the individual's psychological field have relevance to the theme of this chapter, in that some aspect of culture shock is often the precipitating factor in personality disintegration. Complaints about the host culture are indeed an attempt to deal with the problems creating the personality disorder. Facets of the host culture are the least threatening subjects to deal with verbally, and the first ones to be contended with in the unraveling process necessary to reveal the "core" problems. If there is a possibility of diminishing the mean value of the Life Change Units, through paraprofessional help, by alleviating the stress factor as it occurs, then we may be able to obviate the high illness risk factor. I am not denying the current general psychiatric opinion that culture complaints are not the real problem in a personality disorder; I am proposing that the discussion of these complaints has the twofold effect of alleviating mounting stress and offering the individual the opportunity for personal insight and growth.

For those seeking cross-cultural effectiveness, Stewart (1971) proposes four goals: establish conceptual cross-cultural bridges; induce an attitude of cultural relevance; facilitate self-understanding; and identify facilitating and interfering factors. For example:

> The concept of the individual self is an integral assumption of American culture, so deeply ingrained that Americans ordinarily do not question it. They naturally assume that each person has his own separate identity which should be recognized and stressed. . . . When confronted with people who do not identify the self with the individual, Americans react with bewilderment, since the idea of the self not being located in the individual is culturally preposterous for most Americans. Yet the Japanese point of reference seems to be the network of obligations among the members of a group—the social nexus. The consequence of this definition of the self is that congeniality in social interaction becomes the predominant value. To varying degrees a similar assumption pervades through the Orient. The stress on the relations among individuals rather than on the individual himself can be summarized in the concepts of "face," "prestige," and "respect." [What an American may] suggest as objective and practical courses of action may be rejected to spare someone's face. (pp. 66–68)

Under these circumstances, an American may feel frustrated by the rejection, but by recognizing the importance of the social nexus, the American in Japan can establish a cross-cultural bridge, decide to propose courses of action which are relevant to the Japanese cultural assumption, seek to understand his own reactions, and recognize those factors that help or harm the situation. This type of introspection does not come easily to many people, even with the help of literature pertaining to cultural assumptions and differences. Discussion with others in a structured learning situation is more fruitful.

Werkman (1972) states: "Some complications [of overseas living] may result in overt psychiatric disorders, others in character distortions of varying degrees. Many of them can be avoided, minimized or resolved through anticipation, open discussion, informed planning and decisive action" (p. 992). The current lack of facilities for such action must be frustrating to the individual seeking help, and the only alternative in many locations—medical evacuation—can be very damaging to the ego. The stigma of medical evacuation (return to the States for psychiatric treatment) must be a very distressing experience, not just for the patient, but for his family as well.

Paraprofessionals: A Logical Source of Therapy

In a discussion of why it would be advantageous to devise paraprofessional systems of preventive mental health programs or therapy for Americans abroad, there are several factors to be considered. First and foremost is the large number of educated individuals who are abroad because they are accompanying their spouses, whose work has taken them abroad. Upon arrival in a new city, these people are in a position to restructure their daytime activities, and there are many who are both capable of and interested in self-fulfilling involvement of this type. The paraprofessional as well as the client is offered an avenue of personal growth and human understanding; "a better separation of those factors in personality that are culturally rather than biologically determined becomes possible" (Seward 1960, p. 16).

Many cities, of course, have professionally trained psychiatrists and clinical psychologists, but various barriers exist that may prevent the expatriate from seeking their help. For instance, professional therapy is permitted to people holding security-sensitive jobs only after satisfactory completion of a rigid security check of the therapist. There is also very often a cultural inhibition, an overidentification with ethnic differences. The troubled person may, however, be prepared to discuss with someone of his own culture the very cultural factors that are keeping him from seeking professional help or helping himself, and eventually, according to the degree of his need, help him to seek it. This notion of degree is relevant to the personal evaluation of the importance of the problem; several "minor" problems (change in work conditions, residence, schools, recreation, social activities, number of family get-togethers, eating habits) may not seem worthy of a psychiatrist's help. Considering that many American families move from one culture to another as often as every two years, there is room for the accumulation of a massive amount of minor stresses, and little opportunity to find and profit from relations with an empathic friend.

When considering mental health issues, the first question is whether the problem is external or internal, that is, can it be solved by the establishment of specific programs and regulations, or is it one of dependence or lack of insight requiring some kind of talking-out exercise? The specific, focused problems are best handled by special action committees. Paraprofessional assistance here is imaginative, usually spontaneous, and action-oriented. Some examples are the development of a bank of skills drawn from the pool of available community resources, the making of a film or videotape aimed at easing the teenage reentry process into stateside schools, and the establishment of child-care facilities during parent orientation courses. The foregoing are actual instances of this type of paraprofessional activity among U.S. government foreign service families today.

Internal problems, on the other hand, must be dealt with according to the degree of dichotomy between behavior and awareness. The strategy used to bridge this gap is not analytical in the Freudian sense. Rather, it depends heavily on a discussion of the alternatives that the local community has to offer. Thus, the technique consists of a sociotherapeutic bringing-into-awareness of new possibilities, aimed at the solution of difficulties in life-style. For example, paraprofessionals among U.S. foreign service families are working sociotherapeutically in assisting parents and children in the choice of schools and curricula abroad, emphasizing techniques of maintaining continuity within the educational experience and the importance of preparing the children for the new educational setting. They are running spontaneously formed workshops on women's consciousness-raising, values-clarification exercises, and more general, open-forum dissent channels sanctioned by management. Working together with professionals on the sociotherapeutic level, they are organizing and running retreats and seminars focused on the reentry phenomenon, assertiveness training, community diagnosis, and action planning techniques. Most of these paraprofessionals, if not all, are working for no money, filling a need in a grass-roots way as expatriate families react to the inadequacies of the system and to socioeconomic changes such as women's liberation and inflation. The various endeavors tend to be short-lived because of lack of sustained support. The energetic originators of programs move away or lose momentum because of lack of positive feedback from management.

Within the Department of State in Washington, a Mental Health Advisory Committee was recently established. It is comprised of professionals from the Medical Division and professionals and paraprofessionals from among foreign service families who have been trained through the community action courses. Its purpose is to serve as a central communications point for all the community action programs run by professionals and paraprofessionals abroad. Owing to the retirement of its founder, the committee is now floundering from lack of support from management and lack of self-image. Its membership needs to be expanded to include representatives from personnel and policy planning, and it needs funding. Management is reluctant to fund the committee, basically because management has not developed an appreciation for the value of paraprofessional assistance in mobile societies. I hear an overconcern with concepts such as expertise and authority. Though this reaction is to be expected among conservatives who have not thought through the role of community support systems available to the geographically stable, it does not help the many families who are medically evacuated back to the States.

As a general rule, any attempt to treat severe personality disorders should be made strictly under the supportive aegis of the experienced professional, wherein the built-in safety feature of his presence protects the patient from the paraprofessional's sometimes unavoidable mistakes. However, it should be noted that Poser (1966) studied the effects on hospitalized chronic schizophrenics of lay therapists, as opposed to psychiatrists and psychiatric social workers, in group therapy, and discovered that lay therapists achieved slightly better results. Margaret Rioch offered an explanation by suggesting that professionals are "engaged not simply in treatment of the mentally ill, but in pushing back the frontier of knowledge" (Rioch 1966, p. 291).

An intervention technique that may be particularly appropriate to cross-cultural settings is the procedure of cotherapy, or the use of more than one therapist to treat the client. In cross-cultural cotherapy, the disturbed expatriate is presumably avoiding medical evacuation and would prefer the opportunity for rapid recovery. The local professional could call upon the assistance of the paraprofessional—a cultural cohort of the client—for a quicker interpretation of cultural versus interpersonal conflicts, and because his schedule might not accommodate the patient's desire for concentrated therapy. The immediate therapist-therapist and patient-therapist feedback "facilitates rapid insight and growth while maintaining the prolonged intensity of concentration on a single patient which is impossible in the one-to-one relationship and which is rarely manifested in groups" (Piaget and Serber 1970, p. 116).

This advantage over orthodox therapeutic relationships stems from several unique factors in cotherapy. The presence of two or more therapists facilitates the interpretation and handling of transference and countertransference. There is a decidedly purer therapist role definition. "Individual therapy can result in ambivalences within a patient regarding his unconscious interpretation of the therapist's own role. In co-therapy the ambivalence can be externalized and resolved: The dominant therapist invokes a father image; the supportive therapist, a mother image. . . . In particular, love-hate ambivalences can be worked through more efficiently" (Piaget and Serber 1970, p. 114). Therapeutic impasses which may result from transference or counter-transference difficulties or therapist oversight are more easily resolved. Furthermore, Dryud and Rioch (1953) have reported that cotherapy may result in increased therapist motivation, providing the patient with a more dynamic interaction. Yalom and Handlon (1965) have noted a "humanizing" effect on the patient. As the client recognizes that the therapists do care and want to help and that there is no absolute and singular solution, he realizes that the real source of help is internal and that like his therapist, he must accept the "responsibility in spite of uncertainty" that is a major and necessary component of mental health.

Past instances of local professional therapists working with American paraprofessional assistants have been rare. This special kind of leader-disciple partnership is time-consuming and demands a considerable degree of cross-cultural openness on the part of both therapists. Local professionals trained in the United States are, by virtue of their own experience, more prone to this relationship than others. As the word spreads that this innovative approach to therapy is successful, more professionals will consider this possibility, for the relative loss in time and money is more than compensated for by the creative invigoration of the new therapeutic process. During my own experience as a supportive therapist in cross-cultural dual therapy, I noted on several occasions that patients were acknowledging the therapists' capacity to relate openly to each other in the patient's presence as an effective cross-cultural model. Patients also appreciated the opportunity during one-to-one sessions to discuss the absent therapist's in-culture and cross-cultural identities.

The overall effectiveness of paraprofessional help is contingent upon public awareness of paraprofessional availability. I strongly recommend that business and government management reassess their tendency to ascribe adjustment problems to that nebulous nomenclature over which they have no control—"social change"—and that they develop a policy which would draw attention to and fund paraprofessional programs. Consular officers, teachers, members of the medical community, missionaries, and the paraprofessionals themselves are the first to know of the resources available to a community. Local newsletters and bulletin-board announcements should be used to inform the general public. The dissemination of information concerning availability of paraprofessionals is vital to the success of any program. Insufficient public acceptance of the paraprofessionals would have an adverse effect on the morale and willingness of the paraprofessionals to become involved in this important activity.

Training

Training for the paraprofessional expecting to work with Americans abroad should be carried out in the United States. The optimal arrangement would be to use the facilities of an established center of a hospital or university already teaching basic communication skills in small groups, preferably through microcounseling or a similar technique incorporating practice interviews and videotape analysis. By using observational media, the trainees are better able to translate behavioral events into theoretical concepts, and conceptions of therapists' activities into behavioral events. The trainee who reviews videotaped interviews with the trainer—first model interviews, then taped sessions of his own—has the opportunity to recognize errors, to receive suggestions for more appropriate interviewer behavior, to apply these new skills in the ensuing interview situation, and then to recognize the consequences in client response. Matarazzo, Saslow, and Matarazzo (1956) classified interviewer errors into three main types—errors of focus, faulty role definition, and faulty facilitation of communication—which may be readily recognized and corrected through the use of videotapes and microcounseling and then incorporated into a behavioral approach to training. These skills are put to advantageous use in any interviewing situation, from helping a student understand the factors affecting his faulty study habits to helping the depressed patient develop more satisfying patterns of behavior; they are well tailored to the individual who does not know beforehand of the exact paraprofessional activities he may be called upon to engage in at his point of destination.

Cultural material may be handled individually according to the individual's destination. Suggested reading material may be readily obtained from the language departments of colleges and universities. Courses on American culture, foreign civilization, and psychological anthropology are effective in raising one's level of awareness of cultural assumptions.

Since there is no consensus of opinion concerning the necessary before-training capacities of the paraprofessional, individuals who display a desire to become paraprofessionals and who wish to develop their empathic communication are generally accepted for training. Anthony and Wain (1971) report that pretraining ability in empathic communication tends to predict post-training ability ($r = .35$), but also (and more to the point in relation to training) that the ability to profit from empathy training tends to predict the ability to profit from further empathy training ($r = .61$). Grief and Hogan (1973) discuss empathy in terms of interpersonal adequacy and, through the use of the California Psychological Inventory, have isolated three dimensions or attributes of this trait: a tolerant, even-tempered disposition; an ascendant, sociable interpersonal style; and humanistic sociopolitical attitudes.

In view of the established positive value of the paraprofessional, those individuals whose talents lend themselves to counseling should explore the possibilities of training to become paraprofessionals before departure to their new cultural situation. It is almost certain that channels of personal growth will be open to them as they engage in paraprofessional activity. The availability of funds is another question; the purse-string controllers—management—need consciousness-raising. Until paraprofessional effectiveness gains the sort of public acceptance now accorded to professsional therapists, researchers, and hospital and community health administrators, the establishment of a working situation for the trained professional will place demands on his capacities for enterprise and innovation.

But the need exists. Transient American communities are growing larger. Some personal problems are common; more are unique and individually intertwined with common problems to such an extent that they are best dealt with by a trained person who is available locally and who can offer the patient a viable alternative to denying his problems, relying on folk therapy, or considering medical evacuation.

References

Anthony, W. A., and Wain, H. J. Two Methods of Selecting Prospective Helpers. *Journal of Counseling Psychology*, 1971, *18*, 155–156.

Dryud, J. E., and Rioch, M. J. Multiple Therapy in the Treatment Program of a Mental Hospital. *Psychiatry*, 1953, *16*, 21–26.

Grief, E. B., and Hogan, R. The Theory and Measurement of Empathy. *Journal of Counseling Psychology*, 1973, *20*, 280–284.

Holland, J. V. Preventive Psychiatry for Children on a Community Basis. Exhibit presented to the 25th Clinical Convention of the American Medical Association, New Orleans, 1971.

Holmes, T. H., and Masuda, M. Psychosomatic Syndrome: When Mothers-in-law or Other Disasters Visit, a Person can Develop a Bad, Bad Cold. Or Worse. *Psychology Today*, 1972, *5*, 71–72, 106.

Holmes, T. H., and Rahe, R. H. The Social Readjustment Rating Scale. *Journal of Psychosomatic Research*, 1967, *11*, 213–218.

Kiev, A. *Transcultural Psychiatry*. New York: The Free Press, 1972.

Matarazzo, J., Saslow, G., and Matarazzo, R. The Interaction Chronograph as an Instrument for Objective Measurement of Interaction Patterns During Interviews. *Journal of Psychology*, 1956, *41*, 347–367.

Piaget, G. W., and Serber, M. Multiple Impact Therapy. *Psychiatric Quarterly*, 1970, *44*, 114–123.

Poser, E. G. The Effect of Therapists' Training on Group Therapeutic Outcome. *Journal of Consulting Psychology*, 1966, *30*, 283–289.

Rioch, M. J. Changing Concepts in the Training of Therapists. *Journal of Consulting Psychology*, 1966, *30*, 290–292.

Seward, G. *Clinical Studies in Culture Conflict*. New York: The Ronald Press, 1960.

Stewart, E. C. *American Cultural Patterns: A Cross-Cultural Perspective*. Pittsburgh, Penn.: Regional Council for International Education, 1971.

Szasz, T. S. *The Myth of Mental Illness*. London: Paladin Books, 1972.

Werkman, S. Hazards of Rearing Children in Foreign Countries. *American Journal of Psychiatry*, 1972, *128*, 992–997.

Wyler, A. R., Masuda, M., and Holmes, T. H. Magnitude of Life Events and Seriousness of Illness. *Psychosomatic Medicine*, 1971, *33*, 115–122.

Yalom, I. D., and Handlon, J. D. Multiple Therapists in Resident Teaching. *Journal of Nervous and Mental Disease*, 1965, *41*, 684–692.

Gerd Seidel

Cross-Cultural Training Procedures: Their Theoretical Framework and Evaluation

Introduction

One of the most significant phenomena of our times is international cooperation in the worldwide process of planned change. The critical point of the process is the transfer of technical know-how and experience. However, it is now widely recognized that it is difficult to transplant technical methods into the soil of other cultures, because these techniques are the products of a certain cultural history.

Attempting to transfer and adapt foreign technical skills into other cultural systems has caused a lot of problems, especially for and by the mediating person—the foreign expert—who represents the human connecting link in this process of change. These problems include understanding and/or defining his proper role, developing appropriate communication styles, and achieving personal adjustment to an alien cultural environment. The factors growing out of the changing conditions and relationships between nations, combined with many basic problems involved in contact, communication, and cooperation between contrasting cultures, make it incumbent upon foreign experts to develop an appreciation and understanding of these cross-cultural difficulties and to acquire some of the necessary abilities, such as an increased awareness and sensitivity to cultural stimuli and better human relations skills. The training of personnel involved in the process of mediating between different cultural systems is therefore regarded as indispensable by all parties concerned.

In this chapter, we will first review the different approaches to cross-cultural training from a historical perspective. Then the main training objectives will be identified, and a concept of learning which has successfully guided our work will be described. This will lead into a treatment of the theoretical framework underlying the training programs and its derivation from social-psychological concepts of attitude change and behavior modification. In the next section, we will summarize some of the methods and techniques which have been used in current programs. Finally, we will review some of the basic aspects of evaluating cross-cultural training programs.

Historical Perspective

When the representatives of six national training institutes met at Bad Honnef, Germany, for a workshop on training in cross-cultural communication in December 1975, they were surprised to discover that they all had gone through nearly identical phases in their cross-cultural training programs during the last ten years. In the first phase, lasting up to the late sixties, the cultural orientation programs consisted of area orientation studies in which the participants were provided with facts and figures about a country's history, geography, culture, social structure, political system, and so forth. This "information-giving" approach was regarded as sufficient for effective work in a new cultural setting. Thus, the early operations of the training centers relied on traditional information-transmission programs emphasizing content rather than process. Based on feedback from the field, it became obvious that the information-transmission approach was not making the necessary impact on those attitudes and behaviors related to the problem of living and working productively in a different culture. Effective cross-cultural training must result in more than an understanding of the foreign language and an increased intellectual knowledge about the people of the host country. Not being aware of the cultural bias of their values, beliefs, attitudes, expectations, and behavior, the experts were not prepared for the problems which their own cultural dependence might create for them in an alien cultural environment. This created difficulties in adjustment, feelings of isolation and loneliness, and a good deal of unanticipated frustration. It was agreed by the responsible parties that an innovative approach to cross-cultural training was needed.

The essence of the new training programs became the simulation of situations that participants in intercultural cooperation typically face, enabling the trainees to examine closely their reactions to these events. Information-giving was accorded only a minor place in these programs. This approach did not intend to change attitudes by force, as was sometimes misunderstood by critics. But it aimed to encourage the trainees to become aware of their own attitudes and how they have acquired them, how they affect their actions, and how they are perceived by others, and to create a learning atmosphere that provides the individual with preconditions and opportunities to change his attitudes if he wants to. The procedure was based on the assumption that understanding oneself and being aware of one's own socialization is a first step toward understanding others, and is therefore the basis for skill in both interpersonal and intercultural relations.

T-group methodology played a great part in this phase. Although most of the persons directly involved in training felt that they were on the right track with this "sensitivity" approach, there was increasing reaction against it, especially from the outside. The arguments criticized a variety of aspects,

Table 1. Evolution of Cross-Cultural Adaptation Programs

	Phase I (1968–71) Information	Phase II (1971–74) Training	Phase III (1974 –) Learning
GENERAL GOAL	To prepare an expert and his family adequately to live and work in a new cultural environment	To prepare an expert and his family adequately to live and work in a new cultural environment	To prepare an expert and his family adequately to live and work in a new cultural environment
CONTENT	Area orientation studies about host country; information on project; information on living conditions; administrative details	Improvement of behavioral skills; emphasis on personal and cultural awareness and "learning how to learn"; emphasis on process of learning rather than content	Information-giving and skill development; improving special abilities and skills; providing the trainee with tools for analyzing his situation; problem-solving
METHODOLOGY	Information-giving approach; traditional lecture/reading approach; one-way communication	Variety of "human relations" training techniques; T-groups, sensitivity training; simulation games	Integration of a variety of learning approaches; participants are creating their own learning, corresponding to their needs and interests. Task-oriented.
ASSUMPTION	Information transmission of facts is sufficient for the individual to adapt successfully to the new culture	Changing of behavior and attitudes is necessary in preparing trainees for an overseas assignment	Program should offer a variety of cognitive and affective activities, enable the participant to identify his optimal way of learning, and give support for integration

from invasion of an individual's privacy and the alleged impossibility of modifying attitudes and behavior in such a short space of time to the absolute irrelevance of such an approach for cross-cultural preparation.

Given these reactions, the client organizations felt that perhaps the training programs should again focus on hard, factual information. The training centers, however, did not turn back. But in response to the criticism, there was a change in philosophy and methodology, culminating in the third phase in the development of cross-cultural training programs. The emphasis has now shifted from personal awareness of general behavior and attitudes to the self-examination and improvement of specific abilities and skills, such as the accurate perception of others, listening ability, acting on feedback, and so on, and to the analysis of how these variables affect the cross-cultural situation of the experts. The assumption is that this focus better respects people's privacy and avoids sensitivity-type explorations into an individual's personality.

In addition, attention has been paid to improving the quality and integration of the various parts of the training program. Great efforts were made to create an optimal learning climate for the participants during the training procedure. The approach is now trainee-centered rather than trainer-centered and focuses on problem-solving rather than on the memorizing of facts, although relevant informational content is considered important. However, the focus is more on the process of learning, to prepare the participants for continued learning on the job. Assuming that individuals learn in different ways, the training programs should afford people a variety of ways to learn what they need to learn. In effect, most of the training programs today are a judicious combination of the extreme positions that developed in phase one (information transmission) and phase two (behavior-change emphasis), acknowledging differences in individual needs and learning styles and at the same time retaining both the information and the training focus of those earlier approaches.

DEFINING SOME PROBLEMS

It is a fact that many seemingly well-planned technical aid projects, staffed by professionally well-trained and capable foreign experts, have failed because of lack of understanding and inability successfully to transfer technology across cultural barriers. It has always been agreed that volunteers should be given some training before going to a developing country, but the idea of training experts for their work in the field is relatively new. Living and working in a new cultural environment with different rules and unfamiliar ways of thinking is a difficult and emotionally demanding task. So it is not surprising that investigators evaluating the performance and problems of experts in the developing countries have concluded that it is usually the human problems associated with working in a different culture that are likely to be critical in the success or failure of an assignment.

There is evidence that those experts who are least effective in their relationships with host nationals and who demonstrate little insight in their alien culture experience are also the ones who claim no difficulties in their personal relationships and who tend to minimize the importance of the cross-cultural dimensions. Consequently, despite the importance of the human factor, it is not surprising that it is often difficult to make the trainee who is participating in a training course aware of the importance of the cross-cultural aspects of his work. The extent of this problem often depends on the profession of the expert. If he is a technician, he is especially likely to be concerned primarily with the adequacy of his technical proficiency and with little else. At best, a trainee may be curious about the facts and figures of the country of destination and its customs, climate, geography, living conditions, and so forth; but any attempt to give the trainee a perspective that will help him deal with the social-psychological aspects of his work is likely to be viewed as too abstract, too remote, or too simple-minded.

Furthermore, the traditional assumption that information-giving will enable a person working in an alien culture to make the necessary adjustments has not proven to be so. On the contrary, too often stereotyping and false expectations result from the transmission of so-called factual information. Such a traditional approach ignores the trainees' own cultural biases, values, behavior patterns, attitudes, expectations, and the problems these might create for him in another culture. The expert must be able to anticipate how he might react when all the familiar supports of his own culture are removed, and find ways to cope with the ambiguity of the daily life situations with which he will be confronted in the host culture. So, to be relevant to the problems that the expert will encounter in his new environment, the training program must increase and develop the trainee's tolerance of ambiguity. This kind of training does not merely attempt to change attitudes. Rather, it encourages the trainees to become aware of their attitudes, the influence of their education, and their own process of socialization and of how these affect their actions and patterns of behavior in general. Therefore, understanding oneself and one's own culture is a first and necessary step toward understanding alien cultural systems. To open the trainee's mind for the cross-cultural dimension of his work, it is necessary to take the individual's learning biography into account.

A cross-cultural training program should also help the experts anticipate role conflicts concerning the political dimensions of their work in the host country. Many professional development experts avoid considering the political implications and the moral basis of their work. But the expert cannot evade the moral and political implications of his role, since his work so obviously is related to fundamental decisions about the objectives of the host society. The principal moral question which he has to face is whether to work for a particular government or not. The rather narrow moral issue which the foreign expert has to decide is the extent to which his objectives and those of the government have to coincide before he is prepared to lend his professional talent to that government. In his political role, he has to decide as well whether to support that government in the political field.

In all countries there are some gray areas—areas of uncertainty where powerful, clear-cut interests are not involved and where a trade-off may be possible between growth and equity. Sometimes, also, the political leadership of the country may pay attention to the views of the expert. But normally this gray area is relatively limited. So how hard should the expert push, and what objectives should he push for, keeping in mind the risk that strong advocacy may end his employment and usefulness? Another crucial consideration relates to the point at which he should state that the objectives of the government differ too much from his own and that therefore he must resign. And if he contributes by his technical competence to the improvement of the efficiency of the system, does he strengthen the status quo and simply delay a change in the structure, a change which could bring about either greater equity or growth, or perhaps both? Is the technician justified in accepting a political-economic framework with which he disagrees, and thus in providing support for its perpetuation? Does he in fact make a moral decision by working with governments and accepting their politically set goals?

These are some of the questions which have to be reflected in a program preparing trainees for an overseas assignment, to make them aware of the complexity of the political and moral implications of their engagements and to encourage them to define themselves as mediators between cultures in the worldwide process of international cooperation.

Training Objectives

Given the aforementioned difficulties and problems confronting personnel working overseas in an alien cultural environment, we think that a cross-cultural training program should try to realize the following objectives. For pedagogic and didactic reasons, it is sensible to derive certain specific goals from the general objective "to live and work in a new cultural environment" in order to shape and give substance to the training program.

The common components of most training programs are designed to enable the participants:

> to attain a practical working knowledge of a particular foreign language;
> to acquire management and interpersonal skills in an intercultural setting;

to achieve a better understanding of their own culture as a basis for
increased sensitivity to an understanding of the culture of assignment;
to accept and to be tolerant of values, beliefs, attitudes, and behavior
patterns that might be quite different from their own;
to communicate more effectively with persons from other cultures as
well as from their own;
to develop a more creative and effective approach to problem-solving
and goal-setting by the application of modern management techniques;
to acquire new learning skills that will enable the participants to
increase their interest in continued learning during the cross-cultural
experience, and to provide them with techniques to do so;
to reduce problems of adjustment by achieving heightened self-understanding and self-awareness, thus increasing their ability to perform
within the requirements of a new cultural environment; and
to acquire new learning skills that will enable them to become sensitive
and to respond appropriately to the subtleties of the new culture.

THE CONCEPT OF LEARNING

To translate these objectives into a training program requires a suitable
learning setting for the trainees. The trainer should always be aware of the
assumptions underlying his particular approach to training and of the relations of these assumptions to the objectives. These assumptions about learning determine to a great extent, implicitly or explicitly, the training strategies
that are selected to achieve the objectives.

The major types of training programs have already been reviewed—the
traditional information-transmission approach versus an approach that
emphasizes process and experiential learning. As we stated earlier, in the
third and current phase, there seems to be a tendency toward a combination
of both approaches.

The traditional approach to learning will not be described here in detail.
Basically, it is characterized by information transmission and is primarily
cognitive in both content and process. The participation of the trainee is
more passive than in the experiential model, and consists primarily of rote
learning of content material.

Experiential learning, on the other hand, focuses on the active learning
of the material necessary to solve problems or interpret experience (Wight
1969; Wight and Hammons 1970), and the problems are usually of the open-
ended variety, with more than one possible solution. There is very little testing for retention of facts, other than as reflected in application to problem-
solving and through discussion—very often discussion among the trainees
rather than with the trainer. The experiential approach requires considerable

interaction between the trainer and the trainee and among the trainees. The training is designed to be trainee-centered rather than trainer-centered, and shifts the focus of attention from the trainer to the trainee. It focuses on learning rather than training, creative thinking and problem-solving rather than memorization, and responsibility for initiative and exploration rather than conformity. The stress is on the process of learning and on preparation for continued learning.

Experiential learning is thus emotional as well as intellectual, and involves behavior analysis and skill practice. It should enable the trainee to be an effective and independent learner by providing him with a system of learning operations that are independent of settings, persons, and other information sources not available in another cultural environment. Therefore, the utmost goal of a training program should be to enable the participant to generate his own learning as needed in a new setting (Harrison and Hopkins 1967). The experiential model, as it is described by Wight and his colleagues, relies heavily on observation and sensitive, accurate perception, but it would also include any of the traditional ways of imparting information, such as lectures, reading, demonstrations, feedback, and so forth. But used with the experiential model, these processes become more interesting and the data more meaningful and relevant for the trainee.

The responsibility for making effective use of available resources and for the collection of data is the trainee's. Therefore, he is not provided with information or facts for which he does not recognize a need or which he does not understand. By this learning approach, the participant is encouraged actively to seek information he would like to have toward the solution of problems he can already anticipate, and thereby develops a better understanding of the future situation. Experiential training is structured to leave space for reflection, discussion, analysis, and evaluation of the experience. The assumption is that we seldom learn from experience unless we assess the experience, preferably with others who might not share our particular biases or perceptions. Sharing experience with other participants helps the trainee learn to be more objective and to explore various alternatives in the analysis of his experience.

These processes bring about insights, discoveries, and understanding. All this is then incorporated into the individual's conceptual system, with which he construes the world and through which he views, perceives, categorizes, evaluates, and seeks experience. Generalization logically follows conceptualization. In this way, the trainee develops a better understanding of himself in relation to the experience and thus in relation to similar or related past and future experiences.

One of the main advantages of the experiential learning process is the extent to which the learner's abilities are involved: the process is *behavioral* (action, experience, problem-solving, information-gathering); *affective* (feelings, emotions, reflections, reactions); and *conative* or *goal-directed* (need identification, goal-setting, planning). Thus, the whole person is involved in the learning process. It is assumed that the more these various abilities are used in the learning process, the more effective the learning.

As has already been mentioned, in contemporary practice, the traditional and the experiential methods have been combined, with resulting increased effectiveness of the programs. If an information-transmission approach is used, attention must be given to preparing the trainees to receive the information. The content of a lecture is most effective if it is meaningful to the trainees in terms of their own perceived needs or goals. If the trainees' goals are not consistent with the goals of the training program, this is a problem that can be handled within the experiential model by exploring the conflict as a significant experience and a problem to be solved. The trainers will sometimes have information they consider important for which at least some of the trainees will not recognize a need. If this is the case, it is up to the trainer to attempt to create the conditions or a situation that will help the trainees recognize the need, rather than to force the information on the trainees whether they want it or not.

THE SMALL GROUP AS A CONTEXT FOR LEARNING

For trainees to learn group process skills, the functioning of the group itself becomes an object of study and analysis. The intent is to provide a setting where practice can lead to greater understanding and increased competence, by developing in the trainees certain participatory and observational skills.

The specific objectives are to assist the participants in their understanding of small-group functioning and the processes by which groups make decisions and accomplish objectives. Thus, a successful trainee learns how to increase the accuracy of his perceptions of group difficulties, increases his understanding and practice of leadership functions, enhances his problem-solving and decision-making skills, and learns how to communicate more confidently and competently as a participant in various group settings. These objectives call for new roles for both trainees and trainers within a small, group-centered learning environment where responsibility for progress and change can be shared by all participants. People cannot fully learn from one another until they have established a measure of rapport and some degree of mutual trust, support, and respect. When the trainees trust others to respect their own personal growth and learning, when they realize they have support if they experience difficulties in new explorations, then the climate is conducive to learning. Under these conditions, each member of the training program can confront several new views of himself and have an opportunity to develop new insights and behaviors.

The trainer has an important task in this respect. Because he is initially active in structuring the activities and explaining the concepts, his behavior will in large measure influence the climate of the group. The role of the trainer is to teach, but to teach in a special way. It is not sufficient for him to expound cognitive material; he must be able to present the concepts and constructs in a manner that guides and evokes rather than lectures and instructs. He structures the training so that the trainees will follow the experiential process, and supports them when they do. It is his responsibility to provide relevant experiences, problems, data, and information and to structure the training so that the trainees will treat the experience, problems, data, and information in the way described in the experiential model of learning.

Furthermore, the trainer helps each participant develop skills or perform effectively, and he works with each individual to help him continuously improve his performance. Additionally, he emphasizes cooperation and teamwork, so that the group can assist in the development of each team member and each individual can contribute as much as possible to the effectiveness of the team. Thus, the trainer serves primarily as a facilitator and a resource, and the small group itself becomes the main resource and the context for the learning experiences.

This leads us to a consideration of the *group-dynamics aspect of learning*. Group dynamics are always present whenever there is interaction between persons, whether of a verbal or of a nonverbal nature. These interactions can be viewed from the standpoint of individual psychology or from the standpoint of the *group*, as is done in social psychology, where the individual is seen primarily as a group participant. Insight into group dynamics can help the trainees in the group discern their behavior and the happenings in the group. This knowledge and experience promotes social learning and helps the group to reach its goals.

The group-dynamics approach should be understood in this last sense. Group dynamics—not the process, but the method—can have an instrumental function in promoting learning and work processes in groups. As we pointed out, group dynamics are very potently present in all groups. Therefore, the question is whether the participants in groups should be manipulated by group processes or by manipulators of group processes, or whether they should be qualified to recognize what is happening in the group in order to be able to influence the group themselves and actively plan the learning and work processes within the group.

These qualifications can be acquired through an active acquaintance with group-dynamics methods and procedures. We envision the following goals for group members with this group-dynamics method:

1. Sensitizing them to interpersonal occurrences in the areas of communication and social behavior in the group.
2. Reflecting upon their own behavior (through self-perception and feedback from others) and recognizing the effects of their behavior on others, individually and as a group.
3. Learning new communication techniques and behaviors.

Group-Dynamics Exercises

There are a number of problems which crop up in every group, such as communication patterns and style (including the problem of the absolute nontalker); working style of the group during problem-solving tasks; style of leadership and cooperation; and decision-making as practiced by the group and its effect on the group. Group-dynamics games can provide trainees with planned experience. Being games, however, their real-life relevance may not be immediately apparent. But the games do have the advantage that participants are often willing to talk about their strategies and behavior after playing them. It is up to the individual to determine whether or not the game provides him with any experiences which he can apply to his working habits in groups.

Some of the best-known games of this sort are the tower-construction game (cooperation game); the prisoner's dilemma game and the NASA game (decision-making in groups); exchanging roles; and other feedback games. The ultimate goal of these exercises is to sensitize the individual to disturbing processes which occur in groups, in order for him to be able to recognize them and isolate them in real settings. This is the first step in getting to the heart of general difficulties in a group. These exercises therefore give trainees the opportunity to experience problems which are encountered in every group, but without the risk involved in a real situation. Thus, they enable participants to experiment with their own behavior.

Theoretical Framework of the Programs

The ultimate purpose of almost every cross-cultural training course, beside the transmission of knowledge, is insight into one's attitudes, followed by attitude change and behavior modification. Thus, the courses attempt to structure relationships and situations conducive to attitude change. A number of theoretical and conceptual formulations concerning attitude change may be identified, implicitly or explicitly, in the various training approaches, including those of Kelman (1958), Verba (1961), and Festinger (1957).

Kelman distinguishes among three methods by which attitude change may be achieved: compliance, identification, and internalization. Compliance occurs when an individual accepts influence from another person or from a group because he hopes to achieve a favorable reaction from the other. He may be interested in attaining certain specific rewards or in avoiding certain specific punishments that the influencing agent controls. This aspect of opinion change is generally operative only at the beginning of the course. The arriving trainee is not sure what is in store for him at the training course and may initially adopt or express opinions designed to match those of the instructors or to gain their approval. This kind of compliance, however, declines with time, and is replaced by compliance with the norms of the group, which means the trainee group as a whole. During the period of the course, the trainee group usually becomes the most salient reference group for its members, and its influence can be very strong. Now it is the group which gives or withholds rewards, acceptance, status—thus enforcing compliance to the group position.

As a consequence, one method of attempting to achieve attitude change is to be concerned with the norms of the group as a whole, to be aware of the group's structure, its natural leadership, and the processes taking place within it, and to intervene in the group in order to create the desired attitudes. This is in recognition of the fact that the staff of the training course has no power to enforce compliance as far as attitudes are concerned; only the group's rewards and punishments are effective in this area. With the reduced importance of the instructor's compliance-inducing function, there now comes into play the second element of Kelman's triad, that of identification.

There is ample evidence that course participants develop an identification with staff members. *Identification* in this sense means a desire to be like another person, to model oneself after him, and is naturally to be expected in a situation of this kind. The staff members or other objects of identification have succeeded in what the trainee aspires to. The trainee is disposed to adopt the attitudes of the person with whom he identifies, to attempt to emulate him, sometimes even to fall into the danger of idealizing him. This places a heavy burden on the training staff. Their own attitudes, in particular toward other cultures and other people, can provide a model for the trainees to copy. The trainer must therefore have a dedication to his task, since he cannot imbue his trainees with idealism which he does not feel or with goals which he does not share.

Kelman's third mode of opinion change, internalization, is also plainly present in the training courses. By and large, those who participate in training courses come with the intention of improving their own abilities and preparing for their overseas assignments. Consequently, the opinions and attitudes encountered during the course are not usually at variance with their own set of values. Given the will to move in a particular direction, new ideas and methods of doing so are absorbed with little difficulty. Of course, this is not always the case. The rigid, authoritarian, demanding person may have difficulty in accepting the value of cooperation and democratic decision-making, but may, in the attempt to copy the staff member with whom he identifies, nevertheless behave in the desired manner, even if his underlying attitude remains negative or skeptical.

The three patterns of attitude or opinion change discussed above are a *description* of the process. They happen to the trainee with little conscious effort or control on the part of the instructor. More important is an examination of the active methods used in making aware and changing the attitudes of trainees. Behavioral theories hold—and training experience confirms—that little attitude change is produced by mere exhortation, new information, or appeals to logic. The experiments by Lewin (1947a,b), and their subsequent elaboration by Verba (1961) into a "participation hypothesis," point to the fact that people who participate in a decision tend to carry it out more fully than those not involved. The training programs therefore employ a good deal of group discussion and decision-making, both as a didactic device and for the value changes they produce; the advantages, problems, solutions, new forms, methods, and devices are discussed by the trainees.

Useful as this method of attitude change is, it is not always easy to apply. Verba points out some of the limitations and dilemmas inherent in the participation hypothesis. One such problem Verba terms "enforced democracy," expressed by the question "Can people be forced to be free?" Participants accustomed to an authoritarian milieu, and therefore unable or unwilling to participate in joint decision-making, may not be amenable to the kind of attitude change proceeding from this method. The second problem Verba calls "pseudo-democracy," which is when the group leader has a particular goal in mind and uses the group discussion as a means of inducing acceptance of that goal.

The implication here is that while the scope of decision-making may be necessarily narrow, the decision should be truly that of the group and not of the leader. Few training courses, however, can really allow participants to make all the decisions concerning the course, and in some cases the limitations of time, staff, money, knowledge, or experience may narrow the area of real decision-making by the participants to marginal and unimportant items.

The third limitation of the participation hypothesis is that although decisions are theoretically capable of satisfying everyone, many decisions in fact leave some members of the group dissatisfied. As a result, the attitude change might well be in a direction opposite to the one anticipated.

Each of these methods of deliberately changing attitudes is used to a greater or lesser extent in every course. However, the major method of attitude change attempted implicitly or explicitly in almost every course is based upon Festinger's (1957) theory of cognitive dissonance. Simply stated, this theory holds that when people choose to do or say things in clear contradiction to their previous statements, behaviors, or opinions, tension is created within the person because of the dissonance between their beliefs and their behavior. Such tensions may be reduced in a number of ways, one of which is the disavowal of previous beliefs or statements; that is, changing one's previous attitude to conform to the new behavior. The actual structure of the training course is based upon placing the trainee in a situation where he will choose to adopt behaviors and attitudes at variance with those previously held.

There is, however, one serious limitation to the use of the theory of cognitive dissonance in the training courses. When a group has created new patterns of behavior which result in a change in attitude, the continued support of the group is of prime importance. Course participants who move to new intellectual or attitudinal positions in training centers in their own country lose the support of the group when they disperse, and consequently may find it difficult to maintain the new attitude. Therefore, we think it extremely necessary to continue the learning process with follow-up programs, such as in-country orientation courses. By far the most important but most neglected aspect of behavioral change processes is the appropriate generalization of established patterns of behavior to new situations and their persistence after the original controlling training conditions have been discontinued. As Bandura (1969) points out, the generalization and persistence of behavior can be facilitated by three different means. These include transfer of training, alteration of the reinforcement practices of the social environment, and the establishment of self-regulatory functions. After participants have adopted new patterns of behavior, the next phase in the program may require direct training in self-reinforcement. This is achieved by gradually transferring evaluative and reinforcing functions from trainers to the individuals themselves. In order to develop these self-regulatory functions, it is necessary to provide ample opportunities for participants in the training program to enact role behaviors toward peers that are ordinarily performed by instructors. Specifically, this entails delegating progressively more of the standard-setting, evaluative, and reinforcement functions to members of the group as they progress in the program.

In order to enhance participants' willingness to adopt new role behaviors, increased privileges and rewards are associated with increased responsibility for guiding member behavior. Active participation in decision-making, the application of rewards and sanctions for regulating the behavior of peers in accord with institutional standards, and the performance of counterattitudinal behaviors are expected to exert greater influences on values and preferences than a program in which contingencies are simply imposed on covertly resistant trainees. When individuals function as change agents for members of their own group, they not only achieve modifications that might otherwise be strongly resisted, but they also advance the treatment of their subordinates by providing models for desirable modes of behavior.

Content, Method, and Techniques of the Training Programs

Content and method are so interwoven in most of the cross-cultural training courses that it is difficult to separate them, even for the purpose of discussion. The specific methods and techniques can be incorporated into any of the general methodologies and theoretical frameworks discussed before. Although most procedures were developed for some specific program, they can easily be adapted for use with a different approach. We would like to present here in brief summary a number of methods or techniques which we regard as being fundamental and typical of current cross-cultural training programs, and try to show their relevance to the kind of learning concepts and theoretical frameworks we have been discussing.

A major problem for the training staff is the selection of relevant content from a great amount of available information. The material selected should motivate the trainee, give him information that will be meaningful and useful to him in his role as an expert in a new cultural setting, and awaken in him an interest in and excitement for the alien cultural environment. The training staff has to find an approach that will reach each person. If this is too difficult to achieve, the program should at least appeal to as many people as possible.

A great many cross-cultural exercises have been developed especially for use in cross-cultural training. We will present a number of exercises that have proven to be effective for cross-cultural training and have turned out to be suitable for transmitting factual and relevant information in a way that is comprehensibly involving and meaningful to the trainees. It is the responsibility of the training staff to select those exercises that would be most suitable for their program, to select the appropriate content for each exercise, and to plan a program based on a logical, sequential, and developmental relationship among the various exercises.

CRITICAL INCIDENTS

The critical-incident technique was originally developed by Flanagan (1954). By an incident we mean any observable human activity that is sufficiently complete in itself to permit inferences and predictions to be made about the person performing the act. To be critical, an incident must occur in a situation where the purpose or intent of the act seems fairly clear to the observer and where its consequences are sufficiently defined to leave little doubt concerning its effects.

For the purpose of preparing experts for their overseas assignments, the ideal incident must describe (1) a common occurrence in which a Westerner and a host national interact; and (2) a situation which the expert finds conflictual, or which he is likely to misinterpret. Critical incidents are obtained by asking experts and host nationals with whom they come into contact to describe some specific intercultural occurrences or events that made a major difference in their attitudes or behavior toward the members of the other culture. These may be pleasant, unpleasant, or simply nonunderstandable occurrences. The primary purpose of these exercises is to introduce the trainees to typical kinds of situations they will find themselves in as experts and to allow them to explore their possible reactions to these situations. A secondary purpose is to provide the trainee with an opportunity to see how his perceptions, values, judgments, and expectations of another culture compare with those of the other trainees.

CULTURE ASSIMILATORS

Culture assimilators are similar to critical incidents, but are in essence a programmed approach to learning about a culture. Supporters of this method claim that actively involving the learner in discovering for himself whether he has understood each fragment of knowledge in a well-designed program not only gives the trainee the pleasure (reinforcement) of achieving the right answers, but the trainee and the trainer have immediate checks on progress.

The culture assimilators are derived from the concept of "subjective culture" (Triandis et al. 1972), which is a cultural group's characteristic way of perceiving its social environment. The perception of roles, norms, values, and their behavioral consequences are the determinant factors of subjective culture. The culture assimilator consists of more than a hundred incidents of intercultural conflict. After each incident, there is an opportunity for the trainee to analyze the causes of the problems occurring in the text. The trainee makes attributions about the causes of the behavior described in the incident. There are four attributions; one is a typical attribution made by members of culture B and three are attributions made by members of culture A. To train members of culture A to understand the point of view of members of culture B, program directors ask trainees to select one attribution for a particular incident. When the trainee from culture A selects an attribution typically made by members of culture A, he is told that it is not the best way to think about the behavior of the member of culture B, since there are other and better ways to explain this behavior. When the trainee finds out the corresponding attribution which explains the behavior of members of culture B, he is praised and told why it is correct (Triandis 1975).

The following excerpt from the Arab Culture Assimilator (Training Research Laboratory, University of Illinois, Urbana) describes the technique of this kind of programmed instruction:

An Arab student asked his American co-workers in his laboratory if they wanted to go to lunch with him at the Student Union. They agreed, adding that it was time to eat, and they all chatted as they went to the Union where they got in line at the cafeteria. When they reached the cashier's station, the Arab student, who was first in line, paid for all of them. When the group got to their table, his two co-workers insisted on giving the Arab student the money for their lunches. The Arab refused it, but the Americans insisted; and the one sitting beside him swept the money off the table and dumped it into the foreign student's pocket. Later, the Americans commented that the Arab student had been unusually quiet and reserved while he ate his lunch.

If the Americans had analyzed this incident correctly, they probably would settle on one of the following explanations for the Arab's behavior during lunch:

1. The Arab graduate student must have had an upset stomach.
2. It is the Arab custom not to talk during meals.
3. The Arab student had wanted to pay for their lunches, and he was hurt that they wouldn't let him.
4. The Arab student felt the Americans thought he was too poor to pay.
5. When he was away from the lab, the Arab had nothing to make conversation about.

You chose 1: "The Arab graduate student must have had an upset stomach." This is a bad choice. Apparently you missed a key point. A stomach upset can come on suddenly—but if it does, would one continue to eat and watch others do the same?

You chose 2: "It is the Arab custom not to talk during meals." Sometimes people may want to eat in silence, but if such is their mood, why would they suggest that other people eat with them? While the members of some cultures do dine in silence, this is not the custom with members of the Arab culture.

You chose 3: "The Arab student had wanted to pay for their lunches, and he was hurt that they wouldn't let him." Right. Most Americans would not, under the circumstances, interpret the Arab's invitation (an ambiguous word, isn't it?) as implying that he intended to pay for their lunches. However, in Arab culture, a suggestion that others join you in eating is an indication that you are inviting them to be your guests; it is a gesture of hospitality and generosity.

No wonder the Arab student was upset! As the situation evolved, it was for the Arab basically a case of the guests' supplying their own food after they had accepted his invitation. Aside from the confusion the student must have felt over the apparent inconsistencies in the behavior of the Americans, he probably also felt that their behavior was a deliberate rejection of his hospitality, and therefore of his friendship as well. All over the world, acceptance of generosity and hospitality involves a more or less rigid obligation to repay in an approximately similar form sometime later. A generous Arab, when thanked, may say, "Don't thank me; you will repay me someday." An American refusing an invitation to be a guest is much more likely to say, "Let's go Dutch."

You chose 4: "The Arab student felt that the Americans thought he was too poor to pay for all the lunches." Incorrect. You have overlooked significant information which should have indicated to you the correct solution. This thought may have passed through the Arab student's mind, but it would probably not be the first one, nor the one mainly dwelt upon. One of the other alternatives would provide a better explanation of the young man's behavior. Reread the passage, noting carefully what happens and how each of the people involved behaves toward the others at each point in the episode.

You chose 5: "When he was away from the lab, the Arab had nothing to make conversation about." Wrong. Your answer is inconsistent with the information given. Since we've all met some people as narrow in their interests as this, is this choice culturally relevant? Furthermore, this choice practically contradicts the situation as described in the passage.

Research concerning the effects of training with these culture assimilators indicates that the method has some desirable effects, but not as many as the designers had hoped. The main positive results are in the cognitive field, such as understanding the logic of a certain cultural system, and in improving intergroup relations in the specific contexts covered by the situations in the exercises, which of necessity can only sample the many possible instances of cross-cultural contact.

CASE STUDIES

In the most general sense, case studies are descriptions of human situations with a temporal and developmental span, in which a whole complex of determinants of behavior are at work. Trainees are asked to diagnose these situations, to analyze them in terms of why events happen as they do and why the people involved act as they do. Case studies can be regarded as extended critical incidents, giving more information and covering a particular situation in greater depth. Consequently, more cultural background can be introduced to the trainees with this method.

But case studies reduce the trainee's responsibility for moving from a diagnostic judgment to action as a part of a changing and developing situation. The behavior analyzed is the behavior of someone else; the situation judged is a situation of which the trainee, strictly speaking, is not a part, though his own thinking about the situation is pressed toward closure, made public, and analyzed. In order to compensate for this disadvantage of the case-study method, at the Area Orientation Center we usually use a modified form which we call the dramatized case study, as illustrated in the following example.

Problems with Counterpart Mercado

This is an introductory case study dealing with problems of leadership, techniques for the analysis of management styles, and rational methods in organizing and decision-making in a developing country.

Part of the responsibility of Project Manager Wischnik is a slaughterhouse (a meat-packing plant). According to planning, it should accomplish the following:

1. Put the cattle of the region on the market at prices in line with costs and real market conditions;
2. Stimulate the improvement of stock farming (cattle breeding) through a differentiated pricing policy for high-quality meat;
3. Increase production by trying to get better prices through selling to big markets and bypassing intermediate steps in the distribution chain;
4. Improve the profitability of the cattle trade by price-fixing, in accordance with standards to be set up with the help of the project.

Only thirty to forty cattle can be slaughtered at a time, because the work of the slaughterhouse personnel has to be carried out under the following constraints and conditions: The laws of the country demand that the cattle be in the corral twelve hours before slaughtering. Because of the tropical heat, the killing has to begin at 4:00 A.M., to make use of the cool morning hours. Subsequently, the meat has to be stored for forty-eight hours in the cold-storage house to reach a temperature of $2°$ Celsius, according to regulations. The meat then will be transported to the country center by a chartered plane. Flying time is about one hour. As the plane does not have a cooling system, it has to be loaded in the early hours of the morning, preferably at around four o'clock, to reach the capital not later than eight o'clock.

Among the team of German experts, the veterinarian, Dr. Ruck, is responsible for the slaughterhouse and for the marketing of the meat; he is also the person who built up this part of the project. His counterpart is the native agriculturalist Mr. Mercado, who joined the team seven months ago.

One Sunday afternoon around six o'clock, Project Manager Wischnik comes to Dr. Ruck's house and begins the following discussion:

PM: Dr. Ruck, I have just come from the slaughterhouse. Would you please explain to me why there are no cattle in the corral yet? You know, that slaughtering is to start at four next morning and the chartered plane will arrive Wednesday. If we can't start in time, one of two things will happen: either we won't be able to get the correct temperature for the meat, and that means trouble with the officials, or we're forced to let the plane wait till Thursday—and you know best what that will cost us.

Ruck: I know all of this, Mr. Wischnik. What I do not know is why you come to me to tell me these things. After all, it was your idea to give my counterpart, Mercado, full responsibility for the slaugherhouse.

PM: That is correct. But I took it for granted, naturally, that you would have managed to train him in his new job within six months to avoid the grossest blunders, at least. And apart from that, I took for granted that you would come to his help in case of an emergency.

Ruck: Mr. Wischnik, let's get a few things straight between us. I was against Mr. Mercado's taking responsibility for the slaughterhouse from the beginning. You know best what troubles we had to build up this part of our project. And then, there is still too much work to do. I suggested that we acquire a German butcher, and then we could have shown you how to run a slaughterhouse. What will happen when Mr. Mercado is in charge of everything, you can see right now. But some people seem to think they can cut costs by refusing to renew our contracts. They press handing over the project to the natives.

PM: You'll have to admit that Mr. Mercado's training is excellent. He studied at a university known to be one of the best in the field of tropical stock farming. And he had one and a half year's training in Germany as a scholarship holder in the best slaughterhouses and marketing associations.

Ruck: And that's exactly what is wrong with him. That's why he seems to believe himself to be the biggest shot around, always knowing everything better than we do. But as for practical experience and calculation of costs—well, he doesn't have the slightest notions of that. Let me remind you of his spectacular experiment in making sausages. I'll admit that the sausages didn't taste all that bad. But he needed too many additional workers, and to run a small mincing machine he used our big fifty-eight-kilowatt generator for a whole afternoon—and all that to make fifty kilograms of sausages! You've just got to watch how our Mr. "Ingeneer" walks through the slaughterhouse: white outfit, necktie, and always on guard never to dirty his hands. If you had only let me have my way, he would have had to wear rubber boots and a butcher's smock, and I would have made him take the butcher's knife into his very own precious hands. He would have had to start from scratch. After all, that's the way we learned our job. I myself didn't mind lending a hand in slaughtering in case of an emergency.

PM: I was against that with good reasons. You know for a native university graduate it's an impossibility to do practical work. Why, he would lose face, and his authority.

Ruck: I don't agree with you. I didn't lose face when I took part in the dirty work. Anyway, I think we make a hell of a hullabaloo about our counterparts in this project. It's our job to create something worthwhile here and construct something that can be measured and seen. Could you kindly tell me how I am to construct an economical model plant when I'm supposed to consider the feelings and personal needs of every counterpart?

PM: Dr. Ruck, that's a delicate question. But time presses, and at the moment I'm only interested in how we got into this jam and how we can get out again at shortest notice.

Ruck: Well, I can imagine what happened. Mr. Mercado simply forgot to remind the farmers yesterday that slaughtering is to begin tomorrow. These people promised to bring their cattle a week ago, but you know how unreliable they are. I made it a habit to remind them of the arrangement a day before the cattle were to be brought here. But Mr. Mercado boasts a far better knowledge of his fellow countrymen. I'll take good care not to interfere with him, and will therefore not talk to these people myself. Mr. Mercado would tend to see that as an unadmissible interference into his area of responsibility.

PM: I have already asked Mercado whether he talked to the farmers. He told me that he wouldn't have an opportunity to do this anyway, as you have reserved the only available car, the Land Rover, for yourself. He says he didn't see the car either today or yesterday, and claims he doesn't know where you went with it or what you did with it.

Ruck: Better and better. Should I ask Mr. "Ingeneer" for leave? It's a car belonging to the crew of the German technical aid program, and you yourself made me responsible for it. You should be glad—considering the driving habits of the natives—that I take care of the jeep the way I do.

PM: Dr. Ruck, we won't reach agreement in this way. I don't see any other solution at the moment than taking cattle from our own stock and bringing them to the slaughterhouse so that the killing can start in time tomorrow. But it is my impression that several matters need to be straightened out between yourself and your counterpart. I expect you and Mr. Mercado to come to my office at nine o'clock in the morning on Tuesday. I do hope we can clear up this whole unpleasant affair once and for all.

After the trainees have read the case study, they are required to complete the following:

1. Analyze the relationship between Dr. Ruck and Mr. Mercado.
2. How does Dr. Ruck see his duties, and in what way does this affect cooperation with his counterpart?
3. What led up to the situation at hand?
4. What do you think of the handling of the matter by the project manager?
5. Work out suggestions for a durable solution of the conflict.
6. If you could take the place of the project manager, how would you discuss the solution with Dr. Ruck and Mr. Mercado?

From our experience, this dramatized case study has proven to be effective in introducing problems of intercultural management to the participants in training programs.

ROLE PLAYING

A limitation of the methods described so far is that the trainee is merely an observer of, and does not participate in, the situations that he is learning about. One way in which participation can be introduced into the training laboratory is to simulate incidents by role-playing them. Critical encounters are presented to the trainees, and they are asked not to talk about the situation, but to assume the roles of people in it and to enact the developing situation toward some sort of resolution. Other trainees as well as the trainer observe the actual behavior as it is dramatically developed. Observations are made public, along with the inner feelings and thoughts of the actors. Faults in diagnosis, faults in action on diagnosis, and discrepancies between diagnosis and actions are located and clarified through analysis and discussion. This method brings the process of diagnosis and action into close relationship within the training experience. It brings the trainee's own behavior and actions into the open for analysis and guided practice. Many of the personal projections into the role that the trainee played are revealed in the action and analyzed in the discussion of the action.

Because role playing helps participants achieve insight into their own and others' feelings, it has been widely recognized as a method of helping people to broaden their understanding of and empathy with others. Perhaps the most important value of role playing is that because it is a way of presenting human-relations problems in the context of a training group, members can experiment with their behavior, make mistakes, and try new skills without chancing the hurts that experimentation in real-life situations may involve. In this artificial environment, the learner can try out new behavior in the presence not of judges, but of colearners.

Contrast Culture Role Play

The primary purpose of this training is to develop an awareness on the part of the trainee of his own cultural values, assumptions, and expectations and of their consequences in interactions with persons from other cultures. In this approach, it is assumed that awareness of one's own culture should develop a relativistic perspective and increased sensitivity to, understanding of, and tolerance for other cultural norms and values (Stewart, Danielian, and Festes 1969). The procedure consists of the trainee playing the role of an American adviser, while an initiated assistant confronts the American's cultural assumptions with contrasting positions. The role playing is observed by the other trainees, and the session is followed by a semistructured discussion in which the trainee and his partner are interviewed, the intercultural phenomena of interaction are analyzed, and implications are drawn for overseas performance (Wight and Hammons 1970).

Cross-Cultural Simulation Games

A good illustration of this kind of training method is the "BaFa-BaFa" simulation game. As this game is very sophisticated, only an outline can be given here. It is explained to the group that the specific purposes of the simulation will become evident as the simulation progresses, but that in effect, the experience is intended to teach some basic facts about what is meant by the term *culture* and some of the characteristics of cultures. A further intention is to create feelings which are similar to those a person is likely to experience when he comes into contact with a different culture, and to give the participants experience in observing and interacting with a different culture. After this general orientation, the participants are divided into two groups: the Alpha culture and the Beta culture. Each group selects a person who will travel to the other culture to observe their ways and how they behave and to figure out the rules that govern the behavior of the other group. The observer is not allowed to ask a member of the other culture about the rules; he is restricted to observation and, later, to trial and error. As in the real world, a person living in a new culture has to learn the different rules and reasons for various behaviors. In the game, after both cultures are well established, the observers travel to the other culture. Then they return to their home culture, describe what they saw, and report any ideas they have about the values, customs, and rules of the other culture. The next phase is for the groups to exchange visitors and see if they can interact successfully with the other culture. Once everyone has had a chance to visit the other culture, the game is ended, and the implications of the experience are discussed.

The strength of the simulation is that it allows the director to enable the expression of the feelings, anxieties, misperceptions, and counterproductive attitudes of people who by choice or circumstances are required to interact with another culture. Another advantage of the experience lies in being able to help trainees realize that the people with whom they are dealing may belong to a different culture and be operating under another set of rules.

The exercises which are presented here give an overview of methods and techniques actually in use in cross-cultural training programs. The ultimate purpose of all these exercises is to contribute to the understanding of cultural systems. They were derived from an experiential concept of learning and focus on the development of awareness and effective, appropriate behavior. They are most effective if the small group is used as the major pedagogical medium.

Evaluation of Cross-Cultural Training Programs

Research has made it clear that successful learning is at least as dependent upon the quality of the instruction as it is on the personal characteristics of the learner. Therefore, it would be very one-sided to examine only the learner. The instructional system needs examination as well. Only when it has been proven that the instruction has been of good quality can we place the burden for failure upon the trainee.

However, there are grave institutional, psychological, and even political barriers to the evaluation of instructional systems, that is, to a testing of their quality. For one thing, each of us has been conditioned from early childhood to look for the causes of failure in our own laziness or lack of intelligence, not in the lack of quality of the instruction or in the qualifications of the teacher. This attitude persists into adulthood and outlives the transition of roles from learner to teacher, so that teachers in adult education and trainers conducting cross-cultural training programs often react aggressively when even the possibility of low-quality instruction is mentioned.

Nevertheless, there are several reasons why the evaluation of systems will be inevitable in the future. The increasing differentiation of educational programs and the increasing costs of education give rise to the question, how much instruction and what kind of instruction do we get for our money? Evaluation of programs does not make individual evaluation superfluous, but complements it.

This raises the question of how, and by what instruments, changes can be measured. People interested in the effects of training would be the trainees themselves, the trainers, and the organization which initiates the training programs. While the first two parties may have a more subjective interest in the evaluation of the training programs, the organization would be interested to get a more objective picture, thus tending to employ outside evaluators. In fact, all these different groups should take part in evaluating the entire system. The trainee must be convinced that the course had desirable effects and that he learned something to his advantage, as a prerequisite for his willingness to apply the things he has been taught and to modify his previous behavior patterns. In much the same way, the trainer must be convinced that he can create desirable effects, if he is to continue with his efforts. The organizations have to be assured that these effects are not subjective, but that actual improvements in behavior and skills have been achieved in accordance with the goals of the organization.

An ideal evaluation procedure should cover (1) the measurement of the trainees' performance levels, their attitudes, and their amount of information about the host country before starting the course (ex-ante evaluation); (2) changes in the trainees during the course, manifested in actual behavior in the various seminar activities such as role playing, discussions, and problem-solving (built-in evaluation); and (3) long-term effects in real-life situations, such as the ability to apply cooperation and communication techniques and to cope with difficult and ambiguous situations in new cultural environments (ex-post evaluation).

This brings us to a main difference between evaluation and traditional examinations: evaluation is not a task which needs always to be performed by "examiners." The test of the quality of both the instruction and the learning processes can be taken over by the persons involved, in their own interest. There is a distinction, therefore, between self-evaluation and external evaluation, with program evaluation relying equally on both kinds. This distinction permits us to classify evaluation into four main types:

1. *Self-evaluation by the learner:* The learners test their progress and see which qualifications they have acquired.
2. *External evaluation of the learners:* This may be conducted either by the actual trainers or by neutral examiners who have no interest in justifying their instruction.
3. *Self-evaluation of the instructional system:* This occurs frequently when the trainer and participants in a training course decide to include an evaluation phase. A minimum would consist of an informal discussion; there are a number of other possibilities actually in use in training procedures under the name "course criticism," for which questionnaires have been developed.
4. *External evaluation of the course:* Particularly in the Anglo-Saxon countries, public agencies have developed cost-benefit analyses of training programs, and the term *accountability* is used to define the obligation of the agencies.

The different types of evaluation will now be described in more detail.

SELF-EVALUATION BY THE TRAINEE

This function is derived from the right of the individual to participate in decisions concerning his education and profession. In order to make such decisions in as enlightened a manner as possible, one must have adequate information concerning one's own resources. In addition, the self-evaluation of trainees can help them achieve a better understanding of the objectives of cross-cultural training. However, this function is justified above all else by the psychology of learning, which has proved the positive influence of reporting success back to the learner (reinforcement).

Besides the general demand for autonomy, there is still another justification for this type of evaluation. Lifelong learning is a modern social-cultural development which requires that we learn without the presence of a teacher. The self-evaluation of learners is an important part of this autonomous steering process. The process of self-evaluation does not differ much from other evaluating processes as far as the instruments are concerned. The difference lies in the greater attention that is paid to informing the participants as to which instruments are suited to which purpose, how they can be judged, and how the data which are acquired are to be interpreted.

EXTERNAL EVALUATION OF THE LEARNER

The evaluation of participants in cross-cultural training programs is highly congruent with the traditional view of examinations. This type of evaluation is justified on the one hand by the desire of the donating country for a technical expert who will work in an aid program to have the appropriate qualifications, and on the other hand by the right of the recipient country to get an expert who will be able to work in a new cultural environment without causing too much harm during his stay. The most obvious and common method of evaluating the graduates of training courses is to test them on the material contained in the course. A lot of questionnaires have been used as pre- and post-tests to measure the degree of change produced by training courses in sections such as interpersonal communication, good observation, task skills, responsiveness, relation to the group, and self-awareness. But most of the research findings are limited in their applicability and usefulness. This might be partly the fault of the methodology, and partly because of the lack of valid and reliable testing instruments.

SELF-EVALUATION OF THE TRAINING PROGRAMS

This refers to instances where developers and users of the programs themselves are interested in collecting data as to the quality of training. The motives may range from a desire to justify the training program as it is constituted to the wish to improve it in a self-regulating manner. The necessity to justify training programs is not simply a monetary question; it involves the right of the trainee to have his expectations regarding the program fulfilled. The goal of improving the program is deduced from the general principle of functional rationality: that training programs should realize their goals as far and as well as possible. It is easy to recognize that the evaluation of training programs requires collecting data on the achievement of each learner. The next step is to prove that these achievements were a result of the course and not of other influences outside the training program.

But the self-evaluation of the training programs cannot limit itself to measuring the achievements of the learners. It must attempt to gather information on the expenditure of time, effort, and money for various devices, on the qualifications of the trainers, as well as on any secondary influences on the environment which the program may have. If the institutionalizing of self-evaluation as a long-term function in order to bring about improvement is intended, then the evaluation procedures will have to keep in tune with the program changes—not only the instruments, but also the methods of data processing and interpretation.

Evaluating courses is more difficult than evaluating trainees, since both expectations and criterion variables are less clear. It is possible to judge training courses somewhat intuitively, based on previous experiences. This might be termed a "relative" definition of success. Using this method, a course is judged as better or worse than the previous year's, or all preceding ones; the Asian course as more or less successful than the African one; the course on intercultural communication as of greater impact than the one on task skills. Given the large number of variables affecting the success of each course, the ability, experience, and level of participants, the quality of the staff, and diverse external circumstances, it would seem more advisable to try to determine in advance what would be considered success for each particular course and to establish a priori the method of measuring it. In essence, this is what most of the training staff do, even if on a necessarily somewhat intuitive basis.

EXTERNAL EVALUATION OF TRAINING PROGRAMS

This type of evaluation has as its main purpose usually either criticism or comparison. A main variable in this type of evaluation is the perceived legitimacy of the evaluator and his qualifications. Whereas the measuring stick in self-evaluation is the goal of the system itself, so that the evaluators measure the system in terms of the functions which they ideally ascribe to it, external evaluation is oriented to outside standards. This is particularly true of comparisons between programs—for example, between traditional and innovative training models. It is inadequate in such cases to measure both models in terms of the goals of one of the models; the evaluating party must endeavor to find criteria which are fair to both systems. Technically, the evaluation procedures and instruments for both self-evaluation and external evaluation hardly differ. But the social-psychological and organizational conditions under which the evaluations are implemented differ radically, especially when the external evaluation is felt to be an imposition.

It is important that the criteria by which success is to be judged have been agreed to by all the parties concerned. In a complex administrative structure such as a government department, views regarding the ultimate goal of a training program may vary from level to level and person to person. When others to be consulted include a department of another government as well as the trainers and trainees themselves, it may be possible to define the criteria only in terms that are so general as to render them incapable of measurement. This leads us to a second problem, that of defining the qualities or attributes to be measured in evaluating success. This in turn raises the questions of what instruments are to be used in such measurement and what general methodology is to be followed. Unless such agreement is secured, much effort and expense can be swept away at any given level in the evaluation process with the claim that the methodology did not make proper use of the instruments, that the instruments did not properly measure the attributes, that the attributes do not represent the goals under consideration, or that the wrong goals were examined.

Research has revealed that training programs are liable to suffer two kinds of distortions to which evaluators should be particularly sensitive. The first is "goal displacement" or "goal substitution," which occurs when knowledge is not transferred or attitudes are not changed in the desired manner; under these conditions, the course tends to be judged on the basis of the friendships it has created, the group feeling it has instilled, or the prestige and self-confidence it has bestowed on its participants. The second effect is to shift attention and effort away from results and to concentrate on the process. Particularly when the results cannot be easily measured, a mythology often grows up around the method. Thus, more hours are assumed to create more learning; better staff will raise the level of attainment; better selection of candidates will result in better-trained experts. To use the language of small-group theory, the maintenance goals related to improving the internal relationships and workings of the group take priority over the task goals.

Conclusion

Relative to other fields of applied psychology, the theory and practice of cross-cultural training is still in its infancy. Nevertheless, substantial advances have already been made, and the field has a promising future.

Up to the present time, cross-cultural training has drawn only implicitly on the concept of cultural mediation for a definition of its goals and its criteria of success. Yet the expert (who is the main participant in training programs) is by virtue of his role in an ideal position to fulfill a mediating function. If the substance of the present book has any relevance to real-life events, then the next major development in the theory and practice of cross-cultural training will occur when cultural mediation is explicitly introduced as a program goal; when cultural mediation becomes an explicit criterion of success; and when cultural mediation explicitly enters into the selection of training methods and procedures.

References

Bandura, A. *Principles of Behavior Modification*. New York: Holt, Rinehart, and Winston, 1969.

Festinger, L. *A Theory of Cognitive Dissonance*. Evanston, Ill.: Row, Peterson, 1957.

Flanagan, J. C. The Critical Incident Technique. *Psychological Bulletin*, 1954, *51*, 327–358.

Harrison, R., and Hopkins, R. The Design of Cross-Cultural Training: An Alternative to the University Model. *Journal of Applied Behavioral Science*, 1967, *3*, 431–460.

Kelman, H. C. Compliance, Identification, and Internalization: Three Processes of Attitude Change. *Journal of Conflict Resolution*, 1958, *2*, 51–60.

Lewin, K. Frontiers in Group Dynamics: Concept, Method and Reality in Social Science; Social Equilibria and Social Change. *Human Relations*, 1947a, *1*, 5–41.

_____. Frontiers in Group Dynamics, II: Channels of Group Life; Social Planning and Action Research. *Human Relations*, 1947b, *1*, 143–153.

Stewart, E. C. *American Cultural Patterns: A Cross-Cultural Perspective*. Pittsburgh, Penn.: Regional Council for International Education, 1971.

Stewart, E. C., Danielian, J., and Festes, R. J. *Simulating Intercultural Communication Through Role Playing*. (HumRRO Technical Report 69-7). Alexandria, Va.: Human Resources Research Organization, 1969.

Triandis, H. C. Culture Training, Cognitive Complexity and Interpersonal Attitudes. In R. W. Brislin, S. Bochner, and W. J. Lonner (eds.), *Cross-Cultural Perspectives on Learning*. New York: Wiley, 1975.

Triandis, H. C., Vassiliou, V., Vassiliou, G., Tanaka, Y., and Shanmugam, A. V. *The Analysis of Subjective Culture*. New York: Wiley, 1972.

Verba, S. *Small Groups and Political Behavior*. Princeton, N. J.: Princeton University Press, 1961.

Wight, A. R. *Cross-Cultural Training: A Draft Handbook*. Estes Park, Colo.: Center for Research and Education, 1969.

Wight, A. R., and Hammons, M. A. *Guidelines for Peace Corps Cross-Cultural Training: Specific Methods and Techniques*. (Contract No. PC–23–1710). Washington, D. C.: Peace Corps, Office of Training Support, 1970.

Part III

The Mediator and
Social Change

Introduction

This section deals with the practical consequences of mediation. Probably the most evident application of mediation is in the sphere of social action and social change. In societies striving for new forms, the role of the mediator is to defend and preserve the core elements of the cultures under pressure, particularly if the impetus for change comes from external sources. However, it should be emphasized that preservation does not mean the freezing of a society in its existing mold. On the contrary, cultural preservation that is consistent with mediation is an active process and involves culture growth and culture-building; but this development occurs within the traditions that give a society its stability and continuity, and the mediator's function is to protect these components which constitute the heart of the culture. From the perspective of mediation, therefore, social change is a variation on a basic theme rather than a series of discontinuous innovations— a point of view expressed by all of the contributors to this section.

The idea of culture-building comes out most clearly in Ritchie's account of the work of Maori mediators in New Zealand. Ritchie employs the concept of cultural myths to denote those elements in a society that give it its identity and stability and prescribe its future development. These myths and the persons who interpret them serve as mediating bridges between the history of the culture and its unfolding destiny; or, in Ritchie's language, they are the prophets of the future as well as the priests of the past. The chapter contains a series of case studies of prominent Maori mediator-innovators who fulfilled this bridging function. These mediating men and women had three important features in common: they realized the futility of resisting the introduction of outside influences; they found the means to integrate and synthesize these outside influences with the core of their indigenous heritage, demonstrating that societies can modernize without losing their traditions; and they were energetic and practical men and women who were able to get things done, in particular, to persuade their people to accept change on terms consistent with maintaining the core myths of their society. In a very real sense, these mediators were instrumental in preserving the integrity of their culture while at the same time enabling the Maoris to participate in the fruits of modern technology.

The following chapter considers Australia's emerging multicultural society. There are many similarities between Australia and New Zealand. Both are island nations in the Pacific; both were settled by people of predominantly British stock; and both are in the process of establishing pluralistic societies that include a large array of ethnic and cultural groupings. However, there are also many important differences between the two countries. In particular, they vary substantially in the treatment that was meted out to their original inhabitants. This is reflected in the different categories of mediators selected for analysis by the Australian and New Zealand contributors.

Whereas Ritchie's mediators were all members of the indigenous, receiving culture, Throssell's account of the development of a multicultural society in Australia is presented through the contribution of members of the dominant transmitting group. Unlike New Zealand, Australia did not have available, or did not avail itself of, the services of indigenous mediators in the formative years of its existence. In fact, cultural mediation has a relatively recent history in Australia. As Throssell indicates, the dominant majority stands in potential mediational relationship to three major cultural groups: the descendants of the original aboriginal inhabitants; the migrants from many lands who have settled permanently in Australia; and the large number of overseas students and other "temporary" residents whose visits often extend over many years. It is only in the very recent past that the ethnocentric attitude of the dominant majority toward these groups has softened. Australians are now slowly beginning to accept the intrinsic worth of the outsiders' cultures, but much of the impetus for building a pluralistic society comes from official government policy, itself goaded in part by world opinion.

Throssell considers the role of government departments and civil servants charged with implementing formal multicultural policies. The chapter contains interviews with highly placed official mediators who speak about their challenges, problems, and achievements; and Throssell also describes the work of his own department in promoting cultural and technical cooperation. The analysis indicates that in Australia, official mediators have made some impact on that society's dealings with its aborigines, migrants, and resident aliens; and there is no reason to believe that the same claim could not be made about other countries with legislation supporting cultural pluralism. However, ultimately, government policy cannot be divorced from the general social forces that shape a nation's destiny. The effectiveness of official mediators is therefore likely to be greatest in communities where the concept of a multicultural society is already latent but not yet expressed or translated into action. Under these conditions, official mediators can act as catalysts and facilitators for community efforts to establish multicultural institutions and practices. Many governments are now beginning to assume as their proper function the encouragement of cultural diversity among their citizens, and mediators will have an increasing part to play in implementing these policies.

In both Australia and New Zealand, the indigenous inhabitants, or original "insiders," had to contend with "outsiders" who possessed a greatly superior technology. The contest was unequal, and the newcomers very quickly became the dominant "insiders," to the detriment of the integrity of the indigenous cultures. In response, and initially as a rearguard action, there emerged in both countries mediators whose abiding concern was to preserve the cultures of the various minority groups, including subsequent waves of immigrants. As both Throssell and Ritchie have shown, this campaign is still being fought today, although the terms are now much more equal. However, not all social change occurs under siege conditions. Many exchanges of cultural manifestations take place between groups who enjoy roughly similar status and power and who have a joint interest in the outcome of the transaction.

The chapter by Sullivan illustrates the role of mediators in the management of social change under these latter conditions. Sullivan describes the meeting of two cultures in the school systems of non-Western countries that accept foreign (mainly American) children. The outsiders are the American children attending these schools, their parents, and the few American teachers on the faculty. The insiders are the local children and their parents and local faculty members. The two groups are united in their desire to provide the best possible education for their children, but differ substantially with respect to educational philosophies and practices. Under these circumstances, the clash of cultures can become a very personal matter, but since neither group is in a position to dictate to the other, the situation is conducive to mediation. The function of the mediator is to foster a dialogue between the representatives of the two intersecting cultures and bring about a synthesis of the most desirable aspects of each educational system into a new form that is acceptable to both groups. Sullivan extends her analysis to explore more general issues, such as the practical limits to mutual adaptation, the rights of each group to force or block change in a system in which they both have a heavy investment, who should be expected to change and who should not and whether "insiders" have any particular claims, and the role of the mediator in these dynamics.

The chapters in this section bring out that persons mediating social change are highly involved in the practical world of affairs. Although not insensitive to the demands for mutual understanding and cross-cultural empathy, the primary concern of these mediators is to reconcile and synthesize disparate cultural practices. Their involvement is informed by the consideration that concrete action is to follow from the encounter-action that may have far-reaching consequences for the participants and their societies.

The most frequent pattern in the diffusion of cultural manifestations is unidirectional, with powerful societies having an inordinate influence on groups not commanding equal resources. The pattern implied by the principles of cultural mediation is to resist absolutely innovations that will threaten the integrity of a culture. However, the world is an interdependent and open social system, and it would be futile and undesirable to block all transfers of cultural manifestations. The function of the mediator is to select carefully, and if necessary to modify, those exogenous practices that are consistent with the indigenous values and customs of the receiving society and that will make a positive contribution to the quality of life of its people. The mediator will also promote the two-way exchange of cultural manifestations so that each culture may be enriched, and will try to eliminate situations where one society is cast in the role of donor, while the other adopts a mendicant attitude.

S.B.

James E. Ritchie

Tama Tu, Tama Ora: Mediating Styles in Maori Culture

The saying Tama tu, tama ora *is frequently heard in the oratory of the death ceremonial.*

Literally, it can be translated "Man stands, man lives." Which is interpreted to be "Tell me what a person stands for and I will tell you how that person lived." In other contexts, tu *means to be engaged, vigorously committed, to initiate, to instigate, to serve; but* tu *also keys in the god of war, Tumatauenga, who in the carve-up of creation claimed victory over human life. Through him comes death, so as a person is at death, we can evaluate that life. Tumatauenga rules over death in opposition to Tane, who rules over life. As an ordinary word,* tane *means "man," as does* tama, *so the battle between life and death forces is redolently contracted in this proverb.*

Introduction

I shall use the term *culture* in no very special way. It is unfashionable as well as unnecessary to attempt to define words with precision for purposes that cannot be precise. I want to talk about the cultural conditions that make meditation possible, not about words, and so I appeal to the shared meaning of the term *culture* and hope that we have converse.

If anyone wants more, I invoke the older uses of the term, which refer to that which gives common identity to a people, both in time and over time. I will not quibble if you respond that I am speaking more of civilization or tradition than the sense of culture to which anthropology lays claim. My meaning is close to what Benedict (1934) called a pattern; others, the *zeitgeist*, the spirit or genius of a people; or indeed, to use a disparaged but still useful term, their national character.

No one will wish for precise definition of the term *change*. But much that is spoken of as culture change is not that at all, rather merely the substitution of some element of daily life for another without alteration of anything fundamental. Replacing earthen pots with stainless steel may alter culture patterns, but more frequently it does not. Numerous and repeated changes may occur in, say, political systems without disturbance to the basic set of premises that lie behind behavior.

I will reach for common understanding rather than add technicalities or specialized jargon to these discussions. What I have to say will, I hope, be more familiar than unfamiliar, truer in a consensual sense of instant recognition than at some level of testable significance.

There are, it is generally recognized, two basic processes in culture change. Only two? That may seem surprisingly few, but innovation and borrowing really exhaust the possibilities. Innovation refers to inventions within a tradition, whereas borrowing is the process of "trying on to see if it will fit" that goes on incessantly as cultures meet, adapt, merge, and accept or reject what each has to offer the other. I take a special view here, for I exclude the situation where by force or coercion a people are required to accept something foreign or alien. Others would, moreover, add many more terms, speak of "efflorescence," of "cultural lag," and many more ways of trying conceptually to grasp what seems (and indeed is) a daunting complexity of cultural processes.

But we are concerned with the mediator, not with the itemizing of possible cultural processes. The mediator is either seeking within a single cultural tradition to bring about the adoption of what seems to be a new and unique way for people to accomplish something, or he or she is working to introduce what seems a better—though foreign—idea, technique, or practice and integrate it into the existing tradition.

Other authors in this book have dealt with the special qualities of character of a mediator, if indeed there be any that can be spoken of in a universal sense, and with the techniques of mediation that may or may not have seemed to work in facilitating innovation or borrowing. Consequently, I do not want to focus on the personality of the mediator or on methods of introducing innovations; but I can hardly discuss either the abstractions of culture change or particular examples without mentioning them. However, my main aim is to see if anything sensible can be said about the cultural conditions that lead to successful innovation or borrowing. In doing so I am not sidestepping the argument about where culture change originates—whether in a social nexus of need and creative instability, or in the charisma of a great person (or even a lesser, but effective, person). Obviously, times and persons are complexly related as cultures change, and we are unlikely to do more than engage in sophistry to prolong discussion further on this matter.

It is, however, far easier to see the innovator or the broker in the mediation process, and so our somewhat simple minds make the person the figure and the cultural context the ground. I do not want to exclude that perspective, but I do want to switch it around and see if we can find what it is, in preexisting cultural conditions, that creates fertile ground for cultural growth. And here I will have to refer to cultural forces which are not themselves part of the mediation process, for a new way will emerge or be adopted when the load of not changing becomes too great, or when appeal is made to the cultural prescription that permits change, or in other ways that we will discuss. Under these circumstances, it may not matter much who the mediator is or what personal characteristics he or she may have for the process of change to take place.

I want to take the cultural-determinist view. Cultural conditions make or break the mediator. But what are they? This is the central question which I seek to answer, and I shall do so by speaking mainly of the cultures that I know best, my own and that of the Maori of New Zealand. From time to time, the focus will widen to include Polynesia and possibly even further, to include other Pacific cultures. More specifically still, I want to draw on three periods of time, brief decades of momentous change: the first at or about the time of initial contact with Europeans, the second at and just beyond World War I, and the present. In each period, there were mediators both native and European, both successful and unsuccessful. It should be noted that the two cultures, though each was radically changing in every one of these phases, nevertheless remained in their own respective traditions.

Myths and the Stability of Cultures

There are within cultures powerful prepotent selective factors which maintain the nature of the culture and prescribe possible futures. Only by the most complete, repressive, and coercive control can their expression be blocked. Only by massive and total cultural onslaught, by active and determined assimilation or extermination, can they be destroyed. You may call them *values*, for as contact and comparison bring self-awareness through selection and rejection among new alternatives, they may be expressed as statements of the ultimate good or the intrinsically desirable. You may call them *themes*, though the term has a literary, rather undynamic, and play-acting quality that I do not like. I prefer to think of them in terms of the myths through which they are so clearly and frequently portrayed. For most of humankind through most of history, it is in myth that they have their most profound expression.

Myths are made, too. Their presence is signaled every time someone says, "We are the people who . . . ," and finds a fellowship who nod agreement. They are not behaviorally true, necessarily, except at the level of belief. People do not always act in the ways they might wish to be seen to be acting. But what a people believe themselves to be is not invalidated by lack of performance in keeping with the belief. Were that not so, who would need rationalization, denial, and all the other mechanisms of defence in the use of which humanity is so complexly skilled?

For example, consider in the tradition of the United States the minute-man, the frontiersman, the cowboy, the moving frontier, *Stagecoach, High Noon, Bonnie and Clyde*, Kerouac's *On the Road*, Kesey's Merry Pranksters, *Easy Rider*. That sample of cultural images evokes a myth—or maybe several. Or the Boston town meeting, Faneuil Hall, Abe Lincoln, a party convention, donkeys, elephants, and impeachment—all that evokes another. Or Edison, Henry Ford, the Manhattan Project, Bucky Fuller, the safety pin, science fiction; what does that give you? This is the sort of stable cultural core to which I refer when I speak of prepotent selective factors at the mythic level. The charisma of the mediator arises from a conscious or intuitive identification with and manipulation of these sorts of themes.

The present state of a culture may be sensed by seeking to understand how the old state of culture is expressed in projective myths. A change of tense from present to past is a sure sign of a culture in trouble. When a Maori mother says to me, "We Maori people are more affectionate towards our children than are Pakehas [Europeans]," that is a statement which, whether true or false, has heart in it. Change the *are* to *were* and you see immediately what I mean. The statement made in present time offers a program for change, a charter for new practices to validate it. Stated in the past, it betokens cultural loss, low morale, a sense of drifting rudderless at the whim of the winds of change.

Myth as a Mediating Bridge

Any ideological statement, to have widespread commerce or motivating effect, draws implicitly on the mythic charter.

An old Maori man speaks to me at a tribal meeting in the country. He said: "We send you [the university] our young people and you are like a *taniwha* [a predatory monster; a chieftain of status]. We send them to suc-ceed. They fail. You throw back at us the husk of what we once would proudly own and raise in our own enlightenment [*Whakamaramatanga*]." He is caught between the paradise lost and that not yet regained. I am caught between his expectation—reasonable, because to him the university is a *whare wananga* (house of knowledge) sanctioned by the past of both our cultures to do a particular job—and the unfulfillment of his and my desire that it should do so. My hope and his hope are for an outcome neither of us can accomplish, another paradise lost and not yet regained. I am a mediator. So is he. The state in which we existed in that moment could be one of torment: between cultures, between time, between satisfaction—a hell.

"Old man," I said, "can't we sit down with these young people and work this out?" And we did, not in the sense of finding a solution, but in the sense of reducing our mutual but different pain. With wit and with sincerity and with young people around us, we proclaimed that somehow paradise was still a possibility, and whether we were in it or not, we were where we were together. There were similarities enough in institutions, in metaphor and language, in situation and experience, for the communication to be real. He had spoken of his fears and the realities on which they were based. I had spoken only to accept them, not to dispel them. On that, the way ahead depended, not on longing for the past, nor on denial of the present, or in fantasy about the future.

This is the first intercultural prerequisite for success in mediation. All cards down, do we still have a game to play? Let's work it out. Every mediating act depends on that.

The old man calls on a myth, the fabulous *taniwha* of which his people say, *He piko he taniwha he piko he taniwha.* He speaks of the river along which they live: at every bend a chieftain dwells, or, at every point a new ritual of greeting, of supplication, of tribute or encounter must be observed, with the ever-present danger of error and its consequence, disaster. His metaphor keys in what he knows that I know of his mythology. I know the code, and so I know the reach of his feelings of threat and loss and apprehension. The metaphor, the myth, conveys more potentially and powerfully than in any other way the basis of that which is to be discussed. We walk and talk over that mediating bridge of myth, and so we understand and are understood.

In an ordinary day in the life of a mediator, there may be hundreds of such events. They become so general that they pass unnoticed until one stops, pauses to consider, and sees the underlying structure of the mediating exchange. A multitude of questions arise as soon as one begins to think about the cultural basis of mediation. Why is it that an innovation at one point in time fails, but at another succeeds? Why is it possible for a person to be an effective innovator at one time, yet not at another? Is there a link between the role of the mediator and the Levi-Straussian concept of mediation?

For Levi-Strauss (1963, 1969), myths exist to mediate between a pre-existing or existing state and some imagined (or possibly real) state in other time—then, not now, whether past or future. In doing so, along the way, myth mediates between levels of explanation (for instance, experiential-existential, universal-particular) and modes of thought (such as physical-metaphysical, concrete-abstract, or people-of things).

The mediating person, either as a prophet of the future or a priest of the past, is moving or would wish to move himself or herself as well as others from now to then. Or, in another case, the mediator may wish to move a cultural element or trait from one culture to another, one time to another time. Sometimes, as in the introduction of people or when moving personally into new cultural situations, the mediator is moving not in time, but in cultural space, or even in geographical space. Can anything general be said about such mediation?

Does the successful mediator use myths or create them? Clearly, if the mediator is innovating within his or her own culture, the use of potent mediating symbols may be quite a conscious process. General Booth raised the "army of salvation" at a time of great sociological change, in which the control systems of his society (both sociological and psychological) were imperiled. It was a powerful trick to use the conjunction of the imagery of the army (stable in a world of change), the myths of the warrior/hero/prophet of the Old Testament, the sense of personal battle against sin in the New Testament prophets, and various saints (Paul, Augustine) to refurbish the institutions of Protestant religion. His and later his daughters' charisma reek of mythic meanings.

Florence Nightingale, at about the same time, used some of the same mythology—the war against pain and disease—and from within the Army created a new profession, that of the nurse, the ministering angel who was supposed to work selflessly and in personal sacrifice for the salvation of the body through the modern science of medicine. The hypochondria that confined her to her bed, the nurse needing (but rejecting) nursing herself, with its overtones of the unsavable savior, the potent power in the Judeo-Christian cycle of the martyr myth, demonstrates a mediating device. I could state this in terms of psychopathology (which would get us nowhere). But to see it as a necessary mediating device is perhaps more useful.

More recently, Forrestal's being overtaken by paranoia in the Dulles era of the Cold War is an example of a person overwhelmed by the mythic dimensions of his own indulgence in mediation that was unsuccessful. The mediation proved destructive in a personal sense, because that was the only alternative. That which he sought to mediate toward—almost certainly a vision of utter and awful apocalyptic war between Russia and the West—was an untenable other state, an unreal and unacceptable future. No one could afford to allow the secretary of the Navy and chairman of the Joint Chiefs of Staff to actualize that personal myth of savior through battle. No one, not even Dulles himself, could afford that the rhetoric become the reality.

So there seems to be a sense in which the choice of myth, given the social forces around the person, creates the possibility of success or failure in the mediator role. For the innovator, that choice is crucial. The myth allows transcendence of the personal limitations, the frailties, and the failings of the individual. It creates a buoyant sweep of effectiveness, and sets up the nature of the reinforcers that will work to induct others into the new way and support the mediating behavior of the agent of change.

This draws us back into the nature of the available cultural myths, the transpersonal models of action and conduct, that a person may employ. Myths are potent not by any magic or mystic force, but because they awaken confidence based on historical precedent. Winston Churchill's style drew upon, and activated, traces of the battle leaders of the British tradition: Henry V at Agincourt (or at least Shakespeare's version of him—itself heavily mythic), Drake, the Iron Duke, Nelson, and back beyond them to the Celtic king or queen, heroes and heroines whose reality is almost totally obscured by myth-making. The charisma of Adolph Hitler drew, similarly, on the tribal warlord tradition of central and northern Europe, the dynastic, autocratic monarchs and their chancellors. The awful assurance with which Hitler assimilated mythic elements to his purpose created a Wagnerian drama of terror, repression, hate, and slaughter, all in the name of order and control. We recognize the Goths, the Vandals, the Huns, and the Dark Gods of the northern parthenon: the man stood in his own tradition; admired it; took one side of its cultural prescription of character as his character, his justification and model. By identifying his person with its continuity, he *changed* his society dramatically, and in a most distorting and devastating way.

Thus, we can see that whatever the nature of the innovation, its desirability or undesirability, there are not only available myths, but also among them some that have more power than others. The successful mediator has an intuitive understanding of this and is renewing and refreshing those myths most earnestly desired, those that call for refurbishment in his time.

All this, of course, is itself within the universal framework of the myth of eternal return. The confidence that flows from the innovator who, while doing something utterly new in his tradition, yet seems older, wiser, and more traditional than he really is (or reasonably could be) brings to his action a strong self-fulfilling prophecy. The future is assured because we know the assurance of the past. No wonder that in recent times a Boston Irish immigrant family founded a political dynasty at the highest levels of American politics. No wonder that there is magic in the name of Rockefeller.

It follows that within-culture mediation will be achieved by the actions of those who are close not to the character of the times, but to the cultural tradition; that the person who would seek success in changing the surrounding society should study the cultural products of the past as much as contemporary economics or sociology; and that the day of the humanities is by no means over, for in a cultural sense, such products are as useful and as significant as any social-science statement of probabilities—maybe more so.

What, then, of the intercultural mediator? Is he required to be possessor of both traditions, manipulator of two mythic sets? It is tempting to attribute his success to his position at the intersection, but is this real? I am raising questions that lie far beyond the ordinary realm of empirical social science; but one thing that that body of knowledge states with great assurance is that an individual becomes the creature of his culture, and it is a formidable task even to realize what that means, let alone change its impress. True, some may transcend that state to become creative within their tradition. The inter-cultural intellect of a Nabokov, or indeed of Levi-Strauss himself, consti-tutes not a denial of that fact, but its affirmation. By some trick or set of tricks, the voice may be heard in the language of a new culture, but what speaks is the sense of the home culture, sounding new and dramatic for that fact.

To know the metaphors and idioms of another's world is certainly useful. Without them, intercultural communication can only be about the prosaic world of technology, interaction without meaning. Culture is the context that gives action meaning, as Michael Cole (1975) has reminded us. When I say something from my world to another, I need to know how to activate "you" in "yours" as distinguished from "me" in "mine." Something more than technical accuracy in verbs and nouns and the other bits and pieces of language is needed to do that.

At the widest level, this problem is the same as that encountered by any two people communicating. We deceive ourselves in thinking that because we use the same words, we have the same understandings. If, however, I want to be as sure as I can that you know what I intend, I must attend to your attending and check your understanding against my intention. Yet if I do this incessantly, I will cease to say anything like what I intended to say. If I stop attending to you, then you will judge me insensitive, maybe even arrogant or worse. And you will stop listening and not understand. To be at least successful to a pragmatic degree, I have to compromise, make assump-tions, monitor your comfort, your interest, your responding. More than anything else, I must care about you as much as I care about what I want you to know or understand.

This brings us to another possible truth about intercultural mediating: if I am too obsessed with caring for the other, I may become a nuisance, a missionary, and be rejected. Or worse still, the other may become so con-vinced by the mediator's sincerity (or power, or skill in persuasion) that he permits acts of exploitation and becomes destructively dependent on the mediator.

Let me turn now to some data. The material from which I have selec-ted the examples that follow is vast. All that I can do is to present the briefest of sketches of the cases I have in mind. More, much more, is available. As I select, I am setting up information that will make cer-tain issues emerge. In that sense, the presentation is biased, but the bias is necessary if the examples are to speak to the process of cultural mediation.

Case Studies of Mediation

RAUPARAHA

Te Rauparaha was born around 1768 at an inland North Island settlement in
New Zealand. His father was highborn in the line from Toa Rangitira, progen-
itor of one of the major tribes of the Waikato Tainui confederation. His
mother, less well born, was from another major group, the Ngati Raukawa.
He was not the firstborn and had not, therefore, great expectations. He
suffered an insult to his wife that led to quarrels with other Waikato tribes,
the direct result of which was that he tried to form an alliance against central
Waikato. To strengthen his position, he sought the new weapons and fighting
techniques of the Pakeha (Europeans).

Various adventures followed, including an apparent apprenticeship in the
new warfare with Waikato's greatest enemy. This ultimately led to a decision
to gather his people together and trek south, over three hundred miles, taking
with him in migration eight hundred men and their families. These people
established conquest in their new locality in a fertile, pleasant coastal plain,
where Te Rauparaha founded a new community. Now he was living cheek
by jowl with the new, burgeoning Pakeha township of Port Nicholson (later
Wellington), and the association was not inauspicious, though not always
peaceable. The ship *Tory* gave him a royal salute on arrival. He signed the
Pakeha treaty that established the rule of the British over the land. He shel-
tered a Church Missionary Society (CMS) mission under his aegis, more for
its educational value than for religious reasons, and he ruthlessly suppressed
opposition to the new teaching, even though he held to his own religion
till the end.

TAMIHANA

Rauparaha's son, Katu Te Rauparaha, was born during the migration, the
offspring of his father's most significant political-marital liaison. He it was
who traveled north to get the CMS to send a missionary to Otaki, and at the
age of twenty he was baptized "Tamihana." With his friend Matene he
became a traveling apostle of the gospel, sailing around the whole North
Island coastline, spreading the word. When he settled again in Otaki, he
sought to establish what seemed to him a model of English country life:
dressing well; living in European-style houses with rooms, steep pitched
roofs, and chimneys; and striving to show in every possible way his accom-

plishments in the new culture. He even visited England and had a child christened in Windsor chapel. He established a secondary school for his people, a college on the model of Eton, and was ordained a priest and endowed the mission and school with land. His sheep farm was reportedly well managed and successful. Governors and legislators sought his counsel and he died, much honored, in 1876.

On his return from England, Tamihana rejoined his friend Matene Te Whiwhi to take up a new crusade—to unite the scattered and divisive Maori tribes under a king. He carried this idea back to the people of Lake Taupo, in a sense a cousin tribe to his mother's, whose chief was in his view a likely claimant for the title. That man refused and pointed him north to the tribes of his father's group.

WAHAROA

There he offered the idea to their chief politician, Te Waharoa Tarapipipi. Waharoa was one of a triumvirate of Waikato power, a man essentially of peace but caught between the more powerful Maniapoto to the west and Potatau Te Wherowhero to the north. It was astute to seek Waharoa as the first approach to Waikato, because his influence was innovative and far-reaching, and his political position pivotal.

Waharoa stood across the Waikato river, a profound presence in that arterial waterway to the heartland of the country. He had grown up to be his father's successor as leader of one of the most feared groups in the area. But in 1838, when his father died, he was baptized and turned his people toward peaceful development, agriculture, industry, and the mission teachings. He established flour mills, schools, a printing press, and urged his people to develop strong local control to exclude land grabbers, rumrunners, and musket traders. Under his charge, his people became notably prosperous, widely literate, and most energetic in their innovative responses.

When Tamihana Te Rauparaha and Matene Te Whiwhi came to Te Waharoa, he saw the symbolic significance of their proposal and called the tribes to a series of meetings, which finally resulted in the election of Potatau as king. At first only Waikato gave allegiance, but slowly the Kingitanga gained strength and significance. Potatau Te Wherowhero was old, and died a year after his ascension.

WHEROWHERO

Te Wherowhero had been early to respond affirmatively to Pakeha trade and missions, welcoming both to his territory between 1824 and 1826. He married his daughter to a trader at Kawhia, but continued the old style of conquest and warfare right up to the Treaty of Waitangi which, though he never signed, he recognized and even welcomed. The year after the treaty (1841), Governor Hobson took Te Wherowhero to Wellington to confer with Te Rauparaha. He urged his people to ask the missionaries for seed, stock, and schooling, and he offered to open his lands to settlement. He wanted the wealth and power of the new way.

When the settlement at Auckland was threatened by the northern tribes, Te Wherowhero moved his residence and a substantial population there to help Governor Fitzroy with the defense of the town. He helped the government quieten Te Rauparaha when the latter had been arrested and taken from Otaki in order to protect Wellington from his threat. When Te Wherowhero died, Waikato was rich in honor, in material goods, in settlements, and in production, and strong in friendships and hope. He was succeeded by his son, who became Potatau II but is remembered by his people as Tawhiao.

TAWHIAO

Given the nature of Pakeha culture, it was inevitable that the relatively closed lands of Waikato, rich and growing more prosperous each year, should be envied. So a variety of factors led to war. Waharoa and Tawhiao certainly did not want conflict, and could have kept Waikato in peaceful development, trading with the Pakeha to the north. But greed is greed. Waikato's power, progress, literacy, and organization were perceived as a threat by the commercial barons of Auckland. Waharoa sought to fend off conflict by making clear the three critical actions which, if the government took them, could lead to war. Simultaneously, the government did all three. Waikato was routed, their lands seized and occupied. Behind their king, they retired to the hills, there to construct a new way, and till 1882—that is, for fifteen years—the king was a symbol of renewal, return, and protest against dispossession, depression, despair, and defeat.

Tawhiao welcomed the great protest leaders, Te Ua Haumene, Te Whiti, Tohu, Te Kooti, Aperahama Taonui. He reestablished the tradition of prophecy and was a considerable composer of *waiata*, the chant song that links the present to the past in mythic language. All that he could regain from the Pakeha was pardon and amnesty. But he began to fight for compensation for seized land and for the doctrine that the protection of land should remain in Maori hands: "We can live without roads, railways, or courts, but we could not live without our lands." He led a deputation to England seeking redress, though unsuccessfully.

To him we owe the present structure of the Kingitanga, its preservation of ceremonial, and the meticulous correctness of traditional observance.

But he also constructed the social means by which the Kingitanga has come through to the present with astonishing vigor. He published his own newspaper, founded settlements and villages, personally rejected a pension, and kept his people from dependence on handouts. In one famous speech, he stated that the government was his enemy, not the Pakeha. "The officials must leave the country, but the bakers, carpenters, and storekeepers remain. I will look after them," he said, and though he never got that chance, his concern for his own remains legendary.

From him, the line descends through Mahuta, Te Rata, Koroki, to the present encumbent, Te Ariki Te Atairangikau. He founded many institutions: the close family advisers of the king called the Kahui Ariki (the King's Cloak); the Te Kaumarua (council of twelve); the offical religion, Pai Marire; the observances of *kawa* (formal etiquette or procedure); the Runanganui, or conference of local committees of *marae* (tribal meeting places); the modern decorated meeting houses and dining halls; the annual tribute visits to loyal *marae*, termed *poukai*; the celebration of the reenactment of the coronation each year; the rituals of oratory (*whai korero*) and associated chanting (*waiata*). All these and more continue and continually adapt.

Just beyond the turn of the century, there emerged among the then much depressed Maori population a group of self-conscious Maori innovators who established the cultural basis of a resurgent *Maoritanga*. Most of them came through the church boarding school Te Aute, a land-endowment college for the education of young Maori men. (One, however, was a woman, Te Puea, and we await a full biography of her.) Their linkages, the interweaving of their lives, demand both more space and skill than I can bring to the task of documenting and reporting, but in brief compass I shall try to record the essentials.

These people self-consciously created the conditions of their own success, drawing on the readiness in those around them to change and meeting head-on the circumstances that they found. There is a strong sense not of their charisma, for that they only found as they developed their *mana*, but of "throwness"—the almost blind acceptance of the necessity to mediate, of the inevitability of their decisions embracing that into which they were locked. Call it duty, if you will; call it service; neither term expresses the energizing effect, the charge of reinforcement, that doing what must be done brought to their lives.

NGATA

Apirana Turupa Ngata was born late in his mother's life, in circumstances so unusual that his career was marked as special. On the day he was baptized, the *tohunga* who had removed the seven years of barrenness in the marriage of his parents died. His father recorded the fact in his diary. Ngata was reared by Major Ropata, a man who had fought for his people through dark days and troubles.

The record says that Ngata entered Te Aute College in 1884 and later university, taking his first degree in 1893. Later still, he took his master's degree in political science and completed a law degree as well. By 1897 he had prepared himself, and in that year called a conference of young Maoris to begin the work that had to be done.

He entered Parliament in 1905 and remained a member till 1943, serving in the cabinet in a number of portfolios. In the 1930s, he set up land consolidation and development schemes, reestablished a school of carving, personally stimulated and saw built nearly thirty carved meeting houses, and drew Maori funds together in a national program for purposes of land development, farm training, education, and community welfare. He revived the language, traditional oratory, and the *marae* as a setting for it and as a place for political and social discussion and action; rejuvenated the dying tradition of song and chant; and invented an entirely new song and entertainment tradition. He was president of the Polynesian Society, established the Board of Ethnological Research, and published two volumes containing hundreds of chants and songs together with notes explicating their allusions.

All this was done through the mastery of two processes, the parliamentary system and community action. Activity in both earned him a rich harvest of envy and hostility, coming to a head in the Native Affairs Commission of 1934 which was, in a veiled way, a pretty direct attempt to check his leadership of a resurgent Maori nationalism and cultural spirit. His skill in manipulating the machinery of government grew through his career, as he met and mastered incredible difficulties and faced reluctance to the point of blatant discrimination. Yet his pace, energy, and strategy were irresistible.

The community action program was developed from those early days at Te Aute when he and his friends formed a traveling task force trekking the country in the school vacations, urging improved health, hygiene, housing, and cultural revitalization. He used the language both of tradition and of Christianity, marshaling religious as well as secular support. In forging the quite modern idea of the action song team (traveling and making money from entertainment), he showed a keen syncretism of spiritual and cultural appeals, raising funds while raising morale. His memory was phenomenal, as also were his eloquence and pithy skill in metaphor.

Like everyone else, I was more than once subjected to his quite autocratic sharpness and bullying manner, for he castigated anyone who failed to meet his standards. He bore in on his people with hard, tough language which appealed to duty, service, honoring the traditions of the past, and creating a future for the young. "The Old Man," we called him, but to his death he could exhaust anyone of any age who tried to match his energy.

There are many extant stories of the way he took old forms and bent them to new purposes. Old songs acquired new significance. New songs were made to serve old purposes. In building new meeting houses, he had to innovate all the time and reach for any available idea, a bit of myth, an ancestor's *mana*, switching and swapping around traditions to get the people to support his wishes. In doing all this, he had the support of many other young Maoris.

POMARE

Maui Pomare was with Ngata at Te Aute and joined in that traveling caravan. Pomare saw health as a vital prerequisite for his people's resurgence. He went to the United States to train in medicine, graduating in 1899, but came back to New Zealand, not to practice, but to penetrate and change the administration of health services. He established Maori health officers in Maori communities, and got the people moving in reestablishing community councils. In 1911, he too entered Parliament, rapidly achieved cabinet rank, and set up two Royal Commissions on native affairs. Through these he sought redress of land confiscation, and thus helped to establish a new economic base for cultural revival.

With a Pakeha collaborator who had the literary skills which he lacked, Pomare set about collecting and publishing myths and legends, learning as he did so the technique of adding these to his already powerful oratory. Like those of Ngata, his speeches are a potent mixture of forthright directness laced with poetic allusion of great power.

Pomare had a trick of imputing wisdom to the past to shame his people into action, as for example in the comparison he drew between the stinking open privies common in so many places and the putative airy cleanliness of the old-style outhouse over a cliff, river, or stream. I doubt whether anyone really knows what pre-Pakeha privies were like (my guess is that most people used the bushes), but Pomare was not one to trifle over the authenticity of the traditions he invoked if doing so made the point and helped control disease. He did it in the correct language, and knew what he was doing.

BENNETT

On the religious front, several of the Young Maori party, as they called themselves, set to work, but it was Frederick Bennett who stands above all. He became the first national bishop of Aotearoa, claiming as his see the

Maori people wherever they were and (at times one might think) almost whatever their religion.

Bennett had grown up in Rotorua when tourism was leaving his people a burned-out and dispossessed remnant of what they had been. He was picked up by a bishop traveling through the area and whisked off to a parish school in Nelson. Later, ordained as a lay preacher, he did not restrict himself to the business of preaching, but deeply and actively involved the people in community work. He was responsible for the building of at least fourteen churches, some of them decorated and carved in Maori style. He fought the curse of liquor, which had played such a strong role in destroying the economic and social basis of Maori life. He almost personally sang his way toward better standards in the tourist and entertainment industries, calling on his people to have pride in what they were doing. And all the time he was using the church to help the other young leaders build a national sense of renewal. Again, his oratorical flair drew on the Maori tradition, and though he rarely spoke publicly in Maori, his style was clearly derived from the mythico-poetic forms of *whai korero*.

Strongly individual though he was, Bennett returned all the time to the theme of community building and to the peculiar blend of competition and cooperation that Maori communities contained. Quite consciously he drew on this ambiguity, combining it with the parable of the talents and Christian duty. Like Ngata, he had no hesitation in pushing people into a guilt-motivated sense of community service. And he laid the foundation of a vigorous young Maori clergy that other faiths subsequently emulated.

Ngata, Pomare, and Bennett were all men of arts and letters, and you might at this point think that I am arguing for the necessity of a university education to make mediation of this kind possible. I most certainly do not mean to imply that. It was true that these men and others like them—Te Rangi Hiroa and Rewiti Kohere, to name but two—followed that route. But others did not. Pei Te Hurinui, for example, moved directly into the field of land dealing, fighting for the retention, consolidation, and use of the people's major economic asset. James Carroll filled a long life with political service (in the House of Representatives from 1887 to 1912, and from then in the upper house, the Legislative Assembly, till 1926). Carroll was never near a university. Tipi Ropiha, who rose to become permanent head of the Department of Maori Affairs, began his career as a chainman in a bush surveying team.

TE PUEA

Te Puea Herangi must stand as a representative for the women in this group, but she would stand alone in any company. She had status, since her mother was the eldest daughter of Tawhiao, the second Maori king. Tawhiao had banned Pakeha schooling following the confiscation of the Waikato lands, and Te Puea therefore was not sent to school till her mind had been shaped by her father in Maori lore. She learned to speak from orators steeped in the meanings and mysteries of the past. *Then* she topped all this off with a brief but full four years at regular school.

Te Puea's clarity and directness of speech were as effective as any man's, and when she chose to do so, she could roll up her sleeves and set to man's work, even the hardest, such as scrub-cutting. By these skills, matching words to actions and fighting always to bring community to her people, she won through, even past the hostility and rejection of her own kinsman King Mahuta.

By sheer force of energy, Te Puea was instrumental in buying back land close to one of the most sacred places in Waikato, and there she began, from rude, harsh scrub, to rebuild a ceremonial center, Turangawaewae, a *marae* that today is acknowledged as the most elaborate, vital, and growing place of conference and ritual in all of Maoridom. Her carvers and crafts people worked without pay to build it and furbish it with proper decoration. Her work and style continue. Over very recent years, a new, fully carved war canoe capable of holding sixty paddlers has been added to those previously carved, and a new building that has cost half a million dollars contains (among other decorations) a mural that is a superb masterpiece of artistic syncretism, welding old forms to new means of expression.

Since the sacred place had no tribe as such, Te Puea gathered around her the orphans of the people and herself raised a new tribal base, who work at the *marae*, maintain it, and support its activities. She rebuilt the *mana* of women, and in farming laid the foundations of an economic base for the people and the place. Today that *marae* regularly hosts gatherings of several thousand people, and her presence lives on in its style and accomplishments.

Mediator Style in Maori Culture

I said earlier that I was not intent on focusing on the charismatic or other qualitites of the mediator. Yet it may seem that I have chosen so far to concentrate on singular and remarkable people, aristocrats, an elite. That they were. But beyond those whom I have chosen, I could call into this argument many, many more whose efforts have produced a resurgent, living transformation in contemporary Maori culture. What I have to say about all of them could be said by documenting the lives of any of them.

In more recent times, there has been a similar wave of regenerative leader-ship. One such recent mediator, Dr. Maharaia Winiata, wrote of the role of the Maori leader, acknowledging in his book (1967) the institutional and situational nature of the mediator role and process. John Waititi did much to renew the role of Maori language in education and laid the foundation of what is now a widespread development, at all levels, of language teaching. Mr. Robert Mahuta at my own university is building a program of action research that in style and content fits into the pattern I have been recounting.

John Rangihau and others have gone back into the structure of their own tribes to rejuvenate the transmission of the old cultural material of myth and tradition, song, oratory, and custom, while at the same time to build a more secure economic future for their people. Some of the latter-day leaders have borrowed extensively from the rhetoric and strategies of Black Power and nationalism in other indigenous groups, but the aim, the objective, has been as it has always been: the restoration of community and continuity, adaptation, borrowing, innovation—not pride for the sake of pride, but to connect now with then in both past and future.

Twenty years ago, in an attempt to understand these processes, I analyzed leadership and followership in Rakau, the Maori community in which I did my first field research (Beaglehole and Ritchie 1958). I recognized four settings in which leadership could be seen: the traditional, the neotraditional, the modified Pakeha, and the wholly Pakeha. Four categories of leadership itself—by elders, by family heads, by young leaders, and by young people's leaders—provided a matrix of role and situation that brought form into the field data.

That analysis was systematic and smacked of the social-science ideas of the fifties. It served to express the complex, varied, variable, and rapidly adapting patterns that I observed. What it failed to do was to recognize that the categories were arbitrary and the development of effective mediation resided not so much in roles or in persons as in the community processes from which these derive. It was also very idealistic, seeing Rakau in a transitional mode as though some other, more stable state had once existed and could exist again. My own data, reexamined, denied it then and deny it now.

Rakau as a scene called forth responses from people stylistically similar to those great names I have called to the record here. It was uncouth to regard leadership in Rakau as inadequate or confused just because the situation did not support glory. So now I want to try again, to seek in these new data, over time and across grossly dissimilar processes, something of generality that identifies the successful Maori within-culture mediator and that can be extended, I hope, cross-culturally.

Let us look first at the circumstances that made it possible for these men and women to be people of vision. There is, to start with, the cultural model of the people called *matakite*, those who have the gift of vision. Pakeha commentators, for their own cultural reasons, have emphasized the extrasensory or supernatural powers of *matakite*, viewing them as readers of portents, visionaries, soothsayers. The within-culture Maori prescription is far wider, far more ordinary than this. The power of transcending immediate, mundane circumstances to project a possible future is widespread. Anyone can be or become a seer, but some are better at it than others. Thus, while the power of *matakite* was especially characteristic of those whose role verged on the shamanistic, the capacity was a general one, and anyone of foresight, or in a moment of vision, could be said to be *matakite*.

To be a visionary, it was necessary to live or have lived close to the cultural core. My cases are marginal or alienated only in an abstract, not in a psychological, sense. Nor was there any occurrence in any of them of that process which Hagen (1962) calls status withdrawal, the removal of support that forces innovators into the mediator role. These people led from a double competence which they deliberately built and carefully maintained and promoted.

Tamihana Te Rauparaha went on his journey to England with this in mind, and with the same interest began to model his life-style on that of the missionaries and gentry. He could do so because the strong parental model of his father had already made him adept in his own culture. Waharoa similarly took on the model of the Pakeha political strategist. In his recorded writings and speeches, he made significant use of the imagery of the Old Testament and of the prophets and lawgivers, and he had a conception of the rule of law quite alien to his own history. With an almost anthropological sense of culture change, he saw that the old ways ordered things in a manner not now tenable.

The young men of the Young Maori party at the turn of the century deliberately sought the *mana* and power of the alien culture by seeking qualification in its major institution of status, the university. But among themselves, no less deliberately, they returned to some part of the cultural core. They set themselves definite tasks: Ngata, to record the songs and poetry and by annotation make their richness known and knowable; Pomare, the task of recording myth and legend; Buck, material culture; Carroll, the investigation of land title and tenure that required the study of *whanaunga-tanga*, of genealogy and kinship. Te Puea's task was more action-oriented—the reestablishment of the *marae* Turangawaewae and documentation of the Kingitanga. Each task was a voyage deep into cultural significance, so that each person might feel a growth of power within his or her possession of the culture. Each was also a salvage operation, and involvement in it brought the person into contact with the remnants of the seemingly dying congregation of elders.

In this way, the identification of these men and women with the historicity of their culture and heritage was established and never lost, even though most spent years at a time away from their folk, living in urban settings, even overseas. They reestablished for themselves, and in doing so, for others, a sense of cultural "home," a psychological base. Each task required the extension, command, and application of the symbols that lie at the core of the culture—of the balance between things *tapu* or sacred and those that are *noa* or ordinary; of *mauri*, the spiritual essence, and *mana*, its status manifestation; of *aroha*, at its most abstract the warm embrace of kin and friendship, at its most mundane *homai no homai*, the chain of reciprocal giving. And many more concepts carrying a high charge of cultural significance were involved and invoked.

These mediators set themselves the task of mustering the language and of loving and fashioning it into a powerful medium of communication. The oratory of the parliamentarians among them, even in English, emptied the lobbies and bars and packed their colleagues into the House. Fred Bennett's wit and subtlety brought him international recognition at the Lambeth Conference and among his fellow bishops, as much as with the general population. The booming resonance of Bennett's delivery made every sermon a listening pleasure. These people loved their language. They had a profound respect for words, for style, and an urgent need to be understood.

While the tradition of literacy in European culture was respected and indeed envied and admired, these mediators had a profound sense of their own cultural history. They also knew that in traditional societies, a sense of history is not the privilege of a few or something locked within an elite, but the weft in the ordinary life of ordinary people, across which the warp of daily events weaves. This brought to their actions a sense of immediacy and involvement in the minutia of the mundane world. These lofty people dreaming dreams of establishing a king, of resisting the power of the Pakeha, of staging a cultural renaissance, got down and grubbed out the brambles and gorse, took up hammers and saws with the builders, got alongside their young people in action song and *haka* teams, and *worked*.

In order for anything to be possible, it had to be economic, whether it was a scheme to establish Maoris as small dairy farmers or to employ people to carve and decorate houses. Te Puea's establishment of a new tribe at Turangawaewae was seen by sentimentalists as an almost saintly devotion to the orphaned ones in her tribal area. But it was also sound, hard-headed sense, for there was work to be done, and hands were needed to accomplish it.

This example also shows a sense of how things work in the Maori world and illustrates the social machinery of successful action. No Pakeha I know has a real command of this; for these mediators, there was an acutely conscious sense of how to get things done. It was not always successful because in many cases, they had to get extra information. (Matene Te Whiwhi and Tamihana Te Rauparaha cruising the country in search of a king is a fine example of that.) Their sense was not magical or intuitive, but wholly cognitive, including the hard-headed problem-solving, researching, and argumentation without which the seeming miracles could not have occurred.

These mediators were concerned with the hurt their people were (and are) suffering. There simply was no room for mere careerism. All around them, people's lives were being wrenched and torn, their assets destroyed or taken from them, their children and old folk dying, their sacred places desecrated, their food sources alienated and ravaged. Within the language and its symbolism, with recourse to the anguish of the past and to its mythic heroes, they could say things about this more powerfully and freely than could Pakeha politicians or preachers. For any of these people, no issue was minor, no cause too trivial, no injury petty. To build the status of mediator, the pain of the people had to be reduced.

For them all, there was a price to be paid: sacrifice of their own personal concerns, certainly; but more than this was the often bitter necessity of choice. Daily they faced dilemmas that could not be left unresolved. They were people whose living was invested with competence in choosing, in making decisions. To some it might seem that in doing so they cut a bold swath, often choosing neither wisely nor well, leaving in some a feeling of resentment. Tamihana Te Rauparaha's gentlemanly aspirations were mocked. Waharoa's peacemaking left him at one point lonely and alienated from his folk, yet still distrusted by the Pakeha generals and politicians. Ngata was often accused of being anti-Pakeha. He replied that he was not, but that he was pro-Maori. He felt the injustice that he should be criticized for that, as though loyalty to one's people were a crime. Te Puea's resistance to the conscription of Maoris to fight in World War I led to suspicions that she was a German spy! They carried on. There was a job to be done. Time was short. Decisions had to be made.

All the time, in each case, there is displayed a skillful use and construction of structures of support. For all these people, there was a strong sense of real community, of the necessity to work face-to-face in real time with real people. When an issue came up, it had to be related to the real community. Who were the people affected? Who needed to be consulted? Who could not be passed over? Who was most able to help? Who could rally the needed people? How could the people raise the necessary money? There was no dependency on remote agencies, on government funds, on abstract authority; no talk of how little community now really exists. Build it; consolidate it; make every venture a confirmation that community does exist, can continue, has the will, the resources, the solution.

For themselves, at each of the three periods I have described, these mediators formed what Margaret Mead (1964) has called "clusters," self-sustaining, superconscious groups. Among themselves, they cared for each other's concerns. Their letters show this. They not only cared for the health and effectiveness of whole communities of people, but in themselves formed a community of mediators. And when a cry for help came from one of their number, they rallied.

To anyone looking at this work, at their lives, it seems that they lived among a constant onslaught of ambiguities and that they survived and thrived on conflict. In a profound sense, they were people of principle, but in every case one can cite examples where principle was laid aside. They could live with inconsistency, undismayed.

That looks like a peculiar quality of personality until you look closer at the cultural supports for such a capacity. In a vast number of ways, the culture of the Maori gives precedent for and sanction to just such a state. For one thing, very basically, a person in an ambilateral kinship system always has ambiguity regarding which line he or she *really* belongs to, the maternal or the paternal. When a Maori dies, there is always debate and argument about who should have the right to bury the body. One may be in a state of *tapu* at one moment, *noa* the next. The culture was built to contain conflict, to express it, but not especially to resolve it. In history, tradition, and myth, the heroes are those who broke through and beyond the culture constraints of place, folk, role, and status. Maori proverbial sayings richly support this essential ingredient in innovation. This situation creates ambiguities and consequent anxieties, indeterminancy, strangeness, novelty. My cases could sustain levels of ambiguity and unresolved issues, yet still be people of choice and action. They turned conflict into an asset. In the Western tradition, their selflessness might be seen as saintliness, but each and all were far from being that.

In none of my cases did wealth follow from the mediating effort. In all there was an increase in prosperity for the people, of an immediate and direct kind: food for the hungry, jobs for the workers. It is probably unlikely that any community can accept a mediator whose actions result in personal gain. The supraindividual sense of personal commitment rules it out entirely. Yet none of the Maori mediators became personally impoverished through that commitment. The barefoot saint may appeal to those who can accept reward in heaven, but the mediator here on earth must satisfy his or her own needs as well as those of others.

Some ran close to self-destruction through the consuming fire of the energy they burned up in their efforts—indeed, all suffered periods of illness that might be laid to exhaustion just as easily as to any other physical cause. Peter Buck, on his last return to his homeland, was dying with cancer and knew it, but hardly anyone else did. Te Puea, in her later years, took to her bed after each major *hui* or gathering at Turangawaewae and rested on the social support she had built and had so generously earned. Ngata, when I knew him in his retirement at Waiomatatini, would not himself have husbanded his waning physical health, but was held in care and love by those around him so that he could always appear in public with the quickness and assurance that his people knew and loved.

This supraindividual concern was not achieved or maintained by otherworldliness or neglect of the individual interest. Rather, it arose through these. What is so consistently and insistently present in the records of these people is their persistent return to the task, working away at the details till the problem could be transcended. And that meant, in the first instance, application to problems capable of solution. I do not know how they developed such a sense, nor whether the problems tackled were solved because they could be or because they were forced to become tractable by sheer tenacity. My guess is that all these people were good listeners, good at carefully assessing what was possible and what was not. They attended to detail and constantly broke up the insoluble into attainable subgoals. As models of good problem-solving, they could grace any textbook on the psychology of thinking.

In the onrush of their innovating and borrowing, they nevertheless allowed themselves time to demonstrate that new ideas, new media, new techniques work. In this way, they maintained a positive manifold of ensuing success. For some, this was not easy, for there were dark days and troubled times. Not the least of the techniques was a powerful assurance that people can be modern and yet remain within the tradition; that the tradition itself, in its most general, most abstract, most metaphysical sense, could incorporate modernity. Ngata used wax-cylinder recordings in the early twenties to record *waiata*; he seized on the new ethnography as an aid to his people, rather than rejecting it as interference; he constantly urged that only by publishing books could literacy become more than an on-graft. The people should read of their own culture as manifested through their own writers, poets, and historians. In 1928, he urged that the university introduce Maori studies and Maori language, though it was nearly 30 years later that this was done.

It was as though by returning always to powerful central cultural sanctions that the details and trivia of change could be transcended. The groups I have chosen to present contrast strongly with the charismatic religious leaders, whose genius lay elsewhere and who were not, by the complex definition I am building here, mediators. Always there was a flexibility of movement, in and out, to and fro, between and within cultures. No one could challenge the understanding by Tawhiao of both worlds, nor his assurance and sense of *mana* in each. Pomare's biographer (Cody 1953) called his study *Man of Two Worlds*, and that idea is a powerful support for action in itself.

In Maori, the concept of *turangawaewae*, of having a place to stand, whether on the land one owns, in kinship status, or in terms of personal competence, is a core idea. Tamihana used it. So did Waharoa. Te Puea made it material in her *marae*, the footstool of the kings. Ngata urged young Maoris to move deliberately into the Pakeha world and lay claim to its knowledge and skills, and then to return better equipped to serve the people: "Stand firmly with one leg in each culture." Even today, young Maori spokesmen and women repeatedly remind the Pakeha that Maoris are now possessors of two sets of cultural understandings and are the richer for it. Because they had mediators who could and did learn a second culture, they have learned how Pakehas think far more and far better than Pakehas have learned how Maoris think. Buck spoke as often and as proudly of his Irish father as of his Maori mother.

Thus, *turangawaewae* has been stretched and extended to transcend the limitations of nationalism or the blinkers of ethnocentricity. Adroitness in battle, the weaving and ducking that meant survival, has been extended. To beat the Pakeha, you must be more agile, more wily, more subtle than your opponent. Ngata used that analogy, and on one occasion employed the symbolism of a good backline rugby football player to make his point. Politically, my cases were always engaged in a sort of guerrilla warfare, so that by the time attack came, they were somewhere else, in a new position, working on a new project.

Where, you might ask, were the Pakeha mediators in this saga of culture change? Were there any at all? Of course there were, thousands of them. Some clearly identified with Maori aspirations, like the ethnologist Elsdon Best, who spent over a decade in a bush camp recording Tuhoe lore, or Cowan, who from a king-country background became Pomare's close friend and literary collaborator. I have chosen to stack the facts in selecting within-culture mediators for study. No Pakeha, however, achieved the kind of regard my summoned ghosts acquired. None entered into the extension of Maori cultural consciousness that the latter achieved and that has become the major resource of Maori people as they master change today. None could become, in the eyes and minds of the people, exemplars of the mythic heritage. It just is not possible.

The Pakeha mediators are also so very different from each other, lacking the "cluster" cohesion of a common cultural core. But of the external mediators I can voice one strong hunch. They were often successful, but perhaps only through their impact upon within-culture mediators, in whom they induced a response within the cultural code. If that is so, we have only occasional record of it, as when Hadfield, the missionary, supported Tamihana Te Rauparaha in his educational enterprises; or when the governor turned to Waharoa to seek the means of reconstruction after the Waikato land wars; or when Pomare and Ngata undertook to negotiate reduction of opposition to the road through the Urewera Tuhoe wildlands.

There is a chain reaction in any change involving many mediators. Along this chain, in successful cases of induced change, we might see successive steps toward linkage with ever deeper significances, ever deeper layers of cultural meaning in terms of which people come to accept change "in their bones."

I have chronicled little indeed of these lives and used them unashamedly for my purposes. Perhaps what can summarize the complexity best is to say that these people were good human beings, responding closely and well to the competitiveness and the cultural verities of their situations. That said, I might seem to have said nothing—or to have said it all.

Conclusion

In this chapter, I have tried to show that in Maori culture, there existed a mediator style which was a character prescription for innovative action, sanctioned by myth and validated by consensual agreement and results. While some societies are more change-oriented than others, I suspect that mediational styles exist in all cultures. If this is so, then by looking across a range of societies, one might find correspondences that could lead to a general prescription of mediating capability. In a sense, the collected papers in this volume have begun such an inquiry.

Perhaps because I am a psychologist, I see the skills involved as being highly similar to those of the community psychologist who is engaged in therapeutic intervention. Be that as it may, success in mediation seems to require a *culture-building* orientation. The mediator must temper vision with pragmatism; he must pay close attention to cultural resources; he must be able to apply old methods to new situations; and he must be sensitive to the capacity for accepting change—now fast, now slower—within the life-style of the person or group concerned. Above all else, the successful mediator must be tuned in to the satisfactions and dissatisfactions, the joy and the pain of those with whom he or she may be working, and to the overriding fact that successful change is seen in action and not in attitudes and arises from a real increment in the competence of those who are served.

References

Beaglehole, E., and Ritchie, J. E. The Rakau Maori Studies. *Journal of the Polynesian Society*, 1958, 67, 132–154.

Benedict, R. *Patterns of Culture*. Boston, Mass.: Houghton Mifflin, 1934.

Cody, J. F. *Man of Two Worlds: A Biography of Sir Maui Pomare*. Wellington: Reed, 1953.

Cole, M. An Ethnographic Psychology of Cognition. In R. W. Brislin, S. Bochner, and W. J. Lonner (eds.), *Cross-Cultural Perspectives on Learning*. New York: Wiley, 1975.

Hagen, E. *On the Theory of Social Change*. Homewood, Ill.: Dorsey Press, 1962.

Levi-Strauss, C. *Structural Anthropology*. New York: Basic Books, 1963.

_____. *The Elementary Structures of Kinship*. Boston, Mass.: Beacon Press, 1969.

Mead, M. *Continuities in Cultural Evolution*. New Haven, Conn.: Yale University Press, 1964.
Winiata, M. *The Changing Role of the Leader in Maori Society*. Auckland: Paul, 1967.

Sources Consulted

Buck, P. He Poroporoaki. *Journal of the Polynesian Society*, 1951, *60*, 22–31.
_____. Tributes to and Speeches by Sir Peter Buck. *Journal of the Polynesian Society*, 1951, *60*, 223–254.
Gorst, J. F. *The Maori King*. London: Macmillan, 1864.
Kohere, R. T. *The Autobiography of a Maori*. Wellington: Reed, 1951.
McLintock, A. H. *An Encyclopaedia of New Zealand*. Wellington: Government Printer, 1966.
Ngata, P. Journal Extract. *Journal of the Polynesian Society*, 1950, *59*, 280–282.
Ramsden, E. *Sir Apirana Ngata and Maori Culture*. Wellington: Reed, 1948.
Rickard, L. S. *Tamihana the Kingmaker*. Wellington: Reed, 1963.
Ritchie, J. E. *The Making of a Maori*. Wellington: Reed, 1963.
Schofield, G. H. *A Dictionary of New Zealand Biography*. Wellington: Government Printer, 1940.
Schwimmer, E. The Mediator. *Journal of the Polynesian Society*, 1955, *67*, 335–351.
_____. *The Maori People in the Nineteen-Sixties*. Auckland: Paul, 1968.
Sutherland, I. L. G. (ed.). *The Maori People Today*. Wellington: New Zealand Council for Educational Research, 1940.
Te Hurinui, Pei. *King Potatau*. Wellington: Polynesian Society, 1959.

R. P. Throssell

Toward a Multicultural Society: The Role of Government Departments and Officials in Developing Cross-Cultural Relations in Australia

Introduction

In the conventional view, social values change gradually as a result of spontaneous movements within society. The twentieth century has proved the inaccuracy of this generalization. It may be true that we continue to hold the superstitious beliefs of the past, that we continue to devote ourselves to futile tribal combat to the point of extermination, that the beliefs in a divine Earth Mother have persisted throughout the thirty thousand known years of the history of *Homo sapiens*. But during this century we have seen, too, many examples of a fundamental change in the attitudes of communities and in the beliefs and character of human societies, largely manipulated by the organs of government. Social change can no longer be regarded solely as a matter of natural evolution. The example of Nazi Germany and the transformation of the German people under the all-pervasive pressures of the "master-race" ideology should be a clear enough reminder of the force and danger of governments' power to effect change in human beliefs and attitudes.

This is not to say that governments are the sole instruments of change, or even the major determining factor. For example, in Western society, the transformation of the customs of private commerce has been accomplished without any help from the bureaucrats. The practical morality of a previous generation which held that one should save to buy what was needed, one should make do, "a stitch in time saves nine"—these attitudes have been totally replaced by the credit-conscious, "buy it now" conventions of the present day. Built-in redundancy is accepted and even welcomed by consumers who would be outraged to be regarded as credulous.

The greatest transformation in human attitudes has taken place without the help of government: the sexual revolution that followed the introduction and mass distribution of oral contraceptives in the Western world. But the application of this aspect of modern technology to the problems of the developing world, and perhaps to the survival of modern civilization, will be very much the concern of governments.

AN AUSTRALIAN EXPERIENCE

I propose, in this chapter, to examine the impact of government activity on social change in the area of cross-cultural relations. In particular, I will be concerned with the role óf officials as cultural mediators and with the function of government departments as mediating institutions. I will limit myself to some examples of official activity in one country—Australia. I do not suggest that Australian experience in cross-cultural communication is representative, nor is Australia submitted as a model. Australian activities may be neither appropriate nor adaptable to the requirements of other circumstances, and I am sure that those who are involved in the development of cross-cultural communication within several Australian government departments would agree that we have done little more than make a beginning. However, in some ways, Australia serves well as a subject for laboratory study. Our social environment is circumscribed, our history confined to a brief two hundred years. The major influences upon Australian society are well known, well documented, and sufficiently recent to be recognizable and understandable today.

In this chapter, I will be presenting some illustrations of what has been done by government departments and officials in the sphere of relations between different cultures within Australian society and beyond. The perspective will be historical and trace past and present attitudes toward the original inhabitants of Australia, the reciprocal impact of successive waves of immigrants, and past and developing attitudes toward other peoples.

Cultural Influences

To simplify for the purposes of analysis, there have been four distinct cultural influences in the development of Australia: first, the aborigines, the original intruders upon the continent some forty thousand years ago; then, the British settlers, convicts and free, and their descendants, who comprise the dominant ethnic and cultural influence within the society; since the Second World War, the New Australians, the non-British migrants; and representatives of the world outside, the Asian neighbors.

There are atypical factors in the Australian background. We have been singularly insulated from diverse external influences. Few relatively advanced communities share our prolonged search for national identity. Compare our image of ourselves with the reality. We believe ourselves to be an island continent, one people, enjoying a common cultural heritage, united under one flag, speaking a single language. We accept the traditional national stereotype of the long, lean, sunburned Australian of the outback. The facts are very different: we are a people comprising ten million Australian-born, two and a half million migrants, and one hundred thousand aborigines. The aborigines alone speak sixty distinct languages. The migrant population shares fifty-two different languages. Eighty-five percent of the Australian population lives in the cities.

There are four other elements in the population statistics that will affect Australia's future policy and programs relating to cross-cultural communication:

1. Australia's population appears likely to reach stability at about 17.2 million in some sixty years' time, according to estimates presented by W. D. Borrie to the 1975 session of the Australia and New Zealand Association for the Advancement of Science (ANZAAS).
2. Australia's urban aboriginal population is predicted to double by the year 2000, to a figure of 285,000, at constant fertility and mortality rates, according to the first report of the National Population Enquiry. (Some 33 percent of the aboriginal population is currently living in urban areas.)
3. According to evidence presented by Professor Zubrzycki before the Committee on Community Relations (Department of Labor and Immigration 1975), almost 40 percent of the Australian population is of migrant extraction. That is a higher proportion of the population than the United States of America experienced at the peak of its immigration intake in the decade ending in 1910.
4. Australia's present population of 13 million faces an estimated population among its Asian neighbors of 2156 million.[1]

Together, these facts make an accommodation between the dominant culture and other elements in our society a necessity.

THE BACKGROUND

The influences of the past are more relevant to a discussion of contemporary cross-cultural experiments than speculation about the future. I will choose three threads from the fabric of our two hundred years' story, the strands that form the cultural influences I have already identified. The same three themes will later reemerge in my account of current official activity. They are official relationships with the original inhabitants, our attitude towards newcomers, and our view of outsiders.

The First People

Ironically, in view of its subsequent consequences, the original policy of the first governor of New South Wales toward the aboriginal inhabitants was entirely benevolent. Governor Phillip was directed in the original instructions, quoted by Professor Manning Clark in his *History of Australia*, to "open an intercourse with the natives, and to concilliate their affections enjoining all subjects to live in amity and kindness with them, to ascertain their numbers, to punish those who wantonly destroyed the natives or interrupted their several occupations, and report in what manner intercourse with them might be turned to the advantage of the colony" (Clark 1974, p. 80). There was no intention to conquer or subdue. Of course, the British settlers in New South Wales and Van Diemens Land had no real cause to campaign against the aboriginal inhabitants. There was no organized resistance. There was no armed force to prevent the establishment of the convict colonies. Nevertheless, it was the purpose of the British colonists to bring to the "lesser breeds without the law" the benefits of British civilization.

Governor Phillip carried out his instructions faithfully. Manning Clark describes their results: "In the beginning Phillip made all the traditional gestures of goodwill: he smiled with compassion; he gave them presents of hatchets and other articles; he ordered his men not to fire on them, except when absolutely necessary. For a season the aborigines responded with affection and even with veneration as the white skin and the material power, status as leader, and that quite fortuitous gap in his front teeth gave him some little merit in their opinion." (Clark 1974, p. 116).

Whatever the intentions, the results of the original policy toward aborigines were disastrous. It was based on a total lack of understanding, and an utter and unquestioning conviction of the superiority of the white man's way.

> Yet the aborigines remained aloof, out of reach, elusive, practising a standoffishness which puzzled and exasperated the bearers of such gifts. They remained shy in the company of the white man, though they had been treated with kindness and loaded with presents. They seemed either to fear or to despise the white man, too much to be anxious for a closer connection. The more the white man learned of their way of life and view of the world the more they were puzzled: they observed no degree of subordination in their society; they remained strangers to their religious rites and opinions. By the end of February, however, the aborigines inferred from the building that the white man intended to stay. At the end of that month they stoned white men who attempted to land in one of the coves of the

harbour; they stole the white man's tools; they stole his food; on 30 May they murdered two rushcutters and mutilated their bodies in a shocking manner. Such behaviour quickly changed the white man from a delighted observer of the picturesque and the quaint into a partisan defending his civilisation. After six months one of them wrote of the aborigine as a creature deformed by all those passions which afflicted and degraded human nature, unsoftened by the influence of religion, philosophy and legal restriction.

The behaviour of the white man was equally disgusting to the aborigine. To teach the aborigine the ways of the civilised, Phillip instructed his men to gather as many as possible to witness a flogging. The few aborigines who watched manifested only symptoms of disgust and terror. In this way the efforts to concilliate their affections and to diffuse amity and kindness degenerated into theft and murder as goodwill was pushed aside by the more primitive passions of an eye for an eye and a tooth for a tooth. (Clark 1974, p. 116)

Newcomers

The relationships of the first Australian settlers with newcomers were hardly more promising. The First Fleeters were overjoyed to receive the supply ships bringing food and news of home, but as each successive transport brought hundreds more mouths to feed from the government stores, welcome was tempered with resentment. Initially, the New South Wales colony was nothing more than a place of temporary exile, a larger and bewilderingly strange prison which only a few visionaries could recognize as a home of free men. Governor Phillip had such a vision of the future, despite the clear intentions of the British government to use the place simply as a dumping ground for convict deportees displaced from the newly independent American colonies: "What was taking shape before his eyes was the future of the territory as a free society. He wrote of it in the grand manner: 'There can be no slavery in a free land, and consequently no slaves," (Clark 1974, p. 77).

But as the settlers found consolation in vast landholdings, free convict labor, and growing wealth, some came to accept New South Wales at least as a temporary home. To the new generations of settlers born in the colony, and to the freed convicts with little option but to remain, it became native soil. There were few willing visitors; those who were brought from Britain by duty or the promise of grants of land larger than the English counties found that they were regarded with amiable contempt as "new chums." The British-born, ever safe in their superiority, considered the colonials a rough, uncultivated breed, dubbed them "currency lads," for the local coinage they were paid, to distinguish them from the true blue (and somewhat more valuable) "sterling."

The mutual raillery appears innocent enough. It seems a common attitude between colonists and colonials. I have found parallels in the attitudes of Brazilians to the Portuguese immigrants. It continues to this day. It is significant only in that it may illustrate a tendency to seek differences between people, indeed even to manufacture them, when, as in this case, both share common race, language, religion, and culture.

The discovery of gold in the mid-nineteenth century livened outside interest in the Australian colonies; for the first time they were faced with the influx of a substantial number of non-British immigrants, including a large number of Chinese. The reaction was rapid, aggressive, and totally negative. The basis of hostility to the Chinese was primarily economic: they worked the life-or-death hours of a coolie laborer, found gold when others were "unlucky," saved their findings instead of "splashing" them, worked for a pittance. To these grievances were added the fears bred of ignorance, isolation, and the British tradition of racial and social superiority. In 1857, a select committee was set up by the legislative council of Victoria to draft legislation "to control the flood of Chinese immigration settling in this Colony, and effectively prevent the goldfields of Australia Felix from becoming the property of the Emperor of China and the Mongolian and Tartar hordes of Asia" (Brisbane 1975, p. ix).

The committee estimated that forty thousand Chinese, including no more than five women, had immigrated. "Stories of viciousness and the seduction of white women grew, mixed with opposition to inter-marriage. To these were added the sins of opium smoking and gambling and the threat of smallpox and other diseases. In this period there is striking disparity between police and other professional reports which emphasize the inoffensiveness of the average Chinese citizen, and the attitude of the lawmakers and the press" (Brisbane 1975, p. ix).

Anti-Chinese feeling culminated in a riot involving three thousand persons at Lambing Flat in New South Wales in 1861, when the Chinese were beaten, robbed, and scalped by whites. The Immigration Restriction Act, the basis of the so-called White Australia policy, was adopted in the first year of federation in 1901. It remained in effect until 1966. "Although there has been significant relaxation since 1966 on the question of non-European migration to Australia, official policy discriminated in favor of Europeans until the election of a Labor Government in 1972" (Department of Labour and Immigration 1975, p. 45).

The demand for cheap labor led to the introduction of indentured black workers, recruited by trickery or force from the Pacific Islands, to work the canefields of Queensland when convict labor was no longer available. With ironic illogicality, the reaction of Australian labor unions was directed against the unfortunate Kanaka victims of a system which at its worst was little better than slavery.

Australian antipathy toward the strangers in the land was not confined to those of darker skin. At the time of the Great Depression, similar resentment toward Italian shopkeepers flared into violence on the western Australian goldfields at Kalgoorlie. The xenophobia, hostility, intolerance, or simple lack of concern for newcomers was deeply rooted in a people who otherwise took pride in their reputation for warm hospitality to their own kind and boasted an easy-going nonconformity with social convention. Even without the goad of unemployment to make foreigners a scapegoat, Australians preserved a contemptuous disregard for the immigrants that official policies pressed upon them in the name of development or defense. The first refugees from Nazi Germany were known as "reffoes." The early postwar immigrants from the Baltic states became "Balts." Until quite recently, the only attempt to reconcile Australian society to the newcomers lay in the thesis that, like medicine, it was necessary to have them: "Populate or Perish!"

The Outsiders

The British colonial heritage is at the source of Australia's attitude to Asia. Australians knew Asia (insofar as there was any awareness of Asia at all) through the outposts of empire: from Hong Kong to Singapore, from Rangoon to Cairo. The White Australia policy, which for as long as it existed determined Australia's approach to foreign relations, was firmly founded in the imperial tradition.

The outbreak of war in the Pacific in 1941 and the Japanese attack on Darwin seemed to give credence to the old terrors: the nightmare of the "yellow peril" had become stark reality. On 16 December 1941, the prime minister of Australia, John Curtin, said:

> Never shall an enemy set foot upon the soil of this country without
> having at once arrayed against it the whole of the manhood of this
> nation in such strength and quality as to show our determination
> that this country shall remain forever the home of the descendants
> of those people who came here in peace in order to establish in the
> South Seas an outpost of the British race. Our laws have proclaimed
> the principle of White Australia. We did not intend that to be and
> it never was an affront to other races. It was devised for economic
> and sound human reasons. It was not challenged for forty years. We
> intend to maintain that principle. (Hansard 1941, p. 1068)

Paradoxically, it was the reality of the Pacific war that exorcised the myths of British supremacy and white superiority. Irrespective of the Allied victory, Australia had learned the absurdity of the propagandist image of Japan, and came to know at last the significance of Australia's place in Asia. On this basis, Australia was able to develop a more valid relationship with its neighbors.

Perspectives from the Present

Prejudice, discrimination, xenophobia, naked racism, and persecution to the point of genocide are poor foundations on which to build a multicultural society. Nevertheless, it was from that basis that Australia has made, in the decade of the seventies, the first tentative steps toward a real understanding of the ethnic streams within its own community. Of course, there were always the individuals of goodwill, generosity, and kindness who were able to deal with their fellows with tolerance—even among the bureaucrats! Very occasionally, someone emerges from history with compassion that goes beyond mere tolerance to genuine understanding. But the gulf between the cultures of the Old World and the ways of the native people of Australia was immense. The pressures for survival in the new land and the need to adapt to a strange and apparently hostile environment left little room for the luxury of compromise.

Increasingly, the scholars and academics explored the ways of the "strangers." Little by little, the poets came to see them with compassion. The old suspicion, fear, and hatred gradually disappeared. But it was not until very late in Australia's history that the writers were prepared to lead community attitudes. Only in 1928 did writers such as my mother, Katharine Susannah Prichard, begin to see the aborigines as fellow human beings, without patronage, without condescension, without false charity. Even then, her tragic novel of love between a white man on a northwest cattle station and an aboriginal woman, *Coonardoo*, was condemned by decent society as being immoral.

The assumption that Australian society must be based solely upon white British-Australian traditions was never seriously questioned until the decade of the seventies. Official policies toward the aborigines, migrants, and foreign neighbors softened, but continued to be based upon the predominance of White Australia as an article of faith, as firmly and unquestioningly accepted as the Christianity of the founders. Official attitudes toward the aborigines became more protective rather than exploitative. Immigrants were welcomed, but on the basis of their assimilation into White Australian ways. Australia's relations with neighboring countries were primarily directed toward the metropolitan powers for as long as the colonial regimes retained control in Southeast Asia and the Pacific. There was little awareness of the Asian peoples and their cultures until the second World War demonstrated the fallibility of the colonial fable.

The turning point in attitudes occurred when, under the leadership of Dr. H. V. Evatt as minister of foreign affairs, Australia took the initiative in the United Nations to support the Indonesian independence movement against Dutch "police action." In the postwar years, Australia publicly acknowledged its association with Asia—and used the traditional instruments of diplomacy to keep Asia at a distance.

However limited the immediate purposes of the past policies, and however circumscribed their achievements, they did mark the beginning of understanding, and eventually led to the realization of Australia's multicultural national character. The protection of aborigines did lead to the demand for more effective measures to preserve their integrity as a people. The mere presence of migrants in the community and the attempt to assimilate them did lead to the infusion of an awareness of different cultures. Contacts with Asia through diplomatic relations, through foreign aid programs, and through the presence of overseas students in Australia awakened Australian consciousness of Asian cultures. Thus, the concept of a multicultural society as a stated aim of government policy (Grassby 1973) is the product of evolving attitudes. It is not solely the creation of the "Great Reformation" of 1972-75, the years of the Whitlam Labor government.

Many threads from the past drew together during the three years of Labor government under E. G. Whitlam. There was a deliberate reaching out toward the achievement of national identity and a break with the symbols of dominion and colonialism. Her Majesty the Queen accepted the style and title of Queen of Australia. There was an aggressive assertion of Australia's independence and an attempt to shake off foreign cultural and economic dominance. We saw strong support for indigenous art and literature, with the stated intention of establishing an awareness of national identity. Australia's recognition of her cultural diversity coincided with her awareness of her national identity. We had first to know who we were. The extent to which the multicultural society is accepted by government and nurtured by the organs of government, the extent to which Australia accepts its diversity, may depend in part upon the extent to which a common image of Australia survives.

For the present, there is no coherent, comprehensive policy of cross-cultural conciliation. A surprising range of activity in diverse areas has been undertaken by government departments, often directed to separate objectives, but adding up to an interrelated series of initiatives with a broadly common purpose. There is no evidence of conscious coordination. Often the activities associated with cross-cultural contact are inconsistent with the more conventional programs continuing within the same department or partner departments.

The new attitude toward aborigines was epitomized in the views expressed by Dr. H. C. Coombs, chairman of the Council for Aboriginal Affairs, in the George Judah Cohen memorial lecture to the University of Sydney in 1972. Dr. Coombs had made a study of four separate aboriginal communities. He presented a clear and penetrating view of the aborigines' life-styles and the possibility of realizing their very varied aspirations for the future. He concluded: "There is no evidence to my eyes of any of the aboriginal groups having chosen or being prepared to choose, as official assimilationist policy in the past assumed they would, to live by the same standards and to pursue the same purposes as White Australians" (Coombs 1972, p. 25).

With scholarly detachment, Dr. Coombs exposed the attitudes of the aborigines and of white Australians. He acknowledged the Australian community's fear and distrust of differences within our society and the wholly unwarranted value we place upon conformity with the ways and standards of "the Australian way of life." He explained:

> The essential difference, I believe, lies in the attitudes of the aboriginal to what we call "land" and "nature" to which we give meanings that he thinks barbarously insensitive; in the relatively low values that he puts on things that are not charged with what we describe as "symbolic" or "spiritual" values; and in his ideas about social obligations between persons.
>
> In his own world the aboriginal did not see "man" as one thing and "nature" as another. He was *of* nature. He saw the earth itself, plants, animals and men, the clouds and the stars—indeed all natural phenomena—as a living system of social life. It was not just a scientific or philosophical system but one in which and by which man must live consciously and reverently. Long before Terence said "nothing concerning man can be alien to me" the aboriginal was asserting and living by the faith that "nothing in all nature can be alien to me." It is true but inadequate to say of all aboriginal life that it was "in harmony with nature." The harmony came from man being in thought, word and deed of nature itself. . . ."
> (Coombs 1972, pp. 27-28)

Despite the shame of the past and the misunderstandings and failures of present policy, Dr. Coombs was cautiously optimistic about the future of the aboriginal communities in Australia:

Only the aborigines will determine the pattern of that lifestyle and the degree to which it will be achieved. Whether it is to be won from us in bitterness and in conflict or whether it develops in an honored and welcomed diversity in the fabric of our national life can, however, be for us to decide. If *our* vision of Australia is generous enough for us to see and enjoy the differences of this so different civilisation *we* may learn much from it, and *their* dreams may be realised in friendship and respect. If they are, it is my belief that our lives will be the richer for it (Coombs 1972, p. 29).

Dr. H. C. Coombs was among the first to become a Companion of the Order of Australia. He is a distinguished scholar and was formerly a leading public servant, governor of the Reserve Bank of Australia, and an advisor to successive governments on economic affairs. An unassuming man of quite extraordinary modesty, Dr. Coombs has contributed notably to many fields of Australian endeavor. His achievements have been not only in the realm of the economy, but also in such diverse areas as the arts, through the Australian Elizabethan Theatre Trust and the Australia Council; the Australian National University, of which he was both a founder and first vice-chancellor; the Snowy Mountains Authority; and aboriginal affairs. In many ways, Dr. Coombs fills the role of the mediating person to perfection. He combines a breadth of mind, penetrating intelligence, compassion, and humility with a desire to understand and to communicate this understanding. In addition, he has considerable influence with government, particularly in those areas where decisions are made and implemented.

A more direct, if less radical, influence upon the development of policy has been exercised by the Department of Aboriginal Affairs, particularly by its permanent head, Mr. Barrie Dexter, secretary of the department (under various names) since its inception in 1968. Mr. Dexter acknowledges a personal debt to Dr. Coombs, but as a senior administrator, he has been confined by the conventional limits of his position and at the same time confronted with conflicting demands for change. He has explained, in an interview with the author for inclusion in this volume:

I do operate also at this other level of Government decision. Quite frankly there are decisions taken sometimes with which I find it difficult to agree, but then I am a Public Servant of long enough standing to know that it is the Government's right to make those decisions. Up to the point that the decision is made, I will battle as hard as I can for what I believe to be the aboriginal aspect of the matter. Once the decision has been made, I have little option but to implement it; but I don't think that is an abandonment of one's conscience or responsibility, that is just the way that our style of democracy works. So in a sense my greatest advocacy or mediating at the Governmental level must come before the decision is made. Of course if I believe that a decision is a very wrong one, I can always go back and try and battle against it again, but only through the Governmental machinery, not by outside means. To that extent my role is inhibited. I suppose if one looks at it from the point of view of my being a pure and simple advocate of the aboriginal people, to that extent one must agree with your initial proposition that my responsibility to the Government is the major responsibility.

I believe I find it possible, in my own conscience, to reconcile these two aspects of allegiance to the Government and allegiance to the aboriginal people; although often I have had to be distressed personally at decisions that have been made. (Dexter 1976)

Dr. Coombs's influence upon the policy of the Australian government was not directly acknowledged when the former prime minister set forth the views of his government in a statement to the Australian Aboriginal Affairs' Council meeting on 6 April, 1973:

The basic objective of my Government's policy is to restore to the aboriginal people of Australia their lost power of self-determination in economic, social and political affairs. . . . An opportunity for self-determination and independent action would serve little purpose if aborigines continued to be economically and socially deprived. The Government therefore plans to help them as individuals, groups or communities in crafts, trades or professions and as business entrepreneurs. To this end programs of socially valuable special work projects, vocational training, grants and loans in support of enterprises will be actively promoted. (Department of Aboriginal Affairs 1976, p. 22)

While Coombs's objective of a society in which the aboriginals' dreams could be attained in friendship and respect remained implicit, the Labor government turned first to improvement of the legal and material conditions of the aboriginal people. In a policy statement in February 1975, the government undertook to legislate against all forms of discrimination as part of a program to provide equal rights and opportunities for all persons. The Racial Discrimination Act received Royal Assent on 11 June 1975. At the same time, the government promised that aboriginal history and culture would be introduced into Australian schools as an integral part of the history of Australia. (This objective had not been achieved before the change of government in December 1975.)

A high point in the education program was the move toward the establishment of a bicultural community. The key was language. In 1973, bilingual education was introduced into the schools of a number of Northern Territory aboriginal communities. This followed the acceptance of a recommendation of a working group established by the Department of Education. The essence of the bilingual education program was the emphasis placed on teaching in the local aboriginal language as well as in English and the incorporation in the school curriculum of aspects of both cultures, the aboriginal and that of the wider Australian community.

The Northern Territory bilingual education program is not merely a literacy program, in which literacy is first achieved in the local vernacular in order to facilitate a subsequent transition to literacy in the dominant language. Rather, once the children achieve their early educational goals, including literacy in both languages, both the local vernacular and the national language are employed as languages of instruction throughout the entire period of schooling, each being used in its appropriate place. Thus, the bilingual education program is very definitely intended to be not only bilingual, but also bicultural, the school becoming an integral part of the community which it serves. The aim is to produce students who have competence in both *languages* and both *cultures*.

The program began in 1973 with five schools. Another seven schools were introduced in 1974, and a further five in 1975. At the end of 1974, it was estimated that approximately six hundred aboriginal children in the Northern Territory were attending classes in which a bilingual approach had been adopted. Although this represents remarkable progress, the experts do not consider it practicable to achieve the ideal of establishing even basic literacy in every aboriginal child's mother tongue. The number and complexity of languages and dialects is in itself a problem. Further, in only a few communities is a single language or dialect spoken. Many of the languages have never been recorded and even fewer analyzed. For many languages, literacy materials have not been developed. Competent teachers are not available from many of the language groups. Nevertheless, it is clear from the results achieved, even at this early stage, that the bilingual education program is a strategy toward the achievement of a bicultural community which may have application in other areas (Tryon, 1975).

The policy of the Liberal and National Country parties, announced on 25 November 1975, immediately before their return to government, specifically endorses the objectives of a bicultural society. It declared: "We recognize the fundamental right of aborigines to retain their racial identity and traditional lifestyle, or where desired to adopt partially or wholly a European lifestyle; we will promote cross-cultural understanding and co-operation by a continuing process of community education for all age groups to ensure a high level of mutual tolerance, trust and enterprise than has so far marked our history."

COMMUNITY RELATIONS

Australia's official attitude toward migrants changed after the International Convention on the Elimination of Racial Discrimination, which entered into force on 2 January 1969. Article 7 of the convention obliged the parties to undertake measures to combat prejudice which led to racial discrimination, and to promote "understanding, tolerance and friendship among nations and racial or ethnic groups." Prior to that time, Australia earnestly believed in "the ideal of one Australian family devoid of foreign communities, thus preserving our homogeneity and solidarity as a nation" (the prime minister of Australia to the premier of Victoria in 1949; cited in Grassby 1973).

Australia did not immediately become a party to the International Convention on the Elimination of Discrimination, but the Immigration Advisory Council in March 1973 considered a report by the Department of Immigration on discrimination against migrants and decided to appoint a committee to enquire into the question. The then minister for immigration, Mr. A.J. Grassby, decided to expand the role of the committee to consider the more general question of the exploitation of migrants in Australian society. With its expanded terms of reference, the committee was known as the Committee on Community Relations. On 11 August 1973, Mr. Grassby published a pamphlet entitled "A Multi-Cultural Society for the Future" in which he set the tone for future discussion of the question. The paper stated:

> A social philosophy that presupposes the submergence of all ethnic diversity in a melting pot—at a time when current migration is continuing to infuse new members—also seems out of touch with the realities. Naturally, individuals are always free to move in society in whatever circles they prefer, but doctrinaire views should not inhibit that freedom. The corporate life of ethnic groups represents a great deal more than the single totality of their individual members' lives and activity. To an extent, they have created their own national image. They have brought with them a common history and culture, an ideology different from the Anglo-Saxon. They perceive different goals and pursue them in their own traditional ways. In short, they lead a way of life which, while in living touch with its ancient forms and impulses, is imperceptibly coming to terms with—or at least learning to co-exist with—that of many other ethnic groups in our society and of course with the "Old Australians." Such pluralism is not operating within a time scale, but looks ahead far into the future (p. 9).

A bill providing a legislative base for the ratification of the International Convention on the Elimination of Racial Discrimination was introduced into the Australian Parliament in 1973, but failed to pass both Houses of the Parliament before its dissolution in 1974. At the 1974 elections, Mr. Grassby paid the penalty of the reformist and the innovator. He was faced by determined opposition from an anti-immigration lobby, including a group of candidates who went to the lengths of having their names amended by deed poll to include the words *White Australia* so that this slogan would appear on the ballot paper. Mr. Grassby was defeated with a 12 percent swing against him. He was appointed by the second Whitlam government as commissioner for community relations. In this capacity, he prepared the bill relating to the elimination of racial and other discrimination, which was subsequently passed by both Houses of Parliament and entered into effect in 1974.

The policy espoused by Grassby in his paper on the concept of a multicultural society was endorsed by the former prime minister in a statement made to the Good Neighbor Council of South Australia in July 1974:

> We do not want migrants to feel that they have to change their own characteristics and imitate and adopt completely the behaviour of the existing Australian society. We want to see that society enriched by the cross-fertilization that will result from migrants retaining their own heritage. The old approach of individual assimilation is no longer Government policy. We are concerned with the integration of ethnic communities into the broader Australian society. By strengthening those communities we strengthen the whole society.

It fell to the Committee on Community Relations to refine the definition of a multicultural society and to develop the strategies and procedures by which such a society could be achieved. The committee accepted the definition of Michael Banton, a leading authority on the subject, that "a plural society is one in which there is a common realm of political rights and social valuations together with separate spheres of community living" (Department of Labour and Immigration 1975, p. 48). In the committee's view, pluralism implied first and foremost mutual tolerance and respect for cultural differences by all the members and institutions of Australian society. The committee's report explained further that as an objective for migrant settlement, cultural pluralism suggested a duality, one objective pointing to the need for maintaining ethnic distinctiveness and the other to sharing in the common realms of political rights and social values. In order to achieve such a situation, the committee agreed, it was necessary for a change of attitude to occur on the part of the people of Australia. The Ecumenical Migration Centre of Fitzroy arrived at the same conclusion in its paper on "Recommendations for a Multi-Cultural Australia": "The time is overdue for the people of Australia to become more aware of the rich traditions of the many cultures in

Australia and to recognize that this cultural diversity endows all Australians with a great variety of human experience" (Department of Labour and Immigration 1975, p. 52). The committee added that it was even more important for all Australian institutions, and certainly government ones, to be so structured as to meet the reality of this cultural diversity.

The committee proposed a new program of community relations to help people living in Australia to understand and to reconcile the interests of different groups. The committee suggested that to be socially relevant and practically useful, especially to ethnic groups, a community-relations program should attempt to reconcile within the constraints of a democratic society the need for harmony and consensus as well as the need for social change.

The main responsibility for the implementation of the proposed community-relations program would fall upon the grass-roots organizations, that is, the Community Resource Centres. Their functions were to include the development of resource materials for community education programs. Each education program would have as its goal the recognition of human dignity, the development of fair-mindedness and respect for the peoples of other groups, and the acceptance of differences. The methods to be employed by the Resource Centres were to include the provision of teaching aids and display materials; the development of contact with community organizations; the arrangement of short training courses for adult and youth group leaders; the preparation of special materials, seminars, displays, radio presentations, and so forth; the publication of guidelines for group leaders in running community-relations workshops; assistance in the conduct of joint functions; and the use of the media to convey the multicultural image.

The recommendations of the Committee on Community Relations were thus sweeping in their philosophic range and detailed in their practical implications. It is too early to know what results will in fact be achieved. The final report was presented to the Senate in 1976. No policy decision has so far been announced by the present government. Action to implement the committee's findings has been deferred, pending the report of the Administrative Review Committee on the staffing of the Australian public service.

In the meantime, the commissioner for community relations, Mr. A. J. Grassby, appointed by the previous government, is supported by a small secretariat. He has determined that his office will have three major priorities. The first is the education of teachers and students at all levels. He has decided to enlist the aid of teachers so that they may understand and disseminate information on the multicultural nature of Australian society and the importance of Australians' relating to it. To this end, he proposes to encourage multicultural courses at universities, colleges, and other educational institutions. He hopes to persuade state education departments and the Catholic education system to introduce second languages for Australian children on entry into primary school. He has responded to requests from educational institutions to deal with racism when it has manifested itself among either students or teachers. As the second priority, the commissioner for community relations seeks the cooperation of trade unions and employers. As a third priority, individual cases of discrimination will be investigated and dealt with by the commissioner for community relations (Grassby, interview with the author for inclusion in this volume, 1976).

It is unlikely that any one person could claim sole authorship of the concept of a multicultural Australia. But it is quite clear that the acceptance of the idea and its development in practical terms would have been greatly retarded if Mr. Grassby had not seized the idea, pursued it with all of his effervescent energy, secured its recognition as government policy, and proclaimed it to the nation with such exuberant enthusiasm that it both galvanized the immigrant communities to realization of their own future and provoked his opponents to savage reaction.

Personally, Al Grassby is virtually the converse of my previous model of the mediating man. He is a politician, relatively young, long associated personally with the migrant communities in his own home district, without great claims to scholarship, a man of boundless energy, flamboyant, and unafraid to flout convention. He is ready to seize upon a daring idea without undue concern for detail and to champion it at large with all of the overwhelming force of his own volubility—and the government's information resources. He tends to be more concerned with the grand strategy than with the skirmish line. Without him, the multicultural idea would have remained a notion. Because he ensured the acceptance of the idea by the establishment, the time for a multicultural Australia was seen to be now. His espousal of the policy of a multicultural Australia prepared the way for the patient definition of ways and means by officials and the establishment of a climate in which the process of mediation can proceed productively. More of a pathfinder than a mediator himself, Mr. Al Grassby performed a facilitative function, without which the process of mediation can degenerate into futility.

Responding to an interviewer's questions about the part of the private citizen, the politician, and the public official in the development of new attitudes toward Australian society, Mr. Grassby stressed that the individual has a most important role in making the multicultural society a harmonious reality. He found, however, that he could contribute most effectively himself as a politician.

> The politician can do a great deal. But of course there is a great tendency where there are problems, where there are really difficult problems to be faced up to, there is a tendency not to face them, because if you make a commitment, then somebody is going to be unhappy. You can't please all the people all the time. You're not able to preach tolerance and write nice letters to the bigots. You can

write constructive letters to the bigots, but you can't agree with them or even appear to agree with them.

Now, I think there is a great tendency by many people to avoid debate, I'm talking now at the political level; to avoid debate; to avoid recognizing the challenges. In the past there has, I think, been in Australia a great deal of just plain public cowardice, because it was assumed that some of the vocal groups, extremist groups, racist groups, pockets of prejudice, were in fact far more powerful than they have ever been. And so, if a Member or a minister received from one of the dozen racist organisations in the country a letter taking him to task in stern terms, signed by a retired general perhaps to give it a bit of status, with a couple of medals for something or other, then there was a tendency to think, "My goodness, I'd better shut up on that issue because people are disapproving." Well, then you must challenge them, and challenge their disapproval, and if they're wrong, tell them.

Q: It was such a group that had a good deal to do with your own defeat in 1974, wasn't it?

GRASSBY: Yes. I suppose every extremist organization in Australia (a whole dozen of them), they all came and took part in '74. They did it publicly, privately, at all levels. They had a field day, and there's no doubt that even though they were mostly outsiders, in fact almost exclusively outsiders from every state in Australia, they had a marginal influence, which in a tight situation was probably just enough to tip the balance against me. I accept that.

Q: Mr. Grassby, the public official may not be able to achieve quite the sweeping changes as the politician, or primarily the minister, can, but he is insulated a little from those sorts of extreme pressures, is he not?

GRASSBY: Well, it's a very challenging question to answer because, speaking again very personally, I find it very different being a minister of state with authority to make decisions on all these matters, and being a commissioner that has a limited authority, as all public officials must have. I find some frustrations in that. I must be quite blunt. There is a world of difference between deciding and recommending, so I must plead some frustration there.

How much can the public official do? A great deal; particularly if he's a public official in this sphere. He must be completely and totally uncompromising in his objectives to implement his legislation.

Q: Tell me, do you think that changes in attitudes can be promoted by government action, or are they something that comes more through the influence of the society itself, or the media—or the churches, or the writers? Or is this something that can be modeled by direct government action?

GRASSBY: Well, I think—I think there's got to be leadership, you can't just wait for something to happen spontaneously. I don't think it happens spontaneously. Even the storming of the Bastille wasn't spontaneous. You know, there were a few fellows who knew exactly what they were doing and I think that's fair enough. You've got to have leadership. I think governments can give leadership— they can't *do* it, no, of course they can't.

Q: Where do you think we have got to so far, and where do you think we can get to in—well, let's say the foreseeable future, in your lifetime, in my lifetime?

GRASSBY: Well, I think we've come a long way in a very short time. We've come along the road from a society which was a colonial society, a closed, isolated colonial society almost based on the "master-race" concept, and we've come from that to a recognition that it's got to change—and it has changed. I'm talking about a recognition at the political level, the parliamentary level, and very often among the most perceptive top administrators of the country. They perceive that the nation has changed, that the old attitudes just must go. So, I think you've got an informed—you've got an acceptance of change; not too sure where they are going. I'm not saying that they've done all the things that they need to do, but they've accepted the fact that the past is no more.

(Grassby interviewed by R. P. Throssell, Canberra, 1976.)

FOREIGN RELATIONS

Diplomacy itself is a form of intercultural mediation. However, the purposes of diplomacy insofar as they encompass the interpretation of the aspirations and policies of one government to another government are directed to national self-interest. The same may be said of many of the international activities of national governments, including such self-interested functions as trade and the gathering of intelligence. I take the objectives of cross-cultural mediation to be somewhat broader. I will in this section identify three avenues through which community-related cross-cultural mediation is pursued in the field of foreign relations: the role of international organizations, cultural-relations policies, and overseas student exchanges.

The United Nations Educational, Scientific, and Cultural Organization (UNESCO) provides an international model for cross-cultural communication. "Intellectual cooperation through the communication of knowledge, the comparison of experiences, and the exchange of ideas is the basis of all

UNESCO work" (Australian National Commission for UNESCO 1974, p. 3). Australia's participation in UNESCO is channeled through the Australian National Commission and a range of specialist committees. The objectives of the organization are furthered through national seminars, the provision of overseas consultants, the exchange of views through professional journals, and personal channels of communication.

In 1974, the Australian Education Committee of the National Commission for UNESCO convened a seminar on intercultural education in the Asian Pacific region. The participants were specialists in social-science curricula from some twenty countries of Asia and the Pacific. The seminar clarified the basic principles of intercultural education, surveyed resources for intercultural education, and explored means of regional cooperation.

Within Australia, positive steps have been taken toward the implementation of intercultural educational policies. In 1972, an Asian Studies Coordinating Committee was established to stimulate and improve the teaching of Asian languages and courses about Asia in Australian schools. The committee turned first to the tools of understanding, namely language and factual information. Workshops have been held for teachers of Asian languages, Indonesian, Japanese, and Asian history, and social studies. Filmstrips have been produced on Malaysia and Indonesia. School texts have been commissioned. The Sydney University Intercultural Studies project, concerned with the preparation of publications and audiovisual materials, has been supported by substantial financial grants. A publication on Indonesia has been prepared by the Australian magazine *Hemisphere*, and twenty thousand copies have been circulated to state departments of education throughout Australia. A bibliography and resource book on Asia for secondary schools has been published in four volumes. The committee has subsidized the introduction of courses in Japanese, Chinese, and Indonesian at Australian universities, and has assisted in the training of teachers through the provision of travel grants for study abroad (Asian Studies Coordinating Committee 1976).

The Department of Foreign Affairs explains: "Cultural relations promote mutual understanding and assist in the furtherance of foreign policy objectives. The whole thrust of diplomacy is to advance the national interest by negotiation of political, economic and defense issues. By promoting mutual and reciprocal understanding through cultural programs, we create an atmosphere in which these objectives can more hopefully be pursued. In short, if we are to work with and achieve results from people very different from ourselves, we must understand them and they must understand us" (Department of Foreign Affairs 1976). In furtherance of this policy, Australia has established cultural agreements with ten countries and is in the process of negotiating further agreements with five countries. Agreements have been concerned primarily with the countries of South and Southeast Asia with which Australia enjoys the closest diplomatic relationships.

In general, cultural agreements imply a broad definition of cultural co-operation. In practice, they usually encourage exchanges in specific areas: exhibitions; performances of the arts; exchanges of students, teachers, and courses of study; exchanges of radio, television, and film programs; tourism and recreation; and cooperation in the area of science and technology. Agreements frequently provide for exchanges of publications between libraries, museums, and archives and the encouragement of the translation of works of literature from the language of one country to that of another. Many agreements provide for regular meetings between the signatory parties, through the medium of mixed commissions, to prepare a program of activities for the following year.

At the suggestion of the Australian ambassador to Japan, Mr. K. C. O. Shann, a special device has been adopted to supplement the purposes of cultural cooperation with Japan in a major way. An Australia/Japan Foundation has been established by act of parliament, with the objectives of deepening and broadening contacts between Australia and Japan in all fields, including business, academic, cultural, scientific, and trade-union activities, thereby fostering an understanding of each other's problems and cultures. The foundation aims to achieve its objectives mainly through people-to-people contact, rather than by exhibiting aspects of Australian culture covered under the cultural agreement with Japan.

Overseas Students

Some fifty thousand overseas students from Asia, the Pacific, and Africa have studied in Australia since the end of the Second World War. The prime minister, Mr. E. G. Whitlam, acknowledged in an address at Adelaide University in March 1974 that the overseas student programs had been a major factor in transforming the xenophobia of the Australian community and in moderating the antipathy engendered throughout Southeast Asia by the so-called White Australia policy (Whitlam 1975, p. 15).

Improved understanding by the community of overseas students is largely the result of familiarity. These students are no longer objects of curiosity on Australian campuses or cities. In part this understanding represents the achievement of a careful, unostentatious program of community involvement in student affairs, sustained under official guidance over a period of some twenty-five years, since the introduction of the Colombo Plan in 1950.

The policy underlying official Australian contacts with overseas students is based on principles quite distinct from government interest in aborigines or migrants. It is explicit policy that overseas students are temporary sojourners. Thus, the Australian government is concerned to ensure that overseas students are not alienated from their homelands and their native culture. Their orientation to Australian society is based on the need to know the community in which they live and to study more effectively in a strange environment. The students are expected to return to their homelands on completion of their studies and to make an effective contribution to economic and social development. The Australian government does not want to see a development-assistance program become instead a source of "brain drain" from the countries it is attempting to assist.

From the wider view of Australian foreign policy, the overseas student program aims to extend goodwill between Australia and the developing countries of Southeast Asia and the Pacific. In order to further the goodwill objective, the overseas student program attempts both to inform the Australian public about the countries from which the students come and to give the students, and through them their homelands, a more sympathetic understanding of Australian society.

Largely as a matter of necessity, the Australian Development Assistance Agency has relied principally on community organizations and student bodies to carry out this task. The initiator of these measures was in this instance neither a bureaucrat nor a politician. In the mid-1950s, Lady Casey (then Mrs. Casey), wife of the foreign minister, established the first Coordinating Committee for Overseas Students in Melbourne. Coordinating committees have since been established in all other capital cities and in some regional centers. They consist of representatives of voluntary organizations such as service clubs, Rotary, Apex, Jaycees; church organizations; charitable bodies; international friendship societies; and the national student organizations. Two general bodies of overseas students—the Overseas Student Service (OSS) of the Australian Union of Students (AUS) and the All African Students Congress—also play a prominent part in the activities of these groups.

The coordinating committees fulfill housekeeping functions essential to the personal well-being of overseas students in a strange society. They assist with the meeting and greeting of overseas students at the time of their arrival. They arrange accommodation and inspect premises in order to ensure that they meet a desirable standard. They counsel both students and landladies on behavior designed to achieve mutual respect and understanding. Voluntary organizations participate in and sometimes organize orientation functions in order to assist new arrivals to learn the rules and regulations and the modes of behavior of the community in which they will live. They arrange hospitality, provide for financial assistance in times of emergency, and offer legal assistance through a panel of lawyers. They cushion the more apparent causes of disorientation through assistance with language problems and host-family schemes designed to introduce the overseas student into Australian family life. In the process of administering these schemes, the coordinating committees attempt a form of cultural mediation through familiarization of Australian hosts with the society of the students' homelands and through preliminary guidance of the students themselves as to Australian social customs.

The role of government officials in this activity is central to its success. The establishment of coordinating committees has been primarily a function of the International Training Section of the Department of Foreign Affairs, and subsequently of the Australian Development Assistance Agency. Officials convene public meetings for the establishment of coordinating committees, suggest a constitutional framework within which the committees may operate, provide the secretarial and administrative support for the committees' activities, and give policy guidance to ensure consistent programs and approaches to overseas students' problems throughout Australia. The government provides funds for administrative support and for the coordinating committees' major activities, and itself conducts a large part of the routine operational functions and professional counseling. In collaboration with voluntary organizations, government departments assess and review the various overseas-student welfare programs through the mechanism of annual conferences among the representatives of government departments, the voluntary organizations, and the principal overseas student bodies.

Although a very great deal was achieved over the previous twenty-five years, it became apparent at the time of the creation of the Australian Development Assistance Agency in 1974-75 that the voluntary organizations were an ineffectual medium for significant cross-cultural communication between the Australian society and the overseas student body. Students' leaders demanded a greater role in the formulation of welfare programs and regarded the existing activities as patronage and charity. A vocal element among the students insisted that the opportunities for study abroad offered by the Australian government were theirs as a matter of right. They claimed to have an equal contribution to make to Australian society, and accordingly insisted upon civil rights equal to those enjoyed by Australian students. The student bodies, or the more active elements in their leadership, demanded a controlling role in the management of the coordinating committees and the conduct of welfare programs.

In practice, however, the student organizations lacked the capacity, time, and sustained interest to conduct an operational welfare program. Individual overseas students were under considerable pressure in their study programs. Some saw their activities in the overseas student organizations as a political exercise upon which they could sharpen their own ambition. Interest in student affairs fell away after they had graduated and returned to their own countries, or in some cases became Australian citizens. Dawn Beresford-Wylie, a welfare officer of the Australian Development Assistance Agency and once secretary to the Overseas Students Service, describes the problems of communication through the students' eyes:

Overseas student organisations are run on entirely different lines to Australian student groups—I believe they are more democratic. One rarely finds the power blocs and railroading tactics common to AUS. I believe that AUS found this exasperating many times, and I believe that overseas students are always at a disadvantage in meetings conducted by Australians. . . . This may not apply so much to the African students. I learned very quickly not to interfere with the way overseas students conduct meetings. I realised very quickly that it would be fairly easy to exercise superficial control, but that their acceptance of statements and ideas was based on politeness and a desire not to hurt rather than anything else.

I recently attended a meeting which brought it all back to me. The predominantly Australian executive quickly stopped an attempt by a Malaysian student to give a policy speech on his nomination for the position of president. I thought it was sad, because they did not understand that this would be the norm at any meeting conducted by Asian students, and there is no doubt that he lost a considerable amount of "face" that day. I hoped the rest of the Asian students would come to his defence, but the only reaction was a sea of embarrassed grins.

Whilst I can see the value of the coordinating committee and councils and appreciate the aims of the department in giving support to these bodies; whilst I appreciate that there are many committed and concerned individuals on these bodies and they do promote the welfare of the students, I do not think we appreciate how dangerous they can be. They are seen as an arm of the department, and whilst membership is open to overseas students, they are still conducted along Australian lines, and very little is done to sensitize the representatives on councils to have a proper regard for the nature of overseas students. In my experience of these bodies in Western Australia, Victoria, and New South Wales, this results in a situation where students are patronized and shouted down. It is not difficult for students to transfer these attitudes to the officer from the department who may be present in the capacity of secretary-convenor.

Perhaps our attitude to committees is reflected in their attitudes to the students. If we are going to continue to support them, we should be looking at ways of educating them. Frequently, this is where student leaders' attitudes to the department are determined. I do not support the view that these bodies have maintained a consistent regard for the welfare and well-being of overseas students in general. From my experience in the states and from recent comments . . . we are often put in the position of virtually having to remind them of their aims, pulling and pushing them to do those things which we advertise as services provided by the Australian community, and having to walk a thin line in attempts to be diplomatic with them. Do we have a similar regard for the students? It appears to me that in general, these bodies expect students to conform to Australian standards and that short shrift is given to those who do not. This is why so few students participate in councils and committees. (Beresford-Wylie interviewed by R. P. Throssell, Canberra, 1976.)

The effectiveness of the voluntary organizations' contribution depended largely upon the ability, enthusiasm, and initiative of individuals. In some cases, dedicated and devoted volunteers became disillusioned by what they saw as the student spokesmen's ingratitude. Others, more determined, perhaps less sensitive, became diehard committeemen inclined to impose their notion of what is good for overseas students willy-nilly. More and more, the weaker voluntary organizations came to depend on official financial support for their activities and official initiative in the planning, preparation, development, and conduct of welfare programs.

It was in the light of these events that the Australian Development Assistance Agency determined, early in its existence, to move toward a more professional welfare program for overseas students. This scheme depended upon the provision of adequate staff and funds for the conduct of welfare programs for overseas students. In the event, neither staff nor funds became available. In the meantime, it remained necessary to rely upon the good graces of the voluntary organizations. Nevertheless, it is my own conclusion that only official organizations have the longevity necessary to sustain a consistent and effective intercultural program directed to a transient population such as the overseas students.

Several attempts have been made to involve the voluntary organizations in a more direct intercultural role. The need for genuine dialogue between the student body and the Australian community has long been recognized by the Annual Welfare Conference. Several papers on this topic have been presented, including German (1973), Hodgkin (1969), and Robinson (1970). In 1970, the conference recognized "the need to familiarize organisations and the Australian community with the background of Asian, African, and Pacific countries as a means of improving the welfare arrangements for overseas students in this country." The following year, it was reported that the most significant recommendation to the coordinating committees related to the question of explaining to the Australian people the cultural backgrounds of overseas students. Specific action had been taken in a number of states. In particular, South Australia reported on a "Festival 71" student function in

Adelaide which was attended by over 80,000 people. The Australian-Asian Association also had been active in providing speakers and occasions for making contact. The conference happily congratulated itself that action in that sphere had been effective. But by 1972, no new program was reported.

It appears that the primary role of voluntary organizations is in the provision of community services through which, over a considerable period of time, intercultural communication may be achieved indirectly. Official organizations, for their part, will no doubt continue to regard the provision of material welfare services as having first call on limited resources, until such time as the development of intercultural understanding becomes a policy objective of government.

Conclusion

A French diplomatist once said, "The best instrument at the disposal of government will always remain the spoken word of an honest man." Perhaps in these more complicated times governments look rather to organizations; but individuals, separately or together, remain the source of ideas from which human society evolves. Some of the individuals who have contributed at various levels of government to Australians' awareness of themselves, and to their understanding of three of the strands in the emerging pattern of their society, have been used as illustrations of the part played by officialdom in the emergence of a multicultural Australia.

This should not be taken to imply that government has the sole, or pre-eminent, role in the development of a multicultural society, in Australia or elsewhere. This study has not purported to examine the influence of political ideology, public opinion, or religion, or the role of the press, the arts, and the educational institutions in the formation of community attitudes to other cultures; all have an influence, to a greater or lesser degree, at differing stages in national development, as do the accidents of past history, over which the present has no control. Undoubtedly, the actions of governments and their servants either stimulate the development of harmonious communication between cultures or inhibit understanding. But the origins of government policies and the personal attitudes that motivate government officials lie within the very communities over which they exercise jurisdiction.

Notes

1. These figures were compiled in 1975. In the interim, the population of Australia is estimated to have reached 14 million.

References

Asian Studies Coordinating Committee. *Report to the Australian Education Council, December 1975.* Canberra: Department of Education, 1976.

Australian National Commission for UNESCO. *Biennial Report, 1973-74.* (R74/1575). Canberra: Australian Government Publishing Service, 1974.

Brisbane, K. The Yellow Peril. Introduction to J. Romeril (ed.), *The Floating World.* Sydney: Currency Methuen, 1975.

Clark, C. M. H. *A History of Australia.* Melbourne: Melbourne University Press, 1974.

Coombs, H. C. *The Future of the Australian Aboriginal.* The George Judah Cohen Memorial Lecture. Sydney: University of Sydney, 1972.

Department of Aboriginal Affairs. *Annual Report, 1974-75.* Canberra: Australian Government Publishing Service, 1976.

Department of Foreign Affairs. *Submission to the Committee on Administrative Review.* Canberra: Department of Foreign Affairs, 1976.

Department of Labor and Immigration. Committee on Community Relations. *Final Report.* Canberra: Australian Government Publishing Service, September 1975.

German, G. Cross-Cultural Communication and Its Implications for the Host Family Scheme. *Proceedings of Conference of Coordinating Committees and Welfare Organisations, 1973.* Canberra: Department of Foreign Affairs, 1973.

Grassby, A. J. *A Multi-Cultural Society for the Future.* Canberra: Australian Government Publishing Service, 1973.

Hansard. House of Representatives, 16 December 1941 (Vol 169). Canberra: Australian Government Printer, 1941.

Hodgkin, M. Overseas Students: Attitudes and Points of View. *Proceedings of Conference of Coordinating Committees and Welfare Organisations, 1969.* Canberra: Department of Foreign Affairs, 1969.

Immigration Advisory Council. Committee on Community Relations. *Interim Report.* Canberra: Department of Labor and Immigration, August 1974.

Racial Discrimination Act, 1975 (No. 52 of 1975). Canberra: Government Printer of Australia, 1975. (14224/76.)

Robinson, P. The Role of the Coordinating Committees in Introducing Australians to the Cultural Background of Asian, African and Pacific Countries. *Proceedings of Conference of Coordinating Committees and Welfare Organisations, 1970.* Canberra: Department of Foreign Affairs, 1970.

Tryon, D. T. Bilingual Education in the Northern Territory. *Education News,* 1975, *15* (2), 44-50.

Whitlam, E. G. Australia and Asia: The Challenge of Education. *Asian Seminar Proceedings* (March 1974). Adelaide: University of Adelaide, 1975.

Margaret W. Sullivan

When in Rome . . . But Who's Roman? The Mutual Adaptation of Cultural Outsiders and Insiders

When you are in Rome, live in the Roman style: when you are elsewhere, live as they live elsewhere.
—St. Ambrose to St. Augustine, late fourth century

"Foreign teachers who dress in sloppy ways teach our children to be disrespectful. We don't like that."
—Sierra Leonean parent

"What does wearing jeans and flip-flops have to do with whether or not I'm a good teacher? Besides, no one has the right to tell me what to wear."
—Peace Corps volunteer

"That Miss Velez is impossible! The class is bedlam. All she wants them to do is memorize what she says and she can't even say it in proper English."
—Cebu International School (CIS) parent

"What am I supposed to do? Mrs. Benito gets mad if I ask questions. When I say I don't understand, she just tells me exactly the something over again."
—CIS student

"The children are so rude. They always make noise and they don't do what they are told."
—CIS teacher

These snippets of conversation are the stuff of conflict and confrontation that can result when people from different cultures must function together. Much is written about social change as cultural systems collide. Let us consider what happens, however, at the level of individuals. There is a proliferation of people from differing value systems who live and work together on a day-to-day basis: international civil servants, expatriate businessmen or technicians and their families, volunteer teachers, foreign students, host-country officials, counterparts, neighbors. Such people are cogs in the wheels of technological revolution, social collision, and cultural change. These broader external forces often determine the goals, directions, and parameters of individual cross-cultural interaction. Whatever change results is not necessarily what was intended, but rather a by-product of these complexities. The crux of personal intercultural encounters which go beyond casual meeting is whether or not there is change, who changes, to what end, and in what manner.

Not everyone changes, of course, for there are those who never leave their cultural cocoons. The loudmouth who demands hot dogs and tomato catsup wherever he is, the biddies who retreat to bridge tables and complain about the "natives" as they sip gin and tonic, and the grandmother who refuses to speak to her New World grandchildren in any but the mother tongue are stock characters on the cultural migration circuit. Frenchmen have a perhaps undeserved reputation for making no effort to communicate with foreigners whose French is less than perfect.

Conversely, others obliterate themselves in the new culture. The missionary's son who became a follower of a local guru and sat unkempt and begging in front of the temple down the road from his father's church is but one example of "going native." The youth sauntering down the streets of Monrovia or Singapore sporting mirrored shades, flapping bell-bottoms, and six-inch soles copied from Hollywood movie magazines is the other side of the coin.

For many people, however, the meeting of cultures results not in retreat and isolation or in total immersion, but rather in mutual cultural adaptation. Cultural adaptation is the process by which individuals rooted in diverse ways of doing and evaluating come to some form of common ground. At its worst, it is grudging and harmful. At its best, it is mutually respectful and creative. Because it can involve deep feelings, cultural adaptation is a process which is easier to define abstractly than achieve harmoniously. As well as challenge and growth, it often involves puzzlement, confrontation, resentment, stress, the overcoming of ill will, and at least the examination, if not the alteration, of deeply held values before some measure of understanding and accommodation can be reached. To be successful, it must begin with the awareness that different people do the same things in different ways. Having understood this, the individual needs to learn to respond to the other culture in its own terms, and herein lies both the joy and the stress.

To examine various aspects of cultural adaptation, it is perhaps helpful to think in terms of "insiders" and "outsiders." In any particular situation, the insiders are the people of the country and culture: this place is where they live; their ways are How Things are Done; their reality is How It Is. The outsiders are the foreigners or sojourners. To the insider, the outsider's ways are basically irrelevant, but they may be interesting, strange, unnatural, incomprehensible, and perhaps threatening and downright abhorrent. To the foreigner, the outsider, it is the insider's ways that are interesting, strange, inscrutable, perhaps abhorrent, but nonetheless ever present and encroaching, while his own are self-evident, natural, and right.

As they interact, both insiders and outsiders function not only in the frameworks of their respective cultures, but also within the dynamics and imperatives of the particular task or program which brings them together. The goals of the task, the way it is structured, and the reasons why the individuals are involved in it will all affect the cultural adaptations which are made.

Although the insiders and outsiders may have much in common, their areas of difference can foster non- or miscommunication, conflict, and stress. Opening communication, lessening conflict, and alleviating stress can lead to some form of cultural adaptation and personal change. While many people can and often do work through these problems on their own, mediators—that is, people with feet, eyes, and tongues in both or the many cultures involved— facilitate the process. Rarely, however, is the cultural mediator a detached adviser to the situation. In day-to-day intercultural living, it is much more frequent that mediators are also participants, but with a difference. The difference is in being aware of and objective about the various cultural patterns, forces, and values at work in the particular situation, and therefore being able to act as a translator. The mediator must juggle mediating, or (perhaps more accurately) "facilitating understanding," with participating. How effectively he does this is partly a matter of how able he is to function in the dual role and partly a matter of how amenable to mediation the situation is. Ideally, there is not just one mediator; there are mediating insiders and mediating outsiders.

While each interaction is unique, complex, and situation-specific, perhaps it is possible to make some generalizations. In today's world of instant communication and raised cultural consciousness, it is no longer socially or politically acceptable for outsiders to force their culture down the insiders' throats. In most situations, the need to adapt is not one-sided. Nonetheless, one general aspect of adaptation is whether it is the insider or the outsider on whom the major pressure to change falls. One can frequently make a case for the necessity for the outsider, the foreigner, to be aware of the need for adaptation and the requirement to make a larger share of the adjustment. While it is often not easy, he may anticipate that the onus is on him and that the insider will expect or demand it of him. If the individual foreigner does not adapt at least in some measure, he will remain isolated, and while programs in which he is involved may be partially successful in the short run, their long-run prognosis is doubtful. A more difficult situation arises when people in their own country, insiders, find themselves in a position where the need is for them to make fundamental adjustments to the outsiders. The most complex interaction of all arises when two cultures both view themselves as insiders and the struggle is over land and cultural survival, as Ritchie and Throssell have shown elsewhere in this book.

In any intercultural situation, whether it is one in which outsiders or insiders are flexible, there are levels of cultural adaptation ranging from the superficial (for example, forms of good manners) to adjustment in deeply held values. There are also individual differences—what seems superficial or irrelevant to one person may be profound and fundamental to someone else. One person's problem might be another's nonproblem. Cultural mediators can be helpful to both insiders and outsiders at many levels of cultural adaptation, but in the final analysis, the individuals involved must make the adaptation.

In the simplest forms of adjustment, the outsider can learn to fold his hands to his chest and bow his head, to bow deeply, to kiss a friend on both cheeks, to rub noses, or to shake hands, as the good manners of the host culture demand. If he is aware that such differences exist, he can learn merely by observation. Cultural mediation at this level takes place when a newcomer reads a guidebook or asks questions of the old-timer over a cup of coffee, or when a local landlady includes her foreign tenants in a family wedding, or when the houseboy urges his "madame" to take eggs when she goes to visit her father. Learning the new forms and when to use them may be unsettling and confusing, and for some the task may be too much. But on the whole, it is not too troublesome when there is a common underlying value between the two cultures. For instance, most people value good manners, although they may express them in different ways and lay greater or lesser stress on their role in social intercourse.

Adaptation is much more complicated when the values involved are deeply held and offer less area for common ground. By examining in detail the examples of cultural confrontation presented in the introduction to this chapter in the form of conversational extracts, we can perhaps come to a clearer understanding of the complex nature of mutual cultural adaptation and of the interlocking roles of insiders, outsiders, and mediators. I have chosen these examples in part because I know the particular situations well, and in part because the educational process, from which they are drawn, is one about which people of all cultures feel strongly. Schools not only teach factual knowledge, they are also one of the major inculcators of social and cultural values in the young, and as such represent something special and inviolable in most parents' minds. Educating one's young is an area in which even the most adaptable traveler tends to be more rigid than he might be under other circumstances.

Outsider Adaptation

"THE DISCIPLINE THING"

The classroom is airy, although the paint is old. There is a blackboard and a few flyspecked pictures on the wall. About forty-five lively eyed, shining chocolate-faced teenaged boys in white shirts and khaki shorts are crowded at desks for twenty-five. The teacher is one of many recently arrived, highly motivated Peace Corps volunteers (PCVs) come to supplement the national staff by teaching science, math, or English. His hair is longish, his beard bushy, his shirt clean but casual and made of gaily patterned local tie-dye, his patched jeans washed but not ironed, his shoes battered sneakers. The PCV steps out of the room for a minute, leaving the students with some work to do. The classroom erupts into a babble of sound. An indigenous teacher—dressed in a long-sleeved white shirt, a tie, smartly cut, neatly pressed slacks, his leather shoes the latest style with high heels—strides into the room. "Pupils, stand up!" There is sudden silence. The teacher proceeds to administer to each student two strokes with a cane. When he hears of it a little later, the PCV is deeply shocked at the caning.

While the particular situation is fictitious, the values represented are real, and their conflicts constitute areas which have caused particularly deep soul-searching for education volunteers in Sierra Leone.

"The discipline thing" is a clear-cut collision of values. Sierra Leonean society is very hierarchical and authoritarian. Caning as a major instrument of discipline is used at all levels of instruction and elsewhere in the society, and always has been. It is used to make children behave and as a punishment for giving the wrong answers in class. By the time they get into secondary school, pupils expect and respond to it. A pupil is expected to wail loudly while being caned. For the volunteer, who is frequently a product of very permissive, democratic upbringing, with very little corporal punishment in the home and a school system in which it is frequently illegal, the idea is both abhorrent and literally outrageous. It is *wrong*. For many, a personal emphasis on gentleness and nonviolence which motivated them to become volunteers heightens this feeling. To American teachers who have been heavily oriented toward psychology, caning flies in the face of what they have been taught professionally about the harmful nature of violence. They often feel that to resort to caning is a defeat, since an interesting teacher should so motivate pupils that caning becomes unnecessary.

Is there a resolution to this conflict? The Sierra Leoneans, the insiders, do not generally see it as a problem or a conflict, unless the teacher is unable to maintain discipline. Then the problem is the teacher's inability to control the class, not the rightness or wrongness of caning. Caning is how things are done. The real conflict is in the minds of the volunteers, the outsiders. For them, to cane or not to cane is the question. Each must individually decide to what extent he will adapt to the insiders' ways and at what point he cannot modify his behavior without seriously violating something important within himself. This, then, is a case where the pressure to adapt falls primarily on the outsiders.

While it is a new problem as far as the individual volunteer is concerned, it is a continuing one for the Peace Corps. The Peace Corps is well aware that it must serve a mediating function with incoming volunteers if they are to find their tours satisfying and if the Peace Corps programs are to meet the mutual needs of the Sierra Leonean and American governments. A training period is therefore planned for the volunteers' first two months in the country. Some of the trainers—the mediators—are Sierra Leonean teachers; others are volunteers who have been "in country" for a while and who know the ropes. Officials of the Sierra Leonean Ministry of Education are asked to present their concerns. All of them have a vested interest in seeing the Peace Corps program succeed.

Even before the volunteers get into classroom situations, therefore, the in-country training program helps them focus on the questions of discipline and caning, along with other areas of possible cultural conflict. The visiting Sierra Leonean officials and the volunteer leaders stress the need to maintain orderly classrooms. There is lots of talk, not only in regular training sessions but over meals and wherever new volunteers gather:

"I want an orderly class, but I just can't cane."

"I know how you feel. Be firm. Do everything you can to command respect. But you may have to cane. Remember, it is not you who set this pattern and not your responsibility to change it," counsel experienced volunteers.

Most volunteers I talked to left training resolved not to cane and hopeful of being able to change patterns in their school so that caning need not take place. Being forewarned of this area of cultural conflict did not necessarily make the ultimate decisions easier or decide the form of adaptation that the individual volunteer would make, but it lessened the shock and started them thinking before they had to deal with the problem.

The mediation of the Peace Corps staff, both American and Sierra Leonean, was not confined to the initial training period. Every effort was made to maintain open communication between the volunteers and the staff, so that volunteers had someone to turn to when the going got tough, when the cultural-conflict pressure was on and the volunteer need to ventilate, to escape for a while, or to be further aided through cultural interchange. Knowing that one is not alone, that other people feel the same way, is very helpful.

It was interesting to talk to experienced volunteers later in their tours. A few, usually those teaching at the elementary level, had been able to avoid caning altogether by teaching the children other patterns of behavior so that caning was not necessary. The majority, however, had needed at least to threaten to cane. "I avoided it as long as I could," reported Robin, who was teaching art in a Freetown school to fourth and fifth form (tenth and eleventh grade) boys who were bigger than she was. "When I was in Pujehun [a small town], it wasn't much of a problem. But here, one or two of the worst ones kept asking for it. I finally jerked a boy by the ear and asked one of the masters to cane another for me. After that, the class behaved better. But I didn't like it. It took me a long time to see that this was something I couldn't change."

Peter reported much the same thing from his rural school. "I'm big. A firm voice will do most of the time. I like the kids and they know it. They respond well to that. But I've caned one or two—not hard—and the others know it. That's all it takes. I still think there is a better way, but I can't introduce it to the fifth form. The change would have to come in the primary school. The kids just expect to be caned. I can't change that."

Other PCVs reported talking to fellow teachers about caning and not getting very far. The conflict, like many resulting from cross-cultural differences, is not really resolvable. The volunteers who lasted all came to some sort of short-term accommodation, although they tried hard to avoid caning, but very few changed their basic beliefs, and many had their anticaning beliefs reinforced. Some volunteers could not handle the stress and left, although this conflict was usually not enough to precipitate a situation where a volunteer felt that termination was necessary. What will be interesting to see over time is if the volunteers themselves become cultural mediators, by setting an example which encourages some of their Sierra Leonean coteachers to change their values in relation to caning.

THE DRESS ISSUE

The dress issue was a much more open, clearly articulated conflict, not only between Sierra Leonean teachers and parents and volunteers, but also between Peace Corps staff and volunteers. To Sierra Leoneans, looking smart and being appropriately dressed for the occasion is a very high value. The standard of what is considered appropriate is generally derived from styles and proprieties originally set in England, but now very much internalized in Sierra Leonean behavior. Some occasions call for Western dress, others for Sierra Leonean. Neatness, cleanliness, a considerable degree of formality, and the best quality one can afford (or a bit better) are the watchwords. Proper shoes, as distinct from sneakers or "half-backs" (flip-flops), are particularly important. Shirts of *gara* (the traditional tie-dye cloth) are worn for clearly informal, nonworking occasions. Women are only now beginning to wear slacks, and then usually at home or occasionally for shopping, not to work. Most if not all educated women wear Western dresses in the daytime and reserve their *gara* gowns for evening. Students wear uniforms and are taught to keep them neat and clean. In fact, a dirty uniform is a caning offense. Being properly dressed is not only a way of showing one's status, it is a way of showing and commanding respect. Schoolteachers are highly respected leaders in the community.

Many of the volunteers are in their twenties. Their "uniform" at home is jeans and a shirt. Few of them brought dress clothes with them, since they did not own them, did not want to wear them, or thought that in "Sierra Leone—tropics, summer, casual—dressing up will be unnecessary." (This constellation of thoughts is a common reaction, not just of volunteers, but of many Westerners sent to the tropics who in other situations are most punctilious about their appearance.) The PCVs also are generally products of a generation for whom dress is a label which, like long hair, is an inalienable right and an uncompromisable statement of one's being that others have no right to interfere with. Being young, they often do not identify themselves as part of the more respected older and elite portions of Sierra Leonean culture with which the Sierra Leoneans among whom they live identify them. Learning to think of oneself as "Miss— —" or as "Mr.— —" as well as Debby or John is not easy on one's home ground.

To the Sierra Leoneans, the way some Peace Corps volunteers dress is incomprehensible and often distasteful. In fairness, many volunteers are neatly and simply dressed and, while not as formal as their counterparts, very acceptable. It is the sloppy, informal group that is visible and remarked upon. The Americans are assumed, rightly or wrongly, to have money, lots of it; and why anyone with money should dress like a poor man by choice is hard to fathom. Although a large number of Sierra Leoneans are poor, unless they are destitute they manage to look neat.

Additionally, the parents, who view teachers as an extension of themselves, are upset at the example that they feel is being set for their children. For instance, a father bought his son some new sneakers. The very first day, the son came home from school with the backs of the shoes flattened down to the soles and the edges deliberately frayed. "Look, Dad," he said proudly, "Peace Corps." The father was incensed.

Upset about dress and the example of the "disrespectful" American way of doing things that it represents in peoples' minds often outweighs positive feelings about good teaching. The dress issue is a question of people's never getting to judge the content of the book because they are stopped by its cover. Long hair not only has emotional, "hippy" connotations to Sierra Leoneans, it is also downright confusing. "*Na man?*" (Is that a man?), companions of many of the long-haired young men have been asked. (This confusion works in reverse for some women. One female friend with a boyish figure and a pixie haircut was asked at a checkpoint to produce a pass required only of males.)

While Peace Corps dress habits have been a chronic source of friction, at one point feelings were running so high that complaints were made in the newspapers. The issue was used by some Sierra Leoneans as a reason for attempting to remove volunteers from parts of the country and as a threat to close down the program as a whole. Dress was mainly what was latched onto and not the root of the problem, which was more complex. Nevertheless, it made a convenient handle.

As a result of the news story and high-level political pressure, the Peace Corps staff was faced with what seemed a crisis. A directive on dress was issued, followed by a number of regional meetings, at which point a second set of cultural conflicts came into play—those between the staff and the volunteer subculture. Some, but not all, of the volunteers were indignant. They felt that how they dressed was their own business and that no one, not the Sierra Leonean government or the Peace Corps staff (or their parents), had a right to tell them what they could not wear. They resented authority and they resented what they took to be "orders from older people." For some volunteers, the question was perceived merely in terms of authority and not of conflicting cultural values. If they saw it as a conflict in cultural values, it was a part of the continuing one within American culture.

There was a lot of talk for a long time, and the issue is now more or less resolved, at least for working dress, except for a few volunteers to whom dress is still a question of identity on which they are unable or unwilling to compromise. This factor of identity and its concomitant, "doing your own thing," and their significance within American culture, are a key to understanding the long, difficult, and not entirely successful role of mediation in the conflict. When the mediation took the form of authoritarian instructions, it was not mediation at all, although this did help clarify parameters of behavior and force everyone to face the question of adaptation. The successful mediators were for the most part individuals with whom the volunteers identified, empathetic volunteer leaders and, in particular, a much liked and respected Sierra Leonean staff member. Their tack was to spell out the Sierra Leonean values clearly, while at the same time letting the volunteers know that their own feelings were recognized even if they needed to change. Coming on strong usually put people's backs up.

There was a wide variation of response on the part of individual volunteers. Many, of course, had already seen the question of appropriate dress as one of complying with local standards, even if they thought the standards "unreal." It was interesting to watch others, as they got more involved in Sierra Leone generally, becoming more careful and conscious about how they dressed. Those volunteers who never came to terms with their need to adapt to Sierra Leonean values were still fighting their own internal fights and therefore unable to "get inside someone else's head" and respond positively.

Because there is now a clear-cut statement on dress formulated by the Sierra Leonean Ministry of Education and distributed to volunteers before they arrive, the nature of the confrontation has shifted somewhat. Volunteers know what is expected of them, and some who are unwilling to comply do not come. Stated and understood areas of conflict are easier to deal with than those which are not. The group of volunteers which arrived just after the newspaper flurry felt that they were leaned on too heavily about the "dress bit," since they had not been the ones causing the problem. Nevertheless, in part because of the leaning, they began their tours as more sensitive to the cultural issues at stake than were some of their predecessors. However, stating issues and sensitizing newcomers to different cultural values is as far as mediators can go. Whether or not to continue wearing jeans when it is culturally inappropriate is a decision each individual volunteer must continue to make.

Old images die hard. Even though most Peace Corps volunteers are now much more neatly dressed, any hippy on the streets of Freetown is called "Peace Corps." The volunteers who are making an active effort in this area are understandably resentful of the trouble made for them by others.

Both the "discipline thing" and the dress issue are examples of situations in which the outsider is the person needing to adapt and of the kinds of problems he may face, particularly if the changes strike at values which he holds deeply. Part of what the outsider needs to be able to achieve is an understanding of the reasons for the adaptation and that the things he hopes to be able to accomplish by doing so are worth whatever it costs him to make the change. Not everyone does this in quite such an objective manner. For many, adaptation comes about by gradually becoming more sensitive to their surroundings.

But what of the reverse: a specific situation in which the outsiders feel strongly that they cannot adapt, will not adapt, and should not have to adapt and that in large measure, it is the ones who perceive themselves as insiders who must do the major adapting? Are there such cases, and if so, how do these changes come about?

Insider Adaptation

International schools, or as they are sometimes referred to, overseas schools, have developed around the world and are designed to meet the specialized needs of primarily Western, English-speaking children living and being educated outside their own country. The hope is to provide these migratory children with some educational continuity, so that it is possible for them to reenter the home school system adequately prepared. The curriculum and educational philosophy is frequently but not exclusively American, although children from many nationalities attend. Effort is made also to take advantage of the multicultural opportunities provided by their particular setting and student body. Whether or not host-country nationals attend depends on local regulation. In the larger international schools, many, although by no means all, of the educators are expatriates. A fuller description of American-sponsored overseas schools can be found in Luebke (1976), and a comprehensive survey of the psychological and sociological literature pertaining to the education of third-culture children has been assembled by Useem (1971).

To look at it, the Cebu American School in August 1971 was hardly a sea of conflicts. Tall trees shaded a shabby white building raised off the ground by child-high stilts. A porch across the front connected the two classrooms that came out around the rest of the building like parentheses. A low building, an afterthought, sat at right angles to the main school. The tap by the front steps leaked, leaving a mud-lolly that the little children found irresistible. Monkeybars and swings stood along the left edge of the playground. Most of the field was dust in the dry weather, sticky sienna mud when it rained. The windows stood open during the day. Heavy green shutters were fastened tight at night to protect school property from neighboring children. Ceiling fans chunk-chunked to move the sluggish air. The wooden chairs and table-desks were a mishmash of sizes and paints. Blackboards had lessons and childish jokes—"Steven is stupid," "Raoul stinks"—chalked on them. Bulletin boards showed drawings, mottoes, and work papers, and displays placed there by the teachers. The textbooks were American, although many of them were printed just after the Second World War. The library, a dreary corner in front of the principal's office, housed two 1928 editions of the *World Book,* three complete sets of the Bobbsey Twins, most of Nancy Drew and the Hardy Boys, and other storybooks which had been left by departing families clearing out their bookshelves.

Ninety or so children aged between four and twelve, varying from pale pink with blond hair to rich ocher with black hair, stood around the flagpole as the Philippine flag was slowly lowered: "Day is done, gone the sun. . . ." Pert teachers in lettuce-green-and-white-checked blouses and green skirts joined the children, stood on the steps where they were caught as the singing began, or continued to put away books and papers in their classrooms. After the song finished, the children ran for their cars, waiting outside the fence on Gorordo Avenue. They called names, punched each other, or stopped for one last swing, as children do. One or two uniformed nurses waited to escort their charges away in chauffeur-driven Mercedes Benzes; a group of children piled into a repainted red Land Rover; mothers or fathers driving themselves hustled dawdlers; a few of the older, jean-clad boys pedaled off on bicycles; others walked away, either by themselves or with a household helper who came to fetch them. A little later, the teachers drifted out to board *jeepneys* (minibus public transportation).

This ramshackle, rambunctious exterior belied the multiple conflicts which swirled around it. Some were based on personalities; but the roots of many were deep differences in cultural values about people, their roles and appropriate behavior, and education and its functions.

The Cebu American School was founded in 1924 in Cebu City, the Philippines' second city, to provide schooling for the children of Americans working in the islands and children of prominent mestizo families. When it was built, it was one of the few schools in a city which now boasts many. As the years passed, it continued filling a special need for "American" education, although its constituent community altered drastically with political changes in the country and the world.

After Philippine independence, the large American business colony dwindled so that by 1971, there was only one family permanently resident, and occasional temporary ones. The missionary component, always present, grew. All were theologically conservative, mainly representing evangelical sects in the States, although there were also Missouri Synod Lutherans and Swedish Baptists. Some had wide knowledge of and sympathy for Philippine values, languages, and practices. Others were barely accepting of the differences within the missionary group, much less within the rest of the community, either American or Filipino. (Whether to use *debt* or *trespass* in the Lord's Prayer caused continual dissension; discussing evolution was unthinkable.) From time to time, American consulate families added children to the school population, as did a growing number of American medical students with school-aged children. Two British families, one with an English public-school background, the other a mixture of Scots and Irish working stock, and one Spanish family, whose children were first generation Filipinos, completed the expatriate portion of the school population. All the foreign children had traveled extensively, and some had lived in more than one country. Most of their parents, except for a few of the more evangelical of the missionaries, had at least college-level education.

The Filipino portion of the community—or at least that which would make "Filipino" its primary national identification—was equally diffuse. The second and third generations of families who were part Filipino, part American were the descendants or relatives of parents, aunts, uncles, cousins, or older brothers and sisters who had attended the school earlier. One or two families represented mixed marriages in the parent generation. Most of the Filipino students came from socially prominent families, although there was a minority who did not. These prominent families were Spanish mestizo, extremely wealthy by world standards and in comparison to the rest of the Philippines staggeringly so, with social and political connections all over the Philippines. Their children traveled around the islands, and many of them had been abroad as well. At least the men in the families had university educations and often further study in the United States. With very rare exceptions, the Filipinos were Roman Catholic.

While the student population was about half expatriate, half Filipino, the age distribution was skewed. The upper classes (sixth, seventh, and eighth grades) were mainly expatriate, whereas the lower classes were predominantly Filipino. The reason for this was that if Filipino students were to continue in their own school system for secondary education, they needed to make the transfer at the end of the sixth grade. Some made the shift even sooner. For the foreign community, the American school represented the only educational alternative offering their children schooling roughly comparable to what they would receive at home. Parents wanted to keep their children as long as possible before sending them off to boarding school, so these children tended to stay through the eighth grade.

For Filipinos, who had a number of alternatives, the reasons for choosing the American school were complex. Some, of course, were following family tradition. Because these families were socially prominent, the school had a reputation for social, if not academic, superiority. Its "American" curriculum was also thought to be superior by parts of the community at large, although to others, the school was undisciplined and its standards questionable. Along with social distinction, some families wanted their children to be better prepared for the schools they hoped the children would attend in the States. They particularly wanted their children taught in good English, and were concerned by a decline in standards of English in many schools. The sudden influx of Filipino children in the lower grades and the tenacity with which all the families clung to the school were directly attributable to a Philippine government policy of increasing the amount of Filipino language and sharply reducing the amount of English required in the national schools.

The school had ten teachers, including the principal, all Filipino except for one American woman whose salary was paid by one of the mission boards which had children attending the school. She taught math and served as assistant principal, with special responsibilities for guidance and acting as a bridge between cultures. With one exception, the teachers were all women. The principal and three of the teachers had been at the school for a number of years, but the rest were young and just out of normal school. The teachers all had certificates or were taking extra courses to become accredited. Most of the younger ones had been born on Cebu Island, although not necessarily in the city, had been educated there, and had not traveled off the island. Some of the older ones had been the 350 miles to Manila, but none had traveled further than that. While two of the teachers came from the elite and one was from a well-known American-Philippine family, the others were from lower-middle-class backgrounds and looked on teaching as a means to achieving higher social status as well as an increased income. The fact that the school paid some of the lowest salaries of all the schools in Cebu, however, tended to encourage the teachers to move on as soon as they could get a little experience and find a better-paying job. The principal was doing master's-degree work in guidance, understood in theory that there were cultural differences involved in her school situation, and gave lip service to making adjustments for these differences, but when approached on a specific problem usually retreated to "the children must know that they are in a different country and this is how we do it." Two American mothers served as volunteer teachers of art and music, but they were not really considered a part of the school faculty.

While the school at one time had been run by a board, the control had primarily devolved upon its treasurer, an American born in the Philippines who represented one of the city's major firms. When absolutely necessary, two other businessmen were called in to constitute a board. The treasurer was conscientious in his solicitousness for the school, as he saw it. He was committed to showing a profit (professionally he was a comptroller, and a fiscally conservative one at that). He was leery of spending money on educational improvements, and was totally unwilling to answer questions or have his judgment questioned. Tuition was astronomical by local standards, but ridiculously low compared with the costs of international schools in other cities, major or minor. While he controlled the school down to the purchase of the last paper clip (for which a receipt had to be presented), he had no experience with education other than that both his and his wife's parents had come to the islands as Thomasites to establish schools.

About the only thing which was common to this disparate group was that no one was happy with the school. The expatriate parents felt that the school was too rigid but at the same time lacked effective discipline, that the teaching standards were poor, that the children were not encouraged to think, and that the teachers themselves were ill-equipped to deal with the situation. The older expatriate children, particularly those who had not grown up in the school, were bored, resentful of the way they were being treated by the teachers, and condescending about their teachers' English. One or two were openly rebellious. The Philippine parents were quieter, but concerned that their children were not getting what they needed to go on to Philippine schools, that there was not enough firm discipline, and that things were much too free and easy. All the parents, except the very few who were related in some way to the businessmen who ran the school, felt that there was something rotten in Denmark, or at least in the treasurer's office. The teachers felt that they were poorly paid and inadequately respected, that the American children were rude and unmanageable, and that the parents were difficult, since they involved themselves in school affairs in ways other than producing large amounts of food for school parties. The school treasurer was unhappy because people questioned his judgment and wanted to spend money on "educational frills" (textbooks and a library) which he felt the school did not need, or at least could not afford. Concerned parents tried quietly to initiate change and growth of understanding, but to no avail.

The situation might have continued in growing animosity and heated Parent-Teachers Association (PTA) meetings—with one irate parent after another blowing off steam to no useful end, the principal and treasurer saying, in effect, "If you don't like the school, go elsewhere," and the school's giving lip service to meeting everyone's needs and succeeding in meeting none of them—had not a number of things happened externally which eased the logjam and allowed mediation and adaptation to take place. The first was that the principal got the offer of a better job and moved. She was a very capable woman, deeply concerned about the school, but in many ways insufficiently flexible to be able to see the need for or to help initiate the changes that almost everyone else felt were needed.

More important, however, was that following the imposition of martial law, the Department of Education instituted a program of accelerated "Philippinization" of the educational system. New, rigid qualifications for any school to be accredited and maintain a nonstandard Philippine curriculum were set, and a special category of international school was authorized. This made it imperative that the Cebu American School reorganize itself to stay legal, and precipitated a change which put the running of the school into the hands of a new board constituted of parents.

Implementing consciously thought-out change suddenly became a responsibility, rather than something to be fought for. The new board's aim was twofold: first, to foster the growth of a school in the tradition of international schools elsewhere, with an American curriculum and comparable academic and teaching standards, thereby filling the need of the foreign student component; and second, making the school legal under the Department of Education's new rules. The board also took into account that there was a Philippine component whose needs should be met, as long as this was not incompatible with the overall purpose of the new school. As much as the parents would have liked to run two curricula, it was impossible financially, and it was illegal. A choice had to be made. Since the Philippine students had other alternatives and the expatriates had none, it was felt that the needs of this latter group had priority. Thus, the Cebu International School was born.

The new school—for new it was in more ways than its name—faced scores of problems. Lack of money was one, since at least some investment in updated materials would have to accompany whatever changes were made.

Here, one of the previous clashes in what turned out to be values came into a different light. The school was found to have a nest egg of sorts. The treasurer had carefully accumulated a reserve—his own sense of how best to serve the school. Nothing had been rotten in Denmark, secrecy had only made it seem so. Since the parent-run board controlled budgeting, plans were made to use these funds to start a library and to explore whether a whole new building should be constructed. Long-overdue increases in pay encouraged the teachers and provided a tangible symbol of the board's faith in them. But nest egg or no, more money would be needed.

Monetary concerns, while real and serious, were nowhere near as complex, touchy, or crucial as changing the curriculum and teaching methods to make the school truly international. These issues treaded on cultural ground and required patience, goodwill, a sense of humor, and careful planning. The school as it existed could only be described as polyglot. The textbooks and curriculum were basically American, but outdated. Filipino language and Philippine government and history appeared on the class offerings list, but had not been taken seriously. The teaching values were somewhere between what the Filipino teachers *thought* American values were and their own values, learned both in Philippine educational institutions as academic training and, more important, through their own schooling experience. While labeled as an American school, to the Americans the school seemed more truly a Philippine school; to the Filipinos, it was an American school.

While the parents involved had a clear idea of what they wanted to achieve and a fair amount of experience in some aspects of schools, none was a professional educator. The missionary-supplied assistant principal had finished her term and gone home. The charming, very able young Filipino who had been newly hired as principal had a great deal of capacity and had taught at the school for two years, but was not familiar with international schools. An education subcommittee was formed. Its composition was carefully balanced to represent both teachers and parents and the various cultural groups within these segments. The international school in Manila was turned to for guidance. A team came down to help assess the school as it was, both its good points and its weaknesses. One of the major sources of strength was that the teachers were young, enthusiastic, and willing to learn. One of the major sources of difficulty was that these same teachers had very limited experience, particularly compared to their widely traveled students.

But the guts of a school are its teachers. Experienced foreign teachers could not be brought in. So if the Cebu International School was to become international, what in some ways seemed to be the most crucial requirement was an impossibility: to make American teachers out of young Filipinas. This statement is not so xenophobic as it seems. It is based on the assumption that having grown up Filipina, the teachers could be excellent Philippine teachers, but that if the children were to become Americans, they needed to be taught in ways that reinforced American values and thought patterns, which is better done by Americans. It further recognizes that the teaching values and thinking patterns of Filipinas are quite different from those of Americans and teachers in international schools. It should be made clear that there was never any intention to imply that one way was better than the other—only, perhaps, that one was more appropriate for this particular teaching situation. The desire was that the children should emerge from their learning situation conversant with both patterns. The stage was therefore set for cultural adaptation. If the goals of the new school board were to be met, the Filipinas involved would need to learn to adapt themselves to American cultural patterns. In a way, the inside and outside roles had become confused: the Filipinas were in their own country and therefore insiders; but within the school, the cultural base had shifted, and they were suddenly outsiders.

Ways had to be found, therefore, to give all the teachers practical exposure to new ideas. Because there was no experienced leadership, the whole project was pretty much do-it-yourself. The board, and more specifically the education committee, deliberately set out to be mediators in the situation. We were very much involved; we had clear ideas of our goals and a deeply felt, vested interest in the kind of education our children should have. (My husband had been made chairman of the school board. I was a member of the education committee.)

As mediators, the committee did a number of things. The individual expatriate members continued to deepen their personal relationships, not only with the other members of the committee, but also with the entire school staff. The PTA president had a long-standing rapport with the teachers, based on a gently joking manner and a command of Cebuano, the local language. Over a previous two-year period, I had tried to develop a peer relationship with teachers through the volunteer teaching of art classes, so that traditional parent-teacher, foreigner-local, and other social barriers could be broken down. We all strived to do things in a way which respected the principal's and teachers' professionalism and judgment. We tried hard to straddle the cultural differences involved in the need to speak plainly and at the same time indirectly. We talked a lot about what the cultural differences really were, which gave us a chance to find the areas where we agreed—on the need for firm, fair discipline, for instance—but where we might proceed differently in order to achieve this end.

Above all, we had to make haste slowly. This was perhaps the most necessary and the most difficult objective to achieve, since we were anxious to see change, and at the same time, some of use feared change. We found it was necessary to be specific and not too theoretical. "Not so fast" and "Be specific. How should we do it?" were frequent expostulations in our winding and not always calm meetings. A great deal of time had to be spent in communication among ourselves and with the school community as a whole, so that there was opportunity for the new ideas to be explained, consulted about, reacted to, and assimilated. It had to be everyone's school, with no one feeling excluded or steamrollered.

The committee established priorities on a number of levels. It was deemed important to gain as much exposure to outside ideas and influences as we could manage, given our limited financial resources and the isolation of an island 350 miles from the capital city. The principal was sent to Manila—it turned out to be her first trip off Cebu Island—to visit the international school, participate in its in-service teachers' workshop, and to see firsthand the kind of atmosphere and approach to education for which the school was aiming. Her enthusiastic return fired the other teachers, and together they were off. Whenever the opportunity arose to take advantage of outside expertise, workshops were organized, sometimes on only hours' notice. These workshops were particularly important since some of the new ideas could be presented objectively by people who were professionals and not part of the day-to-day situation. They also gave the teachers an opportunity to learn from direct experience, from which both teachers and planners could benefit and grow. Later in the school year, a long-forgotten connection with the East Asian Regional Conference of Overseas Schools (EARCOS) was reestablished. Both the principal and the board chairman attended the EARCOS annual conference in Kuala Lumpur, to gather new ideas and experiences and to take reassurance from the fact that our problems were not unique.

In the fundamentals of altering school practice, two areas were selected for concentration. Teaching methods and their corollary, grading, were an area in which parents were anxious to see quick improvement. Everyone agreed that discipline was a problem. An understanding on the part of the planning group of at least some of the cultural conflicts involved facilitated the changes, although progress was slow and uneven. While the general direction in which the school would move had been decided by fiat, the speed and specifics were worked out first by the parent-teacher education committee, which made the recommendations, and ultimately by the teachers and the principal.

The principal initiated weekly "think sessions," with different teachers put in the role of discussion leaders. This in itself was a break with cultural patterns, since the Philippine society is hierarchical, and subordinates tend to be very uncomfortable in "leading" their seniors. These think sessions gave the teachers a much-needed opportunity to express their thoughts freely, without being afraid of offending the board. These feelings were in turn fed back to the committee through the teacher members, who were able to speak for the group and not just for themselves, thereby avoiding at least some of their own cultural discomfort at saying potentially unpleasant things directly. The parent-volunteer teachers did not attend these meetings unless specifically invited, so that this openness could be maintained. A continuing effort was made to sensitize teachers to American values, and more particularly to have them articulate their own values so that they could see the sources of some of the conflict. While there were differences of opinion about many things, there was not conflict in the unpleasant sense, and the overwhelming feeling of the school at this time was one of creation and excitement.

The first specific change was a revised report card. Highly competitive marking, down to the last hundredth of a percentage point, is a feature of Philippine schools. Lists are published in the newspaper of who ranks first, second, third, and so on in national examinations. Schools print full-page congratulatory advertisements extolling those of their students who finish particularly well. This same spirit of grading had been followed at the Cebu American School. A student in the previous graduating class had been named first by one-tenth of a percentage point over two others, out of a class of nine. The expatriate parents wanted this extreme competitiveness eliminated. They wanted effort to become valued for its own sake. Most of all, they felt that while the extremely competitive ranking might inspire the few at the top to do better, all it taught most of the students was that it was impossible for them to succeed.

The education committee established broad standards of achievement in factual knowledge and effort on which grading was to be based, to replace the traditional percentage scoring method. A new honor roll was devised which recognized students who achieved above a specific level, with names listed in alphabetical order. The honor roll was divided into two parts, one for academic achievement and the other for effort. Gold medals, which had been awarded at the end of the year to the first student in each grade, were eliminated, and certificates were given to each child on the honor roll. It was possible to be on one honor roll and not the other—on just the effort or just the academic list—or it was possible to appear on both.

While the committee established the pattern, the teachers themselves worked out the details. Once they had gone through that process, the teachers understood the new grading system fairly well and accepted it, although some found it hard to divorce effort from achievement. They had previously assumed that a high grade was to be equated with effort, while a low one could not. It was a new concept that some students worked hard and had this effort rewarded, but would still achieve only a "C." High grades were considered a credit to a teacher.

The examination system was also revised, and the importance of tests and the need to do well were de-emphasized. Special times were no longer set aside at the end of the grading period for testing. Instead, more frequent tests were administered and related to the particular teaching material being covered at the time.

Before this system was implemented, a PTA meeting was held to explain what was being contemplated. Since grades and tests are at least as important and as threatening to the parents as they are to the children and their teachers, there was a large attendance, and especially an unusually large turn-out of the Filipino parents. Concern was running high. The principal explained the new system and the reasons for it. While a number of parents, both Filipino and expatriate, expressed approval of the idea, others were worried that because of the lessened importance of exams and grades, the children would not work as hard. Still others were not sure that they would know how the children were really doing. Others were threatened by the loss of the social value of being able to say, "My son was first," although this concern was not so directly stated. The principal kept pointing out that this change was being made because it would benefit all the children, instead of the very few at the top. The meeting closed with many feelings of ambivalence, but there was a general feeling of "Well, let's see how it works."

And so it was begun. Along with the new grading system was instituted a mandatory parent-teacher conference at which the first report card would be given out. This was very culturally threatening because it involved direct confrontation, a social interaction which makes Filipinos extremely uncomfortable. But everyone survived. The principal sat in on some of the conferences, when she felt that they would be particularly difficult for unsure teachers to handle alone. The students liked the new system and responded to the reduced pressure with pride and better results. The teachers, too, found they liked the new atmosphere, although some of them missed the protection they had felt the old percentage system afforded them. By the end of the year, when many more parents than usual were able to walk across the stage with a son or daughter who was receiving a certificate for achievement or effort, even the most reluctant parents were won over to the new system.

The whole question of how people learn, or what different cultures feel it is important for people to learn, translated itself into a continuing discussion of teaching methods, of which grading and testing were but the tip of the iceberg. For instance, the teachers had been used to a system which prized the retention of facts and rote learning (what one person rudely dubbed the "one spoon in, one spoon out, regurgitation method"). The Americans wanted their children to be trained as problem-solvers, using the inquiry method. Each method reflects some national characteristics, if one may use such an imprecise term.

The problem-solving method gave the teachers difficulties, in part because they had themselves been taught facts by their teachers. Nor had they had much experience in problem-solving. They found it threatening, because it raised questions directly and sometimes got them into areas where they did not know the factual answers. Furthermore, asking questions was viewed not so much as questioning facts, but as questioning authority. Workshops were held on the inquiry method. The establishment of a library and the hiring of a librarian, which made it possible for children to do independent research, helped both teachers and pupils to grow in this area. Familiarization programs on the library gave the teachers more confidence in helping children solve problems without underlining the teachers' own shortcomings in this and many other areas.

Perhaps the attribute of American children which made the Filipinos most uncomfortable was their habit of questioning facts and saying, "You're wrong." The Americans, who had been taught to question facts and opinions at home, saw this as just questioning a fact or an opinion and therefore not as a personal reflection that might be embarrassing to the teacher. However, the teachers saw it as not giving sufficient respect to the role of teacher and as a public embarrassment for them, the height of rudeness within their culture. Since questioning was a cultural pattern that the expatriate parents wanted not only retained but encouraged, efforts were made to help the children ask questions in ways which were at least less offensive. While all the teachers got to the point where they accepted the fact that this is how the expatriate children would behave (and that the Filipino children would quickly develop the same pattern), I believe that in their hearts, they continued to be uncomfortable with all but the mildest of these forms of interaction.

The problem of discipline and authority was at least as perplexing as the question of learning, if not more so. The Filipinos had grown up in a world which automatically respected age, authority, and teachers. The foreign children were much more free and easy with adults than the Filipinos. The teachers expected instant obedience, but often found their orders responded to with a "Why?" from children who expected not just to be told what to do, but also to be given a reason for it. In thinking back, I believe that there are different assumptions of responsibility in discipline patterns and different points at which Americans and Filipinos step into a situation. The teachers would say "Stop it" when the noise got a little loud, but if this brought no response, they often would do nothing until the noise was completely out of hand, at which point they would become very harsh. While it was the teachers' responsibility to say "Stop it," they assumed that it was the responsibility of the child to do what he was told. The harshness was triggered not so much by the noise as by the children's failure to carry out an expected obligation. The Americans tended not to say "Stop it" quite so quickly, but when they did, they would follow up rapidly if they did not get the required response from the children. The Americans assumed not that instant obedience was the child's responsibility, but rather that the adults should see to it that they were obeyed. The American children expected the follow-up and were therefore more responsive when they knew it was coming and less responsive under circumstances when they knew it would not.

Another difference in patterns compounded the problem. Most of the Filipinos came from a different social level from the children they were teaching and to an extent stood in awe of their students. In some cases, it was merely because the children were foreigners, and in other cases, because the teachers were acutely aware of the parents' positions. In general, the problem was to give the teachers more self-confidence and also some practical guidance. A number of the American mothers were asked to attend the teachers' workshop one afternoon and talk about how they disciplined their own children and what the relevant cultural cues were. Parents were urged to establish social contacts with teachers, so that the teachers could see how foreign families acted among themselves and remove some of the awe. This was only partially successful, since only a few parents did it, and these were for the most part the same parents the teachers were coming to know better anyway because they were working together on various committees. But even this limited amount of contact was helpful.

Behavior problems with younger Filipino students were different again. In many cases, in their out-of-school hours, these youngsters were largely in the charge of maids, whom they walked all over. Some of these students looked on the young teachers as an extension of the maids. The Filipino children also saw how the Americans responded to authority and sometimes emulated their expatriate peers. Yet their teachers expected them to know their own cultural cues and were completely bewildered when they did not. These children really did not know who they were; they were the real lost souls.

Teachers were not the whole focus of the effort, although they were the main ones. The change program involved the parents as well. Hot and heavy discussions continued. As the school become more comfortable for the Americans and other foreigners, it sometimes became less so for the Filipino parents. The patterns that suited the more liberal of the Americans were less to the liking of the conservative parents. The board and committee members spent hours on the telephone and over coffee answering questions, calming fears, explaining, listening.

It would be nice if this were the best of all possible worlds and if the story had an ending. It does not, however, since the school is an ongoing project with a life of its own, and we moved out of it at the end of the first year. I understand that the new building is now a reality, that all the teachers have had trips to Manila, that some of them have adapted more comfortably and successfully to the new teaching patterns than others, that some parents are happy and some are not—a normal state for schools—and that the principal has become so involved in the concept of international education and the associated specialized skills in cross-cultural mediation that she has taken a leave of absence to study further at the East-West Center.

In retrospect, I think it is fair to say that on the whole, the effort was successful. What the teachers would say, I am not sure. I hope they would agree. The project was not without pain and stress and misunderstanding. I do not know of growth situations which are painless. The fact that Americans are direct and plain-speaking and Filipinos are indirect and avoid open conflict must have caused problems. I know that changing patterns which involved identity and role caused much soul-searching and trepidation. Nor was the stress all between the expatriates and the Filipinos. Ultimately, however, what success there was—and each person involved would no doubt assess that differently—stemmed from the fact that overriding or underlying it all was a basic respect and caring for persons, which I have come to believe is more important than specific cultural understanding. This caring somehow communicates itself even if the forms are wrong, and somehow helps make different forms right.

In analyzing this example in our present frame of reference, it is fair to say that the parents' concern that their children be raised more or less within the parents' educational value system forced the issue. This set up a situation where the insiders, if they were to retain their employment, became the outsiders and had to do most of the adapting. Deeply held concepts of self, the most difficult of all of the personality attributes to change, were involved. Many people acted as mediators. It was important that some were non-involved, impersonal experts, because they were able to transmit some cultural learning nondefensively, which those mediators who were personally involved could not always do. It was, however, very important for the main mediators to be involved, both as parents and as teachers, because mediation as well as adaptation is a personal thing.

One further example is necessary, to draw a distinction between situations in which it is arguably valid that the insiders must change and those in which one clearly cannot expect it. We moved from Cebu to Freetown. Our youngest son was entered into local schools there. Again we found him confronted with many of the patterns of teaching and discipline we had worked hard to change in Cebu. The situation however, was very different. The schools in which he was enrolled were Sierra Leonean schools' designed to meet the educational and cultural needs of Sierra Leoneans, not expatriates. The need to adapt was clearly ours, and most specifically Charley's. Our role was to help him do this and still protect in him the cultural values which he would need at a later time to function in his own society. The problem came in several areas.

"Mother!" He burst into the bedroom one afternoon. "The English teacher is dumb."

"Why dumb?"

"Well, look at this. I wrote: 'She had beautiful skin and a lovely smile,' and he marked it wrong. He says it should be, 'She had *a* beautiful skin and a lovely smile.' That's wrong, isn't it? He's dumb."

A short discussion of mass and count nouns followed—a subtle and not too rational area in the English language where the answer to "Why?" is "Because."

"You're right," said I. "He did make a mistake. You know it and I know it. And you know what is correct. It isn't his language. Let's just let it ride."

Another day Charley came in infuriated because his pronunciation had been corrected. This seemed to call for an answer he could give politely if the situation occurred again, since it hit at his own cultural identification, a very important quality to maintain for a child growing up multiculturally. So we worked out an answer. In essence, it was that yes, the teacher had given the Africanized British pronunciation, but Charley was an American, and under the circumstances, not only was the American pronunciation proper for him, but also the other would not be. The situation never arose again, but Charley felt more comfortable in knowing how to handle the matter if it did.

Caning was an equally difficult problem, but for different reasons. We talked about caning, both giving Charley a chance to ventilate his fears and anger about its use and reassuring him that we too thought it was wrong. However, we also had to help him accept it, since it could not be changed. Charley learned for himself how to control some of it. He just did not misbehave in situations he knew would bring on caning. The first time he was caned, we commiserated with him, after being sure that the caning was for behavior disciplinary reasons, but said, in effect, that this was "their way" and no matter how we felt about it, we just had to accept it. We did say that if he was ever caned for making a mistake, we would go to the teacher and see if something could be worked out, since this so trespassed on our values that we felt compelled to speak out.

Interestingly enough, the following year, when such a situation did arise, Charley would not let us interfere. One of his teachers made the student who answered a question correctly cane the ones who made the mistake. Charley felt that our interference would make him even more different and visible than he naturally was. "I just don't cane the other guys hard," he said. The only time he was caned that he felt was completely unfair was an occasion similar to my earlier Peace Corps example of the entire class being caned for the misbehavior of a small group.

In the Sierra Leonean situation, we were clearly the outsiders and obliged to adapt or withdraw. Our job as parents was to mediate.

Conclusion

What conclusions are there to be drawn from these examples? From my point of view as at least a sometime cultural mediator, they are these: The process of cultural adaptation is not always easy, predictable, or quickly achieved. Nor is it always hard. It comes more readily for some people than for others, and between some cultures, more felicitously than between others.

The insider-outsider distinction is a helpful tool in understanding where the stresses of adaptation are falling in different situations, but I doubt if it is a hard-and-fast rule. I think it is perhaps easier for outsiders to feel the need to adapt, because they know they are strange or foreign to the situation. Insiders are on their own home ground, and therefore the idea of adapting does not occur as quickly to them.

The more deeply held the values, the more difficult they are to alter. Everyone has points beyond which they will not or cannot change. The broader situation in which individuals are interacting is often a controlling influence. Some situations are like steamrollers. In less preemptive situations, the degree to which people see that adaptation under the particular circumstances will help them attain their goals is often the degree to which they are able to adapt, because cultural adaptation is often not the end, but the means. Nor is adaptation necessarily temporary and related to the specific circumstances, although it can alter the course of a person's life. Nonetheless, in my observation, the process of "getting inside someone else's cultural skull" expands the limits of the world in which one lives, even if one does not constantly act upon this knowledge.

Becoming a mediator is often a question of being in the right place at the right time. Mediators carry their own cultural identity with them and function within this framework. They have their own vested interests, and are participants in the situation while maintaining sufficient detachment from it to understand some of what is going on. They too are adapting as they go along. Patience, goodwill, a sense of humor, and above all a basic respect and caring for persons—empathy—which one communicates are the tools of the trade. Mediators can perhaps sensitize those around them to cultural differences, or if they are planning, can plan in such a way that adaptation is fostered. Mediators can form bridges over cultural gaps. But each person must walk across the bridge for himself.

References

Luebke, P. T. *American Elementary and Secondary Community Schools Abroad*. 2nd ed. Arlington, Va.: American Association of School Administrators, 1976.

Useem, R. H. Education of Third Culture Children: An Annotated Bibliography. Studies of Third Cultures: A Continuing Series, no. 1. Michigan State University: Institute for International Studies in Education, 1971.

Epilogue

Stephen Bochner

Intercultural Mediation: A Continuing Inquiry

Although this is the final essay in the book, it is by no means the last word on the subject. On the contrary, in the course of the analysis it became clear that the theoretical model of the mediating person is still evolving, and that there exist vast gaps in empirical knowledge regarding the antecedents, correlates, and consequences of cultural mediation. What the book has achieved is to provide a useful summary of current work in the area and identify the questions that must be posed in order to make further progress. The express purpose of this chapter is to stimulate a continuing inquiry into the topic of intercultural mediation. The chapter brings together in one place the core issues raised by the various contributors to the present volume, draws conclusions where the evidence warrants it, and lists specific areas where further research is required.

When Is a Linking Person Not a Mediator?

Many of the contributors to this book had a problem with distinguishing a mediator from other persons in similar roles. Although there was widespread agreement that mediators serve as links or bridges between diverse cultural systems, different investigators attached their own meanings to these concepts. And although most writers appreciated that acting as a link between two cultures is not synonymous with intercultural mediating, in the main the exact nature of the relationship between these two dimensions did not receive adequate attention. Consequently, the general principle according to which interface roles can be either included or excluded from the category of intercultural mediation has remained obscure, even though most of the contributors assumed the existence of such a principle, and one or two made explicit reference to it.

The aim of the present section is to determine the principles by which a mediator can be distinguished from other individuals located at the interface between two cultures. This will be done by anchoring the concepts to clearly identifiable operations and functions. In particular, it is necessary to specify precisely who is being linked, who is doing the linking, and the nature of the link, as a preliminary to establishing criteria by which certain roles and/or functions can be excluded from the category of intercultural mediation.

There was general agreement among the contributors that mediation can take place between individuals, groups, or societies. There was also substantial agreement about what was the most salient feature of the process. Although different writers used different labels in describing the formal characteristics of the transaction, the common denominator was the purpose of the actor. Thus, most of the contributors regarded the actions of individuals in interface situations primarily in terms of whether the intent and effect was partisan, neutral, or bipartisan.

These two dimensions—the social systems being linked and the purpose of the transaction—provide a framework for establishing a principle whereby linking roles can be categorized as either mediating or nonmediating. The first step was to assemble a reasonably exhaustive list of interface functions, that is, occupational or role categories that have traditionally served as explicit links between different human beings, groups, or societies. Then the functions were classified according to the purpose of the transaction and according to who was being linked. The precise character of the two dimensions, the steps that were used in the classification, the list of interface functions, and the outcome of this analysis are presented in Table 1. The mediating role per se was explicitly excluded from the classification, since the whole object of the exercise was to determine the attributes of mediation without begging the question.

Two main results emerged. First, the analysis indicates that all of the linking functions apply equally at all three levels of generality. There is therefore no utility in making a theoretical distinction regarding links between individuals, groups, and societies, since the same set of principles appears to govern all three sets of transactions.

Second, the analysis revealed major differences among the linking functions when they are distinguished according to the purpose of the transaction. The categories used were partisan, neutral, and bipartisan. Each classification implies different degrees and kinds of engagement by the actor. The partisan actor is concerned primarily with furthering the interests of his own culture, with which he is also primarily engaged. The neutral actor is disengaged in the sense that in his formal role, he is not concerned with furthering the interests of either cultural group. However, he is still engaged with the linking process itself. The bipartisan actor is concerned with furthering the interests of both cultures, and is also engaged with each of these cultural systems.

The distinction between the neutral and bipartisan categories is somewhat arbitrary, which, however, does not greatly affect the present argument. The crucial question relates to whether there is a real difference between those

Table 1. Interface Roles Categorized by the Purpose of the Transaction and the Systems Being Linked

Systems Being Linked	The Purpose of the Transaction		
	Partisan	Neutral	Bipartisan
Individuals	Advocate Ambassador Missionary Persuader Representative Salesman Spokesman	Arbitrator Elucidator Go-between Intermediary Interpreter Moderator Ombudsman Referee Translator	Catalyst Conciliator Facilitator Negotiator Synthesizer
Groups	Advocate Ambassador Missionary Persuader Representative Salesman Spokesman	Arbitrator Elucidator Go-between Intermediary Interpreter Moderator Ombudsman Referee Translator	Catalyst Conciliator Facilitator Negotiator Synthesizer
Societies and Cultures	Advocate Ambassador Missionary Persuader Representative Salesman Spokesman	Arbitrator Elucidator Go-between Intermediary Interpreter Moderator Ombudsman Referee Translator	Catalyst Conciliator Facilitator Negotiator Synthesizer

functions classified as partisan, on the one hand, and those functions classified as neutral and bipartisan, on the other, and what the consequences of such a difference are for the definition of the concept of cultural mediation. A perusal of the table suggests that there are real differences between the functions listed under the "partisan" heading and the functions listed in the other two columns. A further perusal of the table indicates that the functions that have been referred to as "mediating" in the present book resemble more closely the functions that are listed in the columns headed "neutral" and "bipartisan" than the functions under the "partisan" heading.

Thus, a mediator is not a mediator when he is being partisan in intent and effect. More precisely stated, the crucial criterion for distinguishing between mediating and nonmediating links or transactions centers on whether there is some intent of mutuality. Applying this criterion, transactions with a nonmutual intent are excluded from the domain of mediation. Conversely, transactions that are characterized by a substantial degree of mutuality fall within the definition of mediation. In short, the construct of mutuality appears to be the main arbiter between mediating and nonmediating transactions. Mutuality thereby becomes one of the core constructs of the model and hence an important issue in its own right. The next section is devoted to a brief explication of the concept of mutuality.

What Is the Mediator's Reference Group?

The distinction between the neutral and bipartisan categories implies contrasting a mutually neutral actor with a person working to the mutual advantage of both systems. This formulation is not on the face of it altogether satisfactory, since the notion of mutual neutrality suggests mutual inaction, which would be a contradiction in terms when applied to an actor trying to achieve some goal and is in any case not what was meant. What authors in this book have had in mind when referring to some categories of mediating persons is individuals who are neutral with respect to both cultures and disengaged from them, but who at the same time are trying to achieve a goal that will benefit both systems. The best example of this role is the translator, who acts as a faithful and accurate channel of communication linking two systems where previously no such link existed. The intent of such a person is to achieve mutuality between the two groups, even though he will be careful to maintain strict neutrality and noninvolvement with respect to each of the cultures and with respect to the substance of the material he is translating.

The tendency to associate mutual neutrality with mutal inaction and the attendant conceptual problem disappears if the distinction between neutral and bipartisan transactions is set within a social-psychological framework. This can be done by ascertaining who functions as the actor's reference group, that is, the group whose norms, values, and goals guide and inform his behavior. In the case of the partisan actor, the reference group is the person's culture of origin. The bipartisan actor has two reference groups—the two cultures that he belongs to—and his behavior therefore should be consistent with the values of both societies. The distinction between partisan and bipartisan actors in terms of their reference-group affiliation provides an unambiguous operational definition of mutuality: if the behavior of persons in an interface situation is consistent with the values of one of the societies only, then they are acting in a nonmutual manner; if the behavior of persons in an interface situation is consistent with the values of both societies, then they are acting in a mutual manner.

But what about the neutral actor—who is his reference group? A perusal of the role categories listed in Table 1 under the "neutral" heading suggests that the individuals performing these functions probably adopt for their reference group other persons engaged in similar work. In other words, the norms, values, and goals that guide and inform the behavior of the various neutral mediators are the norms, values, and goals that have through custom and tradition become an intrinsic aspect of the respective activity itself. For example, inherent in the translator role is the prescription to convey meanings accurately; ombudsmen are charged with seeing that justice is done to all the parties in the dispute; intermediaries have failed unless they bring the different spokesmen together; and referees do not care who wins, but are very much concerned to ensure that the game is played fairly. Therefore, the correct question to ask is whether the norms of what have here been called the neutral linking function contribute to mutuality. Specifically, if persons in an interface situation carry out a neutral role that has mutally positive consequences, then they are performing a mediating function; if the performance has mutually neutral consequences, or consequences that are negative for one or both of the systems, then it is not fulfilling a mediating function.

What Kind of Mediator Is Effective In
What Kind of Situation?

Implicit in the preceding discussion, and in many of the contributions to this book, is a distinction between two types of mediators. The first type has been referred to as neutral, culturally disengaged, detached, passive, a translator. The second type has been called bipartisan, biculturally engaged, attached, active, a synthesizer. The distinction raises the issue of whether there are absolute differences in the effectiveness of the two types of mediators, and/or whether the type of mediation interacts with the purpose and cultural context of the encounter, so that the engaged style may be more effective under one set of conditions, whereas the disengaged style is indicated in other circumstances.

To date, there is no direct evidence available to shed light on this important question. However, several authors have offered speculative, anecdotal, and tangential accounts which should serve to generate testable hypotheses in this area. In particular, it has been suggested that the disengaged mediator has a special contribution to make when the purpose is disseminating information, promoting mutual understanding, forming culturally relativistic attitudes, producing cross-cultural empathy, and spreading international goodwill; whereas an engaged mediator is more appropriate when the purpose is reconciling disparate cultural practices and/or when some concrete action is to follow from the encounter.

It has further been suggested that cultures differ in the extent to which they construe and value the mediating function, implying that the mediating role may be accepted in some cultures and rejected in others; that some cultures will be more accepting of the engaged mediator, whereas other groups will prefer a disengaged one; and that the cultural identity of the mediating person will interact with all of these variables. These propositions provide a fruitful area of empirical research.

How Does the Mediating Person Achieve His Credentials?

Perhaps the greatest diversity of opinion was expressed in relation to how mediating persons were to be trained and how their function could be legitimized. Authors identified four sets of antecedent conditions for training mediators: (1) a bicultural childhood (for instance, the child of a mixed marriage, the child of a diplomat, a second-generation migrant); (2) an adult culture-learning experience of a general kind (for example, an academic sojourn); (3) a job-related orientation program (such as a predeparture course for Peace Corps volunteers or experts); and (4) a proposal to establish a degree course in cultural mediaton.

The preceding categories have different implications for the process of legitimizing the mediating function. Some authors contended that the mediator's effectiveness will be increased if his role is institutionalized; the mediating person must not only see himself as such, but must be seen by others to be a mediator, with the correct credentials for the job. In practice, this would mean the emergence of a designated mediating role in the international social structure, that is, a profession of cultural mediation with its own set of norms, practices, rewards, sanctions, training procedures, and initiation rites. Other authors had doubts about the desirability of differentiating the mediating role in this way and making it the province of highly trained specialists.

When these authors referred to mediating persons, they really meant mediating engineers, mediating diplomats, mediating housewives, mediating schoolboys, rather than individuals whose primary job description was cultural mediation, and they attributed the effectiveness of these mediators explicitly to the dual nature of their role.

The matter is to some extent an empirical one, and centers on whether the professional or amateur mediating person is perceived as having greater credibility. The authors were all agreed that credibility is a crucial variable in determining the effectiveness of a mediator. But again, the issue is complex, since there may be circumstances in which a professional mediator has greater credibility, and conversely, there may be conditions under which an amateur mediator will be more persuasive. For instance, it is possible that if the interaction is primarily at the level of institutions (that is, government-to-government, corporation-to-corporation), then a person with the official credentials of the professional mediator may be more effective; whereas if the interaction is primarily at the level of interpersonal, informal, and/or small-group contact, then an amateur mediating person may be more acceptable. These propositions also provide a fertile field for future empirical investigation.

What Are the Necessary Personal Attributes of the Mediator?

There was substantial agreement among authors about the personal qualifications that a mediator must possess if he is to be effective in his role. The mediating person was consistently described in the following terms: as an individual who has systematic knowledge of more than one culture; as one who has skills that enable him to overcome the barriers to communication between actors who come from different cultural backgrounds; as a person who has a humanitarian concern for the well-being of the people he is mediating between; as one who respects the indigenous values of the societies he is operating in; and as a person who is concerned with preserving the core aspects of cultural systems undergoing social change.

An unresolved problem relates to how mediators should respond when considerations of cultural preservation come into conflict with humanitarian concerns or, more accurately, when a mediator faces cultural manifestations that contradict his personal conception of what constitutes a humanitarian concern. Specifically, should mediators try to change practices of which they deeply disapprove (corporal punishment in schools, nepotism in the civil service)? Or should they explicitly refrain from making value judgments about cultural matters? The orthodox advice is not to interfere, since cultural practices tend to be interrelated, and tampering with one segment of a culture may have all sorts of unintended and often highly undesirable consequences elsewhere in the social system. Taking the two examples referred to above: banning corporal punishment in schools may undermine the basis of authority on which that culture rests, and eliminating nepotism may weaken a system of reciprocal obligations on which that particular culture is founded.

In practice, individual mediators may not be able to avoid communicating their disapproval of those cultural manifestations that offend their sensibilities, nor resist taking action against indigenous customs they regard as unpalatable. Some mediators may feel that it is their duty to point out that such practices are frowned on elsewhere in the world, and then leave the decision about changing the process to members of the indigenous culture. The problem is very complex, and this is reflected in the lack of consensus among the authors regarding the extent to which a mediator has either the right or the duty to influence the modification of indigenous cultural manifestations.

Conclusion

This chapter had three aims. The first was to summarize the main issues raised in this book. These included defining the mediating person and distinguishing him from other individuals located at the interface between several cultural systems, achieving clarity about the goals of mediation, identifying the reference group of mediators, determining the conditions contributing to the effectiveness of mediating persons, establishing the training and accreditation of mediators, and developing the personal attributes of cultural mediators.

The second aim was to point to areas of needed research and thereby stimulate a continuing inquiry into the topic. With that end in mind, the issues listed above were presented in the form of propositions capable of being tested by empirical procedures. Similarly, the concepts underlying these issues were formulated with reference to specific procedures and operations, thereby leaving room in the theoretical model for subsequent additions, deletions, or modifications in the light of further empirical evidence.

The third aim was to stress the utility of maintaining a constant interplay between theory, practice, and research, to the mutual benefit of all three components. This integrated approach also makes it more likely that the inquiry will be of interest not only to the academically oriented social scientist, but to the practitioner as well.

Throughout the book, issues of theoretical significance were treated in conjunction with the systematic application of the principles of cultural mediation to the solution of real problems in the world of affairs. For these reasons, this book should be judged in terms of the degree of research and theory-building that it stimulates, together with the amount of influence it exerts on the nature of intercultural transactions.

About the Authors

A. A. ALEXANDER is Professor of Psychiatry at the University of Wisconsin Medical School and a Research Associate of the Wisconsin Psychiatric Institute in Madison.

STEPHEN BOCHNER is Senior Lecturer in Psychology at the University of New South Wales in Sydney. His formal interests in mediation began with an East-West Center graduate studentship in 1963-65. He subsequently maintained his affiliation with the Center, and most of his research deals with aspects of the mediating function. He is coeditor of *Overseas Students in Australia* and *Cross-Cultural Perspectives on Learning*, and has published many articles and chapters in the field of social and cross-cultural psychology.

HUNG–MING CHU is Professor in the Department of Neurology and Psychiatry, National Taiwan University.

LEILA F. DANE serves on the Department of State Mental Health Advisory Committee on behalf of the Association of American Foreign Service Women. She has worked as an interpreter in Africa, and more recently as a paraprofessional therapist in India. She is currently completing a higher degree with special emphasis on cross-cultural counseling.

GEORGE M. GUTHRIE is Professor of Psychology at the Pennsylvania State University, where he has been on the faculty since 1949. His interest in mediating activities began with a Fulbright appointment to the Philippines in 1959-60, and was maintained through his involvement in training the first four groups of Peace Corps volunteers who went to the Philippines in 1961 and 1962. His research in the Philippines is mainly on child-rearing practices and aspects of modernization. His early training and experience as a clinical psychologist fostered his interest in the stresses which mediators encounter and the steps which might be taken to prevent or alleviate the stress.

MARJORIE H. KLEIN is a member of the Department of Psychiatry at the University of Wisconsin.

OTTO KLINEBERG is the acknowledged doyen of cross-cultural psychology. His distinguished career spans five decades of scholarship devoted to the theory and practice of improving intergroup relations and international understanding. He has taught at major universities in Europe, Asia, and North and South America; directed projects under the auspices of the United Nations; and has been the president of numerous learned bodies in a variety of countries and of many of the international associations in his field. He has lost count of the number of books and articles he has published, but agrees that the total exceeds three hundred. Many of his publications have been seminal, pioneering a topic. In addition to the four degrees that he earned (which include an M.D. as well as a Ph.D.), he has four honorary doctorates and holds numerous awards and honors, including the Butler Medal and the Kurt Lewin Memorial Award. Otto Klineberg is currently Director of the International Center for Intergroup Relations, in Paris.

BEVERLY MCLEOD has a higher degree in anthropology from the University of Hawaii, which she earned while holding an East-West Center graduate studentship. Earlier, she was an exchange student in Japan, followed by two years in Thailand as a Peace Corps volunteer. More recently, she taught English in Iran. She is currently a doctoral candidate in psychology at the University of California at Santa Cruz.

MILTON H. MILLER is Professor and Head of the Department of Psychiatry at the University of British Columbia in Vancouver.

JAMES E. RITCHIE is Professor and Head of the Department of Psychology at Waikato University in Hamilton, New Zealand. His other positions are Dean of the School of Social Sciences and Director of the Centre for Maori Studies and Research. His work combines the disciplines of anthropology and psychology, and has been chiefly addressed to aspects of social change in New Zealand and the Pacific. An early book, *The Making of a Maori*, is now a classic in the area of Maori community studies. More recently, together with Jane Ritchie, he has published *Child Rearing Patterns in New Zealand* and *Growing Up in New Zealand*.

GERD SEIDEL is a culture trainer with the Area Orientation Center of the German Foundation for International Development, at Bad Honnef in West Germany.

MARGARET W. SULLIVAN is a free-lance writer and painter. She is married to a U.S. Foreign Service officer and is the mother of four teenagers who, like herself, have been raised multiculturally. Mrs. Sullivan was born of American parents in China and lived in Burma and India. Since her marriage, she has lived in Malaysia, Nigeria, Indonesia, the Philippines, Sierra Leone, and, currently, the United States. Mrs. Sullivan is editor of *Everyday Indonesian, A Word and Phrase Book* and author of the cultural "cues and clues" section of *Introducing Indonesia* and of *The Fine Hands People, A Sample of Sierra Leonean Craftsmen and Their Skills*. She is a consultant to the Business Council for International Understanding.

RONALD TAFT recently retired as Professor of Social Psychology in the Education Faculty at Monash University in Melbourne. After receiving a doctorate from the University of California at Berkeley in 1950, he commenced a large-scale program of research into the adaptation of immigrants in Australia, which was reported in *From Stranger to Citizen*. This was followed by a more general investigation of how people adapt to other cultures and how they handle being bicultural. He was awarded the 1975 Medal of the Royal Society of Victoria for his research, which is continuing. He has published extensively in the field of social psychology, including papers on the Australian way of life.

R. P. THROSSELL is Assistant Secretary of the Cultural Relations Branch in the Australian Department of Foreign Affairs.

ENG-KUNG YEH is Professor of Psychiatry at the National Taiwan University and Director of the Taipei City Psychiatric Center.

Name Index

Subject Index